Politics and the Passions, 1500–1850

Politics and the Passions, 1500–1850

Edited by Victoria Kahn,
Neil Saccamano, and Daniela Coli

PRINCETON UNIVERSITY PRESS

PRINCETON AND OXFORD

Published by Princeton University Press, 41 William Street,
Princeton, New Jersey 08540

In the United Kingdom: Princeton University Press,
3 Market Place, Woodstock, Oxfordshire OX20 1SY

Library of Congress Cataloging-in-Publication Data

Politics and the passions, 1500–1850 / edited by Victoria Kahn,
Neil Saccamano, and Daniela Coli.
p.   cm.
Includes bibliographical references and index.
ISBN-10: 0-691-11861-2 (cl. : alk. paper)
ISBN-13: 978-0-691-11861-1 (cl. : alk. paper)
ISBN-10: 0-691-11862-0 (pbk. : alk. paper)
ISBN-13: 978-0-691-11862-8 (pbk. : alk. paper)
1. Political science. 2. Emotions. I. Kahn, Victoria Ann. II. Saccamano,
Neil, 1952– III. Coli, Daniela.
JA71.P6416   2006
320.01'9—dc22
2005028068

British Library Cataloging-in-Publication Data is available

This book has been composed in Sabon

Printed on acid-free paper. ∞

pup.princeton.edu

Printed in the United States of America

10 9 8 7 6 5 4 3 2 1

Contents

Introduction

Victoria Kahn and Neil Saccamano

IN RECENT YEARS there has been a renaissance of interest in the passions in interdisciplinary work in the humanities and social sciences. Scholars have directed their attention to the passions as vehicles of knowledge, as attributes of aesthetic experience, as labile affects or shifting currents that contribute to political upheaval or religious self-sacrifice. The reasons for this affective reorientation are multiple. We might think of it as a reaction to the linguistic turn or the deconstruction of the subject. We might instead think of it as the logical consequence of the focus on tropes and figures: themselves, as ancient rhetoricians tells us, the best means of representing the swerve of affect away from pure cognition, as well as the best means of stirring up the passions of the audience. We might think of the recourse to the passions as a consequence of the interest in the body and the body politic across a variety of disciplines. But there are also less academic reasons for the renewed interest in the passions. At a time when a rhetoric of "terror" is a central feature of our common political life, when political ideologies on the right and left vie to characterize themselves as "compassionate," and when religious passions lead to shocking acts of violence, it is worth reexamining the history of Western reflection on politics and the passions.

This volume begins with the early modern period and concludes with Bentham. It focuses in particular on the new theories of human motivation, the new calculus of passion and interest, that emerged as a result of the social, political, and religious changes that facilitated the transition from feudalism to capitalism. It is arguable, of course, that the passions have always played an important role in Western reflection on politics. Beginning with Plato and Aristotle, philosophers, political theorists, and literary critics have devoted considerable attention to the role of the passions in shaping human knowledge and experience, both individual and collective. At the same time, however, scholars as diverse as Norbert Elias, Albert Hirschman, and Max Horkheimer have argued that the early modern period signals a shift in the conceptualization of the passions, specifically in relation to the political sphere. This volume proceeds from this argument. In the following pages, we briefly set out a framework for thinking about this conceptual shift that may provide a context for the essays that follow.

Elias famously argued that the centralization of political power at court produced a distinctive "court society" that required the sublimation of the passions and the cultivation of manners as the mark of the political elite. As the early modern state developed a monopoly of physical force, so the individual was no longer compelled—or allowed—to gain prestige on the battlefield. Instead, he began to be shaped by indirect forms of coercion, such as the norms of courtly society and increasing rationalization of economic life. At the same time, coercion was internalized: the nobility's increasing dependence on the king or prince was accompanied by a "transformation of human consciousness and libidinal make-up," according to which the individual constrained and controlled himself. For Elias, then, the modern Western notion of the civilized individual cannot be understood "without tracing the process of state-formation" in the sixteenth and seventeenth centuries.[1]

Whereas Elias linked the sublimation of the passions to the civilizing process and "the sociogenesis of absolutism," Max Horkheimer traced the revived interest in the passions to the skeptical and materialist strains of early modern philosophy and to bourgeois ideology. Skepticism about the persuasiveness of older normative discourses was accompanied by a new, naturalistic anthropology, involving the "historical, political, and psychological analysis" of the emotions.[2] For Horkheimer, early modern scientific and philosophical discourses of the passions, especially those of Hobbes and Spinoza, establish a simple naturalism premised on the normative judgment that "for everything in nature, and thus for the body and its indwelling soul, to perish represents the greatest evil."[3] This ostensibly scientific concept of nature is, however, the ideological kernel of seventeenth-century discourses on the passions because the claim that the "self-preservation of each thing is its law and standard corresponds to the social condition of the bourgeois individual." On one hand, the elevation of life itself to the highest good acknowledges the value of material embodiment and the concomitant passions. On the other hand, the recognition accorded material life in these discourses remains nondialectical and ideological in Horkheimer's account because the passion of self-preservation is presented as the motion of an autonomous subject, not one who is conditioned by social and economic factors.

In his influential work on the passions and interests, Albert Hirschman also traced a historical shift in attitudes toward the passions to specifically political concerns. Like Horkheimer, Hirschman considered seventeenth- and eighteenth-century philosophical anthropology and ethics as developing in relation to political imperatives, but he differed about the ideological character of those imperatives, especially concerning the early modern critique of glory. The aristocratic passion for military glory, which was the traditional object and reward for action in the political realm, came under attack from early modern writers as contributing to civil and religious wars and thus as an unacceptable challenge to state power. The new theory of human nature required by a science of politics was characterized by a dynamics of countervailing passions. Against the heroic violence of glory, early modern writers opposed the "dependable" passion of acquisitiveness or greed. Against the desire for self-aggrandizement, they opposed the desire for self-preservation or fear of violent death. This reduction of human nature to its basest passions or interests, and of society to self-interested individuals who bind themselves through contracts, then set the stage for reconstituting the state from the ground up. It also gave rise to a new understanding of the relationship between the public and private spheres, and a new, positive evaluation of everyday life. Yet historically, Hirschman argued, this "denunciation of the heroic ideal was nowhere associated with the advocacy of a new bourgeois ethos."[4] The critique of glory marshaled a scientific, positive approach to politics that initially served to counsel princes in the practice of governing and that only later addressed the conduct of individual subjects, extending scientific discourse from "the nature of the state to human nature" (13).

Both in its emphasis on mere life and its representation of government as artificial (contractual or conventional), early modern political theory represented a radical departure from classical antiquity. In the political culture of ancient Greece, the life concerned only with preservation and reproduction—with the body—was traditionally the life of women and slaves who were excluded from political participation and relegated to the management of the patriarchal household, consigned to purely economic labor and devoted to bare life alone. The inglorious life was private in the sense of privative, enslaved to the necessity of reproducing life itself as the mere condition of political freedom. The equality of free men in a political sense presupposed the inequality of those in the household who were concerned with economics. For a citizen of the polis, to live the "good life" meant to be free from the demands of mere life, and to be worthy of glory meant to master mere life and be willing to risk death for the polis. By contrast, early modern political theory appeals to the inglorious passions of the private individual in an effort to establish a "civil society" in which, as Hannah Arendt put it, "the fact of mutual dependence for the sake of life and nothing else assumes public significance and where the activities connected with sheer survival are permitted to appear in public."[5] For modernity, society is that for which the inglorious life of the ancient Greek household—economics—becomes a matter of public concern. And the reason of the state, in this modern conception, is the protection and preservation of the life of its citizens—a general collective management of economic transactions whose political form is the nation (28). In the classical conception of politics, the category of "political economy" would have been idiotic or senseless because it is a contradiction in terms until the modern period.

In time, the theory of countervailing passions provided the motor not only for a new validation of self-interest and a sanction for economic activity in civil society, but also for the emergence of a new culture of sentiment. Eighteenth-century moral and political philosophers were concerned to manage the conflictive potential of the passions without necessarily advocating the absolutism of state power. The managing of the passion of self-preservation was sought not through the repression of passion by the authority of reason or by the sovereignty of public regulation but through the "discovery" of other, socially beneficent and constitutive feelings such as benevolence, sympathy, and pity. If, in a Hobbesian account, the demystification of heroic virtues as forms of self-love and self-interest required the intervention of an absolute sovereign to provide security, subsequent writers have recourse to moral sentiments precisely to obviate or defer the exercise of state power by aligning the passions and desires of subjects with the imperatives of law. Lord Shaftesbury, for instance, appeals to a moral-aesthetic sense in human nature that gives rise to social affections and allows virtue to be reconciled with what he calls self-enjoyment and true interest. Similarly, Rousseau claims that the natural passion of pity originally takes the place of law in moving subjects to act in ways consistent with morality on the basis of a common, prerational sentiment of humanity. In these and other eighteenth-century writers, the passions hold out the promise of an immanent ethical community insofar as "humanity" becomes a natural sentiment that orients the desire and actions of subjects toward a common good.

Despite their countervailing of the interested passions, the discourses of moral sentiment partly share the skeptical perspective of early modern accounts of the passions to the extent that these discourses continue to derive their ethics and politics from the experiential matrix of individual subjects, especially the fundamental sensations of pleasure and pain. In this respect, moral and political discourses on the passions in the eighteenth century entertain an essential relation to "aesthetics." As a philosophical and critical discourse on art, aesthetics emerges in the eighteenth century in an effort to make sense of sense, to order sensations as judgments, by differentiating the kinds of pleasures and pains elicited by particular works of nature and imagination. Signifying more broadly the material realm of sensation and perception, however, aesthetics was already integral to moral, political, and even epistemological discourses of the eighteenth century. The figurative meaning of taste, as aesthetic judgment, is complexly tied to the literal meaning of taste, as a corporeal sense presumed to have a certain regularity and predictability. Along with the sciences of morality and politics, the logic of art requires that there be a logic of the body and a common sense. As the discourse particularly concerned with the sensations of pleasure and pain that accompany perceptual and imaginative acts and elicit passions and interests, aesthetics does not merely stand alongside morality and politics as another human science in the eighteenth century: it provides for a universal subject of sentiment to support the discourses of moral and political law. From the early modern period to Kant, aesthetic experience is increasingly scrutinized as to whether the particular sentiments of individuals might accord with social virtues and universal humanity. Kant may insist on the autonomy of the aesthetic subject, for whom common sense is only a promise, in contrast to Hume, who makes the social virtue of sympathy essential to aesthetic pleasure. Yet the aesthetic remains crucial to these and other eighteenth-century writers as it is the realm of the pleasures and passions that need to be reflected, represented, refined, educated, or purified in order to make possible ethical and political community.

These accounts of the sentimental, affective, or passionate subject for whom empirical experience or the body is of utmost value signal a historical shift in the political operation of power that Michel Foucault had termed a movement from state violence toward bio-power. In Foucault's well-known formulation of this transformation, state power over subjects is characterized not only by the decision "to make die or let live," exemplified by Hobbes's Leviathan, but by the imperative "to make live or abandon [*rejetter*] to death."[6] Death is the effect of the withdrawal, not just the exercise, of sovereign power. The new, positive evaluation of everyday life as independent of the state makes, in turn, the psychological and physiological conditions of individual subjects of utmost political import. The private life of the subject becomes a care of the state. In this respect, the analysis of the passions forms part of the broader question of the politics of subjectivity examined by recent scholarly and theoretical work.

Some of the essays that follow address, implicitly or explicitly, the crisis of traditional moral and philosophical discourse in the early modern period and the necessity of inventing a new way of describing the relation of private to public selves, subjective reflection, and action in the realm of politics. In the place of traditional notions of virtue and the traditional superiority of reason to the passions, writers such as Machiavelli, Montaigne, Bacon, Hobbes, and Vico begin to reconceive the passions as substitutes for virtue's spur to political action. In contexts of internecine conflict, of civil and religious war, a clear-sighted recognition of the role of the passions in motivating human behavior can itself be a first step in developing a new political rationality, whether the author's purpose is ultimately to control the aristocratic desire to dominate the people

(McCormick), to articulate a space of political agency indebted neither to classical notions of virtue nor to modern reason of state (Hampton), to reinvent philosophy as natural philosophy (Guillory), to bring about a revolution in political theory predicated on a physics of motion and desire (Coli), or to recast the history of the transition from barbarism to civilization (Caporali).

Many of the essays in this volume also address the disciplinary regulation of the body or the ideological constitution of identity from the seventeenth century onwards. Our contributors approach this issue in various ways. The changing discourses on the passions over the course of this historical period indicate, for some, the reach of class politics into affective life. The contestation of aristocratic and absolutist ideology by a bourgeois and liberal ideology can be read in the reevaluation of gratitude or generosity as moral but nominally apolitical passions at the heart of friendship and familial intimacy (Coleman). The ideological imperatives impinging on various accounts of the passions from Descartes to Bentham prompt efforts to displace the corporeal and material conditions of experience in order to give primacy to a self-affecting subject—by blurring the difference between sentiments and ideas, feelings of pleasure or pain and their representations (Armstrong and Tennenhouse); by differentiating between passions, which have some reference to sensation, and internal feelings or reflections, which preserve but supersede the material character of passionate subjectivity (Kahn); and by pathologizing the passions as implicated in the masochism of a voluntary servitude and by distinguishing them from affects that remain linked to sensibility but do not threaten freedom and moral self-legislation (Caygill), to cite only a few examples. Other contributors to this volume acknowledge the ideological and disciplinary role the passions have historically played but also explore whether a discourse of the passions might provide a critical perspective on the politics of subjectivity—whether, for instance, the concept of life might be rethought apart from its role in liberal political theory (Butler); aesthetic experience might expose or incite acts of disidentification rather than consolidate the autonomous subject of bourgeois civil society (Saccamano); and recent attacks on liberalism's exclusion of religious passions and beliefs might be answered by recognizing the progressive potential in liberalism's collective, historical, and contingent understanding of affects in relation to social action and law (Ferguson). Whatever their specific approach to the question of ideology, however, all the essays in this volume reconsider the legacy of the passions in modern political theory and recognize the importance of the history of reflection on "politics and the passions" for modern political debates.

Tempering the *Grandi*'s Appetite to Oppress

THE DEDICATION AND INTENTION OF
MACHIAVELLI'S *DISCOURSES*

John P. McCormick

ONE OF THE MOST anxiously posed questions in the history of political thought is: What was Machiavelli's intention in writing *The Prince*?[1] Was it to advise a prince, or undo him; to encourage tyranny or more subtly moderate it?[2] Quite appropriately, interpreters begin to answer this question by focusing on the book's dedicatee, Lorenzo de' Medici. They then proceed to read *The Prince* in light of how Lorenzo specifically, or a young prince more generally, might receive, understand, and potentially act upon the book's advice. However, few scholars ask the same question, certainly with comparable urgency, of Machiavelli's greatest work, *Discourses on Titus Livy's First Decade*.[3] It's largely taken for granted that the purpose of *The Discourses* is self-evident—to promote republics—and that its immediate audience is obvious—two young friends with republican sympathies.[4] Since Machiavelli dedicates *The Discourses* to friends from his literary circle, the Orti Oricellari, who supposedly share his political predilections, the book is assumed to be a more straightforward and less artful work than *The Prince*. In other words, one need not ponder too deeply the relationship between the book's declared audience and its content.

In this essay, I examine the issue of *The Discourses*' dedicatees a little more closely to draw out what might be one of Machiavelli's hitherto unacknowledged intentions. Cosimo Rucellai and Zanobi Buondelmonti are not simply "friends" or "republicans." They are young men of considerable wealth and good name who, on the basis of lineage, education, and talent, would expect to hold positions of prominence within their polity. Defined in terms of the "appetite" that pursues and acquires such economic advantage and political privilege, and viewed from the perspective of their social subordinates, Rucellai and Buondelmonti are what Machiavelli calls *grandi*: members of a class driven by the "humor" to oppress. Like interpreters who detect a rhetorical strategy in *The Prince*, through which Machiavelli's advice manipulates a prince into tempering or even jeopardizing his dominion over the people, I discern a similar strategy in *The Discourses* with respect to the grandi's domination of the people. While Machiavelli dedicates neither work *to* the people, I would argue that both are very much intended *for* the people; each book is intended to alleviate the people's oppression by their two most persistently malicious political antagonists: respectively, a tyrant and the oligarchs; the one and the few.

Here, I read the first six chapters of *The Discourses* from the perspective of young grandi like Cosimo and Zanobi. In doing so, I seek to open the possibility that Machiavelli uses a hypothetically reconstructed Roman republic to moderate the people's eternal oppressors in all regimes that are not principalities. He attempts to convince the grandi that the best republic is one in which they maximize the material and immaterial benefits they gain from political preeminence in such regimes, and protect themselves from the deleterious results of their own appetite to dominate. Machiavelli advises the grandi, against their natural and learned inclinations, to render themselves more accountable to an armed and politically empowered common citizenry. If followed, however, this advice might eventually make the grandi even more extensively and substantively accountable to the people than Machiavelli lets on. The Florentine's subsequent examples of how the Roman grandi use religion, electoral fraud, and unnecessary wars to manipulate the people may expose, more than serve, grandi interests and machinations.

In the opening chapters of *The Discourses*, Machiavelli establishes the parameters of a political bargain, and ultimately maneuvers his dedicatees into accepting its terms: the grandi constrain their appetite for complete domination of the people at home, granting the latter institutions like the tribunate and practices such as public accusations so that the people may serve as the regime's "guard of liberty"; in return, the young grandi gain the opportunity for increased riches and eternal fame through the pursuit of empire, that is, domination of countless others abroad and even, in the long run, domination of mortality. On this reading, whether Machiavelli really anticipates or even hopes that the grandi make good on this opportunity remains an open question. Roman-style imperialism may be only one of several military options for Machiavelli, and given its role in the republic's collapse, perhaps not the most preferable.

A proper understanding of the dedicatees' identity and what it stands for may allow readers of *The Discourses* to adopt the appropriate perspective when confronting the book's immediate surface. By asking, first and foremost, how the work's declared audience might interpret it, the grandi perspective of the dedicatees provides a hermeneutic key with which readers might unlock the often less than transparent significance of Machiavelli's arguments, assertions, and judgments. Admittedly, this mode of procedure entails considerable speculation: although I try to ground my assumptions historically and with the best textual support I can muster, in many instances I will be compelled to guess how Machiavelli thinks his immediate audience will react to specific passages.[5] Ultimately, I suggest that a proper understanding of Machiavelli's stated audience in *The Discourses* highlights the work's less-than-obvious purpose—the control of elites in a popular government.

It is now widely assumed that Machiavelli writes disingenuously when he flatters Lorenzo in the dedication of *The Prince*. After all, the Medici had dismissed, imprisoned, and tortured Machiavelli after the collapse of the Florentine republic that he served for over a dozen years. But he's taken to be straightforwardly honest in the dedication of *The Discourses* when he flatters Buondelmonti and Rucellai. He tells them that although they are not princes, they deserve to be. In the language of *The Discourses* (e.g., I.12, II.2), this primarily means that they should be leading citizens—magistrates, captains, senators—in a republic rather than, as they presently are, the subjects of an individual prince. Notwithstanding the perhaps unusual use of "princes" plural, this sentiment is not inconsistent with a "republican" understanding of the work, since a republic can be defined as a regime where not one, but more than one, actually governs.[6]

Some might assume more generally that the book's specific addressees are simply private citizens, or just common people, as opposed to the royal dedicatee of *The Prince*. But this easy association of the dedicatees with "the people," and hence republicanism with popular government per se, falls prey to an undifferentiated notion of republicanism, as well as to an historically uninformed understanding of who Buondelmonti and Rucellai actually were, and, even more significantly, what social type they might represent.[7] *The Discourses* is dedicated neither to a single prince—a prince proper—nor to the people, or even to men *of* the people (*popolari*): Buondelmonti and Rucellai are young nobles—*ottimati* in the parlance of the day, grandi in Machiavelli's general usage (*P* 9; *D* I.4).[8] Both come from families with long traditions of influence and command in Florence, and, more pertinently, with well-known biases against any republic that is not a *governo stretto*, that is, a polity within which only the very few, most wealthy citizens rule. The Rucellai and Buondelmonti families were staunch opponents of both the *governo largo*, or more widely participatory republic, within which Friar Savonarola was influential, and the republic under Piero Soderini's chief magistracy that succeeded it. The latter bitterly disappointed them by not fully purging what they considered to be the popular excesses of its predecessor.[9] And yet the class background and social perspective that was Rucellai's and Buondelmonti's political patrimony is generally ignored in the political theory literature that presents them as "humanists and literati," "republican sympathizers," patriots, and, overwhelmingly, just "friends" of Machiavelli.[10]

As a close and valuable aid to Soderini, and as a "new man" recruited to public service from outside the ranks of the ottimati, Machiavelli was certainly *not* considered a "friend" by this earlier generation of Florentine elites, the elders of his dedicatees in *The Discourses*. On this basis we might conclude that Machiavelli not only understands the nature of individual princes, as he suggests in the dedication to *The Prince*—having observed firsthand the actions of kings, queens, popes, and warlords on his diplomatic missions for the Florentine republic, and having experienced firsthand the attentions of a Medici prince upon that republic's collapse.[11] In addition, Machiavelli may have valuable insight into the nature of grandi from firsthand experience. The Florentine ottimati did not resort to violence against Machiavelli, but he certainly endured their constant disdain and derision.[12] While Machiavelli came from a family with an old name, he was not of suitably high birth or sufficient wealth to vote on, or stand for, the highest offices in the republic.[13] And he owed entirely to the patronage of Soderini the diplomatic, secretarial, and military posts usually inaccessible to people of lower social station. Of course, the grandi accustomed to a monopoly on these posts were not terribly pleased with this state of affairs, and are documented as having spit their poison at Machiavelli on a regular basis.[14]

Yet despite good reasons for resenting and mistrusting the wealthy and the well-born in general, some of Machiavelli's best friends in particular were ottimati; most famously, Francesco Vettori and Francesco Guicciardini.[15] More importantly, for our purposes, so were Buondelmonti and Rucellai—even if the relationship between the young nobles and the wry, erudite political veteran was far from perfectly symmetrical: the underborn and unemployed Machiavelli was in debt to one of them, or likely both, financially.[16] Yet it is intellectual credit, not monetary reimbursement, that Machiavelli returns to Zanobi and Cosimo in the dedication of *The Discourses*. Machiavelli thanks his "friends" for having "forced" him to write what he would not have written otherwise. Apparently, excited by Machiavelli's discussions of politics and history at their reading group, the young grandi insisted that he discourse on the topic in writing. And Machiavelli dutifully submits to these friends who command.[17]

So, unlike *The Prince*, *The Discourses*, according to its dedication, was actively solicited by its dedicatees, who happen to be the author's social superiors and intimate friends. And since the young grandi to whom Machiavelli dedicates *The Discourses* are also humanist intellectuals, members of a scholarly circle, they presumably will not scoff at a book on politics that takes a scholarly form. They might even welcome a book that presents itself as a long commentary on a classical text—a book with the full title, *Discorsi sopra la prima deca di Tito Livio*.[18] Indeed, ottimati, whether in *or* out of power, differ from a prince because they can afford to take a bit more time and effort cultivating themselves. Zanobi and Cosimo, like most members of their class, probably do not expect to justify their claims to preeminence with force alone; they probably have some pretensions about really being "the best" citizens. Fortunately for them, both political inactivity under a principality and the political division of labor entailed by grandi domination allow young nobles the time to study and improve themselves. So the full title and academic form of Machiavelli's work might attract rather than discourage young grandi seeking to justify themselves through education.[19]

This analysis points up the fact that unlike a prince, grandi, when in power, "collegially" share the load of ruling among themselves. There is a name for such a regime. Nevertheless, just as "tyrant" is never mentioned in *The Prince*, "oligarchy" is rather scarce in *The Discourses*. In the first three chapters of the latter, Machiavelli refers to those of status, wealth, and command interchangeably as optimates (ottimati),[20] nobles (*nobili*), the few (*pochi*), the powerful (*potenti*), and, in a Roman context, the senate (*senato*). In accord with the apparently "classical mood" set by Machiavelli's title, his prologue and his ostensible fidelity to Polybius's cycle of regimes, in I.2 he seems to abide by a distinction between good and bad kinds of nobility; he distinguishes between rule by optimates and rule by merely "the few."

In fact, young ottimati would be quite flattered by association with the following description of their class, largely derived, but for the significant reference to their wealth,[21] from Polybius: a group who surpassed all others "in generosity, greatness of spirit, riches, and nobility. . . . [who] governed themselves according to the laws ordered by them, placing the common utility before their own advantage; and . . . preserved both public and private things with the highest diligence" (I.2). In the quasi-Polybian cycle of regime transformation, this class of "the powerful" is obeyed and revered by "the multitude" during the elimination of tyranny and the establishment of a noble-governed republic. But, according to Machiavelli's narrative, the heirs of "the powerful" in the next generation respect neither civility nor the multitude's property and women. As a result, a government of optimates is corrupted into a regime dominated by the few, and so they provoke a democratic revolution that is itself, as nobles are inclined to expect, destined to degenerate into "license."

Heartened or perhaps confirmed in their expectations by an approximation of the classical distinction between aristocracy and oligarchy, Cosimo and Zanobi might not be disturbed by mention of the Roman nobility's "insolence" toward the end of I.2. This is, after all, just one particular group of ottimati, not nobles in general, who, as Machiavelli has shown in his apparently faithful rehashing of Polybius, are good, basically. However, they might be surprised that Machiavelli attributes the creation of the tribunes, a magistracy of the Roman plebs, to the insolence of the nobility rather than to the ambitions of the common people—ottimati being inclined to assume that the people agitate spontaneously and unprovoked to take all or part of their political power. The dedicatees are likely even more surprised that Machiavelli promises to show how conflict or disunion between the senate and the plebs made the Roman republic "perfect" (I.2).

Machiavelli still refrains from offering a categorical assessment of the dedicatees as a class at the start of I.3, focusing instead on humanity in general: for political purposes, it must be assumed that "all men [*uomini*] are bad," and that they are ready to vent their malignant spirit as soon as they have a free opportunity to do so. But the immediate example of such malignant evil is the Roman senate and nobility, who concealed their hatred for the plebs during the reign of the Tarquin principality, but "offended them in all the modes they could" once the monarchy was abolished. This "insolence" and the "confusions, noises and dangers of scandals that arose" as a result of the plebs' reaction to it, led to the creation of the tribunes by the two parties, "for the security of the plebs" (I.3).[22] It is important to note that, so far, this is still just an isolated case of preemptively "bad" nobility; and secondly, the "accidents," referred to in the chapter's heading, that emerged in the conflict between the plebs and senate are rather mild (confusions, noises, threat of scandal).

The most casual familiarity with classical writings would suggest that the few are inclined to fear that they will be targeted for expropriation, ostracism, and even violence as a result of conflict with the common people; the example of democratic Athens serving as the chief source of their anxiety.[23] Yet Machiavelli shows here and in the next chapter that as "wild" as tumults became, they never really harmed the Roman nobles: public shouting, street demonstrations, and popular evacuation of the city are frightening to those who only read about them (I.5); and later he claims that the extreme measures taken by the Athenian populace against their elite were perhaps justifiable responses to the experience of tyranny (I.28). Even this early in *The Discourses* it is clear that Machiavelli is teaching Cosimo and Zanobi about the people's nature as well as about their own; in fact, the two lessons seem to be inseparable. But at this point in the text he is more forthcoming about the nature of the people and about the character of the tumults between them and the ottimati than he is about the nature of the latter.

Chapter 4 is devoted to the disunion or tumults that made Rome "free and powerful," tumults criticized by "many," that is, the unnamed classical sources that Machiavelli previously appeared to be following. These authors, taking on the nobles' perspective, pine for an orderly people and blame the latter for civil discord.[24] Why aren't they sensible enough to submit quietly to rule by their betters? But the people themselves are *not* the cause of tumults in Rome, according to Machiavelli. There are two causes of tumults, two seemingly irreconcilable appetites: "in every republic are two diverse humors, that of the people and that of the great, and all the laws that are made in favor of freedom arise from their disunion" (I.4). Here is the first appearance of Machiavelli's universal category for the nobles: the grandi, or "the great." We can assume that "grandi" is his general category on the basis of his judgment that they exist "in every republic," and by cross-referencing this passage to the sociology of "every city" in *The Prince* (P 9).[25] There Machiavelli tells a prince that success depends on establishing his authority with the correct humor of the two, while here free play between the great and the people generates laws that insure liberty.[26] In *The Prince*, Machiavelli immediately defines the substance of the grandi's humor or appetite; while in *The Discourses* he postpones that declaration—even if it's already intimated by particular examples throughout the initial chapters—until the next chapter, I.5.

It may well be that Machiavelli assumes, at this point, that his young dedicatees care more about their welfare in the hypothetical tumultuous contest between themselves and the people than about "the truth" of their own nature. And so Machiavelli assures them with even more specific examples than he proffered in the previous chapter: he insists that exiles, fines, and killings were kept to an absolute minimum in tumultuous Rome, and were spread out over three hundred years (I.4). Moreover, the humor of the people, now revealed, is merely *not* to be oppressed, and they act rambunctiously only when they are oppressed in actuality or when they become suspicious of being oppressed. Hence "the desires of free peoples are rarely pernicious to freedom." Machiavelli cajoles his dedicatees further by insisting that the plebs respond only reactively or passively in most cases anyway. In accord with their nature, the people *refrain* from doing something instead of *actively* doing something: in response to actual oppression, they exit the city or fail to enroll for military service.[27] When the people fear being oppressed, they can be convinced otherwise by a good man, a man of faith, presumably a noble,[28] in deliberative assemblies, the *concioni*. Later Machiavelli will state, perhaps against actual Roman practice, that "any citizen at all" could speak in a *concione* (III.34), hence suggesting that a noble's speech might be contested publicly by a pleb.[29] He does not open this possibility to his young grandi audience at this juncture, preferring instead to concur with Cicero's seemingly authoritative judgment that the people are ignorant—but not so ignorant as to be incapable of "truth" or of recognizing a man worthy of trust; for Cicero, this would certainly mean a member of the ottimati.

However, returning to the exiles, fines, and blood mentioned above, since they are a little more worrisome to a noble than the confusions, noises, and scandals mentioned earlier: even if these costs are kept to a minimum, they may be too exorbitant for a grandi audience to accept unless they are guaranteed a disproportionate reward in return for their risk. (Of course, the chapter leaves open the option that Cosimo and Zanobi simply choose not to oppress the people, or never give the latter cause to worry about the possibility of oppression. Why that course of action would never even occur to the grandi is not revealed until the next chapter, I.5.) Hence, the most intriguing sentence in this section of I.4 is the prospect offered in exchange for allowing the people to express themselves politically, and for tolerating the tumults that necessarily ensue therefrom: cities that do, like Rome, may "avail themselves of the people in important things." The title of the chapter would suggest that these important things pertain to "liberty," which remains undefined, and "power," which may have something to do with, on the one hand, what Rome is most famous for and, on the other, the people's proximity to military matters mentioned in this section.

Machiavelli repeats "the great" as his term for the oligarchic component "in every republic" in I.5. Etymologically, "grandi" or "the great" ought not to be a displeasing appellation for the dedicatees, affiliated as it is with, for instance, grandeur (*grandiosità*), or, a word that will take on considerable import quite soon, greatness (*grandezza*). It's perhaps not as gratifying a label as "aristocrats," yet not so disparaging as "oligarchs." But beyond pleasant names, Machiavelli substantively defines the grandi, and later in the chapter the nobles, by the appetite or humor that drives them to acquire the riches, recognition, and power that they hold, and want more of—the "great desire to dominate." On the other hand, the "ignobles," the people, "*only* desire not to be dominated" (emphasis added). As opposed to classical historians and philosophers, in his general definition Machiavelli no longer professes to define the great in terms of moral probity or meritorious accomplishment. These are the very qualities that young nobles tend to think (or pretend) that they possess, and would like to develop further. These are the very qualities that might have initially seduced the young grandi into tackling such a daunting scholarly tome as *The Discourses*. By chapter 5 of the work, however, they discover that they are defined simply by their appetite to make others bend to their will. The insolence that seemed to be extraneous to the nature of the grandi is now defined as its core.[30]

Thus, since Machiavelli's stated addressees have requested this work, since they have intellectual aspirations, and since they are his friends, perhaps he *can* be more honest after all about his beliefs and intentions in *The Discourses* than he is vis-à-vis his dedicatee in *The Prince*. Even if he must ease them along in the way suggested here, Machiavelli does not permanently hide from his immediate audience what he thinks of them as a class or social type. What is a temporary stratagem in *The Discourses*, is the dominant one in *The Prince*: there Machiavelli never speaks directly on the nature of princes; instead demonstrating by example or, as he did with respect to the grandi in I.3, through generalizations about the nature of "men" (e.g., *P* 15, title).[31] However, after I.3, Machiavelli speaks more frankly about the political nature of his immediate audience, especially in I.5 of *The Discourses*. We do not know whether Zanobi and Cosimo yet recognize themselves in Machiavelli's depiction of the grandi as those with the appetite to oppress. Nonetheless, Machiavelli's straightforward presentation invites them to be honest about it rather than to be ashamed or embarrassed by it. It's just a fact, a natural fact. The instruction, already in progress, will be that they should obey that appetite more prudently so as to satisfy it better, although we don't yet know exactly how.

Chapter 5 also deals with the "guard of freedom" and with what humor those constituting (founding? reforming?) a republic should place it, the people's or the great's. Before delving into this issue, it might be helpful to speculate what Machiavelli means by freedom, or "a free way of life," since he invokes but still does not define it here. What might freedom mean to his dedicatees? We learn in this chapter that they have the appetite to oppress. What are the conditions of possibility for them to act freely, with liberty, on this appetite? First off, we should assume, their regime must be independent of another regime—it cannot be a client or subject state, a satellite or a colony. In such circumstances the prince or princes of a foreign regime would circumscribe the extent to which the grandi will oppress their own people. The same can be said for a domestic prince, who, as Machiavelli demonstrates elsewhere, cannot be secure if he allows the grandi free rein to satisfy their appetites (*P* 9; *D* I.16). Certainly, submission to the reinstalled Medici principality must frustrate the desire of these young grandi to compete freely for public offices, and exercise the command, reap the rewards, and gain the prestige that accompanies them.

So grandi are "free" in the absence of an imperial or princely authority, and, in fact, this is their definition of a republic, an autonomous regime without a single prince. More specifically, given the inclinations of their recent ancestors mentioned above, and based, just for instance, on Guicciardini's depiction of young ottimati in his political writings,[32] we can guess that Buondelmonti and Rucellai think of a republic as a regime where members of the "best families" circulate political offices among themselves. They are free vis-à-vis the people in such a regime by exercising command over the latter through these offices, and by refusing to share such offices with them. The general citizenry might select which of the nobility hold office at any particular time—election being, after all, an aristocratic institution.³³ But the people will not exert any further control on them. Certainly, the highest offices would not be open to anyone outside of these "better families."

Machiavelli points out in I.5 that Sparta and Venice were republics that placed the guard of liberty with the nobles; in other words, they reserved all magistracies for the grandi and entirely excluded the people from political participation. Conventional wisdom among the ottimati in Florence insisted that Sparta and, most especially, Venice were the best republics due to their tranquility and longevity.³⁴ Certainly, Sparta and Venice satisfy the young grandi's definition of liberty: exercising offices on their own terms over the people rather than the terms of a foreign or domestic prince, let alone the people's terms. This is precisely the kind of oligarchic republic that was nearly instituted in Florence when the Medici were expelled in 1494. That is, until Savonarola and Soderini made it more populist in their own different ways: over and against the wishes of the ottimati, Savonarola insisted on establishing an assembly of all the citizens, the Great Council; Soderini retained the Council and, as mentioned above, offered ministerial posts to nonnoble, "new men," like Machiavelli.

Machiavelli concedes the longevity of Sparta's and Venice's "freedom" in I.5. But emphasizing the fact that he is speaking in his own voice on behalf of Rome ("I say"), Machiavelli makes a normative and descriptive argument for granting the guard of liberty to the people. The ignobles desire not to be dominated and so, "having a greater will to live free," have less appetite to usurp or seize liberty. But if Machiavelli's case in the previous two chapters regarding the trustworthy motives of the people has not convinced the ever suspicious grandi, Machiavelli resorts to necessity: the plebs neither *want* to usurp liberty nor have the *ability* to do so. Notable commentators suggest that this move effectively undermines the argument for offering liberty's guardianship to the plebs, since those who cannot usurp or seize something successfully cannot guard it adequately. But is this so? First of all, if by usurpation, one means simply "overthrow," then the people *can* usurp liberty through either license or Caesarism. The grandi know this, and *The Discourses* bears it out at various points. In this regard, it is conceivable that the popular force that is necessary—perhaps insufficient, yet not inconsiderable—to kill all the nobles, or raise up a Caesar to keep the latter at bay, could be enlisted and ordered to defend freedom. And since Machiavelli emphasizes that the people's desires are "rarely pernicious" to liberty, then the grandi to some extent have it in their own power to forestall the emergence of circumstances where it *is* pernicious, where the people would want to usurp liberty. A consistent theme of *The Discourses* is that the people never resort to an attempted usurpation of liberty without first being provoked to do so by the great.

Secondly, even if liberty remains undefined by Machiavelli, clearly it is not a physical object: the people could guard liberty within a republican context without being able to "seize" it, since seizing it is tantamount to extinguishing it. If they resort to either anarchy or tyranny, the people themselves lose the conditions of liberty. The grandi need to be convinced that the people are capable of calculating the following "truth": they will never usurp liberty (overthrow the nobles) when their freedom from noble oppression is greater than the almost nonexistent liberty they would enjoy under conditions of license or tyranny. In light of this, it's not illogical for Machiavelli to assert that "since they are not able to seize it, they do not permit others to seize it," within the confines of republican politics. How do the people prevent the grandi from seizing liberty? They do so through an ensemble of pleb-enabling and noble-constraining institutions, practices, and behaviors that constitute the political concessions that Machiavelli extracts from the grandi over the course of Book I of *The Discourses*, not all of which are enumerated by chapter 5: the examples of pleb collective action mentioned above; the institution of the tribunes; practices such as accusations; deliberative and legislative assemblies; eligibility to stand for noble-dominated magistracies; and—most painfully for the grandi, as it turns out (I.37)—claims on their property as well.[35] In addition, of course, there are the ultimate threats of license and Caesarism to keep the grandi in line.

After making his personal case for Rome as a republic, and for the people as worthy guards of liberty, a speech in which, according to Harvey C. Mansfield, Jr., Machiavelli plays the role of a plebeian magistrate, a tribune even,[36] Machiavelli relinquishes the floor to an unnamed party, first singular, then possibly plural ("he . . . says," "they give as examples"). This spokesman makes the case against Rome and for a noble-entrusted guardianship of liberty. Although taken by a few scholars to be Machiavelli's true opinion, the views expressed by this grandi spokesman amount to little more than the typical "self-aggrandizing pleb" interpretation of Roman history found in Livy before, and in Montesquieu after, Machiavelli,[37] and prevalent among ottimati like Guicciardini in his own day. The speaker or speakers contesting Roman republicanism and the popular guardianship of liberty assert that *both* the "powerful" and the plebs have aggressive ambitions; the former seek to wield "a stick" and the latter are driven by a "restless spirit" to badger the nobility.[38] In fact, they insist that nobles' ambitions may have limits, while the people's, on the contrary, are insatiable, restless, and furious. Yet those who seek so desperately and quickly to subvert Machiavelli's adoption of the popular cause in this chapter miss something terribly important about this little disputation or minidialogue. The noble spokesmen's claim regarding the grandi amounts to an unwitting confession; their claim against the people will be exposed as a calumny.

The spokesmen for the grandi admit in an unqualified fashion the fact that the nobles seek to hold the guard of liberty, that is, exclusive or predominant political power, as a "stick in their hand." In other words, they want office and honors to command and oppress others—literally and figuratively, to beat them. The noble spokesmen, whose perspective would be very close to, in fact, perhaps identical to, that of the two dedicatees, make no pretense of justifying a monopoly of power in the grandi's hands on the grounds that they are "the best," or because they "deserve" it. Through this admission by the noble spokesman or spokesmen, Machiavelli may signal that one or both of his dedicatees have been instructed successfully in the indisputable fact of their nature: it is constituted by an appetite to dominate, period. If there is anything more than a self-serving justification for noble guardianship in this speech, it would be the claim that if given "this stick," the grandi will have their ambitions satisfied "more," but not completely; and they will be given "cause" to be "more" contented, but not necessarily content. In this veiled threat, the powerful offer to disrupt a free way of life *less* if given a weapon by which they can deprive all the other citizens of liberty, but, by their own words, there is no guarantee at all that this will be sufficient for their oppressive appetite. In the case of popular guardianship, on the contrary, there seems to exist the possibility that liberty can be shared, that each class's definition of liberty can be partially satisfied, while there is no such possibility for anyone but the grandi to be "free" when *they* guard liberty.[39]

The noble spokesman would like to divert us from drawing that conclusion, which is why he makes a half-hearted attempt to argue that the grandi appetite to oppress may have limits, that it *might* be satisfied or contented. It is also why he slanders the desires of the people, declaring them to be precisely the opposite of what Machiavelli stated (i.e., the people have *only* the desire not to be dominated) even before he donned, sincerely or not, plebeian or Ciompian rags in his speech on their behalf. The grandi spokesman or spokesmen inflate popular desires to a magnitude even greater than the aggressive ambitions they concede that the nobles harbor. They even render the nobles vulnerable vis-à-vis popular encroachment: The spokesman conjures up the "restless spirit of the plebs" that supposedly causes the nobles to become so desperate that they behave even worse than they might already otherwise. It is the people who make the nobles oppressive, not vice versa! If the plebs are granted any authority at all, as a result of their restlessness and "fury" they will always demand more, just as they did in Rome: from the tribunes, to one consul, then to both of them; from the praetors to the censors to a proto-

Caesar like Marius. They accuse the people of using men like Marius, as if a stick, "to beat down the nobility," and hence of accelerating the destruction of the republic.[40]

Yet, if the grandi's appetite to oppress is not easily contented, as their spokesmen admit, then a politically included people, a people charged with protecting liberty like the Roman plebs, would be forced by necessity to escalate their attempts to contain them in order to prevent the nobles from seizing liberty altogether. To protect liberty, even their disproportionately low share in it, the people will have to acquire more power at the grandi's expense. In two chapters, at the conclusion of this one (I.5) and in I.37, after engaging in complicated evaluations of the people's ambition to protect themselves from domination versus the grandi's ambition to dominate them, Machiavelli indicts the latter as the more dangerous ambition because it is preemptive and provocative.

In any case, aside from the partisanship implied by the perspective of the pleb magistrate that he adopts at the start of this dispute—or perhaps because of it—Machiavelli at its conclusion does not decide for one side or the other, Rome's popular guardianship or Sparta's/Venice's noble guardianship. The grandi may reveal that they want to dominate, but they will never admit that the people do not want the same, an admission that might necessitate that the nobles relinquish to them the guardianship of liberty. Rather than make such a concession of their own free will, they dissemble, deflect, and feign vulnerability ("we're both the same; they're worse; okay, we want a stick to beat others; no, they want the stick; it's they who threaten *us* with sticks!"). Clearly, the grandi will not cede any power to the people out of the goodness of their hearts or on the basis of sound reason. And while Machiavelli seems willing to leave the dispute a tie, he suddenly resorts to an almost unannounced criterion to break the stalemate: the prospect of empire. Machiavelli states rather matter-of-factly that Rome is the model of an imperial republic, while Venice and Sparta are the models for self-contained republics, and the decision for one or the other depends on whether or not empire is desired. After tossing this little bomb into the laps of those whom he's just maneuvered into the admission that they want to oppress, and promising them that he will elaborate on this tantalizing prospect further in the next chapter, Machiavelli concludes I.5 with an examination of who is more hurtful to a republic: those who seek to maintain honors and offices they've acquired or those who seek to acquire what they do not have.

Yet one is tempted to wonder whether a grandi reader can bear to stay with Machiavelli's narrative here, endure what portends to be an abstract discussion without proper nouns for social groups ("that which," on the one hand, versus "that which," on the other hand; "those who," on the one hand, as opposed to "those who," on the other), and wait patiently for a promised elaboration of the imperial/self-contained republic issue "in the following chapter." Having promised to settle, only a page away, a dispute that has obviously vexed them, having confirmed their appetites, and having raised a delectable new way by which they might attempt to gratify them, does Machiavelli expect the grandi to control themselves? Even those grandi who have a traditionalist preference *not* to pursue empire might have a compelling interest in confronting this issue sooner rather than later; after all, their preference, their appetite for a monopoly on the offices of command, still hangs in the balance. But any grandi who did in fact skip ahead would miss the historical playing-out of the dispute that was just concluded, but not settled. A dispute in deeds, so to speak, follows the recent dispute in words. After invoking empire and pointing in the direction of the next chapter, in the final section of I.5, Machiavelli narrates an episode from the Roman republic. He begins with the same declaration, "I say," that initiated the recent dispute, indicating either another partisan affirmation or his own, as opposed to Livy's, historical authority over the episode—or perhaps both.[41]

According to Machiavelli, with the authority of the people, a plebeian magistrate—a dictator in fact—inquired after those who might be attempting to gain the chief magistracies through "ambition and extraordinary modes," an investigation that elicits an insidious response from the nobility. In other words, someone speaking on behalf of the plebs is inquiring into and exposing the nature of the grandi, namely, their ambition to hold the lion's share of offices by any means necessary. While the investigation was targeting "whoever" might be seeking power ambitiously or extraordinarily, the nobles "out" themselves, for it "appeared to them" that they were the objects of the inquiry. Why would that be the case if they weren't in fact "contriving" in such a fashion? The nobles react to the investigation by turning the tables on the plebs, alleging that the latter in general and the pleb magistrate in particular were seeking offices with ambitious intent and through extraordinary means, charging that they are too deficient in "blood and virtue" (birth and wealth?) to ascend to them in an ordinary fashion. It is not *we* the nobles but *they* the ignobles and the men they raise up who behave in an ambitious and usurping manner! (One might wonder how the pleb was made dictator in the first place if he were so lacking in virtue, the cooperation of the senate and consuls being necessary for appointment to dictator.)

Nevertheless, this case of charge/countercharge should sound familiar to anyone who did not abruptly depart this chapter for the new territory of the next. Furthermore, Machiavelli tells us, the charges "spread" by the nobles against the people and their spokesman are so strong—apparently *many* believe them—that the pleb dictator calls a concione and appeals to the people to decide whether the nobility's claims are truthful accusations or slanderous calumnies. There ensues a great debate on whether those without power who attempt to acquire it or those holding power that is already acquired are more dangerous to a republic. The people subsequently absolve the pleb magistrate, and Machiavelli apparently approves, since he makes the following case, as if he were a participant (he seems to place himself "there"). Those who already have are more dangerous than those who seek to acquire, because the nobility bring greater resources and ambitions to bear in the conflicts between the two, and they actually *instigate* the people to want to acquire in the first place:

> Since they possess much, they are able to make an alteration with greater power and greater motive. And there is still this besides: that their incorrect and ambitious behavior inflames in the breasts of whoever does not possess the wish to possess so as to avenge themselves against them by despoiling them or to be able themselves to enter into those riches and those honors that they see being used badly by others. (I.5)

This description of those "who have" confirms the obverse of Machiavelli's description of the people or ignobles in the previous chapter: just as there he asserted that the people had less desire *and* less ability to usurp liberty, here he shows that the nobles have both greater ambition *and* greater ability to usurp liberty.

Indeed, the Roman example bears this out: the nobility's motivation and resources in spreading calumnies through the city effectively put a halt to the pleb dictator's investigation of their designs and machinations, so much so that he resigns his post. Indeed, Machiavelli could not settle the debate between himself and the grandi spokesmen one page before because of their power, both over him individually and over everyone else generally. Perhaps the grandi were stymied temporarily in their permanent conspiracy to secure magistracies and honors for themselves extraordinarily, but they are not punished for doing so.[42] Yet how do we interpret the fact that this pleb magistrate is absolved by a judgment of the people, and that the nobles are thereby effectively censured, formally or informally, by the same? The ambitious motives of the grandi are confirmed, even if their acting on such motives is not punished. But why are the people allowed to pass judgment in a case to which they are party? Should we be surprised that they exonerate their partisan who was making a case for them in the first place? Is this fair? Well, it could be, since Machiavelli later demonstrates that the people are capable of deciding against someone they favor, and who seems to favor them: they sentence Manlius to death (I.24). So, the result in such cases is not a foregone conclusion. Recall Machiavelli's claim that the people are not so ignorant as to misjudge a good man, one worthy of faith, in a concione. But in politics, isn't *every* case one in which the people are an interested party, in fact, *the* interested party, since their vulnerability puts them at disproportionate risk of misery and injury as a result of every "alteration"? Hence, is it not appropriate that the people assume a predominant role in judging these cases? Yet historically the rhetoric of philosophers and the power of the grandi have combined to suppress the people's attempt to play such a role, granting it instead to the grandi themselves.

Returning to the chapter: what are we to make of this pleb spokesman who once held an important office, was forced to relinquish it, but in the end is affirmed by the people? And who exactly makes up this concione that deliberates on the respective threats posed by the people and the great; this deliberative assembly into which Machiavelli has converted the entire conclusion of I.5? The answer might be: any of we readers who are uninterested in empire, or at least not so excited or vexed by the prospect of it that we cannot resist departing in pursuit of it. In other words, everyone except the grandi might make up this concione, which may be why, in their absence, we are free to decide for the people and the people's spokesman, and against the grandi. The latter's resources and ambition usually militate against such a hearing and outcome. The dispute in words earlier in the chapter could not be settled by the people's spokesman; he cannot force such a conclusion on the grandi, who are too strong and resourceful. It must be settled by a seemingly external authority, by empire. In the next chapter, I.6, empire may motivate the grandi in a way that appeals by a pleb spokesman or magistrate cannot. But here, at the very end of I.5, the dispute in fact has been settled by appeal to the people in a gathering from which the grandi might be excluded.[43]

Yet empire has not been absent from the context of our concione in I.5: Machiavelli tells us that the whole controversy began because the pleb dictator was initially appointed to look into conspiracies against Rome being conducted in a rival/subject city, Capua. Presumably, the dictator "followed the money" from external to internal conspiracies. One implication of this is that grandi who govern an imperial republic make themselves vulnerable to pleb attempts at exposing their ambition and scuttling their designs for more pervasive command at home. Grandi who enlist the people in military enterprises may not completely control them in domestic ones. In the next chapter, I.6, when certain minds might be clouded by prospect of empire, Machiavelli mentions that a people enlisted in war cannot be managed in any way the grandi happen to desire. While circumstances where the grandi are excluded completely from political activity are impossible in a republic, empire provides circumstances where the grandi's activity within a republic can be scrutinized and at least temporarily halted.

This dispute in action, unlike the previous one in words, does not end in a stalemate of *judgment*, but it does end in a *political* stalemate. The senate, the nobility as a whole, is indicted but not punished. To be sure, it is a political truth that the status quo ante always favors the grandi. But, with empire as the wedge with which the people can enter political life, might they learn such that they alter the equilibrium of class power more toward themselves in the future? Can they render the grandi's management of them more conducive to their own rather than the grandi's benefit? In both disputes, Machiavelli, like (or as) a pleb magistrate, has exposed the grandi's ambition and resources. Can he teach the people how to serve as guard of liberty against both? We cannot answer that question at this textual juncture as Cosimo and Zanobi await us as we approach the start of chapter 6, and they are not accustomed to be kept waiting. Right now, they are eager to resume their position of perspectival primacy within the work.

Of the entire *Discourses*, I.6 is one of the most closely studied chapters, and I don't intend to add anything to the many excellent existing analyses.[44] Scholars point out the numerous problems with Machiavelli's comparison of Sparta/Venice and Rome, of self-contained and imperial republics, and his ultimate choice for imperial Rome. Sparta and Venice were not so weak as Machiavelli claims: they were not so free of tumult, nor were their "foundations" destroyed by their inability to keep territory they gained when they did expand. Moreover, his description of Spartan and Venetian political institutions seems flawed and woefully incomplete. As for the endorsement of Roman imperialism, in light of the rest of *The Discourses*, the decline of the republic can be attributed partly but definitively to aspects of its imperial expansion: in particular, the prolongation of military commands. This is not even to mention Machiavelli's emphasis on Rome's elimination of liberty in virtuous cities throughout the ancient Mediterranean. Many commentators, on the basis of solid evidence and serious interpretation, conclude that the shortcomings and inconsistencies in Machiavelli's analysis can be attributed to his ultimately unjustifiable preference for the unleashing of human appetite as such, or for the pursuit of greatness in history. On this view, Machiavelli subordinates liberty to the necessity of acquisition and/or a normative preference for greatness.[45]

Does this most puzzling chapter, I.6, look any different when read from the perspective of the grandi dedicatees? At first blush, the chapter disappoints those who turn to it for an immediate discussion of republican imperialism: empire is mentioned in neither the chapter heading nor in the first two, rather long, paragraphs. It's referred to obliquely in Machiavelli's observation that the Venetian grandi or "gentlemen" did not put the populace "to work in things in which they could seize authority." This refers back to both the opposite kind of city that makes use of the people "in important things," mentioned before and, for those who read it, the conclusion of the previous chapter, which illustrates how the people and their magistrates might insinuate themselves into domestic politics through military and diplomatic affairs. In addition, empire, or lack thereof, is pertinent to Machiavelli's discussion, in these passages, of Sparta's resistance to growth. Rather than empire, the chapter continues to investigate the issue of populist versus oligarchic republics—Rome versus Venice/Sparta—but this time from a different angle: whether the "great effects" (*effetti grandi*) produced in Rome could be achieved without the controversies, tumults, and enmities between the people and the senate that produced them.

But what are the great effects presented to the great at this point? The laws that foster "liberty" mentioned earlier? Or the "power" mentioned in the title of the previous chapter and the empire invoked in the penultimate paragraph of it? Much to the frustration of the imperially curious, Machiavelli seems to be treating liberty as the great effect, mentioning both Rome's "free way of life" and Sparta/Venice, who were "free for a long while without enmities and tumults" (I.6). But it seems strange to associate tumults with freedom by pointing out that tumults caused the ruin of Rome's free way of life after the time of the Gracchi. *This* is their great effect? Machiavelli invokes the "time of" the Gracchi rather than the brothers themselves, since he shows later, in the midst of an apparent indictment of the Gracchi, that it was grandi ambition and senatorial avarice more than the brothers' purported demagoguery that set in motion the republic's decline (I.37). He may reproach their method there, but he does not besmirch the Gracchi cause. Yet this issue of grandi oppression and popular responses to it relates directly to the issue of great effects without tumult. How did the Venetian and Spartan grandi exclude the people politically so as to avoid tumult yet restrain themselves from oppressing them so thoroughly that the people neither revolted nor resorted to demagogues?

One could say that the domestic politics of Sparta and Venice appear to be fantasies from a Machiavellian standpoint: in both cities there are nobles who do not oppress the people, either of their own volition (Venice) or because of a kingly separation of the nobles from the plebs (Sparta). Thus, the grandi are free to govern but not oppress. But according to their nature, as Machiavelli defines it previously, can the grandi really be "free" while observing such a distinction? The people, for their part, seem to exist in what is their natural state in both cities: absent oppression by the nobles, they seek neither counteroppression against them nor any part in governing. But on closer inspection, there seems to be a way of governing the people that actually is oppression, oppression that merely goes uncontested: the Venetian people apparently never experienced liberty, and hence it is not that they are unoppressed, but rather that they don't know how to contest grandi governance cum oppression "because nothing had been taken away from them." But people who experience a modicum of liberty under a prince-senate competition, as in early Rome, or under a *governo largo*, as in Florence, will not refrain from challenging grandi domination once they've lost it (cf., *P 5*).

Machiavelli mentions numerous factors that prevent the emergence of tumults in the Spartan case: insulation from foreigners, a small population, equality of conditions, and limits on growth. Two others are the role of monarchy and the status of rank in Sparta. With respect to the latter, Machiavelli observes that the ranks of the city (*gradi della città*) were spread among few citizens and kept at a distance from the plebs. But what kind of rank, which entails both distinction and command, can be kept far away from its subordinates so as to go unnoticed? What kind of grades, gradations, distinctions matter without palpable comparison and contrast? Subordinates must observe rank, see it, in order to acknowledge it as superior if the appetite for prestige in its holder is to be at all satisfied; and subordinates must experience rank, feel it, if its holder's appetite to order others about can begin to be satisfied. Could such unrecognized ranks satisfy the grandi? The answer may be moot in the Spartan context, where a king or kings, "put down in the middle of the nobility," defend the plebs from grandi-generated injury. I would suggest that a regime with such a watered-down exercise of rank, and with a nobility so constrained by monarchy, is not a republic at all, but rather a principality. The upshot of all of this is that Venice is an unrealizable republican model for grandi who wish to dominate a regime in which the people already have enjoyed a modicum of liberty in the past, and Sparta would be an undesirable republican model because it is a trifle too reminiscent of the kind of principality to which the grandi dedicatees already submit. Therefore, Machiavelli has thoroughly discredited the Florentine ottimati's two paragons of republicanism on the basis of criteria derived precisely from their own preferences.

But Machiavelli already may have diverted the attention of his grandi audience away from Spartan and Venetian liberty, that is, mere oppression of the people within their own republic, or at least problematized it, with the introduction of empire. Having described the (unattainable and unsatisfying) liberty of the grandi in Venice and Sparta, Machiavelli proposes that Rome could have avoided tumult only if it imitated the other two by, respectively, not arming the people and not admitting ("opening the way for") foreigners. But in doing both, Rome strengthened the plebs by, literally, putting sticks in their hands and by swelling their numbers. Had it not done so, Machiavelli avers, appealing perhaps to two different kinds of grandi, it would not have come to greatness, on the one hand, and it would have been weak, on the other. This passage establishes the strategy pursued in the rest of the chapter: grandi who are willing to forsake some domination of their own citizens for the greater oppression of others abroad and the greater wealth and fame that accompanies such exploits will cede some domestic political role to the people. Grandi who still cling to a definition of liberty whereby they wholly exclude the people from politics and exercise domination over them will be made to fear that such a republic is inherently weak, and hence in danger of being annexed by another regime, an eventuality that would curtail the grandi's domestic "liberty."

The latter term does not appear in the balance of the chapter, but its realization may yet be Machiavelli's main objective: he entices the grandi to compromise their notion of liberty (the monopoly on "a political way of life" at home) through appeals to the greatness or necessity of expansion, and in so doing, bargains for the people an unnamed and undefined new kind of liberty: a larger role in politics than they had been granted previously in republics; one in which they protect themselves from grandi oppression, and protect the whole regime from the collapse that grandi domination portends. On reflection then, the comparison of the liberty practiced and guarded in Sparta and Venice, on the one hand, and Rome, on the other, may have been inappropriate from the start, since they are qualitatively different in important respects. When liberty is conceived as independence from other regimes, the two models are the same; when it is conceived as the play of domestic forces, they are different in kind. Yet Machiavelli conducted the comparison as if "liberty" in both cases were equivalent, adding the element of empire, to induce the grandi to tolerate a transition from the one kind of liberty to the other.

Machiavelli's choice for Rome, his "belief," as he professes repeatedly at the climax of I.6, in the imperial republican model rules out the possibility of a militarily strong *and* nonexpansive republic. Why might we have cause to doubt his profession of faith in this respect? Well, he uses as the examples of "weak" republics, those with a "weak foundation," Sparta and Venice, republics with the greatest longevity ever recorded. Perhaps their internal liberty pales in comparison with Rome's, but their stability and longevity is incompatible with weakness. Maybe they did not rise to the level of Roman grandezza, but they did not lack for renown. What about the claim that the human condition, the rise and fall of worldly events, necessarily requires expansion or loss? At the conclusion of a highly rhetorical reasoning over self-containment versus expansion, after insisting that necessity *will* compel a republic to expand, Machiavelli remarks in conclusion: "*if indeed* necessity brings [a republic] to expand . . ." (I.6; emphasis added). This is a curiously hesitant way for Machiavelli to discuss a topic like necessity, a topic that he treats so emphatically elsewhere (e.g., I.1).

But given the history of republics, most of which look more like Sparta or Venice than Rome, and based on the political prejudices of the Florentine ottimati discussed above, it's safe to say that all or most of the grandi will *not* be seduced by the promise of imperial glory into tolerating popular inclusion and tumults "as inconveniences necessary to arrive at Roman greatness." Therefore, besides the carrot of glory or greatness, the stick of necessity, the fear that weakness will lead to regime collapse, is required to encourage grandi to accept such inconveniences.[46] At the end of the chapter, Machiavelli reminds his audience what those inconveniences are: a tribunate that enables the people to guard liberty, and provision for accusation (which he introduces) by which any citizen, but especially the tribunes, could bring other citizens to account. So besides being opposed by the plebs and the their tribunes, the grandi are now encouraged to allow themselves to be indicted for specific instances of usurping liberty.

Thus, while appetite and greatness play no small role in *The Discourses*, I would suggest that they are inducements that Machiavelli uses to motivate a grandi audience to pursue empire, not for its own sake, but as a mechanism by which they permit greater popular participation in politics. The Roman model promises more liberty for citizens at home, but diminution of it for republics abroad. The Spartan/Venetian model promises virtually no liberty for most citizens at home, but it does not, for the most part, threaten republics abroad. Machiavelli is quite possibly ambivalent about both, on the one hand, maximum longevity without popular liberty, and, on the other, maximum expansion that destroys liberty elsewhere and corrupts it at home. But he explicitly endorses the model that portends the latter, because it, and *not* the former model to which his dedicatees would already be inclined before undertaking *The Discourses*, encourages popular inclusion.[47]

Expanded popular participation not only improves the lot of common citizens by enabling the people to contest and contain grandi ambition, that is, the practice of liberty, but also helps both grandi and people by better ensuring the longevity of regimes, longevity endangered by the grandi desire to oppress. The grandi must not be allowed to oppress the people so thoroughly that they jeopardize the very regime structure that makes satisfaction of their appetite possible. After all, in *The Discourses* Machiavelli insists that the oppressive appetite of the grandi is the most serious threat to a republic, just as in *The Prince* he states it is a threat to a principality. Republics are usually ruined because the grandi empower a prince to help them dominate the people when laws and institutions are no longer sufficient to this end (I.16). Or they are ruined because the people enlist a prince, foreign or domestic, to protect them from the grandi when laws and institutions no longer do so (I.7). Either way, the fault lies with the oppressive nature of the grandi. In case they miss it, to emphasize his point to Cosimo and Zanobi, Machiavelli frequently insists that *young* nobles (e.g., I.46), in particular, have trouble being satisfied in this desire to dominate the people.

Unfortunately, I can pursue this line of analysis no further within the space at my disposal. If I had the opportunity, I would elaborate on the following themes in the balance of Machiavelli's discourses on the Roman republic: (1) the restoration and preservation of liberty entailed by the grandi's elimination of principality; (2) the rewards of riches and fame that result from the grandi's command of an armed populace in the pursuit of empire; and (3) the prospect that the grandi will continue to hold a virtual monopoly on the chief magistracies (even if the people compete with them for such offices) and will continue to maintain the dominant influence on the policies of a republic. In brief, apropos (1) and (2): *The Discourses* suggest that tyrannicide, and the inclusion of the people in military and political affairs, increase the wealth and fame of young grandi more than does either an alliance between a prince and the grandi against the people, or a simple *governo stretto*—both of which had been the political preferences of the Florentine ottimati, who had either colluded with various Medici princes or sought a narrow oligarchy in the city.[48]

Junius Brutus is immortal for eliminating the tyranny of princes proper in Rome, and for sharply curtailing the tyranny of young princes plural within the republic (I.17, III.3). Brutus decides that the patrimony of liberty is more valuable than progeny with power. Moreover, Machiavelli establishes as exemplary the exploits of subsequent Roman magistrates and captains. Great men like Scipio Africanus (III.21), Cincinnatus (III.24, 25), Fabius Maximus (III.49), and Manlius Torquatus (III.34) gained far more fame than any individuals produced by the Spartan or Venetian republics. Yet Machiavelli suggests that the ferocious participation of the plebs in war *and* politics makes possible both territorial conquest *and* glorious nobles. A popular army is the vehicle the Roman grandi ride to imperial success; and the tribunes, the accusations, and the popular assemblies are the domestic institutions that curb uncontrolled grandi oppression of the people—and, in fact, generally channel their will to dominate into something approximating civically salutary leadership (e.g., I.3, I.18, I.44, III.11).[49]

Regarding (3) above: Machiavelli may assuage his grandi audience's fears that popular inclusion means their own exclusion from places of prominence within a republic. After all, Machiavelli shows quite explicitly how the senate, noble magistrates, and great captains manipulated the people through religion (I.13–15), electoral fraud (I.47, 48), physical appearance as opposed to reasonably persuasive words (I.54), the prosecution of unnecessary wars (I.37), and so on. The question is whether these are genuine instructions to the grandi, or whether, so plainly stated in the vernacular, these are clear guidelines for the people to avoid being manipulated. Who is less likely to know about the methods just described? There are, of course, indictments of the people throughout *The Discourses*, as well—usually focused on the limited capacities of the people rather than any threat to good order that they may pose (e.g., I.44). It would be useful to gauge whether these criticisms are as severe and substantive as those directed toward the grandi—especially in light of similar evaluations over the course of Western political thought. Moreover, it would be imperative to consider whether some of Machiavelli's criticisms of the people, especially those implied in his apparent praise of them in I.58—"The Multitude Is Wiser and More Constant Than a Prince"—were meant to be understood by, and useful to, a grandi audience at all.

Machiavelli provides examples of grandi manipulation of the people that would be obvious to both the grandi and the people who would read about them. There are also examples perhaps too oblique to be recognized or understood by either grandi or peoples. Thus, Machiavelli makes many arguments that were perhaps intended for neither a grandi nor a popular audience; they are intended for, let's say, a philosophic audience. Should we assume that Machiavelli knew that the philosophically inclined who would best locate and identify these passages, if not always the full status and import of the latter, would in fact be servants of the grandi, rather than of the people? Could Machiavelli have anticipated that the only readers capable of nearly intuiting his deepest teachings, or who were best trained to do so, would be partisanly oligarchic in orientation? After the political-philosophic revolution that he initiated, could he conceive that those best equipped to understand him would be those most concerned with reestablishing the alliance between philosophy and oligarchy that he attempted to shatter? Machiavelli's textual sovereignty and spiritual conquest may have met its limit at precisely the point where the modern relationship between philosophy and politics remained thoroughly senatorial rather than becoming tribunate in any substantive way. I venture to guess that he couldn't have predicted that his "philosophic" audience would be overwhelmingly senatorial, as opposed to tribunate, in orientation. Such interpreters of Machiavelli might assume or pretend that they maintain a philosophic position above those of both the great and the vulgar. But they may have overlooked the decidedly oligarchic perspective of the dedicatees of *The Discourses*, and the implications that it may have for the full meaning of the work, precisely because their own perspective is in many ways identical to it, sharing many of the same political prejudices.

Difficult Engagements

PRIVATE PASSION AND PUBLIC SERVICE IN
MONTAIGNE'S *ESSAIS*

Timothy Hampton

> That which the world calls virtue is ordinarily nothing more
> than a phantom formed by our passions, to which we give an
> honest name in order to do as we please.
>
> —La Rochefoucauld

THE SUMMONS

SEPTEMBER OF 1581 found Montaigne in Italy, in the baths. He had left
France the year before, after submitting for publication the first edition
of his *Essais*, and had traveled through France, Switzerland, and Italy on
a trip that was both cultural and therapeutic. He had come to Lucca, the
last of several balneal stops on his Italian journey, as he tried, unsuccessfully, to soak his way out of the pain inflicted on him by his kidney stones.
As he considered options for further treatment, he received a letter, for-
warded from Rome, informing him that he had been selected by the jurists
of Bordeaux to be mayor of that city. His first inclination, he writes later,
was to decline the office. However he accepted and hurried home to Bordeaux, where the call was seconded by a letter from the king, Henry III,
expressing royal pleasure at the selection (which took place, the monarch
notes happily, "without intrigue") and commanding Montaigne to com-
ply "without delay or excuse" [sans délay ne excuse]. By doing so, said
Henry, Montaigne would bring "great pleasure" to his monarch. Failure
to take up his duties, by contrast, would bring "great displeasure" ("le
contraire me desplairoit grandement").[1]
   Montaigne places his account of the summons strategically within the
architecture of the third book of the *Essais*. It directly follows the long
essay entitled "De la vanité," in which he speaks at length of inheriting
the ancestral chateau, and of the vanity of travel. That essay reaches its
climax when Montaigne literally reprints the text of a decree issued to him
by the city fathers of Rome, declaring him an honorary Roman. "Being a

citizen of no city," he writes, "I am very pleased to be one of the noblest city that ever was or will be" (766b) [N'estant bourgeois d'aucune ville, je suis bien aise de l'estre de la plus noble qui fut et qui sera oncques" (979b)]. Two pages later this noncitizen is on his way back to Bordeaux to assume a civic post that his father had held before him.

Scholars of Montaigne's life have underscored the biographical interest of these facts about his travels and his public service.[2] However, we should note as well that the scenario just described is a literary cliché. The summoning of a young man from the errant life of the scholar or tourist to a position of civic or political responsibility is a familiar motif in Renaissance literature. Hamlet leaves Wittenburg to settle things in Elsinore; Prince Hal gives up his revels in Eastcheap to become Henry V; Gargantua and Pantagruel both leave their studies and come to the defense of the homeland. Part of the joke here may stem from the fact at that at forty-eight Montaigne is a bit old to fit the part of a Hamlet or a Hal. Still, it is one of the general strategies of the *Essais* to cast large cultural and literary topoi as autobiographical details; and the scene recalls similar literary moments at which knights or students are reined in and put to work by some sort of political or familial authority. To be sure, Montaigne's assumption of the mayoralty has a biographical dimension since, as noted earlier, by doing so he is following in the footsteps of his father. Yet what he tells us of his father's service is that he found the job burdensome and unrewarding, that it disturbed him and took him from the health and comfort of his rural estate. Thus the father's unhappiness with public service sets the scene for the son's attempt to get it right. In the process, biographical detail and literary cliché overlap to define a site of theoretical reflection on the problem of framing a model of public service that would neither debilitate nor compromise the private self.

Montaigne discusses his mayoral tenure in the tenth chapter of his third book of essays, the essay called "De mesnager sa volonté" (translated as "Of husbanding your will"). It is an essay that has attracted less critical attention than most of the other chapters in the third book. Yet it is crucially important for understanding the relationship of public and private in his work. The most frequently cited passage in the essay is Montaigne's famous claim that "The Mayor and Montaigne have always been two, with a very clear separation" (774b) [Le Maire et Montaigne ont tousjours esté deux, d'une separation bien claire (989b)]. Yet this claim is only one moment in a larger reflection on the conditions of private selfhood. In its specific context, it is followed by a whole sequence of figures—lawyers, accountants, emperors—whose private identity Montaigne considers in relationship to their public functions. The list touches on one of the grand political themes of Baroque culture—the notion that humans are all role players in a vast cosmic drama. Montaigne exploits this theme, but he also claims an authenticity that transcends it. He does so, I will suggest, by carefully circumscribing the terms through which public action might be understood and presenting his own actions as simultaneously serving the public weal and protected from the vicissitudes of passion and violence.

Montaigne had earlier engaged in forms of public service, specifically through his work in the legal profession in Bordeaux. However, he never discusses that experience, and, clearly, it is his service as mayor that he finds of greater interest. Thus Montaigne's entry onto the stage of politics raises questions about the ways in which the discourse of the *Essais* negotiates the relationship between public life and private contemplation, and about how self-cultivation and service can coexist. Indeed, as Montaigne points out in the very first paragraph of "De mesnager sa volonté," public service threatens autonomy. And the meeting point of autonomy and service is the province of the passions, since the passions both shape selfhood and motivate action. As he says in the essay's third sentence: "I espouse, and in consequence grow passionate about, few things. My sight is clear, but I fix it on few objects; my sensitivity is delicate and tender. But my perception and application are hard and deaf; I engage myself with difficulty" (766b) [J'espouse, et me passionne par consequant, de peu de choses. J'ay la veuë clere, mais je l'attache à peu d'objects; le sens delicat et mol. Mais l'apprehension et l'application, je l'ay dure et sourde; je m'engage difficilement (980b)].[3] The rest of the essay suggests that we should take the final word of this passage in its fullest sense. Montaigne engages himself with difficulty; that is, he rarely commits himself, and when he does, it is a difficult process.

We might understand the originality of Montaigne's notion that commitment is "difficult" by recalling the early sections of Albert O. Hirschman's famous study, *The Passions and the Interests: Political Arguments for Capitalism before Its Triumph*. Hirschman posits that Renaissance thinkers tended to offer one of three possible solutions for controlling the passions. These were "repressing" the passions (his example is Calvin), "harnessing" the passions (Pascal, Mandeville), or counterbalancing them with other passions (Bacon).[4] However in "De mesnager sa volonté" Montaigne offers yet another approach to the passions, which is simply to avoid them altogether: "Passions," he says, "are as easy for me to avoid as they difficult for me to moderate" (780b) [Les passions me sont autant aisées à éviter comme elles me sont diffiles à moderer (997b)]. If passion—and by extension the will—cannot be controlled, what becomes important are the strategies of avoidance. These involve controlling the relationship of the will to the things around it—to the institutions and situations with which it interacts. What is at issue is a problem of positioning the self. It is therefore beautifully ironic that Montaigne's articulation of what is in effect a psychology of evasion comes precisely in the essay in which he describes the self as constantly tempted away from "home" by the demon of service to the community. Psychology and topography mirror each other. Having evaded responsibility through travel in "De la vanité," he now returns home to enter public life and seek to evade the worry that accompanies it.

Montaigne's hesitation about commitment may not be merely an effect of personality. It points as well to his position as a member of a provincial aristocracy that is caught between emerging models of centralized political power and the intense, passionate position-taking made urgent by the wars of religion in France. In the middle and later years of the sixteenth century the famous "crisis of the aristocracy" in France begins to impose upon nobles a set of urgent political and ethical choices. After centralized political power began, in the early decades of the century, to erode the traditional autonomy of the provincial nobility, the wars of religion provided that same nobility with an opportunity for reaffirming its independence. The great noble families frequently took religious discord as a pretext for bloody bouts of score-settling and vendetta.[5] We can read this violent background in the king's obvious relief at Montaigne's easy election. Yet at the same time, the relative ineffectiveness and corruption of the court following the death of Henry II in 1559 rendered a strong association with the royal cause potentially disastrous, and the provincial nobility tended to ally itself strongly either with Protestantism or with the ultramontane Catholic extremism of the Holy League. Montaigne alludes to this fragmentation of the public sphere when he notes that his contemporaries allow their passions to place them under the thrall of various charismatic leaders, in the process distorting their vision of the larger political issues underpinning the wars. Excessive service, marked by passion, is destructive to the servant. As he notes, "A friend of mine, a gentleman and a very fine man, nearly drove himself out of his mind by too passionate an attention and devotion to the affairs of a prince, his master" (771b) [Un gentil'homme, très-homme de bien, et mon amy, cuida brouiller la santé de sa teste par une trop passionnée attention et affection aux affaires d'un prince, son maistre (986b)]. Indeed, he goes on, his contemporaries frequently give themselves over to private hatreds that have nothing to do with the ills of the state: "they are stung . . . with a personal passion and beyond justice and public reason" (774c) [ils se picquent de passion particuliere et au delà de la justice et de la raison publique (990c)]. Thus we can say that for Montaigne the crisis of French politics is brought on by the injection of private interest, powered by passion, into the public sphere. It's not only that the passions are political, but that the political, during the French religious wars, is the passionate. In such an atmosphere traditional humanist ideals of public service—grounded in Ciceronian and Aristotelian notions of the polis—appear outmoded or naive, even as the new ideals of retirement associated with Renaissance neo-Stoicism seem to point to a rejection of public life altogether.[6]

"De mesnager sa volonté" offers us the novelty of a meditation on service in the public sphere that is linked neither to the court nor to the vicissitudes of monarchy—those topics that have conventionally interested scholars of early modern political culture. Much has been written on Montaigne's politics and on his role as a member of the so-called Politiques group—that group of moderate humanists which advocated a secular, that is, political, solution to the wars of religion.[7] However, less attention has been paid to the ways in which his own self-representation involves a struggle to define a position for the subject that is both politically engaged and psychologically and emotionally disengaged. The complex interweaving of discourses that underpins this positioning is evident in the very title of Montaigne's essay, which juxtaposes the "management" techniques of home economics with the self-transformative dynamics of traditional moral philosophy. It suggests that Montaigne is trying to work out a new technology of selfhood.[8] The essay draws upon such classical documents of self-adjustment as Seneca's *De Tranquilitate Animi* but blends a reflection on the power of the passions to distort the equilibrium of the soul with a consideration of how to act both effectively and happily in the public service.

The summons to service—the moment of "interpellation," if you will—thus evokes a well-worn literary topos under a new pressure. It recalls a cliché of masculine education applied to a newly complex social and political situation. Yet at the same time it contrasts with the intense self-absorption of the *Essais*. "Few things touch me, or, to put it better, hold me" (766b) [Peu de choses me touchent, ou, pour mieux dire, me tiennent (980b)], says Montaigne in the first sentence of the essay. This gesture of self-correction—"pour mieux dire"—is telling, since throughout the essay he notes repeatedly that, in fact, it is fine if things "touch" us as long as they don't possess us. The difficult thing is to let them touch us without letting them possess us. The space between being troubled and being possessed is the space of effective service. "We cannot distinguish the skin from the shirt" (773b) [Nous ne savons pas distinguer la peau de la chemise (989b)], he writes a few pages later. Yet the halting *correctio*, "pour mieux dire," that marks the entry into the chapter suggests that what is at issue here is both a problem of ethical action and a problem of writing. Montaigne must find a language for describing a kind of public service that is engaging but not entangling. There are few literary models for writing about this middle position, between engagement and disengagement. In the tradition of Aristotelian and Ciceronian moral philosophy that Montaigne inherits, it is through public service that virtue is most effectively demonstrated and that selfhood is most powerfully realized. Fifty years before Montaigne, Rabelais's Panurge, that purveyor of cultural clichés, reminds his friend Pantagruel that his own virtue can be most clearly shown only if he engages in public life. He is distantly recalling Cicero, who writes in *De Officiis* of the importance of public action as both a civic necessity and a way of displaying "greatness of spirit."[9] Even in the Senecan tradition, from which Montaigne drew most heavily in the writing of the *Essais*, retirement from public life is generally depicted as something one does *after* public service, as one looks back on the snares of the political world and cultivates repose. When Montaigne is elected mayor, he has already been cultivating repose for close to a decade. He elects to leave retirement, not fade into it.[10]

Montaigne describes his general approach to public action by stating that one should not refuse public commitment, but that one should take it on without any sense of burden or obligation, "by way of loan and accidentally, the mind holding itself ever in repose and in health, not without action, but without vexation, without passion" (770b) [C'est par emprunt et accidentalement, l'esprit tenant tousjours en repos et en santé, non pas sans action, mais sans vexation, sans passion (984b)]. At one level, the affirmation of a commitment that refuses passion is a commonplace of moral philosophy. In the first book of *De Officiis* Cicero reminds his son that the man who engages in public life must learn to disdain "human affairs" as a way of cultivating tranquility of mind: "Otherwise, how will they live without anxiety, with seriousness and with constancy?"[11] This theme of the disdain for the human world as a precondition of constancy gains new urgency in the context of the French religious wars. The civil and political unrest of the late sixteenth century had produced a revival of classical Stoic thought, and a number of Montaigne's contemporaries had been writing on the control of the passions. The most famous of these was the Flemish humanist Justus Lipsius, whose *De Constantia* is exactly contemporaneous with the *Essais* and explores much of the same terrain as does "De mesnager sa volonté." *De Constantia* opens, in fact, with a reflection on the problem of political commitment in the face of political and civil disorder, as Lipsius is presented fleeing the Flemish wars into philosophical retreat and the control of the passions.

Montaigne reverses Lipsius's scenario. His essay stresses the necessity of public action and the desirability of avoiding the passions. *De Constantia* closes with a reflection on the value of gardens as places of spiritual and physical refuge.[12] For Montaigne, the site of philosophical reflection is the home, which functions both literally and figuratively in his work, referring both to the ancestral castle (from which, he reminds us, his father was drawn into public service) and to a self that is at ease with itself.[13] Indeed, the language that opens the essay is the language of husbandry.

In the third paragraph Montaigne argues that men ("les hommes") are given over to "renting themselves out" [(ils) se donnent à louange] to the public world. They have abandoned themselves to outside forces who now take up residence inside them: "their renters are in their house; it is no longer they" (767b) [leurs locataires sont chez eux, ce ne sont pas eux (981b)]. The reason for this abandonment of the self and its location, he goes on, comes from moral philosophy itself. For it is the teachers and moralists who have instructed men to give themselves over to public service: "Most of the rules and precepts of the world take this course of pushing us out of ourselves and driving us into the public square, for the benefit of public society" (769b) [La plus part des reigles et preceptes du monde prennent ce train de nous pousser hors de nous et chasser en la place, à l'usage de la societé publique (983b)].[14] Thus the humanist emphasis on civic service—a commonplace of moral philosophy since Aristotle and Cicero—turns out to be the spur to a loss of the self. To counter this tendency, says Montaigne, we must "manage the liberty of our soul and only lease it out on the right occasions" (767b) [il faut mesnager la liberté de nostre ame et ne l'hypotequer qu'aux occasions justes (981b)]. Montaigne's use here of the verb "to manage" ("menager") is striking. For this crucial economic term gives the essay its title, which we might translate literally as "Of managing the will." Yet the only time in the body of the essay in which the word appears is in the sentence just quoted. Thus an essay that purports to be about "managing" the will (a problem of self-control) turns out to be about "managing" the freedom of the soul (a problem of social positioning).

This freedom turns out to have much to do with a kind of internalization of the pose of the country aristocrat. Following his admission, cited at the outset, that "Passions are as easy for me to avoid as they are hard for me to moderate" (780b) [Les passions me sont autant aisées à eviter comme elles me sont difficiles à moderer (997b)], Montaigne goes on to add that those who cannot be as constant as the Stoics should take refuge in "the bosom of this plebeian stupidity of mine. What those men did by virtue, I train myself to do by disposition" [qu'il se sauve au giron de cette mienne supidité populaire. Ce que ceux-là faisoient par vertu, je me duits à le faire par complexion]. Philosophers and rustics—the extreme examples of virtue and dullness—are tranquil and happy, he asserts. Those between them suffer. And he goes on to cite Virgil's second Georgic (vv. 490–94), where the poet speaks of the special knowledge of those who "know the origins of things" [qui potuit rerum cognoscere causas]. These are the philosopher, "who can scorn inexorable fate" [qui . . . inexorabile fatum / subjecit pedibus] and the husbandman, "who knows the woodland clan" [ille Deos qui novit agrestes]. Montaigne suggests that whereas others seek knowledge of the origins of things outside the self, he observes the tiny origins of the passions, and learns to avoid them. In this sense, as retired aristocrat, he is both woodsman and philosopher in one. Yet what does it mean to counter "virtue" with "disposition," and to claim that one can "train oneself" "by disposition" instead of virtue?

MONTAIGNE READING: VIRTUE AND EXCESS

Throughout the *Essais* Montaigne insists on the centrality of the public sphere for the definition of the subject. As he writes in "De l'utile et de l'honneste," the first essay in the third book, "Both my word and my honor are, like the rest, parts of this common body. Their best operation is public service; I take that for granted" (604b) [Ma parolle et ma foy sont, comme le demeurant, pieces de ce commun corps, leur meilleur effect, c'est le service public; je tiens cela pour presupposé (774b)]. But there is more to this sense of public service than a moral choice. It is, in fact, the public sphere that controls action and gives acts their meanings. Since desire is virtually impossible to control, he says in the same essay, action must be framed by public institutions: "Will and desires are a law unto themselves; actions must receive their law from public regulation" (603b) [La volonté et les desirs se font loy eux mesmes; les actions ont à la recevoir de l'ordonnance publique (772b)].

Montaigne's position is quite traditional. At least since Cicero, moral and political philosophers had insisted on the importance of the public world as the center of human action, as that place through which human action takes its meaning. As Peter N. Miller has noted, Cicero's argument in the case of Vatinius affirmed that the greatest honor available to a political actor derived from the notion that "the welfare of the State [was] bound up with the welfare of [the] self."[15] Yet under the political pressures of the late sixteenth century, this traditional notion of the political world as the preeminent shaper of action had taken on a new coloration and become intertwined with a new theory—new at least since Machiavelli—which began to privilege the safety and stability of political institutions over the moral disposition of the subject. It is this theory, as Miller points out, that comes to be called reason of state.[16]

Yet Montaigne does not go so far as to advocate a doctrine of reason of state. In "De l'utile et de l'honneste," alluded to above, he considers what will become the classical topos in treatments of reason of state, the moment of the coup d'état, when the prince must act against his subjects in order to preserve the health of the state. In this case, says Montaigne, he accepts that the prince must act in certain seemingly unethical ways, yet it is his hope that the prince will regret those same actions: "If he did it without regret, if it did not grieve him to do it, it is a sign that his conscience is in a bad way" (607b) [s'il le fit sans regret, s'il ne luy greva de le faire, c'est signe que sa conscience est en mauvais termes (777b)]. This slightly sentimental reference to the prince's conscience is telling. For it points to Montaigne's interest—which we will see repeated in a moment—in translating the increasingly impersonal maneuvers of political rationality into personal terms, as if they were carried out as part of a dialogue between sages.[17]

This conventional vision of the relationship between the self and the public world is what seems to be in crisis in "De mesnager sa volonté." Yet we can see the origins of this crisis much earlier on in the *Essais* by turning to the first chapter of the second book, "De l'inconstance de nos actions."[18] For it is there that Montaigne considers the relationship between public action and the classical notion of constancy that is so important to traditional discourses on the passions. "De l'inconstance de nos actions" addresses the relationship of action, passion, and virtue by talking about reading. The essay is centrally concerned with problems of interpretation, and in specific, with the ways in which we can read specific actions as signs of the disposition of the soul. Montaigne is skeptical that actions might represent interiority. Those who try to make sense of human action, he says, are hindered by the diversity of human behavior. In fact, so variable is human action that it seems impossible to bring different actions into harmony with each other and identify them all as parts of "the same shop" (239b) [de mesme boutique (314a)]. A man who is courageous one moment is cowardly the next, such that the pieces represented by his diverse acts cannot be assembled into a whole. Even among the ancients, he notes, scarcely a dozen men were able to define their lives by the "certain and assured pace" [certain et asseuré train] that is the mark of wisdom.

Montaigne states that his own interpretive practice tries to respond to this epistemological uncertainty. He points out that he is generally inclined to say good things about others, and to interpret things "in the best way" (242b) ("d'interpreter plustost en bonne part les choses qui le peuvent estre" [319a]).[19] However, he also recognizes that virtuous actions may be motivated by vicious motives. The pressure of the moment and the impulses of ambition make actions into ambiguous signs—ironic indicators of the absence, rather than the presence, of virtue.

The possible responses to this condition are several. As Montaigne notes in a revision to the text made for the second edition of the *Essais*, readers and interpreters tend to try to counterbalance the dissolution of self into action by choosing as a point of reference a kind of abstract idea of a particular subject, a "universal air" (239b) [un air universel (314b)] against which they sort out and interpret the various contingent moments in which he or she acts. A moment later, in an addition made at the very end of his life, he avers that one must simply divide one's consideration of people from one's interpretation of action. If an act is praiseworthy, he notes, it should be praised—but we must remember that it is "the action alone that is laudable, not the man" (242b) [l'action est loüable, non pas l'homme (319c)]. This is, of course, to empty historical actions of character altogether.

At one level Montaigne's resigned relinquishment of the tendency to always interpret "in the best part" constitutes a turning away from a certain tradition of Christian exegesis that was central to much of French humanism a generation earlier. In his *De Doctrina Christiana* Saint Augustine had stressed the importance of always interpreting in such a way as to promote the rule of charity and the common good. His formulation is repeated often by Montaigne's countryman Rabelais, who, under the influence of Erasmian Christian humanism, advises his readers always to "interpret me in the best way" ("en perfectissime partie"). This hermeneutics of faith is one of the elements of what Rabelais calls "Pantagruelism."[20]

For Montaigne, however, political and intellectual climates have changed in such a way that actions have ceased to signify in the ways they did earlier, and, hence, new hermeneutic strategies are required. He expands on these themes in an essay titled "De la vertu," the twenty-ninth essay of the second book, which explicitly links interpretation to politics. There he makes a distinction between the Stoic ideal of constancy and "the erratic impulses of the soul" (532a) [les boutees et saillies de l'ame (683a)]. Man can do anything, he says, even surpass the gods in certain things. However, he does not do so by virtue. Instead, he is possessed by a momentary excess, "by fits and starts" (533a) [c'est par secousse (683a)]. In the lives of the exemplary heroes of antiquity, he goes on, there are instances of extreme virtue and heroism, "miraculous traits" [des traits miraculeux]. But they are only "traits"—that is, moments (with Montaigne relying on the etymological sense of "trait" as coming from the Latin *tractus*, "carried along"). Even for the moderns, "we who are merely aborted men" [qui ne sommes qu'avortons d'hommes], such moments of excess come occasionally, when we are roused by the examples or discourses of others. However, the results of those impulses are not signs of the true nature of the soul. Rather they are described by Montaigne as passions, as moments that take us completely out of ourselves: "but it is a kind of passion that impels and drives [the soul], and which to some extent tears her out of herself" (533a) [c'est une espece de passion qui . . . pousse et agite [notre ame], et qui la ravit aucunement hors de soy (683a)].

What is striking here is Montaigne's use of the term *passion* to describe the motivation of a the soul when it behaves heroically. For, of course, traditional moral philosophy would call this force "virtue." By calling

virtue passion Montaigne breaks with the Ciceronian and Senecan traditions of moral philosophy on which he draws throughout the *Essais*. For
those traditions virtue is what is supposed to control and police passion.
Montaigne's phrase collapses the distinction between the soul's movements and the force through which those movements may be policed or
corrected. Virtue, which should be a bridle and guide for the passions,
now turns out to be the force incites them. The force that that would
"manage" the will turns out to be the spur that drives it to excess.

This theme is stressed elsewhere in the *Essais* as well. Midway through
the famous "Apologie de Raymond Sebond," the longest of his essays,
Montaigne states that passion is the necessary impetus behind virtue. He
notes that the soul receives powerful shaking from the passions of the
body ("les secousses et esbranlemens que nostre ame reçoit par les passions corporelles" [550a]), but that it suffers no less from its own passions, such that it often has no movement than from its own motion, "the
breath of her winds" (426a) [le souffle de ses vents] and that without such
motivation it can do nothing. Indeed, he ends, "Valor, they say, cannot
become perfect without the assistance of anger" (426a) [La vaillance di-
sent-tils, ne se peut parfaire sans l'assistance de la cholère (550a)]. It is
important that he should end with valor or "vaillance," here since what
is at issue is in part the opposition between a private, intellectual, or moral
virtue, and public military and political virtue. Montaigne strives to blend
his own ideals of aristocratic heroism with the internal, self-regarding
concerns of the Stoic sage.[21]

The context for this fragmentation of virtue is hinted at in Montaigne's
revisions for the second version of "De mesnager sa volonté," published
in 1588. Here he shifts the focus of his meditation to contemporary
events. He inserts two long paragraphs that discuss several notorious political crimes resulting from the sectarian violence of the French religious
wars. These crimes, which would have been well known to his readers,
are the two attempts, the second successful, on the life of the Protestant
leader William of Orange in 1582 and 1584, and the murder of the ultra-
Catholic duke of Guise in 1563. "There has not occurred within our memory a more admirable act of resolution than that of those two who plotted
the death of the prince of Orange" (537b) [Il n'est point advenu, de nostre
memoire, un plus admirable effect de resolution que de ces deux qui con-
spirerent la mort du prince d'Orenge (689b)], remarks Montaigne. In this
formulation, "resolution" emerges as the double of the Stoic ideal of constancy. It produces a direction for the self through time precisely because
it aims at a goal that is outside the self—an end point resulting in a particular act. Montaigne is particularly impressed by Balthazar Gérard, who
went after William of Orange when he knew that an earlier attempt had
failed and that the prince would be well guarded. Moreover, Gérard's

weapon of choice was a dagger, which, says Montaigne, requires more steadiness and is more easily deflected than a pistol. "Certainly he employed a very determined hand and a courage moved by a vigorous passion" (537b) [Certes, il y employa une main bien determinée et un courage esmeu d'une vigoureuse passion (689b)].

Here a "vigorous passion" motivates action that is horrible, but, by virtue of that same passion, admirable. Moreover, in contrast to the disruptive momentary excess seen earlier, passion is finally channeled into determinate action and is contemplated and shaped over time. These references to the violence of religious conflict in Renaissance France bring the crisis of reading virtue set forth in "De l'inconstance de nos actions" into a powerfully immediate context as Montaigne, the moderate humanist, is forced to admire the "heroism" of political assassins. It may be no accident, then, that in the final edition of the *Essais* Montaigne seems to shift the focus away from the ethics of political assassination and back to the problem of how human action may be read as a sign of virtue. At the end of his life Montaigne revises the essay yet again and frames the discussion of assassination with two intercalated references to the world of Islam. In the first he describes a particularly heroic Turkish fighter who declares that his ferocity comes from watching a hare he once hunted unsuccessfully. Despite the many arrows shot his way, the hare never flinched. From the example of the hare, the fighter concluded that we are bound by our destinies and that neither arrows nor blades can turn destiny aside. And the essay closes with an evocation of the "Assassins," a nation living near Phoenicia, where the soldiers are esteemed for their "devoutness and purity of morals" (538c) [devotion et pureté de moeurs (690c)]. Their way of achieving Paradise is to kill someone from the "contrary religion" [de religion contraire]. For this reason they fear nothing and are willing to die to achieve their goal. The late additions to the essay seem to turn away from the problems of reading or manifesting virtue and controlling passion. These "exotic" examples—safely distanced from Montaigne's immediate context—suggest that through the acceptance of one's own destiny—as either limited or defined by the gods—some type of unity of purpose may be introduced into the narrative of human life. Momentary passion gives way to a larger purpose—deadly though it may be.

READING MONTAIGNE: PUBLIC SERVICE AND SELF-DESCRIPTION

"De l'inconstance de nos actions" and "De la vertu" suggest that the passions of politics are inextricably linked to the politics of interpretation, and that interpretation is threatened by passion. Passion, in this context, might be another name for the injection of private interest into the public sphere at a moment when traditional notions of political life are threatened. The language of the passions provides Montaigne with a vocabulary for naming in moral terms a moment when the new political structure of the centralized absolutist state has not yet replaced traditional concepts of the common good. The two essays just analyzed point to the limitations of traditional Ciceronian notions of the public sphere for understanding the intersection of private passion and public action at a time of political crisis. For Montaigne, momentary passion makes constancy impossible, and "resolution" emerges as the demonic inversion of virtue expressed through time. This dismantling of traditional figurations of virtue opens the way for the meditation set forth in "De mesnager sa volonté," the essay mentioned at the outset, and to which I now want to return. The essay falls loosely into three sections. Opening and closing discussions of Montaigne's actions as mayor frame a central consideration of the problem of public action and its power over the private subject. Near the beginning of the central section, Montaigne turns back on the language of selfhood that he has worked out in the essays discussed above.[22] For it is here that he replaces the figure of the self as defining itself through a series of actions—a kind of unfolding through time—with an image of careful circumscription in space:

> The range of our desires should be circumscribed and restrained to a narrow limit of the nearest and most contiguous good things; and moreover their course should be directed not in a straight line that ends up elsewhere, but in a circle whose two extremities by a short sweep meet and terminate in ourselves. Actions that are performed without this reflexive movement, I mean a searching and genuine reflexive movement—the actions, for example, of the avaricious, the ambitious, and so many others who run in a straight line, whose course carries them ever forward—are erroneous and diseased actions. (773b)

> [La carriere de nos desirs doit estre circonscripte et restraincte à un court limite des commoditez les plus proches et contigües; et doit en outre leur course se manier, non en ligne droite qui face bout ailleurs, mais en rond, duquel les deux pointes se tiennent et terminent en nous par un brief contour. Les actions qui se conduisent sans cette reflexion, s'entend voisine reflexion et essentielle, comme sont celles des avaritieux, des ambitieux et tant d'autres qui courent de pointe, desquels la course les emporte tousjours devant eux, ce sont actions erronées et maladives. (988–89b)]

Here, then, is the figuration of the famous "private" self that scholars have seen as first emerging with Montaigne. Montaigne marks out privacy through a critique of desire that is also a critique of the linear model of the self, which struggles to keep itself constant through its "train" or forward movement. The role of passion in destroying that movement, articulated in the earlier essays discussed above, is here recalled by the notion that linear movement is itself error and that the desiring self is lost in a kind of romance wandering into illness. Only self-sufficiency, figured by the image of the circle, can control desire and free the self from the destructive power of passion.[23]

It is within this circumscribed space that Montaigne paints a portrait of the ideal political actor, free from alliances and allegiances, acting not from passion but from his own sense of the exigencies of the moment:

> he who employs in it only his judgment and skill proceeds more gaily. He feints, he bends, he postpones entirely at his ease according to the need of the occasions; he misses the target without torment or affliction, and remains intact and ready for a new undertaking; he always walks bridle in hand. (770b)

> [Celuy qui n'y employe que son jugement et son adresse, il y procede plus gayement; il feinct, il ploye, il differe tout à son aise, selon le besoing des occasions; il faut d'atainte, sans tourment et sans affliction, prest et entier pour une nouvelle entreprise; il marche tousjours la bride à la main. (985b)]

At one level this description draws upon the image of the effective political actor as described by Machiavelli. The feinting agent who controls events by deferring and dissimulating, by seizing the occasion in order to act, recalls the Machiavellian prince, who molds events to his own advantage. Indeed, the image of the archer who "misses the target" but quickly moves on may even draw on Machiavelli's figuration of political actors imitating models as archers trying to hit the bull's-eye, in the sixth chapter of *The Prince*. Yet what is striking is that Montaigne turns the topos of Machiavellian improvisation into a description of a psychological state. What is at issue is not political efficacy, but the care of the self. By improvising and acting in the moment, free of allegiance and passion, one acts "gayly." Machiavellian *virtù*, here read as psychological flexibility, becomes the alternative to what is left of the vocabulary of traditional moral philosophy, in which virtue is really passion and constancy is haunted by the assassin's "resolution."

And yet it is instructive to contrast Montaigne's depiction here of the gay improviser with his description of the risks of public service. If in the earlier essays discussed above action is linked to problems of interpretation, that connection resurfaces again in "De mesnager sa volonté," as he shifts in the final pages to consider his own service. The problem with acting publically may not, it seems, only involve the management of one's freedom. It also involves the way public action is read: "All public actions are subject to uncertain and diverse interpretations, for too many heads judge them. Some say about this municipal service of mine . . . that I went about it like a man who exerts himself too weakly and with a languishing zeal; and they are not at all far from having a case" (781) [Toutes actions publiques sont subjecte à incertaines et diverses interpretations, car trop de testes en jugent. Aucuns disent de cette mienne occupation de ville . . . que je m'y suis porté en homme qui s'esmeut trop lachement et d'une affection languissante; et il s ne sont pas du tout esloignez d'apparence (998b)]. On the one hand, Montaigne asserts moral efficacy of the subject who can manage his passions by not being overly invested in his job. On the other hand, people have criticized him—for not being overly invested in his job. Montaigne here seems to have been misread, to have become the victim of the interpretative malaise I traced earlier in such essays as "De l'inconstance de nos actions." And while he might seem to dismiss the criticism with a quip, his lament about the misunderstanding that attends public action suggests that there is no small degree of impatience and frustration beneath the sunny exterior. Indeed, he goes on to defend himself from detractors who have suggested that his mayoralty was inef- fective and that he was overly passive. "They accuse me of inactivity in a time when almost everyone was convicted of doing too much" (781b) [On accuse ma cessation, en un temps où quasi tout le monde estoit con- vaincu de trop faire (999b)].

Both the jaunty image of the improvising political actor and Mon- taigne's concluding grumpiness about public judgments of his tenure point us back to the beginning of the essay, where Montaigne first broaches the subject of his own political service. The reason he was able to serve the people of Bordeaux without strife or anxiety, he avers, is that he told them from the outset what to expect of them: "On my arrival I deciphered myself to them faithfully and conscientiously, exactly such as I feel myself to be: without memory, without vigilance, without experi- ence, and without vigor; also without hate, without ambition, without avarice, and without violence; so that they should be informed and in- structed about what they were to expect of my service" (768b) [A mon arrivée, je me deschiffray fidelement et conscientieusement, tout tel que je me sens estre: sans memoire, sans vigilance, sans experience, et sans vigueur; sans hayne aussi, sans ambition, sans avarice et sans violence; à ce qu'ils fussent informez et instruicts de ce qu'ils avoyent à attendre de mon service (982b)]. Here we get an ideal vision of honesty and indepen- dence. Whereas his contemporaries are haunted by memory, constrained by allegiances, and driven by ambition, Montaigne simply lacks these qualities and is, as he notes elsewhere in the essay, too old to change. In both time and space he is free of pressure and is reined in only by the bridle of his judgment.

Yet there is an important difference between Montaigne's entry into public service and the Utopian depiction of the improvising actor I discussed earlier. This involves Montaigne's self-description to the city fathers of Bordeaux. In a political space that has been fragmented by conflicting private passions, in which, indeed, virtue itself has become a kind of passion, some sort of new frame for delineating action must be defined that would replace the traditional Ciceronian humanist model of the *cives*. That frame, which both insulates Montaigne from public strife and mediates his relationship to the political sphere, is the compact through which he reveals himself to those who have chosen him as mayor. Like the figure of the circle that delimits the movements of the self, the compact circumscribes the terms of Montaigne's activities, freeing him to perform as the improvising actor in a carefully defined conceptual space. Here we might see a version of the promissory speech act, the giving of one's "word of honor," which is so important both to Cicero's description of public life in the *De Officiis*, and to Montaigne's own descriptions of obligation in the *Essais*. Indeed, we might locate it as part of the chivalric aristocratic code that the recently ennobled Pierre Eyquem bequeaths to his son Michel de Montaigne—a kind of civic version of the feudal oath of service offered by the vassal to his lord and employer.[24] Yet it is none of these things. The moment of compact, where Montaigne cements his relationship to the city fathers, is neither a chivalric oath, nor a contractual obligation—either of which would link it to traditions of political allegiance. Nor again is it a display of oratorical persuasion, which would call to mind traditional links between rhetoric and the passions.[25] It is a simple self-description. Montaigne engages himself with those who have summoned him to service and guarantees the tranquility of soul by talking about himself, "I deciphered myself to them faithfully and conscientiously" [je me deschiffray fidelement et conscientieusement]. In the history of political relations, this gesture places us neither in the context of chivalric fealty or humanist civility, nor yet in some larger structure involving reason of state. Montaigne's gesture might be seen as a strategic attempt to preserve the Ciceronian notion of tranquility of mind in the midst of service, while jettisoning the crucial classical emphases on constancy and community. Instead, we get individuality, the uniqueness of the private subject as the force that binds actor to action. Whether that individuality is the expression of some unique "interiority," as a certain critical tradition would have it, or whether it is improvised in response to the contingencies of the moment may be open to question.[26]

We can see the limits of this approach to the public world when we compare Montaigne's confident entry into service with his complaints, at the end of the chapter, about those who have criticized him: "I had published elaborately enough to the world my inadequacy in such public management" (784b) [J'avois assez disertement publié au monde mon insuffisance en tels maniements publiques (1002b)], he avers. In other words, I told you I was limited, why then do you criticize me for my limitations? Self-disclosure in the political world, it would appear, is not enough. This complaint about the failure of observers to take his admissions into account is followed by yet another shift in terms. Montaigne goes on to assert that if he left any "regret" or "desire," he doesn't care about it anyway—especially since he always promises to do less than he knows he can. This self-justifying description of his relationship to his own self would seem to be at some distance from his opening claim that he "deciphered" himself "faithfully and conscientiously" to the city fathers of Bordeaux. We now learn that he was dissimulating all along, so as not to disappoint anyone. As he says in the closing paragraph, "I am apt to promise a little less than what I can do and what I hope to deliver" (784b) [je promets volontiers un peu moins de ce que je puis et de ce que j'espere tenir (1002b)]. However, this dissimulation seems to have failed, since even under such reduced expectations he has disappointed some.

We may wonder, in fact, what, precisely, Montaigne means by the statement made early in the essay, "I deciphered myself to them faithfully and conscientiously: exactly as I feel myself to be" [je me deschiffray fidelement et conscientieusement, tout tel que je me sens estre (982)]. *Se déchiffrer* is both a verb of interpretation and a verb of description. Montaigne uses it in both senses elsewhere in the *Essais*.[27] It implies both a reading of the self and a writing of the self, both a self-presentation and a self-understanding—two activities that might be said, in their combination, to describe the act of essay writing itself. Yet no less surprising is the present tense of the moment of self-definition, "just as I feel myself to be" [tout tel que je me sens estre]. It suggests that Montaigne's description of himself *then*, to the magistrates of Bordeaux, is of a piece with what he is *now*. This is a surprising move, when we recall that throughout the *Essais* Montaigne returns again and again to the mutability of the self, to the fact that one is never the same two moments in a row. "Myself now and myself a while ago are indeed two" (736c) [Moy à ceste heure et moy tantost sommes bien deux" (941c)], he says in "De la vanité," the essay that precedes "De mesnager sa volonté." Here, beneath the gaze the Other, at a moment when his actions may be, as he puts it, prey to constant misinterpretation, Montaigne suddenly finds a stable self to "decipher." This may relate to the notion, noted earlier, that he is getting too old to change. However, given the insistence throughout the essay on the mutability of action and the instability of interpretation, it also has the function of a rhetorical gesture aimed at claiming a private stability over against a public world that is suddenly in flux. When the institutions of public life no longer guarantee the meaning of actions, an act of writing may help to fix them. Yet the very fact that the phrase is in the present tense and features a verb suggesting momentary impression—"as I feel myself to be" (rather than, say, "as I know myself to be," or "as I am")—underscores the fragility of this claim of essence. It suggests that, like so much in Montaigne, this stability may be produced out of the writing process itself and located in the present of the writing. It stands in unresolved tension with the pastness of Montaigne's various expressions of regret and with his annoyance at those who criticized his mayoralty. Indeed, we may speculate that if "publishing" his defects to the city fathers of Bordeaux had only limited success, publishing essays in which his public service is framed and reinterpreted offers a bit more satisfaction.

"De mesnager sa volonté" closes with a citation from the *Aeneid*, in which the sea pilot Palinurus—a Renaissance commonplace figure for the political leader—is about to fall asleep and tumble to his death.[28] As he gazes around him he expresses his mistrust of the placid surface of the waves that are about to swallow him up: "My trust in such a monster place? / Ignore the meaning of the sea's smooth face, / The quiet waves?" (784b) [me ne huic confidere monstro, / Mene salis placidi vultum fluctusque quietos / Ignorare? (1002b)].[29] This moment of anticipation, coming as it does in the last line of the essay, suggests that Montaigne is happy to have gotten out of public life without falling into the metaphorical sea of disaster. But it may also remind us that the most placid of surfaces, from the glassy sea to the written page of the essay, can conceal turbulence.

"De mesnager sa volonté" offers one of the few moments in the *Essais* when Montaigne appears as a public actor. It repeatedly turns the conventional vocabulary of moral philosophy on its head. It seeks to work out a model for a posthumanist political action, for a form of public service that is no longer built upon a shared public world. Montaigne's response to a political sphere broken up by private passion—in which virtue itself has become a passion—involves the repeated admonition that the self must be protected from distractions, that duty must be undertaken dispassionately. In place of a traditional ideal of constancy we get the figure of the improvising actor, free from allegiance and memory, shaping the moment as he finds it. Next to this ideal, Montaigne depicts his own mayoralty. Yet his own improvisational practice is carefully preceded by an admission of personal shortcomings, as if Montaigne were preparing a stage upon which he might act without consequences. The last sections of the chapter, moreover, hint that this hedging strategy was only partially successful, as the essayist feels compelled to defend himself against those to whom he revealed his limitations at the outset. This need for a supplementary commentary on the mayoralty suggests that political action can never adequately be framed in advance by admonitions or warnings, as generations of moral philosophers have sought to do. It can only be justified retrospectively. Yet the very presence of the hydra-headed reading public, with its "multiplicity of interpretations," suggests that that act of justification, like the *Essais* themselves, is potentially endless.

The Bachelor State

PHILOSOPHY AND SOVEREIGNTY IN BACON'S *NEW ATLANTIS*

John Guillory

> There is no end to suffering, Glaucon, for our cities, and
> none, I suspect, for the human race, unless either philoso-
> phers become kings in our cities, or the people who are now
> called kings and rulers become, in the truest and most
> complete sense of the word, philosophers.
>
> —Plato, *Republic* 473d

> So saith Cicero in great commendation of Cato the second,
> that he had applied himself to philosophy, *Non ita disputandi
> causa, sed ita vivendi* [not so that he might dispute like a
> philosopher, but so that he might live like one].
> —Bacon, *The Proficencie and Advancement of Learning*

PHILOSOPHERS AND KINGS

As a commonplace of Western thought, Plato's notion of the "philosopher
king" lends itself to contexts remote from Greek antiquity. In modern
invocations of this theme, the terms *philosopher* and *king* might refer to
intellectuals in general, or rulers in general; but for premodern societies,
these terms usually name more precisely specified social roles. In Bacon's
New Atlantis, the Fathers of Salomon's House seem to be Bensalem's true
rulers, very like Plato's philosopher kings; yet no one of them is the king,
a difference that gives the fable its peculiar political resonance with contemporary England. Bensalem, we are told, does have a king, though he
makes no appearance in the narrative. This doubling of ruling powers in
New Atlantis is not the least of the work's interpretive puzzles, an aspect
of the narrative that obliquely reflects, even as it transmutes into a correc-
tive utopian fantasy, the developing political crisis of the time, the divided
sovereignty that Hobbes would later identify as a cause of England's civil
war. Sovereignty in England was effectively (though not equally) divided
between king and Parliament, despite the attempt of some theorists to
grasp this sovereignty as unified in notions of a "mixed polity" or "the

king in Parliament." James famously asserted a conception of monarchical power closer to absolutism. Yet if he were as absolute in fact as in theory, he would not have had to abandon Bacon in 1621 to a Parliament eager to strike out at his proxies.

Like Plato, Bacon returned from Syracuse in defeat. Yet England came very close to having a philosopher for a king when Bacon was lord chancellor. For a golden moment before his fall, great power was concentrated in his office and person. Conversely, if Bacon the philosopher ruled almost as a king, he never tired of reminding James that the advancement of human learning was an *opus basilica*, the work of a king.[1] James's bewilderment upon reading the *Novum Organum* betrayed his limitations as a philosopher, the name Bacon embraced after his fall, staking his future reputation on his philosophical writing and not on the considerable achievements of his political career.[2] In *New Atlantis*, written in the years after his impeachment, he wrapped a fable of philosophical power around the hard core of his lived experience, the impossibility in England of transforming the philosopher into a king, or the king into a philosopher.

It has often been remarked that Bensalem's present-day king makes no appearance in Bacon's fable. His place in the narrative is taken by the Father of Salomon's House who "comes in state" to the city where the narrator and his companions have been given asylum. The absence of the monarch might be understood in the terms of Bacon's fantasy as exalting the philosopher at the king's expense. Bacon might have realized his imaginary triumph over James more thoroughly, however, by giving us the fully Platonic figure of the philosopher king. In distinguishing the role of king from that of the natural philosophers of Salomon's House, Bacon reduces the king to a kind of appendix in Bensalem's body politic.[3] The vestigial relation of Bensalem's present-day king to the inaugural figure of King Salomona hints that *New Atlantis* is an example of what Bacon calls in *The Advancement of Learning* "parabolical poesy," a kind of narrative in which the writer designs to "retire and obscure" the meaning of his work (Vickers, 187).[4] This mode of poesy shadows the *arcanum* of government itself, which in the same work Bacon calls "a part of knowledge secret and retired" (Vickers, 286).

As fantasy or parable, the narrative of *New Atlantis* brushes up against certain real conditions of Bacon's social world that limit the reach of the fantasy. Of these conditions I single out in this essay one little remarked by Bacon's commentators, his use of the term *Fellows* to describe his natural philosophers, and the term *college* to describe Salomon's House.[5] The *Fellow* names a person in the collegiate system of Oxford and Cambridge who is by custom and by statute a celibate, a bachelor. The Fellows of the ancient universities were the only legally prescribed celibates in a Reformation culture that had long since repudiated priestly celibacy. Such a figure, a bachelor by statute, could not enter fully into the dynastic, reproductive role that is a given of the monarchical form of government. For this reason the other name Bacon gives to his Fellows, the "Fathers" of Salomon's House, must be read as equally parabolical. Just as the Fellows cannot be kings, neither are they literally fathers: "We have also, as you must think, novices and apprentices, that the succession of the former employed men [the Fathers] do not fail" (Vickers, 487).[6] The unmarried, childless condition of these Fathers is just what draws Bacon into the most deeply fantasmatic aspect of his narrative. The king rules over the state, but the king is *overruled* by Salomon's House, a *collegium* of bachelor philosophers.

Does the social disqualification of Bacon's philosopher from the political title of monarch imply the converse, that bachelorhood is in some respect a qualification for the title of philosopher? Here I hope to demonstrate that what might seem at first an accidental association in Bacon is implicit in the construction of the philosopher as one version of an emergent social type in early modernity, the *lay intellectual*. The familiar figure of the humanist belongs to this general type, of which the philosopher is a later version, perhaps only fully recognized in the seventeenth century.[7] The type of the philosopher exhibits certain features that distinguish him from the humanist, as well as from the cleric, whose social identity was defined above all by the priestly vocation, and in Catholic nations by the institution of celibacy. Bacon's philosopher presents a distinctly early modern profile, a complex of characterological features built upon the humanist foundation but moving beyond humanism to the more focused vocation of the *natural philosopher*. At the same time I argue in this essay that early modern philosophy (not only Bacon's) reaches back past humanism to recapture and transform celibacy into a new practice of philosophical bachelorhood.

Let me offer, then, a preliminary hypothesis for unpacking Bacon's fable: The narrative of *New Atlantis* triangulates between the social roles of *philosopher*, *king*, and *fellow*. The predicate *fellow* divides the philosopher from the king by excluding the philosopher from the dynastic game, even as the fable transfers ultimate political authority to the Fathers of Salomon's House. Bacon does not give this sovereignty, however, to a *single* philosopher, but to the community of single—that is, unmarried—philosophers. Because the single state of the Fellows is also a communal way of life, a fellowship, no one among them is distinguished from the *collegium* by being set above it. The philosophers' communal exercise of political power—the Fellow who speaks with the narrator always speaks in the first-person plural, a literal, not a royal "we"—does not conform exactly to any real-world institutional model, neither the college fellowship nor the mixed polity of England, with its unique codependence of king and Parliament. The sovereignty of Salomon's House is never divided against itself; it speaks with a single voice and will like that of a king, though without the name of the king—or any proper name, as none are mentioned in *New Atlantis*.

This sovereignty is founded, I will argue, on the tacit relation between the social form of the fellowship—a community of single males bound together by what the ancients called *philia* or *amicitia*—and the peculiar identity of these single males as *natural* philosophers.[8] The form of the fellowship is recognizably a version of the humanist network, localized as a college. In Salomon's House we also recognize the fictional realization of Bacon's "great instauration," his reinvention of natural philosophy. The link between humanist fellowship or friendship and natural philosophy at once constitutes the fable and gives it a parabolical political sense. In the century leading up to *New Atlantis*, humanists moved centripetally to the centers of political power; the great counselors and secretaries, including Bacon himself, rightly saw humanist learning as a means of political advancement. The claim Bacon makes for his natural philosopher simultaneously expresses and cancels this desire by asserting a new *identity* of knowledge and power. In an early letter to James, we find Bacon already arguing for the "congruity between the principles of Nature and Policy," and for "making the government of the world a mirror for the government of a state" (*SEH*, 10:91–92). This "congruity" might only be a future possibility, or might only be imaginary (by which we conventionally mean "utopian"); yet it is Bacon's implicit contention everywhere in his work that only natural philosophy can resolve sectarian conflict and alleviate want, that only natural philosophy can bring peace and plenty to the state.[9] The figure who overrules the king in *New Atlantis* is thus both the realization of humanist political desire and the instauration of a successor to the humanist counselor.

Bacon's natural philosopher is not a "scientist," then, but the governor of both nature and the state. In *New Atlantis* Bacon brings this governor onto the stage of princes, and justifies his warrant to rule by exhibiting both his power over nature and his distinctive ethos or way of life. The prerogative of the natural philosopher cannot be revealed in the "frame of Laws" that Rawley tells us Bacon intended to provide in order to complete his fragmentary fable, and which would have brought *New Atlantis* into greater conformity with More's generic pretext. I suggest that Bacon's fragment is in the parabolical sense complete without its "frame of Laws," that it is a narrative analogue to the intentionally fragmentary aphorism. Bensalem's political order is already embodied, aphoristically expressed, in the Fathers of Salomon's House, in the complex of affects and attributes that constitute the ethos of Bacon's natural philosopher.[10] The bachelor state, as we shall see, is the social condition for the cultivation of this ethos.

ALL UNMARRIED MEN ARE BACHELORS

Although the motif of the bachelor philosopher is not so current as that of the philosopher king, it is well known in the history of philosophy. Nietzsche offers an enthusiastic endorsement of this figure in *A Genealogy of Morals*: "Which great philosopher, so far, has been married? Heraclitus, Plato, Descartes, Spinoza, Leibniz, Kant, Schopenhauer—were not; indeed it is impossible even to *think* about them as married. A married philosopher belongs to *comedy*, that is my proposition: and that exception, Socrates, the mischievous Socrates, appears to have married *ironice*, simply in order to demonstrate *this* proposition."[11] The note of the risible is struck by the allusion to Socrates' spouse, the reputedly shrewish Xanthippe. By contrast the unmarried philosophers might best be represented by Kant, whose private life was marked by little drama of any kind. According to anecdote, his habits were so regular that his neighbors could set their clocks by the time of his afternoon walk.

The philosopher in modern Western culture has sometimes been imagined to lead a life in which the absence of incident is the outward sign of thought—the habitus of *abstraction*, the pulling of the mind away from bodies, places, times, and events. On this view, the philosopher's is a peculiar sort of allegorical life, ideally neither comic nor tragic, a narrative with no genre because no event. And yet, as a simple matter of fact, such a life has not always been perceived either before or since Nietzsche as a necessary condition for philosophical thought; and certainly being unmarried has not always been regarded as such a condition. Nietzsche might have mentioned among the exceptions to the bachelor philosophers not only Socrates but, much closer to home, Hegel, whose comfortable *bürgerlich* marriage was no impediment to philosophizing for him. Conversely, many bachelor philosophers, both some Nietzsche mentions and some he does not, led quite worldly lives, neither ascetic nor sexually celibate. Such counterexamples should prevent us from too quickly identifying the unmarried state of some philosophers with the great thematic of asceticism in Western culture, its perennial opposition of mind and body, contemplation and action.[12]

Presently I will return to Nietzsche's conjecture about the meaning of the philosopher's choice not to marry; but it will be necessary first to locate Nietzsche's question—if we are to raise this question above the level of mere gossip—in relation to the long history of philosophy in the West, and specifically to its deflection in contemporary practice from certain of its original aims. In antiquity, the life of the philosopher, so far from being regarded as properly uneventful, was a subject of absorbing interest and hence frequently set down for posterity. We know more about the lives of the Greek philosophers than we do about Homer or Aeschylus or Sophocles. Much of this information comes down to us from the famous third century CE work by Diogenes Laertius on the lives, opinions, and sayings of the ancient philosophers, which attests by its sheer volume to the extent of antiquity's interest in philosophers' lives.[13] As the classicist Pierre Hadot reminds us in his important studies of Greco-Roman philosophy, the ancients were fascinated with philosophers' lives because the philosopher was chiefly concerned with espousing a "way of life." Hadot writes that for a philosophical school such as the Stoics, "philosophy did not consist in teaching an abstract theory—much less in the exegesis of texts—but rather in the art of living."[14] Much the same was true for the Platonists, the Epicureans, the Skeptics. As social types, philosophers were rather like gurus; they attracted small groups of disciples who followed both their teaching about truth or "nature" and their way of life.

Nietzsche was writing in a still living relation to this now alternative and perhaps even defunct philosophical tradition. As Alexander Nehamas has argued, he rigorously rejected the distinction between the value of a theory and the value of a way of life.[15] If philosophy for the ancient philosophers, as for Nietzsche, was above all a way of life, the philosopher himself was a distinct, highly unusual social type; he was, as Hadot observes, *atopos*, unclassifiable, because the philosophical life, the examined life, tended to alienate the philosopher from customary social roles.[16] Philosophers and their disciples were widely recognized for their eccentric styles of life, at once fascinating and disturbing. Nietzsche's insistence on the bachelorhood of the philosopher recalls this atopical status of the ancient precursors, but generalized as a condition of philosophy *tout court*.[17]

If bachelorhood is no longer an enabling condition for philosophy, it does have a peculiar afterlife in twentieth-century philosophical writing, a kind of spectral remainder. When philosophers today discuss what is called an "analytic truth" (in the Kantian tradition a statement that is logically or necessarily true once its terms are analyzed), they sometimes use a version of the sentence: "All unmarried men are bachelors," or "No bachelors are married." This stock example from the logic textbooks was deployed to great effect in Quine's refutation of the distinction between analytic and synthetic truths in his famous essay "Two Dogmas of Empiricism." Equally effectively, J. L. Austin offers the pronunciation of the marriage contract as an example of his "performative utterance," thus locating the performative in the transition from the single to the married state.[18] By the time of Quine and Austin, then, Nietzsche's portentous observation about the philosopher's marital status was transmogrified into a philosophical *example*, retaining only enough of the aura of the *atopos* to produce a small shock of historical recognition (though perhaps not for most philosophers!). Quine's or Austin's use of this example does not affect the validity of their arguments one way or the other; but the example does tell us something about the history of philosophy.

If philosophy remembers its history in its examples, what is it remembering? I suggest that the connection between philosophy and bachelorhood recalls nothing other than the emergence of the philosopher as a recognized social type in early modernity. What makes Nietzsche's remarks in the *Genealogy* so compelling from a historical perspective is that the bachelor philosophers he names cluster for the most part in the early modern period, during the time bounded by Bacon in the seventeenth century, and in the late eighteenth century and early nineteenth centuries by Kant, Kierkegaard, and Schopenhauer. After this point the bachelor philosophers become increasingly rare—among them Nietzsche himself.[19] As it happens Bacon is the one philosopher before Nietzsche most insistent on the connection between philosophy and bachelorhood, despite the fact that he himself married; but Bacon married late in his life, in his forties, to a girl of fourteen whom he married evidently for her dowry, and from whom he lived mostly apart. In the spirit of Nietzsche we might say that Bacon was married, like Socrates, *ironically*. But against Nietzsche, we must assert that the single state of the philosophers is not a transhistorical condition of philosophizing, but rather a largely early modern phenomenon.

Between 1600 and 1800 nearly every one of the greater philosophers was unmarried: Descartes, Hobbes, Spinoza, Locke, Leibniz, Hume, Adam Smith, Kant (the major exception is Berkeley). To this number we must also add the most important scientists, Robert Boyle, Robert Hooke, and Isaac Newton, who would have been known in their own time as philosophers rather than scientists (a term that did not become current until the nineteenth century). In the early modern period natural philosophy could be distinguished within philosophy but not *from* philosophy. Even the emergence of the "virtuoso" or the "experimenter" in the later seventeenth century does not yet single out the scientist as a distinct social type so much as it names certain internal divisions within the pursuit of natural philosophy itself. When we return the virtuosi and experimenters to the social group from which they are retroactively distinguished, we recognize that they do indeed share the features of the philosopher as social type, including a preference for the unmarried state.

The temptation to assimilate bachelorhood to an ascetic motivation, or to the thematic of the contemplative life, is so strong that it will be necessary to invoke Nietzsche again in order to see what else might be at stake in this life choice. Nietzsche conjectures in *The Genealogy of Morals* that the bachelor state of the philosophers, despite appearances, is not a simple expression of Western asceticism, the social norm that the *Genealogy* so aggressively targets. For Nietzsche, the single state of the philosophers rather represents an opportunistic appropriation of an apparent ascetic ideal as an alibi for quite another aim, for what he calls an "an optimum condition of the highest and boldest intellectuality [*Geistigkeit*]" (82). More simply Nietzsche calls this condition "freedom." The philosopher is a bachelor because he wishes to be free from constraint both in living and thinking, not because he wishes to renounce sexual pleasure. The freedom of which Nietzsche writes is not only freedom from the social institution of marriage, from its responsibilities and distractions, but also freedom from constraint in a deeper sense. Marriage can be said to stand in for social institutions generally, inasmuch as these might constrain both freedom of action and freedom of thought. We will see that there exists just such a link between the two kinds of freedom in the early modern period.

Nietzsche's argument also implies that if the bachelorhood of the philosophers does not express the motive of sexual renunciation, then it cannot be modeled simply on the practice of clerical celibacy. In fact Nietzsche does not name any medieval philosopher-priests as exemplary of his theme. The single state of the early modern philosophers is the choice of "atopical" individuals. In this it is quite unlike Catholic celibacy, which developed within a vast institutional structure of coercion and reward, the effect of which was not only to induce the choice to be celibate in significant numbers of persons, but also to exalt celibacy as a higher and holier way of life than marriage. While it can be conceded, then, that celibacy was a diverse practice in Catholic Christianity, in some contexts (the monastic) voluntarily embraced, in others (the regular clergy) compelled despite sometimes considerable resistance, it must also be remembered that from at least the third century CE celibacy acquired and required extensive institutional support.

Philosophical bachelorhood in Protestant nations of the early modern period had no obvious institutional support such as the church rendered to clerical celibacy; it rather had the character of a mysterious congruence of singular choices among otherwise institutionally unrelated persons. I propose, then, that the bachelorhood Nietzsche advocates, and which does indeed characterize early modern philosophers, is the converse predicate of celibacy: it is the *freedom not to marry* rather than the *prohibition of marriage*. In making such a distinction, I do not mean to deny that celibate monks and priests during the medieval era might have been motivated individually by a desire to be free from the constraints of marriage; but this was not the primary rationale for sexual renunciation in clerical celibacy. As a matter of doctrine, celibacy was an imitation of the life of Christ; the argument that priests needed to be free from marital obligations in order best to accomplish their priestly tasks was sometimes adduced as an additional reason for the practice of celibacy, but this motive did not and could not stand alone, without support from the ideal of the *imitatio christi*.[20]

The possibility of philosophical bachelorhood in Nietzsche's sense arises only with the emergence of the lay philosopher in the early modern period, when the choice not to marry was removed from the immediate context of compulsory celibacy—in short, only after the Reformation. But these same historical conditions also make the choice not to marry even more surprising. For if the Reformers brought clerical celibacy into disrepute, they also elevated the married state into a dominant social norm. In the Protestant nations, choosing to remain unmarried, indefinitely or for a lifetime, made less social sense than ever before, because such a choice could no longer be attached to the institution of the celibate clergy, or to the monastic ideal. In Protestant modernity marriage becomes the default life choice, and it is the resolution not to marry that requires explanation or defense.[21] The bachelorhood of the early modern philosophers thus presents us with a nice historical puzzle.

BACHELORS OF SCIENCE

Before I turn to Bacon's defense of philosophical bachelorhood, I will need to sharpen and fill in the picture I have begun to sketch of the bachelor state as a form of social life distinct from clerical celibacy. There are two features of this form that must be understood more precisely in historical context. The first concerns the conditions giving rise to the single life as a desirable life choice for itself, as opposed to those conditions that might hinder individuals from marrying when they wished to do so. The second feature of the single life that must be explained is its connection with the social identity of the lay philosopher, a figure who is, of course, presumed to be male, but is otherwise relatively undetermined with regard to other social categories (such as class).[22]

The major work to date on the connection between bachelorhood and early modern philosophy is the pioneering study by the philosopher Naomi Zack, *Bachelors of Science*. Zack rehearses some of the contexts for single life in the seventeenth century, no one of which, nor the sum of which, seems finally to explain the remarkably consistent bachelorhood of the early modern philosophers. I will enumerate these conditions briefly, drawing from Zack and other historians before turning to Bacon.

Zack's study takes as its point of departure Lawrence Stone's well-known study *The Family, Sex, and Marriage*. The interesting fact (if it is a fact) to emerge from Stone's analysis is that in the early modern period the ratio of single to married persons rose, especially among the aristocracy and gentry.[23] It fell again by the nineteenth century. Though the causal factors are probably many, there is some evidence that for the upper classes a tightening of property transfers on the basis of primogeniture left many younger sons with insufficient means to marry. But there does not seem to be a consistent correlation between this condition and the social type of the philosopher. Robert Boyle, for example, was a younger son who declined to marry despite the fact that he was possessed of a considerable fortune. His status as younger son might have given him greater freedom not to marry.

A second possible causal factor might be identified in the conditions of service, which often precluded marriage. Service comprised a vast number of relations, at many levels of the social hierarchy, from the footman to the most highly placed secretary. Hobbes and Locke were secretaries to important noblemen, but it isn't clear that their service absolutely precluded marriage. The constraints on the desire to marry represented by such conditions as inheritance or servitude underscore the peculiarity of the historical question I am raising. The single state might indicate an *inability* to marry for reasons of income or dependent status; but the bachelorhood of the early modern philosophers seems to be something else, the choice not to marry even when it was *possible* to do so.

More promising for its suggestiveness is the existence in England of that curious social anachronism, already remarked, the celibate Fellow of Oxford and Cambridge. Despite the repudiation of clerical celibacy in reformed England, the Fellows of the colleges continued to be required by statute to be unmarried, a requirement that wasn't lifted completely until the nineteenth century.[24] The insistence on celibacy in the ancient universities may seem bizarre to us, but we must remember that Fellows lived in close quarters with students, often sleeping in the same rooms, and that celibacy might have been perceived as necessary for quite mundane reasons.[25] Nonetheless the celibacy of the Fellows long survived the modernization of living arrangements. The celibate fellowship was the condition for the emergence of a distinct, eccentric social type in England—the don—a figure who supremely exemplifies not celibacy, but bachelorhood. It seems likely that the profession of don came to attract persons who were already disinclined to marry, for whatever reason.

As Zack points out, Locke and Newton were Fellows until middle age; still, they did not marry after leaving their fellowships. While the celibacy of the fellow does not provide a causal explanation for the bachelorhood of the philosophers, it does suggest that, at least in England, there might have existed a socially sanctioned association between the unmarried state and intellectuality even after the priesthood had been decoupled from the institution of celibacy. It was perhaps such an association that accounts for the fact that when Thomas Gresham endowed Gresham College, he specified in his will that the readers for the college be unmarried, and that, should they marry, they were immediately to resign their fellowships.[26]

The question before us, then, is whether the college fellowship was able to model the intellectual life more widely, even for those who were themselves no longer attached to the universities. The possibility of such a modeling function seems to be suggested by the very history of the word *bachelor*, which in the later Middle Ages came to designate the person who attained the preliminary arts degree, what we still call the bachelor of arts. The etymology of the word is only conjectural; it seems originally to have referred to an apprentice knight. By extension it came to define the relation of the apprentice in the arts program to the master of arts. Since the bachelors of arts were all presumably destined for holy orders, and expected to be celibate, the term bachelor came by a still later transference to mean any single male, not just clerks or clerics. With the continued imposition of celibacy on the Fellows of the early modern college in England, bachelors in the first sense, bachelors of arts, were now compelled to be bachelors in the extended sense, unmarried men. Whether these men actually took holy orders was now irrelevant. If the reason for the imposition of celibacy in this context had something to do with the social conditions of the college, as an all-male institution, the question Zack raises is much more speculative: whether noncollegiate philosophers might have signaled their intellectuality publicly by a kind of mimetic celibacy.

Zack is inclined to answer this question in the affirmative: "The required bachelorhood of priests on the continent and academic fellows in England could strengthen an argument for the general association of bachelorhood with philosophy in the early modern period. It could be argued that the prescription of bachelorhood was internalized by philosophers with results that made them different psychologically from men in other occupations" (66). If celibacy was a renunciation university Fellows and Catholic priests accepted as the requisite of their calling, Zack proposes that celibacy was actively embraced by noncollegiate and nonclerical philosophers as a way of announcing their commitment to the life of the mind. At this point, however, one might ask whether the residual identification of the philosopher with the social type of the celibate cleric or Fellow is sufficient to explain what is after all a hugely consequential and nonnormative life choice.

Zack's hypothesis is persuasive up to a point because it resonates with the familiar Western theme of the disembodiment of thought, its transcendence of material conditions. Celibacy seems, of all the possible life choices one might make, the most dramatic confirmation of a life devoted to thought. Steven Shapin has recently made an argument similar to Zack's about the metaphoric significance of other apparently ascetic choices among the early modern philosophers, such as dietary abstemiousness, or a preference for solitude.[27] Ascetic lifestyles, however, were not consistently favored by the early modern philosophers, as Shapin also notes.[28] Though these philosophers were nearly all bachelors, their single lives were far from consistently nonsexual. Bachelorhood implies nothing, one way or the other, about sexual activity. The single state is not incompatible with a sexually active or even promiscuous life. Descartes had a mistress, and Bacon during his bachelor years (also probably during his marriage) was sexually active with his male servants. Even Hobbes boasted in an autobiographical poem written in his old age, "Yet I can love, and have a mistresse too"—though his actual relations with the opposite sex are difficult to determine. The choice not to marry might also express a disinclination to sexual behavior rather than a renunciation of it. This might well have been the case for Boyle, Shapin's chief example of an ascetic natural philosopher. While Boyle's resolute singleness might seem to be of a piece with his ascetic style of life (an image he actively promoted), we might also understand his choice as asserting the freedom not to marry, a liberty masquerading as self-restraint.

There is no question that the ascetic ideal figured largely in the self-identification of philosophers in the early modern period; but I would suggest, in partial qualification of Zack and Shapin, that even the most rigorous adherence to a life of renunciation could be cross-hatched with a complementary motive closer to what Nietzsche meant by freedom. As we are now poised to demonstrate, the freedom not to marry—a freedom in the realm of action—could be associated in the early modern period with another kind of freedom, *freedom of thought*. These two modes of liberty were sometimes closely identified in the early seventeenth century, and it is in this identification of free thinking with free living that we will find a clue to the historical significance of philosophical bachelorhood.[29]

The Freedom of Philosophy

In the most famous sentence of his most famous essay, "Of Marriage and Single Life," Bacon casts the relation between the two choices of his title as an opposition between the states of restraint and freedom: "He that hath a wife and children hath given hostages to fortune; for they are impediments to great enterprises, either of virtue or mischief." Consequently "the most ordinary cause of a single life is liberty, especially in certain self-pleasing and humorous minds, which are so sensible of every restraint, as they will go near to think their girdles and garters be bonds and shackles" (Vickers, 351). In this and the immediately preceding essay, "Of Parents and Children," Bacon plays the elaborate rhetorical game of *in utramque partem*, arguing on both sides of the issue.[30] The choice between marriage

and single life had long been a set subject for such rhetorical perfor-
mances. Thomas Wilson, for example, in his dialectic textbook of 1551,
The Rule of Reason, offers "Should a priest take a wife" as a subject for
rhetorical debate.[31] But subsequent versions of this contest had to confront a supervening social norm. Between Wilson and Bacon, the issue of
the single life was no longer a question concerning the clergy. The decisive
rejection of clerical celibacy in England left the social form of an elected
single life increasingly outside the realm of the normative; it was *atopos*.

In *New Atlantis* the single state is embodied by the natural philosophers
of Salomon's House, and is implicitly legitimated by their resemblance
to collegiate fellows; but elsewhere in the narrative, the single state is
denounced as indulgence in a dangerous sexual license. This argument is
given to the character of Joabin, who has lived both in Europe and in
Bensalem, and who, in the manner of More's Hythloday, makes a number
of charges against European society, including this one: "there are with
you seen infinite men that marry not, but chuse rather a libertine and
impure single life, than to be yoked in marriage" (Vickers, 477). Unmis-
takably here, as in the essays, the single life is a choice; but more than
that, in the choice to be single it is *freedom itself that is chosen*, a liberty of
action so extreme that only promiscuity evokes its extent. Such hyperbole
suffuses Joabin's heated rhetoric, which conjures a numerically impossible "infinite" number of bachelors. If not literally infinite, such an indefinitely large number of bachelors represents a grave social danger, a ram-
pant promiscuity. This version of the single life is just the opposite of
celibacy. Or perhaps it would be better to say that the unmarried state is
a contradictory social form, signifying either an ascetic ideal, celibacy, or
its libertine opposite, promiscuity.

Clerical celibacy itself had long been vulnerable to this contradictory
construction. Its opponents in the early years of the Reformation often
attacked celibacy as an alibi for promiscuity—as it perhaps often was for
the late medieval clergy. The Protestant reformers could depend upon the
currency of this critique, even among some Catholic critics of celibacy.
Erasmus, for example, had already raised doubts about clerical celibacy
on these and other grounds in a published work of 1519, which was condemned before the theological faculty of Louvain.[32] Celibacy was easy
to attack as a fraud, as the mask of promiscuity, despite its normative
superiority as a way of life in Catholic culture.

If the suspicion of single life had its origin in attacks on clerical celibacy,
"libertinism" occasioned nothing less than a major crisis in the early seventeenth century. By this time the concept of the libertine had acquired a
set of associations connected as much with freedom of thought as with
licentious behavior. In France the term *libertins* was widely used with
reference to a group of philosophers and poets who were reputed secretly

to scorn Christianity in favor of skepticism and an epicurean celebration of nature, and who were further said to engage in *débauches* or *banquets* at which they drunkenly espoused their unorthodox opinions.[33] Freedom of thought and freedom of action were compounded in the word *libertin-age*, testifying to the emergence of what we would now call a moral panic.[34] The *libertins érudits*, as these figures came to be known, counted among their number eminent poets, philosophers, and even priests, including among the latter so famous a cleric as Pierre Gassendi, Descartes's interlocutor. Despite his libertine reputation, Gassendi actually lived an ascetic life—celibate, teetotaling, and even vegetarian. But moral panics are not bound by the facts; they betray large social anxieties.

The panic reached its peak in the years between 1619 and 1625. Treatises denouncing the libertines were written by François Garasse and Marin Mersenne, investigations conducted, and several of the so-called libertines were prosecuted, most prominently the poet Théophile de Viau, who was condemned to death in 1623.[35] This penalty was reduced to banishment in 1625 as a result of the poet's important connections at court. Théophile seemed to draw the most fire, because he did in fact lead a dissolute life. He was suspected, probably with reason, of sodomy, a vice often seen as implying blasphemy or atheism.[36] But Théophile was only the most vulnerable among the erudite libertines of the 1620s. In retrospect it seems likely that the real target of the panic was philosophy itself, particularly versions of natural philosophy drawn from the schools of antiquity. The panic was possibly also related to rising tension between lay philosophers and the clergy, a hypothesis confirmed to some extent by the fact that the Jesuits seem to have been the major force behind the persecution of the *libertins*. Their campaign seems to have succeeded in driving Descartes and other philosophers into a more circumspect and self-defended mode of philosophical discourse, particularly when the subject was nature.[37]

The crisis of libertinism coaxed the figure of the philosopher out from behind, as it were, the figure of the celibate priest and theologian. The philosopher emerged from this panic as a distinct social type, as a potentially dangerous or atopical figure. Even though Gassendi himself was a priest, it was as a philosopher that he was condemned for libertinism. His notoriety was a consequence of his bold rehabilitation of Epicurus, whose moral and natural philosophy he hoped to reconcile with Christian theology. If the crisis of the *libertins érudits* has something to tell us about the formation of the social type of the early modern philosopher, it is that this type was born in controversy, in a panic betrayed by the double sense of *libertinage*, freedom of thought and freedom of living.[38]

Bacon could not have been unaware of the crisis in France, which coincided with the period of his impeachment and the composition of *New*

Atlantis.[39] Although England did not suffer a similar panic, this divergent outcome might be attributed in part to Bacon himself, to his long-standing prudent refusal to embrace any particular philosophy of antiquity, as Gassendi did so imprudently with Epicurus.[40] Bacon was especially cautious not to fall into the trap of associating his philosophy of nature with that of continental figures such as Vanini and Bruno, who were condemned for elevating Nature over God as the highest power. Nonetheless, as England's premier philosopher Bacon was committed as much as the *libertin érudits* to freedom of thought—*plus ultra*, after all, was his motto.

If Bacon also believed, like the philosophers of antiquity, that a teaching about nature implied a "way of life," he was cautious about extrapolating from the principles of his natural philosophy to a moral philosophy. Despite the proliferation of moral commentary in the *Essays* and elsewhere, Bacon never developed his moral philosophy systematically; it remained, like Descartes's, a "provisional morality."[41] We do have scattered remarks, however, about the *character* of the natural philosopher, an ethos suggested above all by the association of philosophy with the bachelor state. The most unambiguous expression of this association occurs in *De Sapientia Veterum*, published in 1609, in the chapter on Orpheus. There Bacon presents Orpheus not as a figure for the poet, as he is more usually understood, but for the philosopher. Among the reasons for making this identification Bacon points to the fact that Orpheus repudiated the company of women after the loss of Eurydice: "Also it is wisely added in the story that Orpheus was averse from women and from marriage; for the sweets of marriage and the dearness of children commonly draw men away from performing great and lofty services to the commonwealth; being content to be perpetuated in their race and stock and not in their deeds" (*SEH*, 6:352). The same association between singleness and great works appears in "Of Parents and Children": "The perpetuity of generation is common to beasts; but memory, merit, and noble works, are proper to men. And surely a man shall see the noblest works and foundations have proceeded from childless men; which have sought to express the images of their minds, where those of their bodies have failed. So the care of posterity is most in them that have no posterity" (Vickers, 352). The theme is again sounded in "Of Marriage and Single Life": "Certainly the best works, and of greatest merit for the public, have proceeded from the unmarried or childless men; which both in affection and means have married and endowed the public" (Vickers, 353).

This version of bachelorhood, which is distinguished on the one hand from clerical celibacy and on the other from libertinism, defines the best way of life above all for the philosopher—always for Bacon the *natural* philosopher. As a figure who "marries and endows the public," Bacon's philosopher is morally exemplary without being universally imitable. He remains atopical, and in this sense, the bachelor state refunctions the high social valuation of clerical celibacy as a way of life for the few. As a strategy of legitimation, the refunctioning of clerical celibacy as philosophical bachelorhood gives us a philosopher who is something like a secular saint; but Bacon does not need to put his argument in these terms, which are in any case anachronistic. More usually he will make his strongest claims for the natural philosopher by means of a discreet classicizing gesture, as in this sentence from *Valerius Terminus*: "The dignity of this end (of endowment of man's life with new commodities) appeareth by the estimation that antiquity made of such as guided thereunto; for whereas founders of states, lawgivers, extirpers of tyrants, fathers of the people, were honoured but with the titles of Worthies or Demigods, inventors were ever consecrated amongst the Gods themselves" (*SEH*, 3:223).

Most surprising in this strategy of refunctioning is the apparent demotion of great political figures to the second rank. Bacon gestures here toward an interpretation of technology whose implications lie just beyond his historical moment. *New Atlantis* projects a society in which the political superstructure atrophies as a consequence of universal economic well-being. In the demotion of the monarchical role, Bacon's Bensalem is close to More's *Utopia*, the difference being that Bacon substitutes a technologically achieved productivity for More's communism. Because there is no "political economy" yet either for Bacon or More, the projection of a society without want cannot do without political and religious vocabularies. Bacon thus typically associates his "inventors" with the theme of charity, setting this theme in tacit relation to the biblical narrative—"commodity" remediates some of the harsher consequences of the Fall.[42] In the quotation from *Valerius Terminus* Bacon means by "commodity" that which has made postlapsarian life easier—ample food, fine clothing, housing to shelter against the elements, medicine to ease pain and prolong life.[43] The natural philosopher who succeeds in increasing the store of human commodity is hardly motivated by ascetic renunciation, then, or by any version of the monastic ideal, though he is motivated by the Christian virtue of charity. This theme is ubiquitous in Bacon's work, culminating in the argument of *Novum Organum* that the true end of his great instauration is to "bring it [philosophy] to perfection in charity, for the benefit and use of life."[44]

It would surprise no reader here if I were to remark the naive faith in technology Bacon seems to be expressing; but I suggest that this is only one way to think about his project, and furthermore just as anachronistic as the notion of secularization. Bacon's philosopher is not a scientist in our sense of the term because science and technology are indistinguishable in his natural philosophy. Knowledge is for benefit or use, or it is of no worth to him, and therefore there is no "technology" not subordinate to a moral-religious end. If the natural philosopher is motivated above all by the virtue of charity, his charity is no less Christian for being unlike the charity of the priest. Bacon's defense of the single life for its philanthropic possibilities is the middle term, the copula, that permits him to identify the *natural* philosopher as the true *Christian* philosopher. In order to do natural philosophy as Bacon conceives it, this figure must be free to direct his charity to the benefit of humankind generally. The legitimacy of the natural philosopher can thus be seen to depend crucially on the single life, the freedom not to marry.

Let us now make a first pass at explicating the text of the natural philosopher in *New Atlantis*, a figure we can expect to exhibit the virtue of charity openly, even if the bachelor state remains an implicit choice (along with everything else about this figure's private self, including a proper name). The Father of Salomon's House appears, as we recall, "in state": "The day being come, he made his entry. He was a man of middle stature and age, comely of person, and had an aspect as if he pitied men" (Vickers, 478). There is nothing intrinsically remarkable about the body of the natural philosopher. His middle stature and age, the comeliness that is neither remarkably beautiful nor ugly, direct our attention rather to the "aspect as if he pitied men."[45] In foregrounding this "aspect" or strangely fixed facial expression, Bacon reproduces here almost exactly a passage from the fictional frame of another of his works, the unpublished *Redargutio Philosophiarum* (1608), in which a natural philosopher makes a similar stately entrance before delivering a vigorous refutation of the errors of all former philosophers: "Not long after there entered to them a man of peaceful and serene air, save that his face had become habituated to the expression of pity" (I quote here from Benjamin Farrington's translation of the Latin text, "aspectus . . . admodum placidi et sereni; nisi quod oris compositio erat tamquam miserantis").[46] The similarity of detail is striking enough to raise the question of why it is pity that is fixedly expressed in the face of the natural philosopher. Even though pity is regarded as an emotional state, it is difficult to identify a facial expression specific to this emotion, an aspect or regard.[47] When we feel pity we experience pain at the pain of another; but the outward expression of this pain is perhaps indistinguishable from the expression of emotional pain generally. Farrington rightly senses the oddness of Bacon's insistence on the fixed expression of pity, which he attempts to grasp in his interpolative translation, "habituated to the expression of pity."[48] The same problem of the relation between feeling and expression is even more difficult to resolve in the case of charity, a virtue with which pity is often linked, and which is here implicit as the motive of pity, its underlying ethical support. In any case we can hypothesize that in giving the Father of Salomon's House the single expression of pity, Bacon makes a slightly desperate attempt (the burden of the "as if") to *embody* the virtue of charity in the natural philosopher.

The puzzle raised by the relation of pity to charity is an instance of the larger problem of the relation between feelings (or passions) and *dispositions* or *virtues*, a problem that concerned Aristotle in the *Nicomachean Ethics*.[49] When Bacon invoked pity, he could depend upon the recognition of pity as a passion. Today we tend to regard pity more as an emotion than a passion because we reserve "passion" for the stronger emotions.[50] In antiquity, pity was regarded rather as one of the strongest passions. In the *Poetics*, Aristotle famously identified pity as one of the two chief passions aroused by tragedy—the other, of course, being fear. For the ancients (if Aristotle can be permitted to speak for them), pity had two defining features: First, it entailed a judgment that the person to be pitied suffered *undeserved* misfortune; and second, it presumed that the person to be pitied was *like oneself* in the sense that the one who pities might at some time suffer undeservedly as well. The latter point suggests why the gods were seldom said to feel pity for humans, as they were not subject to the same misfortunes. In the Christian-Hellenistic world, by contrast, all human misfortune is seen as merited because of the fall, though a merciful God suspends judgment about merit by holding out the possibility of salvation. Already in the first centuries of Hellenistic Christianity, the mercy that founds Judaeo-Christian religious belief came to be associated with what the Greeks called pity (*eleos*). Much later Nietzsche could express scorn for Christianity as "the religion of pity."[51] The Christianized conception of pity is closer to what we mean by compassion than to Aristotle's passion; but the concept of compassion, like charity, can be distinguished as a disposition from the schema of the emotions or passions. In retrospect, it would seem that the emergence of a concept of compassion in late antiquity mediated the fusion of pity with Christian concepts of mercy, making it possible thenceforth to confuse the passion of pity with the disposition of charity.

Bacon recovers and deploys these sedimented meanings by attributing the passion of pity to the Fathers of Salomon's House, restoring to pity its fully passional status, even a visible bodily sign or "aspect." Further, the trace of the process by which pity was Christianized can be seen in the assertion of its expressive duration, which gestures toward the disposition or virtue of charity. Yet the pity of the Fathers is less like ordinary human charity for other humans than like what a god might feel, or a human when elevated to a kind of divinity: "inventors were ever consecrated amongst the Gods themselves." The affect of these inventors—the natural philosophers—is a Christianized pity, then, but not exactly the pity either of Christians or the Christian God. For Bacon's natural philosophers have arrogated to themselves a power that might seem to usurp the powers of that God in their control over nature. It is within the power of Salomon's House to undo by "technological" innovation the wound to nature that occasioned the misery of human want, presumably the misery that elicits the Fathers' *misericordia*. The habitual expression of pity thus signals a kind of figurative deification, which finds some cover for its boldness—remember that Salomon's House is also called "The College of the Six Days' Works"—behind the Christian virtue of charity. This is not to say that Bacon's thought here is theologically heterodox, but that his narrative drives inexorably toward the concentration of unprecedented power in the person of the natural philosopher. Pity is the outward face of this immense power, the visible expression of its benign intent, its charity.

The Rule of the Fellows

In *New Atlantis* Bacon gives us, it is said, a scientific utopia. But the strangeness of this utopia is easy to underestimate, along with the strangeness of the figures who seem to be Bensalem's true governors, its mortal gods on earth (as Hobbes liked to call his sovereigns). When Bacon describes the Fathers of Salomon's House alternately as "Fellows" of a college, his contemporaries would have understood something at once quotidian, that the Fathers were like the Fellows of Cambridge and Oxford, and at the same time unusual, atopical. Their single state is not just implied by a casual epithet; it is integral to their very identity as natural philosophers. They are "Fathers" only figuratively; their sons are their disciples. Salomon's House is a college of Fellows, then, but Bacon also calls it a "foundation," which in Renaissance English usually means a charitable institution. In *New Atlantis* Bacon imagines a place or noplace, a topos or utopia, for the atopic philosopher, an institution that would allow the philanthropic possibilities of the single life their maximum play and effectivity. This noplace is at once college and charitable foundation. Rawley captures this dual function in his headnote, when he writes that *New Atlantis* is a fable whose end is to "exhibit . . . a model or description of a college for the interpreting of nature and the producing of great and marvelous works for the benefit of men" (Vickers, 785).

But if Bacon's intention was also to produce a description not just of the college but an entire society, the truncated quality of that project suggests that it was either troubled by a failure of imagination, or that Bacon said all he wanted to say. In either case, the narrative falls well short of the total descriptive mapping we find in More's *Utopia*. In the entire text Bacon speaks at length of only two social institutions, the family and Salomon's House, the one based on marriage, the other on the voluntary association of bachelors. Though he offers us some particulars about

other aspects of Bensalem—its religion, its economy, its political structure, its foreign relations—the relative sketchiness of these details by comparison to what is lavished upon the family and Salomon's House hints
at a parabolical aspect of his text less designed than perhaps overdetermined. In its selection of topics for elaboration *New Atlantis* is arguably
a cryptic and traumatically motivated rewriting of Bacon's essay "Of
Marriage and Single Life," a translation into narrative of unresolved anxieties connected with these two life choices.

Let us begin to read the narrative, then, as a rewriting of Bacon's famous essay, another staging of its *in utramque partem*. I turn first to
Bacon's account of the ritual called the "Feast of the Family," passing
over much of its elaborate descriptive detail, and foregrounding first just
its announced purpose, which is to celebrate any patriarch who "shall
live to see thirty persons descended of his body alive together" above three
years of age (Vickers, 472–73). This is indeed an impressive reproductive
accomplishment. The father of such a family must have at least five children who each have five children in order to add up to thirty descendants
in two generations. Extending the generations to great grandchildren
would ease the math, but this would still be an impressive accomplishment, especially given mortality rates in early modernity. It suggests that
what is being celebrated in the Feast of the Family is the sheer fact of
reproduction, which Bensalem encourages as a population policy, but
which has the quality here of hyperbole or fantasy.

Elsewhere in Bacon's work, we find generation celebrated in the most
extravagant terms, but usually as a *trope* for the productivity of Baconian
natural philosophy. Bacon very much needs this trope, which is everywhere in his work from early in his career. As the Baconian philosopher
tells his disciple in one early text, "what I purpose is to unite you with
things themselves in a chaste, holy, and legal wedlock; and from this association you will secure an increase beyond all the hopes and prayers of
ordinary marriages."[52] When we set this trope alongside the narrative
account of the fertility of Bensalem's families, the latter begins to look like
more like a trope. It is as though the reproductive success of Bensalemite
marriage is yet another figure for the productive triumph of Baconian
natural philosophy.

In the description of the Fellows' achievements in the latter part of *New
Atlantis*, we find unsurprisingly that Bacon celebrates most extensively
the control of the Fellows over generative processes in nature. This is the
essence of Baconian "science." As the Father of Salomon's House boasts
to the narrator, "we make them [plants and animals] more fruitful and
bearing than their kind is; and contrariwise barren and not generative"
(Vickers, 482). Perhaps the very reproductive success of the Bensalemites
can be attributed to the Fellows' total control over the processes affecting

generation.[53] They are responsible, after all, for the health of this society, and their knowledge has already been impressively demonstrated in the care of the quarantined European sailors (a serious matter in plague-ridden Europe). Nor should we forget here how increasingly important population growth was to early modern states. The concern was not Malthusian but just the opposite; they saw the wealth of the nation as increased by the growth of the population. In any case, *New Atlantis* informs us how we might understand "great works" in Bacon, how we are to understand his wish for the philosopher to marry and endow the public. If marriage is everywhere in Bacon—in his Great Instauration he "prepared and adorned the bridal chamber of the mind and the universe" (*Novum Organum*, 23)—this marriage is everywhere a trope. And when Bacon calls his natural philosophers "Fathers," the title defuses the otherwise disturbing or atopical associations of philosophical bachelorhood, the social danger hyperbolically expressed in the depiction of Europe's "infinite bachelors."[54]

These more dangerous associations are the subject of the passage immediately following the Feast of the Family, when the character Joabin takes up the further description of Bensalemite mores. In his quasi-Morean critique of European sexual practices, from which I have already quoted, Joabin declares that Bensalem is the "virgin of the world," that here there are

> no dissolute houses, no courtesans, nor any thing of that kind. Nay, they wonder (with detestation) at you in Europe, which permit such things. They say ye have put marriage out of office . . . But when men have at hand a remedy more agreeable to their corrupt will, marriage is almost expulsed. And there are with you seen infinite men that marry not, but chuse rather libertine and impure single life, than to be yoked in marriage; and many that do marry, marry late, when the prime and strength of their years is past. And when they do marry, what is marriage to them but a very bargain; wherein is sought alliance, or portion, or reputation, with some desire, (almost indifferent) of issue; and not the faithful nuptial union of man and wife, that was first instituted. (Vickers, 477)

Just as marriage in the real world might be said to resist the idealizing and metaphoric role Bacon gives it in his fable, so Bacon seems to acknowledge in this passage a kind of real-world bachelorhood, the moral antithesis of the single life of the fellows. Joabin's diatribe more than glances too at the relation between marriage and bachelorhood in Bacon's own life, since Bacon himself married late, obviously for portion, and perhaps even with indifference to issue.

Indeed, the passage rehearses so closely the particulars of the gossip that circulated freely after Bacon's fall that we might now consider the possibility that Bacon is confronting this matter directly for a reason. But to see what this reason might be, we must also confront directly the worst that was said of Bacon. For that worst indictment of Bacon's private libertinism, we turn to Simonds D'Ewes, who was not so reticent a Puritan as to refrain from committing the details of these rumors to his journal of 1621:

> His most abominable and darling sin I should rather bury in silence than mention, were it not a most admirable instance how men are enslaved by wickedness and held captive by the devil. For whereas presently upon his censure at this time his ambition was moderated, his pride humbled, and the means of his former injustice and corruption removed, yet would he not relinquish the practice of his most horrible and secret sin of sodomy, keeping still one Godrick a very effeminate faced youth to be his catamite. After his fall men began to discourse of that his unnatural crime, which he had practiced many years; deserting the bed of his lady, which he accounted as the Italians and Turks do, a poor and mean pleasure in respect of the other.[55]

The rumors about Bacon's private life, which had been current for years, were no longer confined to whispers; the rumors could now be spoken openly, even published in ballads. Decades later John Aubrey could bluntly conflate Bacon's public and private disgrace in his "Brief Life": "He was a *paederastike*; His Ganimeds and Favourites tooke Bribes."[56] Bacon's contemporaries saw the connection between bribery and sodomy, which might seem accidental to us, as arising from the prodigality of Bacon's way of life, especially his habit of gathering about him large numbers of male favorites, upon whom he spent with abandon and who in turn "tooke Bribes." It is just these two concerns, bribery and sodomy, that enter as though from outside into the text of *New Atlantis*, only there to be disavowed.

The disavowal of sodomy is Joabin's task. He goes on in the passage from which I have been quoting to describe a form of life we might call *singleness within marriage*, a disregard for marriage so total that the very difference between married men and bachelors is erased: "The haunting of those dissolute places, or resort to courtesans, are no more punished in married men than in bachelors." The pageant of vices ends up in Sodom itself, with Joabin's reference to "Lot's offer":

> They hear you defend these things, as done to avoid greater evils; as advoutries, deflowering of virgins, unnatural lust, and the like. But they say this is a preposterous wisdom; and they call it "Lot's offer," who to save his guests from abusing, offered his daughters: nay they say farther that there is little gained in this; for that the same vices and appetites do still remain and abound; unlawful lust being like a furnace,

that if you stop the flames altogether, it will quench; but if you give it any vent, it will rage. As for masculine love, they have no touch of it; and yet there are not so faithful and inviolate friendships in the world. (Vickers, 477)

In nineteenth-century editions of Bacon's work, this passage was sometimes omitted; it seems strangely unmotivated in its lurid fervor. The linking of friendship and sodomy in the same sentence, disavowed by the disjunctive "and yet," confirms our suspicion, which the circumstances of Bacon's fall arouse, that the form of promiscuity or libertinism most to be feared in the single life is "masculine love." At this moment of greatest strain on Bacon's fantasy, the worst accusation against Bacon himself—that he lived as a bachelor even while married, alienated from his wife's bed, indulging in sodomitical relations with his favorites and servants—reappears as the vice that has *no place* in Bensalem. The fantasy works like a disavowal, then, less to protect Bacon himself, perhaps, than Salomon's House, a *collegium* of single males bound together not by blood but by the affective tie of friendship or *amicitia*. It would not do for Bacon's readers to see in York House or Gorhambury, Bacon's own estates, the true model of Salomon's House.

In the next sentences Joabin recounts the courtship rituals of the Bensalemites, which Bacon borrows from More's *Utopia*, with one important revision. While More allows prospective mates to examine each other naked, Bacon gives this function of ocular inspection to a "friend." The marital bond is thus made to depend directly on the social relation of friendship. This moment is structurally related both to the Fellows' remote facilitation of the reproductive success of Bensalemite marriages and to the moment later in Salomon's House when we are told that it is up to the Fathers whether or not they will reveal to the state the results of their experiments. The latter functions as the crucial hinge between Salomon's House and the state apparatus: "And this we do also: we have consultations, which of the inventions and experiences we discovered shall be published, and which not: and take all an oath of secrecy, for the concealing of those which we think fit to keep secret: though some of those we do reveal sometimes to the state, and some not" (Vickers, 487). Nature herself is not to be revealed in her nakedness, not even to the state; such naked truth is instead reported by a friend, the Fellow. Just as the Fathers seem to control from their remote position the very fertility of Bensalemite families, so they seem to control from a distance affairs of state.

If Bacon famously "philosophized like a Lord Chancellor," it might be said conversely that he governed like a philosopher. As counselor to the king, he imagined himself to be the king of the king, a delusion that was cruelly exploded when James sacrificed him to the lupine Parliament of

1621. In *New Atlantis*, the overruling counselor or friend reappears as the embodiment of a fantasmatic sovereignty.[57] The Fathers of Salomon's House decide among themselves what secrets they shall reveal to the state. The secrets of nature become the secrets of state. Thus Bacon achieves, if only in fantasy, his lifelong design of "making the government of the world a mirror for the government of a state" (*SEH*, 10:91–92). This is the sovereignty of Salomon's House, greater even than a king's, as great as a god's.

If Bacon composed *New Atlantis* in the gray afterlife of his public career, the text seems to allude to his fall in one other detail, again for the purpose of disavowal, the refusal of the Bensalemite officials to take tips: "So he left us; and when we offered him some pistolets, he smiling said, 'He must not be twice paid for one labour:' meaning (as I take it) that he had salary sufficient of the state for his service. For (as I after learned) they call an officer that taketh rewards, twice paid" (Vickers, 459).[58] In other contexts, of course, these might be bribes. It was precisely Bacon's defense that the money he accepted did not function as bribes, and that his judgments were rendered disinterestedly; in that sense, he regarded the bribes as very like tips. Bacon does not hesitate to rehearse his most public trauma, just as he rehearses the accusation of sodomy; but at the end of his fable he boldly reinstates the disastrous gift economy that characterized his sexualized relations with favorites and servants. Though the officials of Bensalem refuse to take tips, the Fathers of Salomon's House happily dispense bounty in the other direction. So the narrator reports that after their conversation the Father gives him and his companions a large monetary gift. "For they give great largesses where they come upon all occasions" (Vickers, 488). This is the last line of the supposedly unfinished text, and Bacon's death rendered it a posthumous testament.

It is a gesture of defiance, of justified libertinism. Although Bacon had to immunize the Fellows of Salomon's House from this charge in the worst form in which it was laid at his own door, he reserved for his idealized philosophers the right to express pride in their power over nature, and a delight in the wealth that permits them to bestow largesse on their favorites without fear of bringing the charge of corruption: "These are (my son) the riches of Salomon's House" (Vickers, 486). Hence, despite the severity of the sexual morality prevalent in Bensalem, which would tend to confirm the celibacy of the Fellows, their lifestyle is characterized not so much by asceticism as by a kind of spectacular expenditure. Their celibacy is rather an alibi, a screen behind which can be discerned the freedom of the bachelor philosopher, expressed not as promiscuity but as liberality, largesse.

The theme of largesse must also be seen as a recoding of the great Baconian theme of charity. To bestow largesse or endow the public is the action that answers to the "aspect" of pity, the only visible passion expressed by Bacon's natural philosophers. If we can read that facial expression in its *habituation* as the sign of the philosopher's ethos, we can also read the theme of liberality in the symbolic register of dress, in the very *habit* of Bacon's philosopher, which contrasts in its gorgeousness so markedly with the monastic gray of More's Utopians. Let us return once again, and finally, to the text of Bacon's philosopher: "He was a man of middle stature and age, comely of person, and had an aspect as if he pitied men. He was clothed in a robe of fine black cloth, with wide sleeves and a cape. His under garment was of excellent white linen down to the foot, girt with a girdle of the same; and a sindon or tippet of the same about his neck. He had gloves that were curious, and set with stone; and shoes of peach coloured velvet . . ." (Vickers, 478–79). Reading these sentences in sequence, the link between the habitual expression of pity and the gorgeous habit comes into sharper perspective. The Father of Salomon's House *wears* the expression of pity just as he wears his robe of fine black cloth. The uniform signifies not only his social identity but also his habitus, the bodily expression of his singular ethos. This ethos is very like (with the singular difference of singleness) the aristocrat's demeanor, the carriage of a great lord or prince:

> He was carried in a rich chariot without wheels, litterwise; and with two horses at either end, richly trapped in blue velvet embroidered; and two footmen on each side in the like attire. The chariot was all of cedar, gilt, and adorned with crystal; save that the fore-end had panels of sapphires, set in borders of gold, and the hinder-end the like of emeralds of the Peru colour. There was also a sun of gold, radiant, upon the top, in the midst; and on the top before, a small cherub of gold, with wings displayed. The chariot was covered with cloth of gold tissued upon blue. He had before him fifty attendants, young men all, in white satin loose coats to the mid-leg; and stockings of white silk; and shoes of blue velvet; and hats of blue velvet; and with fine plumes of divers colours, set round like hat bands. (Vickers, 478–79)

This scene of sumptuary splendor is the heart of Bacon's fantasy, a fantasy he was able to live for a time as lord chancellor, when his wealth permitted him to indulge in unsurpassed extravagance of dress, and to keep a household numbering hundreds of servants and retainers, all clad head to foot in expensive livery, down to the finest Spanish leather boots.[59]

When the Father arrives "in state," he is momentarily indistinguishable from the greatest peer, or from the monarch himself. Bacon loved to put on this kind of show as lord chancellor, but the biographical resonance does not reach the deepest level of the parabolical in *New Atlantis*. If we look more closely at this lordly philosopher, he is thoroughly atopical. He lives only in the nowhere of Bensalem. He rules like a king, but he is not one. He parades and dresses like a nobleman, but he stands outside the dynastic system of familial succession. His wealth and title are transferred not to progeny but to disciples, by elective affinity.[60] What binds him to these disciples is the common pursuit of natural philosophy. This philosophy, unlike many of its classical precursors, imposes a way of life that is far from ascetic. These are no barefoot disciples, and their master, we suspect, will deny them nothing. For Bacon, the true philosopher, the natural philosopher, will be like a great lord, bountiful and generous, and his disciples will be clad, if not in Spanish leather boots, then in blue velvet shoes.

Bacon knew that philosophy might be something more than an afterthought of Christianity, just as he knew that the philosopher might be something other than a pseudo-priest. Still, his natural philosopher remains strange to us, neither scientist nor philosopher as we recognize those social types today. Bacon's natural philosopher is meant to rule (or overrule)—but only because he is a *natural* philosopher. He commands nature for the benefit of mankind, for charity, and his charitable life is enabled by his unmarried state. This fantastic fusion of social types—natural philosopher, ruler, bachelor—was possible for Bacon to imagine fully only in the wake of his political trauma. Some elements of the fantasy soon became unavailable even to those who called themselves his disciples, even the members of the Royal Society. In the distance traveled between Salomon's House and the Royal Society, we begin to make out the contours of another, longer historical narrative, to which *New Atlantis* belongs less as a fantasy than as evidence of a certain historical mediation, a transitional moment in the career of the lay intellectual. If Salomon's House realized in its fusion of philosopher and sovereign the political desire long harbored by the humanist intellectual, by the second half of the century the type of the philosopher was propelled into an orbit more remote from the centers of power (though not without acquiring by way of compensation a new kind of power that came to be known as "critique").[61] As for those who called themselves natural philosophers in the Restoration state of Charles II, their king needed to know that they harbored no threatening political desire before he was willing to grant them the title of "royal" or the right to assemble as a "society." The philosophers who succeeded Bacon, whether moral or natural, had no kingdom to rule; but they continued for some time to share with Bacon the one element of his fantasy that required only an act of will to realize, the will not to marry. This singleness continued to offer itself as a sign, at once public and parabolical, of a freedom Nietzsche later celebrated as the freedom of philosophy itself.

Hobbes's Revolution

Daniela Coli

IN THE HISTORY OF PHILOSOPHY Thomas Hobbes has often been regarded as the theorist of absolute power and the inventor of a monstrous Leviathan. Instead, however, as we shall show, power is for Hobbes the central element in all human conduct, marked by passions. From curiosity, the origin of every science, to glory, the object of all competition among men, the conflict between the passion for unlimited power and for the preservation of life is present in every individual. Hobbes founds his system upon motion, the keystone of his whole philosophy. By re-elaborating the role of motion, Hobbes gives a new solution both to the age-old discussions of *phantasia*, which since the *Rhetoric* of Aristotle had continued through the Middle Ages and the Renaissance, and to the seventeenth-century disputes over the distinction between *ratio* and *imaginatio*.[1] Hobbes constructs the concept of imagination as a mental process connected with memory, without which men would be devoid of passions, but also of any talent or intelligence.

Hobbes's theoretical revolution thus brings together two terms, passion and reason, regarded as opposites by the tradition. For him, not only is reason a calculus at the service of the passions, but the very rationality of the calculus is defined by the capacity of passion to guide the imagination and identify the means for reaching the desired objective. This theoretical revolution also involves a linguistic revolution, whereby names have only the property of expressing and fixing our image of them. In Hobbes's philosophy, where there is no room for ontology, universality is a quality referring only to names and not to the things we connect with them, and derives only from the power of the imagination to conceive of them as universal. By thus giving a radical solution to disputes of past and present, the modernist Thomas Hobbes represents, at the very outset of modernity, a rationality critical of the tradition that from Descartes to Hegel was to dominate the West.

HOBBES'S RAZOR

Thomas Hobbes was a philosopher and scientist who was part of a great scientific revolution. He was the last great systematic modern philosopher, capable of moving from treatises on physics, optics, or anatomy to discussions of the circulation of the blood, from translations of Thucydides or Homer to reflections on Aristotle's *Politics* and *Rhetoric*. In his philosophy we accordingly find an anthropology, a psychology, a sociology, a theory of language and of the state. He represented a theoretical revolution, a model of rationality that threw into crisis the wisdom of his times, which instead regarded as decisive for modernity the philosophy of his adversary Descartes, so that even such a prestigious British institution as the Royal Society preferred the experimentalist Boyle to him.[2] Even today, though, his sardonic smile, as Brian Barry notes, hovers over all of our discussions of rationality.[3] Like every great thinker, Hobbes recycles and reworks both the knowledge and the language of his times and certain classical and medieval concepts and doctrines. Suffice it to cite the case of natural law, where the sage of Malmesbury gave a new interpretation to the natural-law tradition, causing Norberto Bobbio to call him the initiator of modern natural-law theory and the precursor of legal positivism.[4]

As is true of every classic, Hobbes's texts are, as Quentin Skinner observes,[5] the worst guide to the wisdom of his times, because classics challenge the commonplaces of their contemporaries. For a classic, immortality becomes both an eternal process and an eternal attempt by the interpreters of subsequent centuries to fit him into their own epoch, or win him for their side. Hobbes too shares in this condition of being a classic. Since in *De Cive* he stated that, if the moral philosophers of his time had done their job with the same results as the scientists of his time, the world would have enjoyed a sort of perpetual peace, and in *De Corpore* presented himself as the Galileo who would make politics a science, it has become a stock theme of Hobbesian historiography to ask whether his work is to be classified as the result of his historical or of his scientific interests. Aubrey tells us how Hobbes fell in love with geometry after coming upon Euclid's *Elements* at the age of forty. But seeking to oppose Hobbes's scientific interests to his historical ones is not at all apt, since he had both historical interests (enough to translate Thucydides' history of the Peloponnesian war), and scientific interests, mediated through Mersenne's Paris circle. Hobbes studied optics, and we know of his friendship with Harvey, the discoverer of the circulation of the blood, and of his relations with physicians, physicists, and mathematicians like Huygens. Science is of outstanding importance in Hobbes's work. For as we shall show, his conception of politics and the theoretical model of the state are founded on an anthropology at the base of which lies physics, and in particular, the concept of motion.

Hobbes's political science, and also his epistemology, should not, however, be understood, as has often happened, as a mechanistic reduction of his thought to a computational method. As we shall show, the importance of the Hobbesian conception of motion, the keystone of his system, has not always been fully grasped. To be sure, Hobbes states in *De Cive* that had the moral philosophers of his time been as able as the scientists to define "right and wrong," we should be living in a world without conflicts;[6] but in *Leviathan* he decisively asserts that if the geometry books had had any political implication whatever, they would have been destroyed and the geometers would be fighting with pen and sword just like the moral philosophers. In *Leviathan* Hobbes explains why the world could never enjoy complete serenity:

> [T]hey [*sc.* men] appeal from custom to reason, and from reason to custom, as it serves their turn; receding from custom when their interest requires it, and setting themselves against reason, as oft as reason is against them: which is the cause, that the doctrine of right and wrong, is perpetually disputed, both by the pen and the sword: whereas the doctrine of lines, and figures, is not so; because men care not, in that subject, what be truth, as a thing that crosses no man's ambition, profit or lust. For I doubt not, but if it had been a thing contrary to any man's right of dominion, or to the interest of men that have dominion, *that the three angles of a triangle, should be equal to two angles of a square*; that doctrine should have been, if not disputed, yet by the burning of all books of geometry, suppressed, as far as he whom it concerned was able.[7]

In *Leviathan* what we see is not a shift in Hobbes's outlook, as Quentin Skinner maintains. For him, Hobbes in his masterpiece changes his mind, loses trust in the power of science to find truths and persuade us of them, and revalues eloquence.[8] In *Leviathan* we see, first, a corroboration of Hobbes's conviction of the different status of the mathematico-physical sciences and of politics in his times. Hobbes intends to make the latter into a science, by founding it on an anthropology in which the passions play the leading part. Second, in *Leviathan* Hobbes reiterates that politics consists of conflict, and that because of the passions conflict cannot be eliminated from the human world. Third, the Leviathan Hobbes proposes to build to avoid the destruction of the human species is the modern state founded upon a political contract with the consent of the citizens. Hobbes, as Leo Strauss wrote, founds the state on the continent of politics discovered by Machiavelli. But Hobbesian man, by contrast with what Strauss thought,[9] is not Hegelian man and does not change his spots (or his DNA) by entering Leviathan, which always runs the risk of breakup through external or internal war, while men always run the risk of falling back into the condition of *homo homini lupus*. It should also be stressed—and perhaps underestimation of this aspect weighs on Skinner's interpretation—that Hobbes, for whom, as for Francis Bacon, science is power, is not Descartes and does not have a Cartesian conception of science.

MOTION, IMAGINATION, AND THE PASSIONS

Hobbes states in *De Homine*: "Thus, it is because we ourselves create the figures that there is a geometry and that it is provable."[10] For the sage of Malmesbury, the same applies to the laws that govern the coexistence of citizens: "the principles whereby what is *right* and *fair* and the opposite, *wrong* and *unfair*, is known, that is, the causes of justice, namely laws and conventions, we have ourselves made."[11] The scandal Hobbes aroused among his contemporaries lies in the very fact that Hobbes is proposing a model of rationality that brings into crisis the concepts of "objectivity" and "universality" as codified in Western thought by Descartes. For him it was essential to differentiate intuition from the "fluctuating evidence of the senses" or the deceptive verdict of the imagination[12] in order to affirm that by deduction we "understand everything that is necessarily concluded from other things known with certainty." Descartes's aim was to show the existence of a rationality able to combine truth and certainty, so as to found a knowledge sure of itself and able to operate in the physical and human world.

Hobbes was no less interested than Descartes in the future of science, and took an enthusiastic part in the scientific revolution under way. In *De Corpore* he cites Copernicus, Harvey, and Galileo, who "was the first that opened to us the gate of natural philosophy universal, which is knowledge of the nature of *motion*."[13] Yet in this very work celebrating the protagonists of the modern scientific revolution he asserts the inconsistency and unproductiveness of a science that claimed simultaneously to give universal, empirical truths and to be able to operate concretely in the world. The difference between Hobbes and Descartes consisted, as we shall see, in their founding two different paradigms of rationality; this difference is also to be seen in Hobbes's theory of the passions and in his decision, by contrast with the Frenchman, to construct a science of politics. To understand the divergence of their positions, one must examine their philosophical assumptions.

Where Descartes's philosophy is "essentialistic," as Karl Popper has argued,[14] (since for Descartes the main problem is to give clear, certain definitions for everything) for Hobbes instead the problem is to know by what means one arrives at formulating the cogito. "Il est très certain que la connoissance de cette proposition: *j'existe*, dépend de celle-cy: je pense, comme il nous a fort bien enseigné. Mais d'où nous vient la connoissance de celle-cy: *je pense*?"[15] Descartes was so irritated with "l'Anglois," as he called him, as to hope his *De Cive*, published anonymously in Paris in 1642, would be condemned by the Church of Rome. But already after Hobbes's criticisms of his *Dioptrique* Descartes had told Mersenne in

February 1641 he wanted nothing to do with "l'Anglois." He never forgave him his critique of the *Dioptrique* and especially of the *Méditations*. Thus, Karl Popper's definition is particularly suited to Descartes's philosophy because Descartes considers the processes of cognitive thought from the viewpoint of their conclusions, so as to establish the certainty of their representations.

Hobbes instead raises the problem of analyzing the processes through which the human system, biological and mental, arrives at representations. To do so, he considers the relation between the phenomena of representation and of perception: that is, the problem of the relation between the "phantasm" of an object perceived through the senses by a subject Peter or John and the process whereby its image is recorded in memory and expressed through the tokens of language. Hobbes's problem is to know the means whereby the human body processes the information received from outside, within a locus circumscribed by the "phantasms" of space and time. We know that Cartesian science, for which certain and universal truths are possible, founds the certainty of knowledge on the theory of innate ideas, and the existence of these on God. Hobbes was no less concerned than Descartes with the future of science, and for Hobbes too certainty was an obsession, but for Hobbes certainty is "the concomitance of a man's *conception* with the *words* that signify such conception in the act of ratiocination."[16] Science is, for Hobbes, in the *Elements*, "*evidence of truth*, from some beginning or principle of *sense*."[17] In fact, for Hobbes, "the truth of a proposition is never evident, until we conceive the meaning of the words or terms whereof it consisteth, which are always conceptions of the mind: nor can we remember those conceptions, without the thing that produced the same by our sense."[18] The concepts that men have formulated using the signs called "names" are concepts they themselves have created by processing the information received in their interactive relation with outside bodies.[19] In the *Elements*, as we know, Hobbes defined cognitive power as the mind's capacity to conserve the images of things perceived by the senses, even in the case of the absence or destruction of the objects previously perceived.

The difference between the theories of knowledge of Hobbes and Descartes lies in the different role they assign to memory. Whereas for Descartes memory mainly has the job of recording the results of knowledge, with a secondary mnemonic function, for Hobbes it has instead the essential role of founding the cognitive power, since without memory there would be no imagination, and hence no knowledge. The idea that knowledge is founded on the human capacity for memory and imagination, without which no form of mental discourse would be possible, entails that the certainty and universality of knowledge do not, for Hobbes, lie in some principle or principles innate in our minds, but are relative to men's images.

Hobbes's revision of nominalism in an anti-ontological sense, making it, along with logic, the instrument of his epistemological convention-alism, is the feature that distinguishes him from Descartes, who sets God up as guarantor of science. In Hobbes's science there is no room for God, since God is unknowable to men and only an object of faith, and science is understood as the conventionalistic construction of a reason not innate, like the senses and memory, "but attained by industry; first in apt impos-ing of names; and secondly by getting a good and orderly method in pro-ceeding from the elements, which are names, to assertions made by con-nexion of one of them to another; and so to syllogisms, which are the connexions of one assertion to another, till we come to a knowledge of all the consequences of names appertaining to the subject in hand; and that is it, men call science."[20] For Hobbes the universality of science, the ultimate goal of which is "the performing of some action, or thing to be done,"[21] is built upon names: "a word taken at pleasure to serve for a mark, which may raise in our mind a thought like to some thought we had before, and which being pronounced to others, may be to them a sign of what thought the speaker had, or had not before in his mind."[22] And as regards universality, Hobbes takes care to state: "this word *universal* is never the name of any thing existent in nature, nor of any idea or phan-tasm formed in the mind, but always the name of some word or name; so that when *a living creature, a stone, a spirit*, or any other thing, is said to be *universal*, it is not to be understood, that any man, stone, &c. ever was or can, be universal, but only that these words, *living creature, stone, &c.* are *universal names*, that is, names common to many things; and the conceptions answering them in our mind, are the images and phantasms of several living creatures, or other things. And therefore, for the under-standing of the extent of an universal name, we need no other faculty but that of our imagination, by which we remember that such names bring sometimes one thing, sometimes another, into our mind."[23] Hobbes can therefore conclude: "From hence also it is manifest, that truth adheres not to things, but to speech only."[24] As Hobbes asserts in the citations from *De Homine* quoted at the beginning of this second section, the in-strument whereby we have created geometry, as also *rightness* and *fair-ness* and the laws governing civil coexistence, is the imagination. From it originate all our passions, without which there would be neither science nor politics. Hobbes intoduced the modern world to a rationality con-ceived of as a system of signs, logical operations, laws and conventions, established by man and able to operate in a commonwealth to serve the survival of the species. The hypothesis of man as artificer of his own universe is not, however, fitted by Hobbes into a teleological conception of human activity. For Hobbes, progress is possible and pleasing, but does not coincide with happiness, which, considered as an ultimate goal, cannot be attained as long as one is alive.[25]

At the base of every phenomenon of the physical and human universe is motion, the keystone of the whole Hobbesian system, but conceived of differently from Aristotle, as Thomas A. Spragens showed in his important book *The Politics of Motion* in 1973. Whereas for Aristotle motion is not possible without an external force, for Hobbes it is *causa sui*. And while in Aristotle it has a teleological function, in the English philosopher it has no other aim than itself. Motion plays a particularly important part in the Hobbesian conception of memory, the imagination and the passions. For Hobbes each individual is so constructed as to be dominated by a continual flow of desire from one object to another, and gaining one is nothing but the stimulus to gain another. All is motion in Hobbes's philosophy, and at the root of his anthropology lies movement, from which arise all our passions, the aim of which is our personal pleasure, every individual being dominated by his own self-interest. By contrast with what Jean Hampton claims, though our search for pleasure is bound up with our biological structure, Hobbesian man does not seek pleasure in the same way that blood circulates in his veins.[26] Hobbes distinguishes two types of movement: vital or biological movement, in which the imagination plays no part, and the voluntary type, impossible without the imagination. Hobbes stresses that the biological movement is "begun in generation, and continued without interruption through their whole life; such as are the *course* of the *blood*, the *pulse*, the *breathing*, the *concoction, nutrition, excretion, &c.* to which motions there needs no help of imagination."[27]

By contrast, regarding voluntary movement, that is, such movements as walking, speaking, moving, "it is evident, that the imagination is the first internal beginning of all voluntary motion."[28] When an object strikes our senses, appetites and aversions are formed, through the pleasure and pain experienced through the senses and fixed in memory, which has the power—described by Hobbes in the *Elements*—to retain the images of perceptions even after the disappearance of the objects. "If a man could be alive, and all the rest of the world annihilated," he states in the *Elements*, "he should nevertheless retain the *image* thereof, and all those things which he had before seen or perceived in it; every one by his own experience knowing, that the *absence* or *destruction* of things once imagined doth not cause the *absence* or *destruction* of the *imagination* itself."[29] In chapter 2 of *Leviathan*, "Of imagination," Hobbes defines the imagination using the image of water moved by the wind: "and as we see in the water, though the wind cease, the waves give not over rolling for a long time after: so also it happeneth in that motion, which is made in the internal parts of a man, then, when he sees, dreams, &c. For after the object is removed, or the eye shut, we still retain an image of the thing seen, though more obscure than when we see it. And this is it, the Latins call *imagination*, from the image made in seeing; and apply the same, though improperly, to all the other senses. But the Greeks call it *fancy*; which signifies *appearance*, and is as proper to one sense, as to another. IMAGINATION therefore is nothing but *decaying sense*."[30] (The metaphor of water stirred by the wind is present in the *Elements* too.[31]) In *Leviathan* Hobbes distinguishes two types of imagination: "This *decaying sense*, when we would express the thing itself, I mean *fancy* itself, we call *imagination*, as I said before: but when we would express the decay, and signify that the sense is fading, old, and past, it is called *memory*."[32] Thus imagination is "decaying sense," while memory is the decayed, vanished, past sense, incapable of acting on the senses, of arousing emotions or activating passions.

Memory and imagination are referred by Hobbes to two different forms our memories can take with the passage of time. In the *Elements* Hobbes notes—recovering and reworking the Augustinian distinction in *De Trinitate* between *phantasia* and *phantasma* in connection with Carthage and Alexandria—that the image of a city familiar to us in every detail can decay gradually in our mind to the point of being recalled as a confused mass of streets and houses, and that this amounts to having forgotten it.[33] Just because the succession of images in the human mind is such as to produce the phenomenon of forgetting, man has, for Hobbes, invented tokens to bring back to mind the thought he had when he established them. Names are in fact "*marks*, or *notes* of remembrance," he writes in *Leviathan*.[34] All our fancies are for Hobbes movements within us, residues of the senses. Sometimes our thoughts proceed without any design or plan, as in dreams. Other times they are guided by some desire or design. As he writes in *Leviathan*: "For the impression made by such things as we desire, or fear, is strong, and permanent, or, if it cease for a time, of quick return: so strong it is sometimes, as to hinder and break our sleep."[35] Desire or fear that does not pass with time, does not vanish, activates our thought so as to reach what we desire or flee what we fear. "From desire, ariseth the thought of some means we have seen produce the like of that which we aim at: and from the thought of that, the thought of means to that mean; and so continually, till we come to some beginning within our own power."[36] These movements, efforts, strivings, to reach what we desire or flee what we fear, these appetites and aversions, before they take shape in action, are the passions.

Departing from the tradition, Hobbes links two terms regarded as opposites, reason and passion, thereby accomplishing a theoretical revolution. Not only is reason for Hobbes a calculus in the service of the passions,[37] but the very rationality of the calculus is defined through the capacity of passion to guide the imagination and identify, through discernment,[38] the means for reaching the desired goal. By contrast with the French and German tradition, the English-speaking one considers passions evaluatively, and does not hold it possible to eliminate them. For Albert Hirschman, what emerges from British thought is a paradigm of modernity in which it is more the passions that shape reason than vice versa.[39] Hirschman recalls Hume, for whom reason is the slave of the passions, at the service of the passions; but Hume had a radical precursor in Hobbes, for whom reason is nothing but a calculus among passions, remote from emphatic *Raison* and *Vernunft*. Even the faculty whereby *"man leaveth* all community with *beasts* . . ., the faculty of *imposing names,"*[40] and of make syllogisms "that we call *ratiocination* or *reasoning,"*[41] is, for Hobbes, born of a passion: curiosity.[42]

From the passion of curiosity arises knowledge, and this is a pleasure for Hobbes the scientist and philosopher. But "to a man in the chase of riches or authority, (which in respect of knowledge are but sensuality) it is a diversity of little pleasure, whether it be the motion of the sun or the earth that maketh the day, or to enter into other contemplations of any strange accident, otherwise than whether it conduce or not to the end he pursueth."[43] The results of curiosity differ, however, according to the individual capacity to apply oneself to an object with constancy and tenacity. A curiosity that leads to interesting oneself in everything, as with a person who, in the midst of a conversation, continually wanders off, opening one parenthesis after another, is mere levity.[44] The pleasure of knowledge, for which "the great and principal delight is represented by the goal," is defined by Hobbes as "lust of the mind," which is more intense than sexual pleasure ("natural lust").[45] "By a perseverance of delight in the continual and indefatigable generation of knowledge, [cusiosity or the lust of the mind] exceedeth the short vehemence of any carnal pleasure."[46] The scientist too, then, feels the attration of power, since every scientist faced with a new discovery is seized with the hope that all gamblers feel when the cards are reshuffled.[47] Happiness is in fact for Hobbes a continuing flow of desire from one object to another, attainment of which is nothing for man but the necessary condition to be able to continue to desire and hope to obtain pleasure. "The cause whereof is," he explains in *Leviathan*, "that the object of man's desire, is not to enjoy once only, and for one instant of time; but to assure for ever the way of his future desire."[48] Just because happiness is the certainty of being able to continue to desire and to hope to obtain still further pleasure, the figure of desire and of happiness is connected with that of power, which represents "a general inclination of all mankind, a perpetual and restless desire of power after power, that ceaseth only in death."[49] As Elias Canetti, who regarded *Leviathan* as his ideal Bible, wrote, Hobbes is the only thinker who does not mask power, its weight, its position, central to all human conduct.[50] The desire for power, central to all human conduct, arises from the desire for pleasure, different for each individual, and from it arise all the passions. And it is from the desire for power that what we today call rationality arises.

THE LOGIC OF POWER

Will, too, is for Hobbes a passion. For it is the result of a process of deliberation that involves the whole sum of movements of appetite and aversion, of hope and fear, which reason calculates in terms of something it wishes to attain or intends to flee from.[51] "In *deliberation*, the last appetite or aversion, immediately adhering to the action, or to the omission thereof, is that we call the will; the act, not the faculty of *willing*. . . . *Will* therefore *is the last appetite in deliberating*."[52] Hobbes therefore found absurd the accusations of the scholastic theologians and Bramhall that he had not distinguished "rational appetite" from "sensible appetite." If will were a "rational appetite" separate from the passions, one could not—he replied to them—understand how voluntary acts that cause harm to the subject who decided them could exist.[53] The distinction seemed absurd to Hobbes, since as he had stated in the *Elements*, in polemic with Aristotle's *Nicomachean Ethics*, there exists no "absolute good" to which the "rational" aspect would tend, or "utility" that the "irrational" appetite seeks. "Every man, for his own part, calleth that which *pleaseth*, and is delightful to himself, *good*; and that *evil* which *displeaseth* him: insomuch that while every man *differeth* from another in *constitution*, they differ also from one another concerning the common distinction of good and evil. Nor is there any such thing as absolute goodness, considered without relation: for even the goodness which we attribute to God Almighty, is *his goodness to us*."[54] It is for this reason, moral philosophers continually dispute with pen and sword to establish "right" and "wrong," and are in unceasing conflict.

This continuous competition caused by the passions also leads to the difference in talents among men. For Hobbes "the passions that most of all cause the difference of wit, are principally, the more or less desire of power, of riches, of knowledge, and of honour. All which may be reduced to the first, that is, desire of power. For riches, knowledge, and honour, are but several sort of power."[55] Elias Canetti wrote that Hobbes took the mask off power, for in Hobbes power is no longer concentrated at a single point, top down, but omnipresent and a central feature of all human conduct. For Hobbes power is not concentrated in a politico-legal institution nor an economic structure, as in Marx, but is an element present everywhere in every aspect of individuals' action and at the basis of all relations of force present in the multiplicity of human relations. Power in Hobbes is like a strategic situation, and just as war is the continuation of politics, so also all resistance to power does not depend on some element outside power, nor does it escape the logic of power, even when revolution comes along and cuts off the king's head. In the *Elements* he had stated: "The *passions* of man, as they are the beginning of all *voluntary* motions: so are they the beginning of *speech*, which is the motion of his tongue."[56] Language is for Hobbes not just the instrument with which we construct our knowledge, but the most important instrument of communication and of sociopolitical engineering. In *Leviathan* he attributed the causes of the English political crisis to the reading of Greek and Latin texts, and stated that the learning of Greek and Latin had cost his country such a bloodletting that it could never have been bought at such a price; and in *Behemoth* he described the seditious preaching of the Puritan ministers.

Thus *Leviathan* is also an analysis, in an Aristotelian sense, of locutions, and Hobbes tackles the rhetorical, political, and moral anarchy of his times, founding the science of politics and of civil coexistence among men. Just because, for each man, "*Good*, and *evil*, are names that signify our appetites, and aversions; which in different tempers, customs, and doctrines of men, are different,"[57] each individual realizes that "man is in the condition of mere nature, which is a condition of war, [so long] as private appetite is the measure of good, and evil." Consequently, "all men agree on this, that peace is good, and therefore also the way, or means of peace."[58] Once contract and sovereignty are made, "*Civil law, is to every subject, those rules, which the commonwealth hath commanded him, by word, writing, or other sufficient sign of the will, to make use of, for the distinction of right, and wrong; that is to say, of what is contrary, and what is not contrary to the rule.*"[59]

But since Hobbes is not Kant and does not identify rationality with an objective order of reality, nor attributes to it—as does Kant—any purpose, and since his epistemological conventionalism precludes us from having objective knowledge of reality, and the motion at the basis of every phenomenon of the physical and human universe is *causa sui* and without any purposiveness, the laws are for Hobbes like the rules of a game, valid as long as the compact that produced the state lasts. "But what is a good law?" asks Hobbes. "By a good law, I mean not a just law: for no law can be unjust. The law is made by the sovereign power, and all that is done by such power, is warranted, and owned by every one of the people; and that which every man will have so, no man can say is unjust. It is in the laws of a commonwealth, as in the laws of gaming: whatsoever the gamesters all agree on, is injustice to none of them."[60] The object of the laws is in fact "not to bind the people from all voluntary actions; but to direct and keep them in such a motion, as not to hurt themselves by their own impetuous desires, rashness or indiscretion; as hedges are set, not to stop travellers, but to keep them in their way."[61] Just because for Hobbes justice and fairness, wrong and inequity, that is, the causes of justice, the laws and conventions, are things we have ourselves made, his revision in an anti-ontological sense of nominalism and his epistemological conventionalism enable him to overcome ethical relativism in political science. He entrusts this science with the task of the survival of the species and human coexistence in a *Civitas* founded on what Hobbes sees as the sole passion able to be set against that for power: the desire for survival.

For Hobbes, as for Machiavelli, men are equally "wretched," and for both, politics is independent of morality; but they have different theoretical frameworks for ordering their worlds of the "wretched." Hobbes's modernity is founded on a critique of Aristotle. Hobbes rejects not only the Aristotelian theory of the natural sociality of men, but also that of natural inequality because, as he says in *Leviathan*, no individual—even the least perspicacious—would be prepared to join a state founded on the principle that some are wiser than others and are destined to rule. For every man, according to Hobbes, feels himself worth at least as much as any other, so that whether they be equal or not, a formal equality must be accepted. The paradox Hobbes puts before us is that men are not able to respect this equality since they are in continuous competition, yet without the presence of even only formal equality they are unable to accept any contract.

Hobbes's Leviathan is founded not by a prince through a war of conquest, but by the individuals who through the contract themselves create the sovereignty to emerge from the state of war. For Hobbes, in fact, individuals are not, by contrast with what Aristotle thought, bees and ants for whom private good does not differ from the common good, but are in continuous competition, and delight in prevailing over others. Dominated by appetites and aversions, men may destroy themselves, or else compete on a basis of *self-interest*; and it is from this competition that the wealth and prosperity of a community may arise. In *Leviathan* it is not the prince who controls the destiny of the *Civitas* by the arts of force and cunning, but the individuals themselves, in the last instance, who are in charge of the fate of the order created through the contract. Where Machiavelli arms the citizens, Hobbes disarms them and makes them responsible. For men are not meek, sociable creatures but *naturaliter* adversaries, so that the order that makes their coexistence possible is artificial and may break down if they do not feel bound to respect the contract made.

We can thus see that power in *Leviathan* is not simply located at a single point, in the institution of the sovereign, but constitutes a web of relations that cuts across all the bodies and institutions without ever being entirely localized in them. Because of this very tendency towards dispersion and atomization of power, a state's order is fragile unless the citizens feel themselves artificers and in charge of the sovereignty created. Moreover, Hobbes knows that for men happiness is not rest, the total absence of passions, of desires, of conflicts, which would coincide with the end of biological and mental motion, namely death. Happiness for men is an endless conquest, it is desiring; and the law of desire is never to be exhausted with conquest. This conception of happiness is also at the root of the antagonism among men. Hobbes's problem is to find a rhetoric for building an artificial order in which competition, the "race of life," can be possible without the self-destruction of the species, for it is the "race of life" that makes men happy and gives their lives meaning.

Hobbes aims to supply rulers with an instrument not just for understanding the circle of their acquaintances, since for this the ancient *nosce te ipsum* or introspection would suffice, but for governing the human race, for which politics must become a science.[62] For this, Hobbes establishes a special epistemological status for political science. It is well defined in *Leviathan*, making politics a science that draws on physics, biology, psychology, law, and logic, as well as history, an extremely useful instrument though not a science. (Indeed, Hobbes is also known as the translator of Thucydides' *Peloponnesian Wars*.) Politics becomes a science, implying an intellectual autonomy of its own.

As regards logic, it has an important task in the Hobbesian system, since for Hobbes we cannot know things in themselves, but only what we say about our "phantasms" (the objects we perceive with our senses in time and space and elaborate with our minds), so that we need logic lest in our scientific discourses our passions prevail. Logic has a role as arbiter in Hobbes's science. It has the same function as the rules of a card game: Hobbes notes that all players at cards want to win, but each card game has a set of rules meaning one has to hold particular cards to win. The rules have the aim of preventing the game being won by force or fraud. Logic in Hobbes has the function of controlling the formal rigor of our discourses.

The same happens in politics, since it is not enough to say *pacta sunt servanda* in order for men to respect them. The sword is needed, but also men's will to respect pacts in order not to throw the state into civil war. For this it must be shown logically that the contract is the only way the individuals themselves can construct the "artificial person" of sovereignty that makes them feel obliged to obey the Leviathan they have themselves created. The laws are for Hobbes like hedges whose object is to guide men's path, but they are alterable, and have to serve the political systems that establish and adopt them. At the root of the civil laws of the Hobbesian state is natural law, the fundamental law of which is the right of each individual to preserve his own life. But Hobbes neither sacralizes nor absolutizes the civil law of the state through natural law, since once the state is founded, the obligation of the citizen to obey sovereignty remains founded on natural law itself.[63] Politics is in fact for Hobbes the realm of the useful, and he wishes to construct an artificial order—whatever its form (democracy, aristocracy, monarchy)—with as its object internal peace.[64]

LEVIATHAN AT WAR

For the first time in history, in the twentieth century war has been legitimated as the instrument for restoring a violated moral and political order. Hobbes can be of great assistance in relocating war in a more realistic dimension. For Hobbes, war does not exist as *bellum justum*, as an instrument for restoring a violated moral order or imposing values considered universal. War is for Hobbes a prerogative of the state for reasons of interest, and the enemy is a *justus hostis*, and enemies *hostes utrimque justi*. Moreover, as we have seen, for Hobbes men call "just" simply what is pleasant and useful for them. Carlo Galli has noted that Hobbes's theoretical radicalism shows that "the modern rationalization of war is a thin, fragile façade hiding the tragic fact that it is politics that cannot do without war."[65]

Hobbes rejects the concept of the *bellum justum* just because he knows the desire for power is central to all human conduct: the desire for power arises from the desire for pleasure, different for each individual, and from the desire "to assure for ever, the way of his future desire."[66] Power represents "a general inclination of all mankind, a perpetual and restless desire of power after power, that ceaseth only in death."[67] Men accordingly engage in conflict over power, but from Hobbes's approach it is clear that this struggle for power concerns the sphere not of justice, but of utility. It should be noted that for Hobbes external war and internal (civil) war are the two causes of dissolution of a state. His whole work is aimed at averting civil war and founding a state in which, though the conflicts inherent in human nature remain, political obligation, founded on natural law, seeks to consider citizenship as an antidote to war. But Hobbes knows that politics and war interpenetrate: he disarms the citizens, unlike Machiavelli, but knows that, since even in the Leviathan the passions that lead to conflict will remain, so will the possibility of war. As he writes: "And though sovereignty, in the intention of them that make it, be immortal;

yet is it in its own nature, not only subject to violent death, by foreign
war; but also through the ignorance, and passions of men, it hath in it,
from the very institution, many seeds of a natural mortality, by intestine
discord."[68]

Just as, in order to emerge from the war of the state of nature, Hobbes
invents a pact on which the state is founded, so by positing the principle
of enemies as *justi hostes* he makes external war become a matter of state
and between states, a result of the same logic as civil war: "when in a war,
foreign or intestine, the enemies get a final victory; so as, the forces of the
commonwealth keeping the field no longer, there is no further protection
of subjects in their loyalty; then is the commonwealth dissolved, and every
man at liberty to protect himself by such courses as his own discretion
shall suggest unto him."[69] For "the sovereign is the public soul, giving
life and motion to the commonwealth; which expiring, the members are
governed by it no more, than the carcase of a man, by his departed,
though immortal, soul."[70]

The Leviathans are not immortal; indeed they may die, because states
are in a fight for power just as individuals are. Hobbes does not clearly
theorize a state of war among the Leviathans, but it can be deduced from
the regulation of the behavior of the citizen of a defeated state. The victor
state dissolves the defeated state, whose citizens have no other way to
preserve their lives but to accept the sovereignty of a foreign state, though
only if the defeated sovereign submits to the victor. "If a monarch subdued
by war, render himself subject to the victor; his subjects are delivered from
their former obligation, and become obliged to the victor. But if he be
held prisoner, or have not the liberty of his own body; he is not understood
to have given away the right of sovereignty; and therefore his subjects are
obliged to yield obedience to the magistrates formerly placed, governing
not in their own name, but in his. For, his right remaining, the question
is only of the administration; that is to say, of the magistrates and officers;
which, if he have not means to name, he is supposed to approve those,
which he himself had formerly appointed."[71]

War is not legitimated by Hobbes as *bellum justum*, as a means for
restoring a violated moral order, but regarded as inherent in human nature and disseminated among both individuals and states—a violent ex-
plosion of the eternal competition for power by individuals and states.
For that very reason Hobbes, while acknowledging the state's *jus ad bellum*, also desires a *jus in bello*, a set of pacts to reduce "the destructiveness
of war, by confining it to the purely military event, aimed against the
enemy's armed forces only, thus excluding civilians, and aimed at exclusively political, but not religious nor social, objectives."[72] Hobbes is quite
clear, as he states in *De Homine*, that men are endowed with weapons
more dreadful than wild beasts' talons because they have language,

whereby they can deceive each other; but he also theorizes the possibility of constructing an artificial order founded on the principle *pacta sunt servanda* and hence also on the possibility of honest communication.

THE POWER OF THE STRONGEST PASSION

Hobbes is so disenchanted that for him the just is only that which men find useful and pleasing. Hobbes knows very well that the various rhetorics of justice are the means whereby men wage their fight for power with the pen, but he also knows that his realistic conception of politics can lead to an artificial order in which peace, prosperity, and science are possible. For Hobbes, in whose opus the words *society, state, nation* do not exist, but *Commonwealth* and *Civitas* do, conflict is individual. It is conflict of the individual with himself, among individuals, between individuals and sovereigns or between communities governed by a sovereign. Hobbes includes civil war among the causes of the end of a state, and is thus not so utopian as to think he can exclude conflict from the very Leviathan founded upon his political science, nor war among the Leviathans. By contrast with Machiavelli, in Hobbes's philosophy social conflict becomes civil war and is the worst thing that can happen because it is an attack on the life of the state and on the safety of all. Machiavelli's model was republican Rome, in which civil war between patricians and plebs led to Rome's greatness. For Hobbes the good of the state does not differ from the common weal, and men delight when they prevail over others. Dominated by appetites and aversions, men may either destroy themselves or else find an order in which to compete on the basis of *self-interest*. This is the fundamental difference from Machiavelli, for whom politics is the art of winning and keeping power by an individual or an elite that holds the whole of a society together through a civil religion.

For Hobbes, it is not a civil religion that keeps a state united, but the capacity for coexistence established by contract among individuals dominated by personal interest. What holds the Hobbesian *Civitas* together, apart from fear of the sword, is the network of passions and interests and the obligation to respect the contract. It is a fragile, artificial order, for which the citizens are in the last instance solely responsible. Hobbes knows that his Leviathan is a mortal god, and may break down when the web of passions and interests leads to civil war. Like Pareto, Hobbes might have said that history is a graveyard of Leviathans, just because human nature cannot be changed.

For Leo Strauss, the irrational desire for power, man's natural appetite, has its root in the pleasure man feels in considering his own power, that is, in his vanity. Accordingly, the origin of man's natural appetite lies not in perception itself, but in a special passion, vanity.[73] But for Hobbes the desire for power is neither rational nor irrational, since it is inherent in the human psychic structure itself, and vanity is for the sage of Malmesbury a sort of madness, because it is a passion for power not supported by any adequate capacity to assess one's own strength and others', an intellectual weakness that leads to an exaggerated conception of oneself. "The passion, whose violence, or continuance, maketh madness, is either great *vain-glory*; which is commonly called *pride*, and *self-conceit*; or great *dejection* of mind,"[74] writes Hobbes in *Leviathan*. In the *Elements* Hobbes notes that the aspiration to glory, "or internal gloriation or triumph of the mind, is that passion which proceedeth from the imagination or conception of our *own power* above the power of him that contendeth with us."[75] This aspiration is a natural sentiment of man: an ambivalent passion, which may also be constructive and produce knowledge and activities that increase the welfare of the human community. When, however, the aspiration to glory is not combined with the effort to reach the objective desired and the imagination confines itself to fantasizing about actions never accomplished, it becomes vainglory. "*Signs* of *vain glory*," writes Hobbes, "in the *gesture* are, *imitation* of others, counterfeiting and usurping the signs of virtue they have not, affectation of fashions, captation of honour from their dreams, and other little stories of themselves, from their country, from their names, and from the like."[76] The passion for glory, complacency about one's own worth, is nonetheless brought by Hobbes into relation with the capacity to calculate if it corresponds with reality. Vainglory consists, instead, "in the feigning or supposing of abilities in ourselves, which we know are not,"[77] and is accordingly a vain and useless passion that may lead to folly.

Conflict among men does not however arise, for Hobbes, from vainglory, but from the natural inclination to power that prompts competition, mistrust, and the desire for glory.[78] Men's rationality is accordingly, for Hobbes, limited, since reason itself is nothing but an instrument of calculation at the service of the passions. It is from a consideration of the conflictual logic of human rationality itself that the pessimism present in the Hobbesian opus derives, as does his awareness of the precariousness of any order whatever. *Leviathan* itself was regarded by Hobbes from the outset as a hypothesis.[79] For Hobbes scientific progress made men more powerful, but could not change their nature, being the product of it. Calm could arrive—he affirms in the *Elements*—only at the end of the "race of life." Accordingly, the philosopher who linked two terms traditionally regarded as opposite, passion and reason, is anything but an exalter of the will to power. While Nietzsche regarded his contemporaries' passions as too weak and sought to arouse them, Hobbes by contrast had been born prematurely a child of fear—for fear of an attack by the Invincible

Armada—and was witness to a bloody civil war. He desired if anything to cool the passions of his countrymen. Nor was he a Rousseau, wanting to change the bourgeois of his times and make of him a *citoyen*, so as to found a nation capable of not awaiting the enemy at the frontier but rising as one man and achieving the *union sacrée*, as Hannah Arendt well saw in *On Revolution*. Rousseau's model is the Roman republic and Sparta. To the French, he held up the Romans and the Spartans as examples: "Un citoyen de Rome n'étoit ni Caius ni Lucius; c'étoit un Romain: même il aimoit la patrie exclusivement à lui." "Une femme de Sparte avoit cinq fils à l'armée, et attendoit des nouvelles de la bataille. Un Ilote arrive; elle lui en demande en tremblant. 'Vos cinq fils ont été tués.' 'Vil esclave, t'ai-je demandé cela?' 'Nous avons gagné la victoire'. La mère court au temple et rend grace qu'elle l'étoit: voila la Citoyenne."[80]

For Machiavelli, as for Rousseau, the model was republican Rome, whose political life was dominated by the conflict between plebs and patricians. For Machiavelli, social and political conflictuality is the necessary physiological condition of the health of a state. The tumultuous history of Rome, a story of bitter civil and external wars, is for Machiavelli proof that conflicts are positive in creating a powerful state. If instead one wishes a state incapable of growth, one should follow the example of Venice, which "avendo occupata gran parte d'Italia, e la maggior parte non con guerra ma con danari e astuzia, come la ebbe a fare la pruova delle forze sue, perdette in una giornata ogni cosa."[81] Machiavelli was thinking of Florence, weak and irresolute, he wrote, because it lacked an army and was prepared to put itself into anyone's hands in order to resolve its internal conflicts.

While for Machiavelli the key to a state's success is continual, even ruthless, competition among the citizens for glory, money, and power, for Hobbes, who had seen the long English civil war, the model for *Leviathan* is instead Lucca, a Tuscan city that since the fourteenth century had been in a position of economic primacy, and in the sixteenth century became legendary for its citizens' commitment to stopping the rise of leaders of particularist groupings. What Machiavelli identifies with politics constitutes for Hobbes a sickness of the state, since what makes a people prosperous, in a monarchy or in a democracy, is the citizens' capacity to obey the sovereign they have created through the contract. As with Ulysses, it is only their capacity to opt for their strongest passion that will decide their future.

Happy Tears

BAROQUE POLITICS IN DESCARTES'S *PASSIONS DE L'ÂME*

Victoria Kahn

> Ut comoedi, moniti, ne in fronte appareat pudor, personam
> induunt; sic ego, hoc mundi theatrum conscensurus, inquo
> hactenus spectator exstiti, larvatus prodeo.
>
> [As comic actors, receiving their cues, don their masks lest
> shame appear on their faces, so I, about to enter on the stage
> of this theater of the world, where up till now I have been a
> spectator, step forward masked.]

IN THE HISTORY OF PHILOSOPHY, Descartes most often appears as the founder of modern epistemology, a scientific discourse whose notion of evidence decisively shaped the subsequent understanding of philosophy.[1] Scholars of Descartes only rarely discuss his late treatise on the passions, written in 1645–46 and published in the last year of Descartes's life.[2] Like his correspondence with Princess Elisabeth of Bohemia and Queen Christina of Sweden, the *Passions de l'âme* is read for its contribution to the fuller study of ethics Descartes did not live to complete. In this essay, I argue that the treatise on the passions should be read as Descartes's prolegomena not only to ethics but also to political theory. If his *Méditations* is about the conditions of the possibility of knowledge, then the *Passions de l'âme* is about the conditions of the possibility of politics. But the two enterprises are not simply analogous. Rather, Descartes's reflections on politics and the passions end up fundamentally recasting his earlier conception of the philosopher-spectator who looks on politics with stoic detachment. Theater in the *Passions* is not simply a metaphor for theory, for a modern, disengaged notion of rationality, or for what Heidegger called the modern world picture. Instead, theater becomes a way of reflecting on the irreducible embodiment of human beings and on the project of strategically manipulating the passions in order to secure social and political order. "In the end," Adorno and Horkheimer write of Spinoza, "the transcendental subject of cognition is apparently abandoned as the last reminiscence of subjectivity and replaced by the much smoother work of automatic control mechanisms."[3] They could just as well be describing the effect, if not the intention, of Descartes.

Of course, the notion that the prince should theatrically manipulate his subject's passions was a familiar one in the Renaissance. Aristotle had discussed the process in the *Rhetoric* and *Politics*. In *De officiis*, the most influential ethical treatise in the Renaissance, Cicero had argued that it is better for a ruler to be loved than feared. In *The Prince*, Machiavelli had scandalously inverted this advice, arguing that—if a prince has to choose—it is better to be feared than loved; and that an effective prince will know how to simulate and dissimulate, to feign virtue and to put on theatrical displays of his power, in order to control his subjects. By the seventeenth century, Machiavelli's advice had been assimilated to (and, to a certain extent, camouflaged by) a Tacitean or baroque tradition of politic advice, which featured the prince as a skillful dramaturg and the dissident subject as a cunning actor. In this tradition, the passions were an object of pragmatic concern, but not of philosophical speculation.

With the seventeenth-century challenges to Aristotelianism by the new science and various materialist philosophies, the passions became a topic of renewed philosophical importance, and this philosophical approach in turn affected political theory. Many early-seventeenth-century writers saw the passions as a source of religious war on the continent, but they also believed that a new minimalist account of human nature—one predicated on self-interest and fear of violent death—could provide the building blocks for reconstructing society. In contrast to Machiavelli, who could also be said to have reduced human nature to its basic passions and drives, the new theories claimed the pedigree of scientific method. In the prolegomena to his great treatise on international law, *De jure belli ac pacis* (1625), the Dutch jurist Hugo Grotius explains that he was driven to compose the work by the conflagration on the continent, but he went on to analogize his method to that of mathematics: "just as mathematicians treat their figures as abstracted from bodies, so in treating law I have withdrawn my mind from every particular fact."[4] Hobbes famously claimed to have done the same in *The Elements of Law* (1640). Praising mathematics as "free from controversies and dispute, because it consisteth in comparing figures and motion only," Hobbes declared he had discovered similar principles of justice and policy: scientific principles that "passion not mistrusting may not seek to displace."[5] And in a later work, he declared that political science was no older than his own *De cive* (1642).

On the basis of this new scientific account of the minimal components of human nature, Grotius and Hobbes advanced a contractual theory of political obligation. Spurred by their passions and interests, including above all their desire for self-preservation, human beings would agree to subscribe to a political contract, involving an exchange of protection for obedience. The new political science thus joined a materialist analysis of human nature with a juridical language of rights. This juridical language encompassed older questions of sovereignty, morality, and agency but re-cast them in terms of artifice and individual consent. Morality was not missing from the new scientific politics, but conceived as a product of human agreement; while political agency was defined as the voluntary transfer of one's rights. In *Leviathan*, Hobbes famously compared the individual's alienation of his rights to the sovereign, to theatrical represen-tation: the sovereign impersonates and acts for the subject, just as an actor impersonates a character on the stage.[6] Whereas Machiavelli used the met-aphor of theater to enhance the prince's agency, Hobbes employed theater to convey the nonmimetic relation of sovereign to subject, and the corre-sponding diminishment of the subject's power.[7]

In addition to the Machiavellian and Tacitean tradition of politic ad-vice, Descartes was intimately familiar with the new scientific discourse of politics. He was also acutely aware of the political conflicts all around him. As a young man, Descartes had briefly traveled with a regiment of Prince Maurice of Nassau. Later, in his correspondence with Elisabeth, he discussed such contemporary political issues as regicide, rebellion, and religious wars.[8] His response to such issues, however, was not to extend scientific method to explicitly political matters, such as war and peace, but rather to confine his speculations to questions of epistemology. This was because "the most perfect moral system" could only be arrived at after the full study of metaphysics and physics.[9] In contrast to both Gro-tius and Hobbes, who proposed new contractual theories of obligation, Descartes declared he would adopt a skeptical "morale provisoire" and abide by the laws and customs of his country.[10] Instead of the new mini-malist language of natural right, Descartes continued to use the more tra-ditional language of Stoic virtue and Stoic detachment when discussing ethical questions in his correspondence[11]—until, that is, he encountered in Elisabeth an interlocutor with a passion for philosophy, who pressed him to apply his scientific rigor to moral discourse and to the contempo-rary political situation. In the course of this exchange, which is, among other things, a kind of trial run for the *Passions de l'âme*, Descartes began to see the relevance of baroque politics and theatrical manipulation for a scientific treatment of the passions. By the time he composed *Passions*, Descartes had arrived at an understanding of politics that was potentially more radical—in the sense of innovative and transformative—than the new, putatively scientific discourse of contract and natural rights. Whereas Grotius and Hobbes sought to apply scientific method to the realm of politics, Descartes adapted baroque politics to his new mechanis-tic science of the body, and in doing so, transformed them both. In this way, *Passions de l'âme* anticipated a new paradigm of government as well as self-government.

Although Elisabeth was first won over by Descartes's work in epistemology and mathematics, she quickly became dissatisfied with his reluctance to speak more directly to political affairs. It was all very well for Descartes to recommend scientific method and philosophical meditation from his retreat in the country, but how was someone who was engaged in the affairs of the world to follow his recommendations? More important, how relevant were his philosophical notions to the daily lives of those responsible for governing? Increasingly, Elisabeth pressed Descartes "to teach princes how they should govern."[12] She sought his advice, as well, about how to deal with the failure of government. As the exiled daughter of Frederick V, the deposed "Winter King" of Bohemia, Elisabeth was all too familiar with the loss of sovereignty—something she registered physiologically as well as emotionally in her aches and pains and depression.[13] Her personal experience was inseparable from her experience of contemporary politics, and both motivated her request for Descartes's therapeutic advice concerning the passions.

In his early letters to Elisabeth, Descartes parried Elisabeth's requests for political advice by appealing to the philosopher's spectatorial relation to current events. Adopting a pose much like that of Seneca in his moral letters, Descartes wrote to Elisabeth that he regarded the turmoil of political events "in the same way that we do comedies."[14] Some months later, in another letter to Elisabeth, he described this attitude of philosophical detachment as having its own pleasures, which he compared once again to a theatrical experience.

> It is easy to show that the pleasure of the soul which constitutes happiness is not inseparable from cheerfulness and bodily comfort. This is proved by tragedies, which please us more the sadder they make us, and by bodily exercises like hunting and tennis which are pleasant in spite of being arduous—indeed we see that often the fatigue and exertion involved increase the pleasure. The soul derives contentment from such exercise because in the process it is made aware of its strength, or skill [*la force, ou l'adresse*], or some other perfection of the body to which it is joined; but the contentment which it finds in weeping at some pitiable and tragic episode in the theater arises chiefly from its impression that it is performing a virtuous action in having compassion for the afflicted. Indeed in general the soul is pleased to feel passions arise in itself no matter what they are, provided it remains in control of them.[15]

Just as the painful exercise of the body gives pleasure because it makes us conscious of our strength or skill, so tears at the theater give rise to contentment because they allow us to see ourselves as compassionate.

Moreover, the soul takes pleasure in all excitations of the passions, as long as it remains in control. Here the argument is not so much that detachment will facilitate practical intervention, but rather that the theatrical experience of, or distance on, one's own passions will facilitate self-regard or contentment. This advice had obvious relevance to Elisabeth's own morose state of mind, but did not address her larger political concerns.

In response, Elisabeth objected that Descartes had conflated theater and life. It is true that we naturally enjoy having our passions excited. But the pleasure we derive from watching sad spectacles depends on the fact that they are not real. If these spectacles were real, and provoked real and potentially harmful actions on our part, she argued, we would not be able to take pleasure in them: "And this, in my judgment, is the reason tragedies please us more, the more sadness they cause, because we know that this sadness will not be so extreme [*violent*] as to lead us to foolish actions, nor so lasting as to affect our health" (110).

In September 1646, Elisabeth grew tired of letting Descartes hide behind the mask of the philosopher. Instead, she explicitly requested that he give his opinion about Machiavelli's *Prince*, and Descartes complied. The letter is a virtuoso political performance, one that suggests that the philosopher-spectator and the theatrical Machiavelli are not as antithetical as one might expect.[16] In the course of elaborating his views, Descartes touched on the major themes of baroque political thought: the legitimacy of reason of state, the management of the people's passions, the relationship between force and ideology, as well as between *virtù* and virtue. Descartes complained that Machiavelli did not distinguish between the prince who acquires power by legitimate means and the prince who does so by illegitimate means. He rejected Machiavelli's "very tyrannical precepts." At the same time, he conceded that "God gives the right to those whom he gives power" [Dieu donne le droit à ceux auxquels il donne la force], and that the justice of an action is determined by the agent's intention. Even the good prince will need to "join the fox with the lion, and join artifice to force" to preserve the state, as Machiavelli had recommended (146). Crucially important to the prince's success is persuading his subjects of the justice or necessity of his actions. This will allow him to avoid their "scorn" or "hatred" (144). Descartes thus accepted Machiavelli's view that the prince must know how to manage the people's passions and turn them to his own political advantage.[17] But he limited the excesses of Machiavellism by presupposing that the prince is not only legitimate but also *généreux*.[18]

In his reference to the prince's générosité or nobleness of mind, Descartes recalls the neo-Stoic ethical ideals advocated by such near contemporaries as Lipsius, Charron, Le Caron, and Du Vair. Here theater is not primarily a figure for illusion and deception, but rather for Stoic self-control. Le Caron declared that "the world is the true theater in which the man who wishes to be called noble and virtuous must exercise himself."[19] Du Vair proposed a model of Christian neo-Stoicism that advocated political engagement, generosity, and heroic self-sacrifice. By the 1640s the term *générosité* would also have suggested the more ambivalent preoccupation with heroism in the tragedies of Corneille.[20] But in its dominant meaning, *générosité* conjured up greatness of soul and the autonomous disposition of the will, which Du Vair described as "a correct disposition of the will to make use of things that present themselves, according to reason" [une droicte disposition de sa volonté à user des choses qui se présentent selon la raison].[21] In these neo-Stoic texts, self-government is the precondition of right political government.

By contrast, in his recommendation of politic feigning in the letters on Machiavelli, Descartes draws near to the baroque *political* advice of the same neo-Stoic authors. In the *Politiques*, which was translated into French in 1590, the Dutch neo-Stoic Justus Lipsius had advocated "a certain praiseworthy and noble [*honnête*] deception" in affairs of state, while in his *De la sagesse* (1600) Pierre Charron offered an extensive account of "political prudence," which dictated a certain indirection for success in politics. As Charron wrote of the sovereign, who must procure "the common good": "It is sometimes necessary to shift and dodge, to mix prudence with justice, and as they say, sew to the skin of the lion, if necessary, the skin of the fox" [Il luy faut quelques fois esquiver et gauchir, mesler la prudence avec la justice, et, comme l'on dict, coudre à la peau du lion, si elle ne suffit, la peau du renard].[22] The ruler must know how to join force and artifice; he must act his part and manipulate his audience, not least of all by staging awe-inspiring theatrical displays of power. Similar recommendations were put forth by Guez de Balzac in *Le prince* (1631) and by Gabriel Naudé in *Considérations politiques sur les coups d'Estat* (1639).[23] In these texts, the art of government is explicitly distinguished from the moral art of self-government. Government is not a matter of law, but of tactics and forces; and theater is not a figure for philosophical speculation but rather politic intrigue.

The letters on Machiavelli thus encompass a twofold attitude towards politics and theater. On the one hand, we find an insistence on the rational self-control of the Stoic sage. Here the letters gesture towards the sublime display of virtue and self-mastery associated with the ideal humanist ruler. On the other hand, we find the pragmatic consideration of political circumstances that authorizes a rationality specific to politics, a baroque "reason of state" divorced from the ethical injunctions of Stoicism. Whence the recommendation of politic feigning and the manipulation of the people's passions. These two aspects of theater—deception and display, the manipulation of force and the celebration of self-mastery—encapsulate the two poles of contemporary neo-Stoic thought. They also, as we began to see in the remarks on theater in the correspondence with Elisabeth, capture the ambivalence of Descartes's account of the mind-body relation.

Descartes's account of human nature in the *Traité de l'homme* illustrates the relevance of baroque political thought, with its complex metaphor of the theater, to Cartesian dualism. In this work, Descartes compares the mechanism of the human body to those mechanical devices that formed part of the theatrical display of the sovereign's power in the royal gardens. At the same time, the treatise shows how Descartes fundamentally alters the traditional early modern understanding of spectacles of state, familiar to us, for example, from Elizabethan processions and the great royal entries of Louis XIII. In Descartes's new garden-theater, the relationship between sovereign and subject is subtly transformed: instead of dramatizing his power through spectacles of state, the sovereign acts from behind the scenes. Instead of consciously imitating the sovereign's exemplary self-mastery, the king's subject is manipulated at a distance through a series of mechanical devices. Here is Descartes comparing the mechanism of animal spirits to the royal gardens:

> Now in the same proportion as the animal spirits enter the cavities of the brain, they pass from there into the pores of its substance, and from these pores into the nerves. And depending on the varying amounts which enter (or merely tend to enter) some nerves more than others, the spirits have the power to change the shapes of the muscles in which the nerves are embedded, and by this means to move all the limbs. Similarly you may have observed in the grottos and fountains in the royal gardens that the mere force with which the water is driven as it emerges from its source is sufficient to move various machines, and even to make them play certain instruments or utter certain words depending on the various arrangements of the pipes through which the water is conducted.

A little later in the same text, Descartes compares the effects of external objects on the senses to strangers entering into the royal gardens and causing—"without thinking" [sans y penser]—the mechanical movements of the figures in the grottos and fountains:

> External objects, which by their mere presence stimulate its [the body's] sense organs and thereby cause them to move in many different ways depending on how the parts of its brain are disposed, are like visitors who enter the grottos of these fountains and unwittingly cause the movements which take place before their eyes. For they cannot enter without stepping on certain tiles which are so arranged that if, for example, they approach a Diana who is bathing they will cause her to

hide in the reeds, and if they move forward to pursue her they will cause a Neptune to advance and threaten them with his trident; or if they go in another direction, they will cause a sea-monster to emerge and spew water onto their faces; or other such things according to the whim of the engineers who made the fountains.[24]

Descartes then goes on to explain that the soul (which has its royal "seat" in the pineal gland) is to the body-machine as the fountain-maker is to his mechanical fountain.[25] In this elaborate comparison of the soul-body relation to the royal gardens, the mechanical play of forces—of the automata—is designed to display the authority of the sovereign/artificer. At the same time, however, other aspects of the scene curiously undermine this authority. With the appearance of the king's subject as visitor to the gardens, the analogy between soul and body, and sovereign and subject, begins to break down: the sovereign's soul may be in control of the spectacle, but the subject's soul is both isolated from and dependent on material sensations that may deceive the soul or subject it to a mechanical play of forces.[26] This play of forces is responsible for theatrical illusion and deception—a deception that cannot fail to suggest its evil twin, the *malin génie*. Ironically, the only figure of authority who actually appears in the scene—Neptune—is himself a mere mechanical effect of pressure on the garden tiles, while the only human agent who appears is entirely deprived of thought: "sans y penser." In this display of control by the sovereign soul, Descartes insinuates what Alain Vizier has called "the existence of an automatism proper to thought," an automatism that Descartes elsewhere calls a "passion."[27] This automatism is both the problem Descartes sets out to analyze in *Les passions de l'âme*, and his proposed solution. But it is a solution that fundamentally recasts our understanding of the political subject. In *Passions de l'âme*, politics is less a matter for the sovereign than for the self-disciplining subject, and discipline is less a matter of neo-Stoic virtue than of indirection and force.

Les Passions de l'âme is not a treatise on politics, but in obvious ways it grows out of the correspondence with Elisabeth. As in the correspondence, Descartes responds to Elisabeth's concerns about "those in charge of governing," who do not have the leisure to examine the most expedient course of action and who are not able to "judge without passion." In both the treatise and the letters, action in the realm of politics poses an obstacle to Cartesian ethics in the form of passions such as "regrets and repentance" that are not easily mastered.[28] In both, the passions are the material of politics, which sovereign and subject need to control. In both, Descartes singles out the passion of religious zeal, which has inspired "the greatest crimes that men can commit, such as betraying cities, killing princes, and exterminating entire peoples just because they do not accept their opinions" (art. 190). As in the Lettre-Préface to his *Principes*, the religious wars resulting from the passion of zeal are one motive for composing *Passions de l'âme*.

So far, this description makes Descartes's text sound like any of the numerous treatises on the passions published during the 1640s in France. These treatises often commented, directly or indirectly, on the contemporary political debate surrounding Richelieu's policies of raison d'état and the court ethos of aristocratic "gloire."[29] One of the most explicit was Jean-François Senault's *L'usage des passions* (1641). Although Senault recommended the use rather than the Stoic suppression of the passions, he also drew on the well-worn trope of the body politic to compare Richelieu's management of the people to the way sovereign reason rules over the passions.[30] In contrast, Descartes avoids this sort of clichéd analogy. Rather than elaborating a comparison between the state and the individual, Descartes celebrates the political benefits of scientific method. Writing with the religious violence of the Thirty Years' War clearly in mind, Descartes voices his hope that a scientific treatment of the passions, a treatment "en physician" rather than as a moral philosopher, will provide a scientific basis for the management of the passions and thus a scientific basis for generosity or nobility of soul, and the promotion of peace.[31]

Descartes begins with a dualist account, according to which the soul is an immaterial substance, while the body is extended. The question is then how to establish a relation between the soul and the body, and the passions are one answer. According to Descartes, the passions of the soul broadly construed are the ways in which the soul is affected or acted on by the body. In this broad sense, the passions include various kinds of perceptions, which Descartes classifies in the following way: perceptions of external objects; bodily sensations, such as hunger or pain; involuntary memory and imaginings; and perceptions that seem to have no location other than the soul itself.[32] These last are passions in the narrow sense of the term.[33] As in the *Traité de l'homme*, Descartes then goes on to give a mechanistic account of how passions arise in the soul by means of "animal spirits" that move the pineal gland. He also provides a functionalist account of the passions as modes of perception of an object's utility or harm. In both cases, we can see the passions as revealing the internal political relations between body and soul. In the mechanistic account, the passions are spirits or forces within the soul that act on the soul's faculties of judgment and will, which must in turn learn to master them (art. 212). In the functionalist account, the passions communicate the body's interests to the soul, moving it to consent and to contribute to actions that preserve the body. The passions also provide the soul with evidence of its relations to others (art. 137, art. 206). From this analysis of internal relations, Descartes moves outward again in part III of the treatise to the social and political relations in which all individuals are implicated. Here the passions are not simply ways in which the body affects the soul; they are social modes of interaction: we relate to our friends and enemies, our fellow citizens and our superiors, with pity, fear, contempt, veneration, cowardice, or emulation.

Although Descartes avoids the body-politic metaphors of Senault and others in *Passions*, baroque politics are everywhere in the treatise. In particular, the baroque political problem of the relationship between force and representation appears in Descartes's discussion of the relations between body and soul. This problem is initially discussed solely in mechanistic and materialist terms: just as the contemporary political question is how to move from force to representation—both how to legitimate the exercise of force and how to make the play of political forces intelligible—so Descartes wants to explain how the mechanics of the body communicates with the incorporeal locus of reason, and specifically what the relationship is between the mechanics of the passions—the play of forces—and the intelligible order of the soul.[34] Ultimately, however, Descartes intends his analysis of the relation of force to representation to raise the question of the relationship between mechanical force and virtue. For humans as embodied creatures, the political question is the following: how are creatures who are moved or determined by their passions also capable of reflection on and control of their passions? What is the relationship between the determinism of the passions and the capacity for voluntary action, which is to say the capacity for virtue, political or otherwise?

The Cartesian ideal of *générosité* or nobility of soul, which involves a kind of theatrical distance on the self, is one answer to this question. In Book III, Descartes tells us that self-esteem, a subspecies of the passion of wonder (art. 150), is a good opinion of oneself. He then explains that one can only rightly esteem oneself if one is generous. Generosity comes from understanding "that there is nothing which truly belongs to him but this free control of his volitions, and no reason why he ought to be praised or blamed except that he uses it well or badly" (art. 153). It also comes from feeling "within himself a firm and constant resolution to use it well, that is . . . to follow virtue perfectly" (art. 153).[35] As both a passion and a virtue, understanding and feeling, generosity is the moral and affective equivalent of the pineal gland—the meeting place of soul and body, philosophy and ethics, knowledge and resolution, virtue and *virtù*. Generosity also establishes a link between ethics and politics, as when Descartes explicitly equates generosity with the political virtue of justice: "For the more noble and generous one's soul is, the greater one's inclination is to render everyone his own," unlike the servile individual who disdains authority, and passes from impiety to superstition and back again (art. 164). Descartes also tell us that the generous are "naturally inclined to do great things, and yet to undertake nothing they do not feel themselves capable of" (art. 156). The potential conflict between an aristocratic ethos of great deeds and the Stoic "undertak[ing] nothing they do not feel themselves capable of" is then displaced by being recast in terms of traditional Christian ethics: the generous "esteem nothing more highly than doing good to other men and for this reason scorning their own interest" (art. 156). Heroic theater is internalized in the satisfying spectacle of one's transcendence of individual interest.

Descartes develops this conceit in articles 186 and 187 on the passion of pity. Descartes claims that those are most subject to pity who imagine the sufferings of others as happening to them: "Those who feel very weak and very much subject to fortune's adversities seem to be more inclined to this passion than others are, because they represent the misfortunes of others to themselves as possibly happening to them; thus they are moved to pity by the love they bear to themselves rather than by that which they have for others" (art. 186). In contrast, the generous man has a different theatrical experience, one in which pity is not based on identification with the sufferer, construed as the love one bears to oneself. For the generous man,

> the sadness in this pity is not bitter; like that caused by the fateful actions we see represented on the stage, it is more on the outside and in the senses than in the inside of the soul—which all the while has the satisfaction of thinking it is doing its duty in being compassionate to the afflicted. Now there is a difference present here: whereas the common person has compassion for those who lament because he thinks the misfortunes they suffer are extremely grievous, the main object of the pity of the greatest men is the weakness of those they see lamenting.

As in Descartes's correspondence with Elisabeth, theater is here employed as a metaphor for a Stoic distance on the passions, a distance that itself yields the satisfaction of seeing oneself as virtuous. The generous man does not pity real-life suffering, just as he does not pity the sufferings he sees represented on the stage; instead, he pities those who experience pity in the wrong way. These sentimental individuals are incapable of the higher pleasure or ethical satisfaction of knowing one is doing one's duty.[36]

Elsewhere in *Passions de l'âme*, however, Descartes complicates this Stoic use of theater as a metaphor for the philosopher's mastery of the passions—his own and others. I have in mind the strange example of article 147. In this article, Descartes distinguishes the passions from what he calls *émotions intérieures*, which are the excitations the soul feels when it reflects on its own perceptions or operations.[37] Although he has just argued that the passions tell us what is beneficial or harmful, he now asserts that "our good and our ill depend principally on inner excitations, which are excited in the soul only by the soul itself."

Descartes gives as his example of *émotions intérieures* the husband who experiences joy at mourning his dead wife:

> although these excitations of the soul [*émotions de l'âme*] are often joined with the passions that are like them, they may also frequently be found with others, and may even originate from those that are in opposition to them. For example, when a husband mourns his dead wife, whom (as sometimes happens) he would be upset to see resuscitated, it may be that his heart is constricted by the sadness which funeral trappings and the absence of a person to whose company he was accustomed excite in him; and it may be that some remnants of love or pity, presented to his imagination, draw genuine tears from his eyes—in spite of the fact that at the same time he feels a secret joy in the innermost depths of his soul, whose excitation has so much power that the sadness and tears accompanying it can diminish none of its strength. And when we read of unusual adventures in a book or see them represented on a stage, this sometimes excites sadness in us, sometimes joy or love or hatred, and in general all the passions, according to the diversity of the objects offered to our imagination; but along with this we have the pleasure of feeling them excited in us, and this pleasure is an intellectual joy, which can originate from sadness as well as from any of the other passions.

The husband feels both sadness, prompted by the funeral trappings and the loss of his customary companion; and remnants of love or pity, prompted by the image that memory presents to the imagination. Descartes goes out of his way to emphasize that these give rise to real tears—"de véritables larmes"—a phrase that recalls his earlier insistence that we cannot be deceived by the passions as we can be by our perceptions (art. 26). Our perceptions of external objects may be falsely referred to those objects, but our passions are always correctly referred to the soul. Or, to put this more colloquially, our perceptions may be inaccurate, but if we feel certain passions, we must actually feel them. Descartes then tells us that this complex of emotions coexists with "a secret" or "intellectual joy"—a kind of metapassion that comes from feeling the primary passions excited in us. This metapassion is one of those *émotions intérieures*, which are excited in the soul when it reflects on its own operations.

What is striking about the description of the mourning husband is that Descartes does not moralize the example.[38] He does not offer a judgment about the husband's passions, as he does in his discussion of pity in article 186. Nor does he represent the husband's sadness as following from a judgment that his marriage was, after all, a good one. Instead, he describes how the husband's tears are prompted by the funeral trappings and the representation of some remnants of love in his imagination. And he describes the secret joy in terms of its power or strength, which overcomes the primary passion of sadness. On the one hand, we have theater; on the other hand, we have force. The juxtaposition of the mourning husband to the experience of reading a book or going to the theater makes it clear that the husband's experience of his wife's funeral, and of his own response, is an essentially theatrical one. The question is, how should this theatrical experience be interpreted?

As though to acknowledge Princess Elisabeth's remark (in the letter quoted earlier) that theatrical experiences are pleasurable because they are not real, Descartes stresses that the husband experiences joy in mourning his dead wife even though (or precisely because) he would be upset to see her resuscitated. That is, his mourning does not necessarily reflect his real feelings about his wife. Descartes's language suggests that his tears are a mere reflex, a physiological response to the funeral trappings and his own imagination: his heart is constricted by sadness; his tears are prompted by remnants of love or pity. This is of course what makes them "real tears," but also what makes them morally problematic. In responding to the funeral and his marriage as though to the theater, the husband is being hypocritical—in the root sense of *hypokrites*: an actor who can take pleasure in his own experience of certain artificially or mechanically induced emotions. The clause, then, in which Descartes intimates that the husband is hypocritical is Descartes's concession to Elisabeth that the feelings prompted by the theater are different from those that would be prompted by the same experiences in real life and are morally problematic for that reason. The irony, of course, is that the husband really *is* at his wife's funeral, he just experiences it as though it were a play.

Descartes then offers us two responses to the hypocritical husband, two responses to Elisabeth's objections about the morally problematic conflation of theater and life. In the first response, he describes the relationship between the passions and the *émotions intérieures* as a calculus of forces. First, he tells us that the husband "feels a secret joy in the innermost depths of his soul, whose excitation has so much power that the sadness and tears accompanying it can diminish none of its strength." Similarly, he tells us that, when we go to the theater, we not only feel discrete passions but "along with this we have the pleasure of feeling them excited in us, and this pleasure is an intellectual joy, which can originate from sadness as well as from any of the other passions." Intellectual joy is a metapassion, a pleasure we take in feeling our own passions or, as the sentence about the husband suggests, a pleasure whose force is greater than any individual passion.

In article 148, Descartes tries to moralize or legitimize this experience of power by linking it to an understanding of "perfection":

> Now, inasmuch as these inner excitations affect us more intimately and consequently have much more power over us than the passions from which they differ but are found with them, it is certain that, provided our soul always has what it takes to be content in its interior, none of the disturbances that come from elsewhere have any power to harm it. On the contrary, they serve to increase its joy, for in seeing that it cannot be injured by them it comes to understand its perfection. And in order that our soul may thus have what it takes to be content, it needs only to follow virtue diligently.

This passage is exemplary of the treatise's indecision concerning the relationship of force to ethics. In arguing that the power of the soul derives from representing to itself the idea of perfection, Descartes seems to be echoing the famous passage from Lucretius, *De rerum natura*, book 2, where the spectator looks on a storm-tossed ship from the vantage of a safe promontory. This passage was regularly cited in the seventeenth-century discussions of tragic pleasure, particularly by those who wanted to advance an amoral account of tragic pleasure as analogous to the pleasure of self-preservation.[39] But in linking this pleasure to an idea of perfection, Descartes also anticipates the Kantian notion of the sublime, in which reason comes to understand its higher destiny by the very fact that the individual can imagine and therefore transcend his own physical destruction. If we read article 148 as a gloss on the mourning husband, we could say that what the husband understands—what gives him intellectual joy—is the recognition that he can't be harmed by his feelings of sadness. Although Descartes qualifies his potentially amoral calculus of forces in the last sentence in the quotation above, by attributing the satisfaction and contentment of the individual not simply to greater power but to the firm and constant resolution to act virtuously, he mentioned no such resolution in discussing the mourning husband. The ethical explanation is belated, and not entirely convincing.[40]

In this light, the distinction between passions and *émotions intérieures* is another manifestation of Descartes's ambivalence about the mind-body relation. In the aftermath of his emphasis on the mediating power of the passions, the idea of *émotions intérieures* appears designed to preserve the soul's inviolability and to guarantee the autonomy of the moral subject, whose virtue is not affected by external events or contaminated by the passions but is instead constituted precisely by the act of self-reflection, that is, reflection on the "free control of [one's] volitions." This notion of self-reflection, uncontaminated by the passions, is what we might call the idealist moment in Descartes. But no sooner has Descartes introduced this distinction than he complicates it by his illustration of the mourning husband. For Descartes's example of the autonomous, self-reflexive master of the passions is not presented in the first instance in moral terms but in terms of greater power. The Cartesian act of self-reflection is less a matter of neo-Stoic autonomy than of a baroque politics of force.

In Book III, Descartes distinguishes between generosity, based on correct judgment, and pride, which is based on false judgment, in a way that has implications for the unruly example of the mournful husband. Articles 157 and 158 suggest that the husband would be wrong to esteem himself for experiencing a passion that has nothing to do with generosity: "whatever may be the cause for which we esteem ourselves, if it is anything other than the volition we feel within ourselves always to make good use of our free will, from which I have said generosity arises, it always produces a most blameworthy pride." Whether the husband feels joy in his freedom from the force of sorrowful passions, or joy in feeling the sorrowful passion, in neither case is this joy clearly linked to a disposition to virtue.

Article 147 thus provides a different account of what it means to have a theatrical experience of the passions from that of the generous man. Rather than serving to moralize admiration or self-regard—as the virtue of generosity does—the example of the mourning husband shows instead the moral ambiguity of such self-regard. For in ascribing the husband's tears to a physiological reflex, the example suggests that the husband cannot equate theatrical distance with Stoic mastery. Instead, the theatrical experience produces—through a relation of forces—a sense of *virtù* or power that cannot be simply assimilated to moral virtue.[41]

We can now see that the example of the mourning husband is part of a historical shift in the understanding of the ethical and political utility of the theater. In the early modern period, the pleasures of tragedy were primarily interpreted in ethical terms: tragedy instructed about virtue and vice both in its explicit plot and in its cathartic effect, by which it purged or moderated those passions that hindered ethical action. Such a moralizing interpretation of tragedy conveyed obvious lessons to both subjects and sovereigns. By the middle of the seventeenth century, this moralizing explanation was being challenged by Descartes's and Hobbes's materialist accounts of the passions. Later in the century, followers of Descartes such as Rapin and Dennis explained the effects of tragedy in terms of the natural delight we take in the "sheer physical stimulation of the animal spirits." But in *Passions de l'âme*, we see that such an interpretation of the theater was not simply an extrapolation from Descartes; it was Descartes's own chosen analogy for the workings of the passions.[42]

Even more important, the example of the mourning husband also suggests a shift in the understanding of the relationship of government and self-government. If we think back to the description of the royal gardens in the *Traité de l'homme*, we can compare the complicated emotional state of the husband to the relationship between the sovereign and subject. In his experience of intellectual joy, the husband is like the sovereign who takes intellectual pleasure in observing the unwitting visitor. Yet, in responding reflexively to the funeral trappings, the husband is also like the visitor to the royal gardens who triggers the mechanical display of waterworks without thinking. In fact, we might think of the husband's tears as a miniature version of the royal fountains. In neither case can the theatrical scene be assimilated to an older model of Stoic self-government. Instead, Cartesian theater anticipates a new model of social and political order in which government is not exercised from on high by a sovereign but rather exercised through indirect mechanisms and diffused throughout the body politic.

The example of the mourning husband in turn bears on our understanding of generosity. As we have seen, *générosité* is a passion insofar as it involves self-love or self-esteem. It is a virtue insofar as this self-esteem is legitimate—that is, based on a correct judgment of the good, and a firm and constant resolution to use one's will to act in accordance with the good (art. 48).[43] Self-esteem for any other reason is not generosity but rather pride (art. 157). The generous man knows how to control his passions and channel them into the service of reason. The problem, of course, as we see in article 147 and elsewhere, is that the passions cannot be directly controlled by an act of the will (art. 45). And this problem leads in turn to the characteristic dilemma of Descartes's Christianized neo-Stoicism. Either virtue is simply defined as the intention or resolution to do well, without regard for success or the practical results of one's actions (art. 146, art. 156), or virtue is defined as, at least in part, a matter of *virtù*, a surplus of power or a strategic manipulation of the passions by means of the passions themselves (art. 45).

In this context, Descartes reveals his discovery of the principle of association or habituation: habituation is the psychological equivalent of the combination of force and artifice that Descartes discussed in the letter on Machiavelli (arts. 44, 50, 107, 211). Just as one cannot will to dilate one's pupils but can trick oneself into doing so by focusing on a distant object, so "our passions cannot . . . be directly excited or displaced by the action of our will, but they can be indirectly by the representation of things which are usually joined with the passions we will to have. . . . Thus, in order to excite boldness and displace fear in oneself, it is not sufficient to have the volition to do so—one must apply oneself to attend to reasons, objects, or precedents that convince [one] that the peril is not great, that there is always more security in defense than in flight, that one will have glory and joy from having conquered" (arts. 44 and 45). In short, "there is such a connection between our soul and our body that when we have once joined some bodily action with some thought, one of the two is never present to us afterwards without the other also being present" (art. 50). Precisely for this reason, the mechanism of association can be used to retrain the mind to have different thoughts in connection with the same bodily stimuli.[44] The soul is once again in the position of a theatrical spectator watching various "representations"; but the spectator here is located somewhere between the Stoic sage and the mourning husband, who only appears to be virtuous as a result of his automatic emotional response. The mechanism of association may ultimately convert *virtù* into virtue, the play of forces into representation, but the cost of doing so is the dethroning of the sovereign soul or Stoic sage who directly masters the passions by force of will.[45]

As we have seen, in exploring the problem of how to control the passions, Descartes alternates between an ideal of generosity or wonder at our capacity to act according to free will, and a mechanistic manipulation of the passions. This alternation is reflected in Descartes's shifting use of the metaphor of the theater. In contrast to the correspondence with Elisabeth, in *Passions* Descartes uses his metaphor of the theater to complicate his own project of mastery and generosity. At times, in *Passions de l'âme*, theater is a metaphor for the Stoic's spectator relationship to the external world; at other times, theater is the locus of a conceptual disturbance— one might even say, a dramatic conflict—between the ideas or representations of the soul and the force of the body-machine. Far from simply asserting a Stoic notion of reason as the remedy for political passions, Descartes gives us an instrumental conception of reason as the manipulator of the passions. In elaborating his principle of association, he even appears to suggest that the body might be a better sovereign than the soul. The Descartes who recommends the principle of association or habituation as the chief discovery of the *Passions* recalls the politic advice of Machiavelli, Lipsius, or Charron. But with a difference. Whereas baroque politics involves a rationality intrinsic to politics, a reason of state, dealing with the passions requires a mechanistic principle of association that undercuts any self-aggrandizing claims to virtue or, for that matter, *virtù*.

The *Passions de l'âme* deserves to be seen as a contribution to and transformation of this early modern politic literature. Although writers such as Lipsius and Charron very often treated the passions moralistically, as something to be stoically mastered or channeled, they were also quite capable of treating the realm of politics in a proto-scientific fashion, as requiring a non-moralizing, dispassionate method of observation and control. As we have seen, in his own scientific treatment of the passions, Descartes applies the insights of neo-Stoic politics to the realm of the passions and, in doing so, transforms them both. Where Descartes differs from his contemporaries is in his internalization of baroque politics.[46] The subject of *Passions de l'âme* is not the prince who rules over his people and territory, but rather the vexed relation of the soul to the body. Although, in some ways, the generous man involves a familiar, even old-fashioned aristocratic ideal of self-mastery, in other ways the text takes as its subject the modern individual, whose body has become a foreign territory, one that requires new indirect techniques of government. These indirect techniques are very far from Descartes's original ambition to establish ethics on a secure scientific basis. But the distance Descartes has traveled should not necessarily be construed as a sign of failure. In internalizing baroque politics, Descartes not only moves beyond the baroque prince's use of indirect techniques to control his unruly subjects. He also moves beyond Hobbes's and Grotius "modern" juridical language of rights, obligations, and consent, to a conception of government and self-government based on units of energy, mechanical operations, relations of forces. Because he transfers the prudential techniques of Machiavelli, Lipsius, Charron, and Senault to the internal politics of body and soul, Descartes's *Passions de l'âme* deserves to be seen as one of the inaugurating texts of a new regime of politics, one inscribed in the body itself.

The Desire to Live

SPINOZA'S *ETHICS* UNDER PRESSURE

Judith Butler

THE DESIRE TO LIVE is not an easy topic to pursue. On the one hand, it seems too basic to thematize; on the other hand, it is vexed enough as a topic to cast doubt on whether one can settle the question of what is meant by the phrase itself. The desire to live is not the same as self-preservation, though both can be understood as interpretations of a person's desire "to persevere in its being,"[1] Spinoza's well-known phrase. Although self-preservation is largely associated with forms of individual self-interest associated with later contractarian political philosophers, Spinoza's philosophy establishes another basis for ethics, one that has implications for social solidarity and a critique of individualism. The self that endeavors to persevere in its own being is not always a singular self for Spinoza, and neither does it necessarily succeed in augmenting or enhancing its life if it does not at once enhance the lives of others. Indeed, in what follows, I hope to establish within Spinoza not only a critical perspective on individualism, but also an acknowledgment of the possibility for self-destruction. Both of these insights come to have political implications when recast as part of a dynamic conception of political solidarity in which sameness cannot be assumed. The fact that Spinoza takes some version of self-preservation to be essential to his conception of human beings is undisputed, but what that self is, and what precisely it preserves, is less than clear. He has been criticized by psychoanalysts who contend that he leaves no room for the death drive, and he has been appropriated by Deleuzians who for the most part wish to root negativity out of their conception of individuality and sociality alike. He has been castigated as well by writers like Levinas for espousing a form of individualism that would eradicate ethical relationality itself. I propose to test these views and to consider in some detail Spinoza's view of the desire to live—not to establish a definitive reading but to see what possibilities for social ethics emerge from his view.

When Spinoza claims that a human being seeks to persevere in its own being, does he assume that the desire to live is a form of self-preservation?

Moreover, what conceptions of the "self" and of "life" are presupposed by this view? Spinoza writes, "The striving by which each thing strives to persevere in its being is nothing but the actual essence of the thing" (IIIP7, 159). It would seem that whatever else a being may be doing, it is persevering in its own being, and at first, this seemed to mean that even various acts of apparent self-destruction have something persistent and at least potentially life-affirming in them. I've since come to question this idea, and part of the purpose of this essay will be to query what, if anything, counters the force of perseverance itself. The formulation is problematic for another reason as well, since it is not fully clear in what "one's own being" consists, that is, where and when one's own being starts and stops. In Spinoza's *Ethics*, a conscious and persevering being does not persevere in its own being in a purely or exclusively self-referential way; this being is fundamentally responsive and in emotional ways, suggesting that implicit in the very practice of perseverance is a referential movement toward the world. Depending on what kind of response a being undergoes, that being stands a chance of diminishing or enhancing its own possibility of future perseverance and life. This being desires not only to persevere in *its own* being, but to live in a world that reflects and furthers the possibility of that perseverance; indeed, perseverance in one's own being requires that reflection from the world, such that persevering and modulating reference to the world are bound up together. Finally, although it may seem that the desire to persevere is an individual desire, it turns out to require and acquire a sociality that is essential to what perseverance means; "to persevere in one's own being" is thus to live in a world that not only reflects but furthers the value of others' lives as well as one's own.

In the Fourth Part of *Ethics*, entitled "Of Human Bondage, *or* The Powers Of The Affects," Spinoza writes, "No one can desire to be blessed, to act well and to live well, unless at the same time he desire to be, to act, and to live, that is, to actually exist" (IVP21, 211). The desire to live well presupposes the desire to live, or so he suggests. To persevere in one's own being is to persevere in life, and to have self-preservation as an aim. The category of life seems, however, to traverse both what is "one's own" and what is clearly not only or merely one's own. The self preserved is not a monadic entity, and the life persevered in is not only to be understood as a singular or bounded life. Importantly, in the disposition toward others, where the self makes its encounter with another, the *conatus* is enhanced or diminished, so that it is not possible, strictly speaking, to refer to *one's own* power without referring to, and responding to, other powers—that is, the powers that belong to others. Similarly, it is not possible to refer to one's own singularity without understanding the way in which that singularity becomes implicated in the singularities of others, where, as we shall see, this being implicated produces a mode of being beyond singularity itself.

For Spinoza, self-preservation is enhanced or diminished depending on the way in which others appear; they arrive physically and they wield the power of reflection. More precisely, they reflect back something about life itself, and they do this in variable ways. Much of the second part of the *Ethics* is devoted to lists of these kinds of experiences. The *conatus* is augmented or diminished depending on whether one feels hatred or love, whether one lives with those with whom agreement is possible, or whether one lives with those with whom agreement is difficult, if not impossible. It seems that self-preservation is, in nearly every instance, bound up with the question of what one feels toward another, or how one is acted on by another. If we are to call this being that one is a "self," then it would be possible to say that the self represents itself to itself, is represented by others, and that in this complex interplay of reflection, life is variably augmented or diminished. Actually, what the self does, constantly, is imagine what a body would do, or does do, and this imagining becomes essential to its relation to others. These imaginary conjectures are not simple reflections, but actions of a certain kind, the expression of *potentia* and, in that sense, expressions of life itself. *This means that the way that we represent others to ourselves, or the means by which we are represented to ourselves by or through others, constitute expressive actions by which life itself is augmented or diminished.* In representing others as we do, we are positing possibilities, and imagining their realization. Life stands the chance of becoming enhanced through that process by which the *potentia* of life are expressed.

If we are to understand this formulation, one that Deleuze clearly facilitated in his early readings of Spinoza,[2] we have to become disoriented by the formulation itself. For it turns out that to persevere in one's own being means that one cannot persevere in that being understood as radically singular and set apart from a common life. To be set apart from the interplay of selves and their reflective powers is to be deprived of the representational and expressive apparatus by which life itself is enhanced or diminished. Indeed, the very meaning of the life that is, finally, one's own to persevere in becomes equivocal in this formulation. So if we are to speak about desiring to live, it would seem in the first instance to be emphatically a personal desire, one that pertains to my life or to yours. It will turn out, however, that to live means to participate in life, and life itself will be a term that equivocates between the "me" and the "you," taking up both of us in its sweep and dispersion. Desiring life produces an *ek-stasis* in the midst of desire, a dependence on an externalization, something that is palpably not-me, without which no perseverance is possible. What this means is that I start out with a desire for life, but this life that I desire puts the singularity of this "I" into question. Indeed, no I can emerge outside of this particular matrix of desire. So, strictly speaking, one should say that *in desiring, I start out—that desire starts me as an "I—" and that the force of desire, when it is the desire to live, renders this "I" equivocal.* Accordingly, the *Ethics* does not, and cannot, remain with the question of individual perseverance and survival, since it turns out that the means by which self-preservation occurs is precisely through a reflection or expression that not only binds the individual to others, but expresses that bind as already there, as a bind in several senses: a tie, a tension, or a knot, something from which one cannot get free, something constitutive that holds one together. So, on the one hand, the problematic of life binds us to others in ways that turn out to be constitutive of who each of us singly is. On the other hand, that singularity is never fully subsumed by that vexed form of sociality; for Spinoza, the body establishes a singularity that cannot be relinquished in the name of a greater totality, whether it be a conception of a common life or a political understanding of *civitas* or, indeed, of the multitude (*multitudo*), a term that becomes important, very briefly, in Spinoza's *A Theologico-Political Treatise*, a work that remained incomplete at his death.

I will return to the question of this relation between singularity and commonality in a later section of this essay, especially when I consider the criticism that Levinas has made of Spinoza, but let us first return to the other quotation from Spinoza with which I began. At first, it seems to be relatively straightforward, namely, that "no one can desire to live well, unless at the same time he desires to be, to act, and to live." It appears that the meaning of this line is to be understood in the following way: the desire to live well calls upon the desire to be and to live, and that this latter desire to live must first be in place for the desire to live well to come into play. According to this view, the desire to live well is a way of qualifying the prior desire to live, and living well is but a permutation of living. This reading is thwarted, however, because Spinoza does not quite say that the desire to live well presupposes the desire to live. He writes that both desires are engaged simultaneously. They both emerge "at the same time." It is as if in desiring to live well one finds that one has engaged the desire to live. Or perhaps one encounters only belatedly the desire to live, only after it makes itself known as the unacknowledged underside of the desire to live well. This formulation also leaves open the possibility that living in the wrong way can induce the desire not to live or, indeed, diminish the organism in Spinoza's sense. This seems to be the sense of what he is maintaining when he makes the following kind of claim: "Envy is hatred itself or sadness, that is, a modification by which a man's power of acting or endeavour (persistence) is hindered."

Spinoza's is a controversial claim, if he is claiming, as he appears to be, that the virtuous life works *with*, rather than against, the desire to live. Of course it may be that the desire to live is a necessary precondition for the desire to live well, and that it also undergirds the desire to live wrongly, and that the desire to live is finally in itself neutral with respect to the question of living rightly or wrongly. But even this last, minimal interpretation leaves untouched the question of whether living rightly might sometimes entail a restriction on the desire to live itself. There is no repressive law that attacks some life force, whether that life force is conceived as the Nietzschean will to power or the Freudian conception of libidinal drives. And there is no sense that the right life might demand that we enfeeble ourselves in the name of morality, as Nietzsche and Freud have both suggested. The account Freud gives in *Civilization and Its Discontents* (1927), namely that living well can come at a cost to the life drives themselves, is not anticipated in Spinoza's ethical reflections. One can argue in a psychoanalytic vein that the desire to live the right sort of life can compromise the desire to live, and that morality requires the activation of a suicidal tendency. This would seem to be in contradiction to Spinoza's explicit views. Indeed, he rejects the notion that anyone might commit suicide "from the necessity of his own nature" and suggests that suicidal desires can only be "compelled by another" (IVP20S, 210–11). Of course, Spinoza distinguishes between forms of pleasure that diminish the desire to live and those that enhance or augment that desire, so he locates the possibility of an attrition of life that is achievable through pleasure and passion more generally. He also links the emotions to human bondage; there is the possibility of passivity and servitude in passion, which, for him, undermine the possibility of both persevering in the desire to live and living virtuously.

That said, however, Spinoza disputes that the desire not to exist can actually be derived from human desire, something he has already and consistently defined as the desire to persevere in one's own being. When he imagines how suicide might be conducted, he writes, "Someone may kill himself if he is compelled by another, who twists his right hand (which happens to be holding a sword)" (IVP20S, 210–11). He also cites the example from Seneca in which a suicide is coerced by a tyrant as a form of obligated political action. The third conjecture he offers is enigmatic since it promises an analysis it does not pursue. There Spinoza suggests that a man may commit suicide "because hidden external causes [*causae latentes externae*] so dispose his imagination, and so affect his body, that it takes on another nature" (IVP20S, 211). This is surely a paradoxical claim, since Spinoza acknowledges that a suicide can take place, that the self can take its own life, but that the self has acquired an external form or, indeed, an external cause has made its way into the structure of the self. This allows him to continue to argue that a person takes his own life only by virtue of external causes, but not by any tendency internal to human desire itself, bound to life as it ostensibly is.

This external cause that houses itself in the self is something for which I cannot have an "idea" and is, thus, an unconscious sort of operation, one that I cannot understand as proper to myself, something that is for me an object or, indeed, an external intrusion. The I is said to have taken on or contracted this externality, and so it has absorbed it through some means for which it has no representation and can have no representation. Indeed, the I becomes something other to itself in taking in this externality; it becomes, quite frankly, other to itself: obdurate, external, hidden, a cause for which no idea suffices.

At this point it may be that Spinoza himself has admitted something into his theory that threatens the consistency of his account of desire, and that he has momentarily assumed the form of some other conception of desire, one that would orient it against life. And though I think here we can see a certain prefiguration of the death drive—one invoked in the commentary on the proposition only to be disposed of quite quickly—I would suggest that there are ways to see Spinoza's unsettled relation to a psychoanalysis he could have never anticipated. There is already, apart from his introduction of this hidden external cause in the life of desire, a manner in which externality works upon desire that modulates its relation to life. I hope to show some of this in what follows, and to suggest that his view, however improbable it may seem in the light of contemporary thinking on the drives or desire in general, prefigures some of the continuing difficulties that beset these discussions.

Spinoza's ethics does not supply a set of prescriptions, but offers an account of how certain dispositions either express or fail to express the essence of humankind as the desire to persevere in one's being. The phrase, "each thing strives to persevere in its being," functions as a description of human ontology but also as an exhortation and an aspiration. It is not a morality in a conventional sense if, by morality, we mean a more or less codified set of norms that govern action. But if, for Spinoza, any morality is to be called virtue and we understand virtue, the virtuous life, as governed by reason, as he claims we must, then it follows that the *conatus* will be enhanced by the virtuous life, and there will be no cost to life, properly understood, if we live well.

Psychoanalysis approaches this question from another angle, since self-preservation comes to represent one of the basic drives for Freud, and this is so from nearly the beginning of his writings. But self-preservation is a drive that is eventually supplemented and countered by the death drive. This has consequences for the way in which Freud thinks about morality. Indeed, conscience harnesses the death drive to a certain degree, so that morality is always cutting away at the life drives. For Freud, it would seem that sometimes the dictates of morality require that self-preservation be suspended or put into question. And in this sense, morality can be murderous, if not suicidal. For Spinoza, however, self-preservation, understood as perseverance or endeavoring in one's desire, provides the basis for virtue, or living well, and he assumes further that living well enhances life and the capacity for perseverance in it. Not only does the desire to live well presuppose the desire to live, it follows that suicidal persons are at risk for some rather bad behavior. For Spinoza, living well might relieve the diminishing sense of life that is a kind of slow suicide.

Such ethical optimism is not only countered by Freud's account of the drives but, from a different direction, by Levinas's conception of ethics. For Levinas, self-preservation cannot be the basis of ethics, which is not to say that self-annihilation should take its place. Both relations are problematic because they set up a relation to the self as prior to the relation to the other. It is this latter relation that forms the basis of ethics in his view. I would like first to conjecture the psychoanalytic rejoinder to Spinoza, and then turn to Levinas in order to understand why he explicitly faults Spinoza for positing self-preservation as a precondition of virtuous conduct. For Levinas, it will turn out, there is no "other" for Spinoza, but only and always the self. But it may be that in reapproaching Spinoza through the lens of psychoanalysis we find a way of adjudicating this quarrel about just how much violence we are compelled to do to ourselves and, indeed, to others, in the name of morality.

Freud's thesis in *Civilization and its Discontents* is that morality, centralized and institutionalized as conscience, demands a renunciation of the life drive. Indeed, the very process by which conscience is formed is the process through which a renunciation and transformation of drive into conscience takes place. In this text, he recounts his argument from *Beyond the Pleasure Principle* (1920) in which he distinguishes self-preserving instincts or, more rightly, drives (*Triebe*), from the death drive. He writes:

> Starting from speculations on the beginning of life and from biological parallels, I drew the conclusion that, besides the instinct to preserve living substance and to join it into ever larger units, there must exist another, contrary instinct seeking to dissolve those units and to bring them back to their primaeval, inorganic state. That is to say, as well as Eros there was an instinct of death. . . . The manifestations of Eros were conspicuous and noisy enough. It might be assumed that the death instinct operated silently within the organism towards its dissolution, but that, of course, was no proof. A more fruitful idea was that a portion of the instinct is diverted towards the external world and comes to light as an instinct of aggressiveness and destructiveness.[3]

Freud makes two claims about life in the course of his discussion of the death drive that are not precisely compatible with one another. On the one hand, he distinguishes life drives from death drives, and claims, in sweeping terms, "the meaning of the evolution of civilization is no longer obscure to us. It must present the struggle between Eros and Death, between the instinct of life and the instinct of destruction, as it works itself out in the human species" (82). But immediately after this statement, he suggests that the struggle itself *is* life, and that life is not reducible to the life drive. He states, "This struggle is what all life essentially consists of, and the evolution of civilization may therefore be simply described as the struggle for life of the human species" (82). The struggle he refers to is a struggle *between* the two drives, one of which is the life drive, but it is also a struggle *for life*, implying that life is a struggle composed of the interplay of both the life and death drives. Life itself seems to be a term that switches between these two meanings, exceeding its basis in the drives, we might say, through a displacement that ceaselessly accommodates its apparent opposite. Indeed, one reason to use the term *drive* rather than *instinct* is that the notion of the "drive" is, as Freud argues, a border concept, vacillating between the domains of somatic and mental representation.[4] In Freud's text, the drive does not stay still (as Laplanche points out in his *Life and Death in Psychoanalysis*).[5] The struggle for life is not the same as the simple operation of the life drive; whatever "life" is said to adhere to, that drive alone is not the same as life, understood as an ongoing struggle. There is no struggle and, hence, no life without the death drive (*Todestrieb*). In that sense, without the death drive there is no struggle for life. If life itself *is* this struggle, then there is no life without the death drive. We can even extrapolate logically that life without the struggle provided by the death drive would itself be death. Such a life would be no life, and so, paradoxically, the triumph of the death drive over life.

So it would seem that life requires the death drive in order to be the struggle that it is. Life requires the death drive, but it also requires that the death drive not triumph. But it would also appear that the death drive plays a specific role in the emergence and maintenance of morality, especially the workings of conscience. For Freud, morality runs the risk of cutting away at life itself.

In "Mourning and Melancholia" (1914) Freud relates that the suffering of the melancholic is enigmatic: the melancholic suffers from loss but does not know precisely what he or she has lost. The clinician sees the melancholic absorbed in something and also losing self-esteem. One may know that one has lost someone or some object, but one cannot seem to find "what" is lost in the one who is lost, or "what" kind of ideal is lost when, say, historical circumstance shifts a political formation, demands a geographical displacement, or introduces uncertainty into the very conception of where one belongs or how one may name oneself. One cannot quite see it, but it makes itself known nevertheless; the loss appears in a deflected form, as the diminution of self-esteem and in the escalation of self-beratement. In mourning, Freud tells us famously, the world becomes impoverished, but in melancholia, it is the ego itself. The ego does not simply find itself impoverished, shorn of some esteem it once enjoyed, but the ego begins, as if inhabited by an external cause, to strip away its self-esteem. Freud describes it as a violent act of self-reproach, finding oneself morally despicable, vilifying and chastising oneself. In fact, this loss of self-esteem can lead to suicide because, according to Freud, the process of unchecked melancholia can conclude with "an overthrow, psychologically very remarkable, of that drive which constrains every living thing to cling to life."[6]

Whereas mourning seems to be about the loss of an object—the conscious loss of an object—melancholics do not know what they grieve. And they also somewhere resist the knowledge of this loss. As a result, they suffer the loss as a loss of consciousness, and so of a knowing self. To the degree that this knowing secures the self, the self is also lost, and melancholy becomes a slow dying away, a potentially suicidal attrition. This attrition takes place through self-beratement and self-criticism, and can take the form of suicide, that is, attempting to obliterate one's own life on the basis of its own felt contemptuousness.

Freud returns to this theme in his essay "The Economic Problem of Masochism" (1924), in which he attempts to spell out the phenomenon of moral masochism and understand its role in giving evidence for the death drive. In moral masochism, he claims, we see the least amount of pleasure at work for the psychic organism; it is unclear whether there is pleasure at all in this state. This form of masochism does not draw upon the resources of pleasure or, indeed, the life drive, and also risks devolving into suicide. The death drive, left alone, will attempt to "disintegrate the cellular organism,"[7] he writes, and so functions as a principle that *decon*stitutes the ego. Although Freud generally understands sadism as an outwardly directed act of aggression accompanied by the life drive, masochism of the moral kind not only turns aggression against the self but dissociates it from pleasure and, hence, life, thereby imperiling the very perseverance of the organism.

This leads Freud to conclude that masochism is a primary expression of the death drive, and that sadism would be its derivative form, a form that mixes the death drive with pleasure and, so, with life. He writes, spectacularly, that "it may be said that the death drive which is operative in the organism—primal sadism—is identical with masochism" (164). Moral masochism, "loosened" from sexuality, seeks suffering and derives no gain from the suffering. Freud postulates that an unconscious sense of guilt is at work here, a sense of guilt that seeks "satisfaction," not, however, a satisfaction of pleasure but rather an expiation of guilt and the death of pleasure itself. Freud explains:

> The super-ego—the conscience at work in the ego—may then become harsh, cruel and inexorable against the ego which is in its charge. Significantly, conscience and morality have arisen through the desexualization of the Oedipus Complex, and suicide becomes a temptation precisely when this desexualization becomes complete. (164)

Moral masochism approaches suicide, but to the extent that self-beratement is eroticized, it maintains the organism it seeks to decompose. Oddly, in this sense, morality works against the libido but can marshal the libido for its own ends, and so keep the struggle between life and death alive. In Freud's words, "through moral masochism, morality becomes sexualized once more" (169). Only when morality ceases to make use of libido does it become explicitly suicidal. Of course, we may want to question this claim, and remind ourselves of that final moment in Kafka's "Judgment" when the apparent murder/suicide of Georg, who hurls himself from that bridge, is likened, by Kafka in his journals, to ejaculation itself.

So for Freud, morality, which is not the same as ethics, makes use of the death drive; by virtue of becoming sexualized as masochism, it animates the desire to live as well. Morality would have to be understood as a perpetually, if not permanently, compromised desire to live and, in this sense, a move beyond or away from Spinoza's claim that the desire to live well emerges at once with the desire to live. Or, rather, with Freud, we might say that the desire to live well emerges at once with the desire to live, but also, always, with the desire to die, if not more explicitly with the desire to murder. In this way, we can understand Freud's remark in this context that the categorical imperative is derived from the Oedipus complex. If I am obligated to treat every other human being as an end in him- or herself, it is only because I wish some of them dead, and so must militate against that wish in order to maintain an ethical bearing. This is a formulation that is not so far removed from Nietzsche's insistence in *On the Genealogy of Morals* that the categorical imperative is soaked in blood.

Freud's view certainly seems to counter Spinoza's, since for Spinoza self-preservation seems always to coincide with virtue. Although Spinoza does make room for a deconstitution of the self or, rather, an attrition of its desire to live, he would surely dispute the claim that virtue is any part of what *de*constitutes the self; the measure of virtue is precisely the extent to which the self is preserved and the perseverance and enhancement of the *conatus* takes place. And yet, this fairly clear position is already muddled by two other propositions. The first is that the desire to live implicates desire in a matrix of life that may well, at least partially, deconstitute the "I" who endeavors to live. I opened this essay by asking whether it is clear in what Spinozistic self-preservation consists, since perseverance does not seem to be exclusively defined as the preservation of *this* singular self; there may well be a principle of the deconstitution of singularity at work. It may not be possible to say that this deconstitution of singularity parallels the workings of the death drive, but the idea becomes easier to entertain when we consider the second proposition at issue here, that it is possible for a self to acquire an external form, to be animated by an external cause and not be able to form an idea of this alien nature as it works its way with one's own desire. This means that the "I" is already responsive to alterity in ways that it cannot always control, that it absorbs external forms, even contracts them, as one might contract a disease. This means that desire, like the Freudian conception of the drive, is a border concept, always assembled from the workings of this body here in relation to an ideation that is impressed upon it from elsewhere. Those alien forms that the "I" assumes come from the matrix of life, and they constitute, in part, the specters of lives that are gone as well as modes of animating an other, assuming that externality internally so that a certain incorporation ensues, one that acts psychically in ways for which one has no clear idea. In melancholy, we find ourselves acting as the other would have acted, using her speech, donning his clothes. A certain active mode of substitution occurs, such that the other comes not only to inhabit the "I" but to constitute an external force that acts within—a mode of psychic operation without which no subjectivity can proceed. Who acts when the one who is lost from life is reanimated in and by the one who remains, who is transformed by the loss and whose desire becomes the desire to infuse continuing life into what is gone, and puts its own life at risk in the course of that endeavor?

Of course, this is not quite Spinoza's thought, though it is something that, in his language and through his terms, we might well begin to think. As we turn to Spinoza's political philosophy, we find that desire is deconstituted from another direction. We can only understand how the desire to live runs the risk of deconstituting the self once we understand the *common life* that desire desires. This common life, in turn, can perhaps only be properly understood if we make the move from ethics to politics and to a consideration of how singularity thrives in and through what Spinoza refers to as the multitude. I would like to approach this conception of Spinoza's through an examination of Levinas's critique of him. In short, Levinas takes Spinoza to represent the principle of self-preservation and interprets this as a kind of self-preoccupation and, indeed, a closing off to the ethical demands that come from the Other. In this sense, Levinas claims that Spinoza can only offer a notion of the social world in which the individual is primary, and in which ethical obligations fail to be acknowledged.

In an interview with Richard Kearney, Levinas makes clear that his own view of ethics must depart from Spinoza's. For Levinas, the human relation to the other is prior to the ontological relation to oneself.[8] And though Levinas does not ask in what self-preservation consists for Spinoza, he seems to assume that the relation to the Other is foreclosed from that domain.

> The approach to the face is the most basic mode of responsibility. . . . The face is not in front of me (*en face de moi*), but above me; it is the other before death, looking through and exposing death. Secondly, the face is the other who asks me not to let him die alone, as if to do so were to become an accomplice in his death. Thus the face says to me: you shall not kill. In the relation to the face I am exposed as a usurper of the place of the other. The celebrated "right to existence" that Spinoza called the *conatus essendi* and defined as the basic principle of all intelligibility is challenged by the relation to the face. Accordingly, my duty to respond to the other suspends my natural right to self-survival, *le droit vitale*. My ethical relation of love for the other stems from the fact that the self cannot survive by itself alone, cannot find meaning within its own being-in-the-world. . . . To expose myself to the vulnerability of the face is to put my ontological right to existence into question. In ethics, the other's right to exist has primacy over my own, a primacy epitomized in the ethical edict: you shall not kill, you shall not jeopardize the life of the other. (21)

Levinas goes on to say, "there is a Jewish proverb which says that 'the other's material needs are my spiritual needs'; it is this disproportion or asymmetry that characterizes the ethical refusal of the first truth of ontology—the struggle to *be*. Ethics is, therefore, against nature because it forbids the murderousness of my natural will to put my own existence first" (24). It would be interesting to find in Levinas a presumption of a natural will murderous in intent, one that must be militated against for the ethical priority of the Other to become established. Such a structure might belie, then, a compensatory trajectory well worth reading, and it would bring him closer to Freud, though, I think, not closer to Spinoza. For though Spinoza's being in its primary ontological mode seeks self-preservation, it does not do this at the expense of the other, and it would be difficult to find something like the equivalent of primary aggression in his work.

Levinas faults Spinoza for believing that through intellectual intuition one can unite oneself with the infinite, whereas for Levinas the infinite must remain radically other. But Spinoza does not say in what this ostensible unity consists, and it leads Levinas to ally Spinoza with Hegel, a move that is disputed by Pierre Macheray and others within the Althusserian tradition. In fact, sometimes this subtle alliance with Hegel becomes explicit when, for instance, Levinas remarks in *Alterity and Transcendence* that for Spinoza, "the revelation of the Infinite is rationality itself . . . [and that] knowledge would thus be [for him] only knowledge of knowledge, consciousness only self-consciousness, thought only thought of thought, or Spirit. Nothing would any longer be other: nothing would limit the thought of thought."[9]

Consider the defense of Spinoza's view of sociality, however, provided by Antonio Negri.[10] It would seem that the subject at issue is neither exclusively singular nor fully synthesized into a totality. The pursuit of one's own being or, indeed, of life, takes one beyond the particularity of one's own life to the complex relation between life and the expression of power. The move from individuality to collectivity is never complete, but is, rather, a movement that produces an irresolvable tension between singularity and collectivity and shows that they cannot be thought without one another, that they are not polar opposites, and that they are not mutually exclusive. The Levinasian tendency to reduce the *conatus* to a desire to be, which is reducible to self-preservation, attempts to lock Spinoza into a model of individuality that belongs to the contractarian tradition to which he is opposed. The individual neither enters into sociality through contract nor becomes subsumed by a collectivity or a multitude. The multitude does not overcome or absorb singularity; the multitude is not the same as a synthetic unity. To understand whether Levinas is right to claim that there is no Other in or for Spinoza, it may be necessary first to grasp that the very distinction between self and Other is a dynamic and constitutive one, indeed, a bind that one cannot flee, if not a bondage in which ethical struggle takes place. Self-preservation for Spinoza does not make sense outside of the context of this bind.

In Proposition XXXVII (37) of the *Ethics*, Book IV, Spinoza makes clear his difference from a contractarian account of social life. There he maintains: "The good which everyone who seeks virtue wants for himself, he also desires for other men; and this desire is greater as his knowledge of God is greater" (IVP37, 218). In a note to this scholium, he considers how contract theory presupposes "that there is nothing in the state of nature which, by the agreement of all, is good or evil; for everyone who is in the state of nature considers only his own advantage, and decides what is good and what is evil from his own temperament, and only insofar as he takes account of his own advantage. He is not bound by any law to submit to anyone except himself" (IVP37S2, 220). But true self-preservation, as he makes clear in Proposition LIV (54), provides the basis of virtue, in which self-preservation takes place under the guidance of reason. Likewise, freedom, understood as the exercise of reason, consists in disposing humans to reflect upon life, and not on death: "A free man thinks of nothing less than of death, and his wisdom is a meditation on life, not on death" (IVP67, 235).

Similarly, the person who endeavors to preserve his own being finds that this being is not only or exclusively his own. Indeed, the endeavor to persevere in one's being involves living according to Reason, where Reason illuminates how one's own being is part of what is a common life. "A man who is guided by reason is more free in a state, where he lives according to a common decision, than in solitude" (IVP73, 238). For Spinoza, this means as well that hatred should be overcome by love, which means "that everyone who is led by reason desires for others also the good he wants for himself" (IVP73S, 238). Here again we are asked to consider the *simultaneity* of these desires. Just as in desiring to live well we also desire to live, and the one cannot quite be said to precede the other, so here what one desires for oneself turns out to be, at the same time, what one desires for others. This is not the same as first determining one's own desire and then projecting that desire or extrapolating the desires of others on the basis of one's own desire. This is a desire that must, of necessity, disrupt and disorient the very notion of what is one's own, the very concept of "ownness" itself.

In the introduction to *The New Spinoza*, Warren Montag notes that "The absolute is nonalienation, better, it is positively, the liberation of all social energies in a general *conatus* of the organization of the freedom of all" (228), and then suggests that the subject itself is "recast [by Spinoza] as the multitude" (229). Negri offers an economical formulation of this conception of the multitude, exposing the irreducible tension between two movements in Spinoza's political philosophy: the one in which society is said to act as if according to one mind, the other in which society, by virtue of its expressive structure and dynamic, becomes irreversibly plural. What this means, on the one hand, is that what we might call the general *conatus* turns out to be differentiated and cannot achieve the totality toward which it aims. But what it means, on the other hand, is that singularity is constantly dispossessed in and by its sociality; singularity not only sets a limit on the totalizing possibilities of the social, but, as a limit, it is a singularity that assumes its specificity precisely in the context where it is taken up by a more general *conatus*, where the very life that it seeks deconstitutes its singularity again and again, though only completely in a state of death.

In this way, we can read the implications of Negri's theory for the rethinking of singularity, even though that is the direction opposite to the one in which he moves. He writes, for instance, "if absoluteness is not confronted with the singularity of real powers, it closes back onto itself" (230). But it would seem equally true to claim that the singularity of real powers is that which, in its confrontation with absoluteness, establishes an irreversible openness to the process of generalization itself. No general will is achieved, simply put. It is thwarted and articulated through the limiting power of singularity. One might even say that in this sense singularity is that which produces the radically open horizon, the possibility of the future itself. Moreover, if the body is what secures singularity, is that which cannot be synthesized into a collectivity but establishes its limit and its futurity, then the body, in its desire, is what keeps the future open.

However, for this singularity—conceived as a subject—to be powerful, for it to persevere in its desire, and to preserve its own power of perseverance, *it cannot be preoccupied with itself*. For Negri, this becomes clear in the experience of *Pietas*:

> *Pietas* is thus the desire that no subject be excluded from universality, as would be the case if one loved the particular. Moreover, by loving universality and by constituting it as a project of reason across subjects, one becomes powerful. If, by contrast, one loves the particular and acts only out of interest, one is not powerful but rather completely powerless, insofar as one is acted on by external things. (238)

Here he refers to love as "a passage so human that it includes all human beings."

Of course, there is the tendency of Spinoza to resolve the singular desire of the subject into a collective unity, and this comes through when he claims, for instance, that "Man . . . can wish for nothing more helpful to the preservation of his being than that all should so agree in all things that the minds and bodies of all would compose, as it were, one mind and one body" (IVP18S, 210). This is a situation, however, for which man *can wish*, but it is this wish, not the fulfillment, that constitutes the ontological condition of humanness. Indeed, Spinoza refers to the possibility of a unity of mind and body through a figure, "as it were," signifying that this unity is only conjectured, but cannot be established on certain ground. Something operates as a resistance to this longed-for unification, and this is linked to his abiding materialism, to the radically nonconceptualizable persistence of the body.[11]

Although Levinas's criticism is not yet met, we can see already that it would be a mistake to read self-preservation as if it were self-preoccupation, as if it were possible without the love that "includes all human beings" or the desire that is at once the desire for oneself and for all others. We might still conclude, however, that the Other is not radically and inconceivably Other for Spinoza, and that would be right. But are the ethical consequences of this nonabsolute difference as serious as Levinas takes them to be? After all, in Spinoza there is nevertheless that which resists the collapse of the subject into a collective unity. It seems that "the Other" is not quite the word for what *cannot be* collapsed into this unity. It is desire itself, and the body. For Levinas, this would be an impossibility, since desire is precisely what must be suspended for the ethical relation to the Other to emerge. This is where the divergence from Spinoza seems most definite. For what cannot be collapsed into collective unity, from one perspective, is what cannot be collapsed into a purely individualist conception of the *conatus*, from another. Desire to persevere in one's being implicates one in a common life, but the body returns as an ineradicable condition of singularity, only to bear precisely the desire that undoes the sense of one's body or, indeed, one's self, as purely or enduringly one's own.

Interestingly, Levinas remarks that "the humanity of man . . . is a rupture of being," and for Spinoza, in a parallel move, it is desire that has this rupture as part of its own movement, a movement from singularity to collectivity, and from collectivity to an irreducible plurality. The disorientation in desire consists of the fact that my own desire is never fully or exclusively my own, but that I am implicated in the sociality, if not the potential universality, of my desire in the very acts by which I seek to preserve and enhance my being. In this sense, the singularizing force of the body, and its disorienting trajectory toward the social, produces a deconstitution of singularity, one that nevertheless cannot fully be accomplished. At the same time, the production of collectivity is deconstituted by this very singularity that cannot be overridden.

So, one might see here that Spinoza provides for a shifting and constant principle of deconstitution, one that operates like the death drive in Freud, but which, in order to remain part of the struggle of life, must not become successful as either suicide or murder. This is a principle of deconstitution that is held in check and that, only in check, can function to keep the future open. There are two points here with which I'd like to conclude, one having to do with Freud, and the other with Levinas.

With regard to Freud, I am not proposing that the body in Spinoza does the covert work of the death drive, but I am suggesting that despite the rather stark differences between the Spinozistic point of view that would identify the desire to live well with the desire to live, and the psychoanalytic view in which living well may actually come at a cost to desire itself, there seems to be convergence on the notion that a trajectory in desire works in the service of deconstituting the subject, comporting it beyond itself to a possible dissolution in a more general *conatus*. Significantly, it is in this deconstitution and disorientation that an ethical perspective arises, since it will not suffice to say that I desire to live without, at the same time, seeking to maintain and preserve the life of the Other.

Spinoza comes to this ethical conclusion in a way that differs from Levinas, but consider that for each a certain rupture and disorientation of the subject conditions the possibility for ethics. Levinas writes:

The face is what one cannot kill, or at least it is that whose *meaning* consists in saying "thou shalt not kill." Murder, it is true, is a banal fact: one can kill the Other; the ethical exigency is not an ontological necessity. . . . It also appears in the Scriptures, to which the humanity of man is exposed inasmuch as it is engaged in the world. But to speak truly, the appearance in being of these "ethical peculiarities"—the humanity of man—is a rupture of being. It is significant, even if being resumes and recovers itself.[12]

If, as Levinas says, citing scripture, the Other's material needs are my spiritual needs, then I am able, spiritually, to apprehend the Other's material needs and put those needs first. For Spinoza, the distinction between material and spiritual needs would not be a secure one, since spiritual needs will end up, within this life, depending upon the body as their source and continuing condition. But it will turn out, nonetheless, that I cannot secure my needs without securing the Other's. The relation between the "I" and the "you" is not, for Spinoza, asymmetrical, but it will be inherently unstable since my desire emerges in this twofold way, simultaneously for myself and as some more general *conatus*. In a way, these two positions, allied with Freud's, concerning the death drive held in check, underscore the limits of the narcissistic approach to desire and lay out a possibility for a differentiated collective life that is not based in violence, eluding the double specter of narcissism or, indeed, property, on the one hand, and violence either to another or to oneself, on the other. But recourse neither to property nor to violence as final value is necessitated by any of these positions.

What I have been exploring here, though, is a set of approaches to ethics that honor desire, without collapsing into the egomaniacal defense of what is one's own, of ownership, and that honor the death drive, without letting it emerge as violence to oneself or to another. These are the makings of *an ethics under pressure*, one that would be constituted as a struggle and one that has "anxiety" rather than conviction as its condition.

Let me mention two trajectories that emerge from this framework, and I'll let them stand as dissonant paths. The first belongs to Primo Levi, whose death is generally regarded as a suicide, although there was no note. He fell or threw himself down the stairs of his apartment and was found dead. The death left open the question of whether this was an accident or a purposeful action. The idea is that either he lost his footing or he gave up his footing. There was no one else there, so the thesis that he was pushed finds no evidence in reality. But I have always been perplexed by this last inference, only because certainly one can be pushed without someone literally there to push you. And the difference between the push and the fall is a complex one, as he himself tells us, for instance, in one of the vignettes he relays in *Moments of Reprieve*. There he speaks about a Jew interned at Auschwitz who stumbles and falls regularly. Levi writes that every time it seemed like an accident but there was something purposeful about the fall, that it enacted some pressure that this man was under, some difficulty staying standing, relying on gravity. And surely we might wonder how it might have been to try to stand and walk in the camps, to rely on gravity and its implicit thesis that there is an earth there to receive you. And surely also if we think about all the pushing that took place there, why would that push cease at the moment that physical contact is relieved? Why wouldn't that push continue to have a life of its own, pushing on beyond the push, exceeding the physicality of the push to attain a psychic form and an animation with a force of its own?

When Levi speaks of suicide in *The Drowned and the Saved*, he writes, "suicide is born from a feeling of guilt that no punishment has attenuated." And following that he remarks that imprisonment was experienced as punishment and then, within parentheses, he adds: "if there is punishment, there must have been guilt."[13] In other words, he offers here an account of a certain guilt that takes hold as a consequence of punishment, a guilt based on an inference that one has done something to deserve the punishment. This guilt is, of course, preferable when the alternative is to grasp the utter contingency and arbitrariness of torture, punishment, and extermination. At least with guilt, one continues to have agency. With the arbitrary infliction of torture, one's agency is annihilated as well. This "guilt" that receives a knowing account within parentheses nevertheless becomes, within his text, a fact, a given, a framework, so that he asks, mercilessly, whether he did enough in the camps to help others; he remarks that everyone felt guilty about not helping others (78), and then he asks his reader and himself whether any of us would have the proper moral armature to fight the seductions of fascism. He comes to accept self-accusation as the posture he must assume with respect to his own actions, actions that were not, by the way, collaborationist.

Levi's guilt comes to frame a morality that holds those in the camp accountable for what they did and did not do. In this sense, his morality occludes the fact that agency itself was widely vitiated, that what might count as an "I" was either sequestered or deadened, as Charlotte Delbo makes clear. It defends against that offense, the offense against a recognition that the ego, too, was decimated. But more importantly, it enters into the cycle by which the guilt, produced by punishment, requires further punishment for its own relief. If, as he claims, "suicide is born from a feeling of guilt that no punishment has attenuated," we might add that no punishment *can* attenuate such guilt, since the guilt is groundless and endless, and the punishment that would alleviate it is responsible for its infinite reduplication. It is over and against this particularly bad infinity, then, that suicide most probably emerges for someone like Levi. But what this means is that we cannot answer the question of whether he fell by accident, threw himself, or was pushed, since the scene of agency had become, doubtless, fractured into those simultaneous and co-constituting actions. He fell by accident, surely, if what we mean by that is that his fall was not the result of his own agency; he was pushed, surely, by an agency of punishment that continued to work upon him; he threw himself, surely, for he had, through his morality, become the executor of his self-torture, believing as he did that he was not and could not be punished enough.

The second and last remark concerning an ethics under pressure, then: we see this ethical difficulty alive in antiwar practices in Israel by those who oppose the occupation of Palestinian lands, or call for a new polity that would leave Zionism behind; the collective efforts to rebuild demolished Palestinian homes; the efforts of Ta-ayush, a Jewish-Arab coalition to bring food and medicine to those suffering within the occupied territories; and the institutional practices of villages like Neve Shalom to foster Jewish-Arab self-government and joint ownership and to create communities and schools in which my desire is not powerful or self-preserving unless it permits for a disorientation by yours, in your power of self-preservation and perseverance. I'll cite to you from an email from a friend of mine in Israel, since I think we can see that it is possible to base an ethics on one's own situation, one's own desire, without the relation to the other becoming pure projection, or an extension of one's self. Her name is Niza Yanay, and she is a sociologist at Ben Gurion University who worries that the Supreme Court has lost its power in Israel, that military rule is ascending, that proposals to relocate Palestinians are being actively debated in the Knesset. She writes,

> In the elections a few months ago a friend and I both voted for the communist party which was a Jewish-Palestinian party but now is mostly an Arab-Palestinian party with almost no Jewish supporters. We felt that it is utterly important to strengthen the power of the Arabs in the parliament, and to show solidarity with them. Sami Shalom Shitrit, a poet and a writer, said in a small gathering before the election that if in 1933 he had been a German and Christian he would have looked very carefully to find a Jewish party to vote for. I was very moved by it, but it also gave me the shivers because we are not that far from 1933.

We are not in 1933, but we are not that far, and it is in that proximate difference that a new ethics must be thought. When discussions of "transfers" of populations have begun in the Knesset and vengeance seems to be the principle invoked on both sides of the conflict, it is crucial to find and value the "face" that will put an end to violence. To be responsive to that face, however, demands a certain self-dispossession, a move away from self-preservation as the basis or, indeed, the aim of ethics.

Whereas some locate the belief that self-preservation is the basis of ethics with Spinoza, and others suggest that Spinoza forecloses the forms of negativity that Freud so aptly describes under the rubric of the death drive, I have been trying to suggest that Spinoza's view leads neither to the defense of a simple individualism, nor to the forms of territoriality and rights of self-defense usually associated with doctrines of self-persistence. Within the Jewish frameworks for ethics that presume the superego and its cruelties as a precondition of ethical bearing or that claim that forms of political sociality are based on the unity of a people, conceived spatially, Spinoza enters with a form of political solidarity that moves beyond both suicide and the kinds of political unities associated with territoriality and nationalism. That he is doubtless still part of an intra-Jewish quarrel on the meaning and domain of ethics seems true, but that he is also outside the tradition, indeed, providing models for working with and alongside that "outside," seems equally true.

But what is perhaps most important is to see that there are the contours of an ethic here in which the death drive is held in check, one that conceives a community in its irreducible plurality and would oppose every nationalism that seeks to eradicate that condition of a nontotalizable sociality. It would be an ethic that not only avows the desire to live but recognizes that desiring life means desiring life for you, a desire that entails producing the political conditions for life that will allow for regenerated alliances that have no final form, in which the body, and bodies, in their precariousness and their promise, indeed, even in what might be called their ethics, incite one another to live.

A Mind for Passion

LOCKE AND HUTCHESON ON DESIRE

Nancy Armstrong and Leonard Tennenhouse

MOST SCHOLARS of eighteenth-century England and America are quick to credit John Locke with being the first to imagine a modern liberal state, where literacy was the ticket for participation in the civic arena and men could assume positions there on the basis of their intrinsic worth. While they grant the modernity of his model of the state, many of the same scholars consign Locke's model of the human subject to the late seventeenth century—there to be superseded during the eighteenth century by Hume, who understood an individual's intrinsic merit to consist not only or even primarily of reason but also and more importantly of his natural affections and moral sense.[1] Thus someone like John Rawls simply reinforces conventional wisdom when he understands eighteenth-century theories of human nature in terms of an opposition between Enlightenment definitions of reason, on the one hand, and intuition, emotion, or imagination on the other.[2] Our reading of Locke will challenge the assumptions that allow one to map the eighteenth century onto this opposition, on grounds that doing so creates a false continuity between early modern notions of the subject and the distinctively modern subject that emerges in eighteenth-century debates concerning the relation of reason and sentiment.[3] Emptying the mind of each and every idea implanted there by the Creator paradoxically provided Locke with the rhetorical foundation for imagining a new kind of individual naturally disposed to be governed only by an aggregate of individuals like him.[4] When he emptied the individual mind of its early modern contents, Locke freed reason both from God and from the passions as they had been defined by humoral theory. Thus, as we hope to show, he opened a category that not only gave rise to a debate about the rational operations of the mind but also encouraged a sustained discussion of what we now call the emotions. While his status as architect of the modern subject diminished precipitously during the nineteenth century, the debate he initiated only gathered momentum. This debate elaborated, challenged, and successively transformed the subject into one predisposed to emotions that he himself could control—an individual, in short, constitutive of the modern state.

To argue that modern theories of the emotions began as a refutation of the humoral model of the passions, we would like to call attention to the figure of *terra nullius*, which Locke used when he asserted that human intelligence began much like "white paper void of all characters."[5] So successful was this figure in nullifying the earlier belief that the emotions were part of one's physical makeup that the idea of a surface yet to be inscribed died out as a metaphor and passed into the register of common sense: of course, one assumes, the minds of children, madmen, and illiterate individuals are either empty or their contents disorganized to the point of illegibility. Lost with the figurative dimension of Locke's rhetoric was the radical nature of his claim. To represent the mind as *terra nullius* was to imagine it as a territory unclaimed by any nation, a territory without an owner. Like a sheet of "white paper," such a territory awaited inscription.[6] In imagining the mind in such terms, he linked sovereignty over the mind with writing upon it through a play upon the term "characters," meaning both characters of the alphabet, or "letters," and the characteristics inhering in one's mind, or "ethos." By means of the figure of *terra nullius*, in other words, Locke represented the mind as something that comes to exist only as the individual receives and orders information gleaned from external sensory experiences. The acquisition of reason in *An Essay Concerning Human Understanding* is, in this respect, exactly analogous to the acquisition of property described in his *Second Treatise of Government*.[7]

The mind is void in two ways. First, it has no characters for someone to own and therefore no owner. On the other hand, if there can be no owner before there is a mind to own, then no individual can exist until he acquires sufficient information to fill the blank page of his mind. What this means is that the individual's existence as such depends on his ability to produce a self-enclosed field of information that belongs first and only to him. But, second, "void" also implies the nullification of ownership, which in this case manifests itself as the erasure of writing. In this respect the figure of the white page "void of all characters" was Locke's way of announcing that he meant to nullify the prevailing modes of culture and build his model of the human mind from scratch. Althusser's analysis of the paradox of self-alienation in Rousseau applies equally well to Locke's use of *terra nullius*, whereby the empty mind cancels out all prior forms of ownership over the subject, in order that he may voluntarily nullify that sovereign ownership and submit to the state.[8]

One key component of the early modern subject is significantly missing from the version of the debate that occupies Book I of *An Essay Concerning Human Understanding*. Rarely in his argument that reason alone is what distinguishes man from the rest of nature does Locke mention the passions. Yet the passions, according to early modern critiques of reason, kept the human mind from understanding the laws of nature and thus from making principled moral decisions.[9] Indeed, even early proponents of the scientific method acknowledged this problem and sought to mitigate it by observing natural phenomena from a position outside of and at a remove from the phenomena observed. By introducing a void precisely where the natural passions had exercised unchallenged dominion over the subject, as it had been represented in literature, theology, epistemology, and political and moral philosophy, Locke accomplished a feat that changed how educated Englishmen and women thought and wrote about the human subject. After Locke, such people invariably imagined two subjects in one: (1) the individual who was subject to the state and (2) the individual intent on expanding the private, internal domain over which he exercised sovereign power. Locke developed his theory of government over the same twenty-year period while writing and revising *An Essay Concerning Human Understanding*. Each theory consequently presupposed and implied the other—a state that protected the autonomy of each individual, his person and property, and an individual free yet predisposed to agree to limit his freedom in the name of civic order and stability.[10] Indeed, Locke's rational individual was the logical precondition for the very government authorized to protect him.

At the same time, Locke enabled his successors to deal with these mutually dependent models of mind and government as if they were in fact independent entities. Authors so different as Adam Smith, Thomas Malthus, Jeremy Bentham, and John Stuart Mill, to name but a few, invoked the logic of the *Second Treatise on Government* in order to adjust the balance between the claims of free subjectivity and the need for political stability to meet the demands of their respective moments in history. Subsequent formulations of the self-enclosed, self-owning, and self-governing subject that took shape in Locke's *Essay Concerning Human Understanding* observed a different historical trajectory. In striving to differentiate the sources of affection and morality from those of reason, such moral philosophers as Frances Hutcheson and David Hume had to distance themselves from Locke's premise that almost everything the mind thought derived by logical inference from ideas that originated in sensations. Even in challenging the primacy of reason, however, these authors were in Locke's debt. Thus, for example, when Hume argued for the primacy of our initial impressions over and above those well-seasoned ideas that piled up in the storehouse of the mind, he was taking issue with certain aspects of Locke's model from within the problematic of individualism that Locke had established.[11] So, too, in arguing that the human passions arose from information provided by the internal senses, Hutcheson was not invalidating Locke so much as appropriating his model of the empty mind in order to challenge Locke's claim that mind was the exclusive domain of reason. Such a double legacy, Foucault reminds us, is the mark of an originary discourse.[12] We intend to show why we have to understand the dependency of Locke's model of government on his theory of the subject in order to explain the enduring ideological impact of that model of the modern state.

DESIRE IN THE FIELD OF REASON

His account of how the mind acquires and exercises reason enabled Locke to explain how men ideally develop into individuals capable of self-government and therefore capable of governing others. To acquire reason, as he tells the story, one fills "the yet empty cabinet" of the mind with information gathered strictly from encounters with the outside world that enters the mind via the physical senses in the form of "sensations" (I.ii.15). In addition to an empty space that can, like "paper," be inscribed or, like a "Store-house," filled with ideas, Locke endows the mind with the faculty of judgment—an ability to classify this information and arrange the categories that result in relations of similarity and difference, cause and effect, greater or lesser importance, and so forth, until the order of the mind mirrors that of the world. Although the human mind, as he conceives it, is potentially reasonable, there is nothing actually present in the mind before its sensory encounter with the world. As a result, reason comes into being only as the mind acquires sensations to classify and arrange. But when it does have sufficient material to develop and eventually to know itself, reason has a relatively clear field in Locke's model, as compared to early modern accounts where the mind is invariably disturbed by passions coursing through the body.

Consider, for example, this passage from Burton's *Anatomy of Melancholy* (1621), which demonstrates how the fact of the brain's being of the body virtually eliminates the possibility of anything like a rational perception of the world:

> To our imagination commeth, by the outward sense or memory, some object to be knowne (residing in the foremost part of the braine), which he mis-conceiving or amplifying, presently communicates to the Heart, the seat of all affections. The pure spirits forthwith flocke from the Braine to the Heart, by certaine secret channels, and signifie what good or bad object was presented; which immediately bends it selfe to prosecute, or avoid it; and withall, draweth with it other humours to helpe it: so in pleasure, concurre great store of purer spirits; in sadnesse, much melancholy blood; in ire, choller. If the Imagination be very apprehensive, intent, and violent, it sends great store of spirits to, or from the

heart, and makes a deeper impression, and greater tumult, as the humours in the Body be likewise prepared, and the temperature it selfe ill or well disposed, the passions are longer and stronger. . . . The spirits so confounded, the nourishment must needs be abated, bad humours increased, crudities & thicke spirits engendred with melancholy blood. The other parts cannot performe their functions, having the spirits drawne from them by vehement passion, but faile in sense and motion; so we looke upon a thing, and see it not; heare, and observe not; which otherwise would much affect us, had wee beene free. (Part 1, Sec. 2, Mem. 3, Subsect. 1)[13]

Burton represents human thought as a physical process. When an object comes to the individual's attention—whether from memory or from observation—that object sets off a chain reaction that Burton describes as the ontogenesis of a disease. According to this model of the individual, his sensory apprehension of an object is always encumbered with imagination.[14] The imagination sends out a distorted image to "the Heart," which calls up the appropriate humors: "in sadness, much melancholy blood; in ire, choller." The stronger the imaginative supplement that the brain supplies, the more confused the idea of the object, until passion completely destroys its grounding in sensory perception, causing us to "look upon a thing, and see it not; hear, and observe not." That those things imagined to give pleasure remain relatively free of distortion by the physical effects of passion only implies that imagination—in this case, by not providing much in the way of a supplement—shapes how we see good objects as well as bad.

To create a model whereby the individual's acquisition and reaction to information received through the senses observes rational principles, then, Locke does more than empty the mind of ideas that circumvented sensory perception because they came from God.[15] Locke also severs the mind's connection to those organs of the body believed to be the source or conduit of the passions: the heart, the spleen, the liver, and even, paradoxically, the brain. Where Burton focuses on the "brain" in relation to other organs of the body, Locke makes a careful distinction between "brain" and "mind" and focuses on the mind as the exclusive terrain of thought.[16] The "brain" experiences a constant exchange of fluids with the rest of the early modern body, which sends at least as much information to the brain through the humors as it received from sensations of the outside world. Locke's "mind," in contrast, receives information only from the physical senses. Housed within a particular body, with which it carries on an exclusive, lifelong partnership, the modern mind has remarkably little connection to the body. By means of "simple *Ideas* taken in by Sensation," Locke explains, "the Mind comes to extend it self even to Infinity. Which however it may, of all others, seem most remote from any sensible Perception, yet at last hath nothing in it, but what is made out of simple *Ideas*: received into the Mind by the Senses, and afterwards there put together" and reproduced (II.xvii.1). With Locke, then, we suddenly encounter an individual mind enclosed within a particular body and yet so cut off from that body as to overturn the priorities of body and mind that an author of Burton's moment took for granted.

To turn the individual mind into the exclusive ruler of the body that it inhabits, Locke translates pleasure and pain from the status of physical responses into "sensations." Until such sensations have been stored in the mind as ideas, we cannot classify pleasure and pain as either good or bad. As with his argument against "innate ideas," Locke seems, in executing this move, primarily intent on taking the concepts of good and evil away from God and placing them squarely in the domain of human understanding. Good and evil develop as other concepts do, from the individual's sensory encounter with the world. In truth, he contends, "they be only different Constitutions of the Mind, sometimes occasioned by disorders in the Body, sometimes by Thoughts of the Mind" (II.xx.2). As he systematically incorporates those thoughts and feelings considered irrational within the architecture of reason, it is only accurate to say that Locke overdoes it. So intent is he on emptying the mind of innate ideas that he stretches the notion of "idea" so far out of shape that his successors— notably Hutcheson and Hume—find it necessary to remove from that category those mental operations that seem naturally inclined to respond to beauty and virtue.[17]

In chapters xx and xxi of Book II of *An Essay*, we discover that Locke has a yet grander purpose than sweeping away the traditional foundations for human behavior. As the entire thrust of his argument shifts direction in this perplexing chapter, it soon becomes clear that in continuing to rethink pleasure and pain, he is not interested in naturalizing the operations of judgment so much as in disembodying the passions and transforming desire. Desire arises from ideas of pleasure and pain, to be sure. Having been formed on the basis of external "sensations," however, ideas come to mediate between the mind and the external world that gave rise to those sensations in a very different way than judgment does. In acknowledging that judgment needs desire to make the responsible citizen, Locke obviously feels his argument has ventured onto slippery ground. To provide a clear sense of how gingerly he reintroduces the passions into his model of mind, we might compare his version with Burton's description of the process by which the passions assert themselves and begin to interact with ideas.

Rather than bubbling up in the organs of origin to surge through heart and brain, the passions according to Locke originate in our sensations of pleasure and pain and take the form of ideas. Love and delight are his clearest illustrations of this point: "any one reflecting upon the thought he has of the Delight, which any present, or absent thing is apt to produce in him, has the *idea* we call *Love*" (II.xx.3). In making love depend on "the thought . . . of delight," Locke removes love one cognitive step further from the body than the idea of pleasure. In this respect, love is neither a sensation nor a simple idea, but a complex idea. Moreover, because pleasure itself does not exist unless and until sensations have been classified as pleasurable, even pleasure is relatively independent of physical sensation, as, for example, when a man takes "constant delight" in the "Being and Welfare of [his] Children or Friends . . . [and] is said to constantly *love* them" (II.xx.5). So, too, with joy, which Locke defines as "a delight of the Mind from the consideration of the present or assured approaching possession of a Good" (II.xx.7). A source of delight might be right before our noses, he suggests, but unless we "consider" it, we cannot experience joy. Even expectation trumps the physical encounter with an object of delight, as we may experience joy just from knowing that such an encounter awaits us.

Indeed, it is fair to say that in moving swiftly through a catalogue of passions from love and joy to anger and envy, Locke conspicuously removes the passions from the body and relocates their source in the ideas of pleasure and pain that we formulate on the basis of our sensations. At times, moreover, he indicates that before we can experience passion, we must have abstracted from our ideas of pleasure and pain a further level of ideation that indicates whether a given pleasure or pain is good or evil. That would certainly put an edge on the feeling we get when experience contradicts our idea of pleasure. This discrepancy between idea and experience produces "uneasiness," which we identify as sadness, anger, envy, and so forth, depending on our understanding of the discrepancy that prompts it. Fear, for example, "is an uneasiness of the Mind, upon the thought of future Evil likely to befal us." Having recovered from an injury, we no longer need to feel pain in order to remain angry and want the person who inflicted that pain to suffer for his deed. Conversely, envy arises from "the consideration of a Good we desire, obtained by one, we think should not have had it before us" (II.xx.13). In none of these cases does the individual respond to the actual sensations of pleasure or pain. The body is all but gone from the picture. The passions originate in ideas of pleasure and pain that have been translated into good and evil and so arouse a form of uneasiness that—except in cases of love and joy—we attribute to the absence of some good. By including the passions in the field of reason as complex ideas several steps removed from immediate sensory experience, Locke has detached them from various organs contending within the body for control of the individual's will. So detached, the passions blend into one another to form a spectrum from positive joy to negative despair that observes the single dynamic principle spelled out in Locke's discussion of desire.

Rather than a positive force in its own right, desire is generated by a discrepancy between one's "idea of delight" and the object whose possession would provide the sensation of delight.[18] This gap identifies the lack of some good that produces a sensation of uneasiness within the individual: "The uneasiness a Man finds in himself upon the absence of any thing, whose present enjoyment carries the *Idea* of Delight with it, is that we call *Desire*, which is greater or less, as that uneasiness is more or less vehement" (II.xx.6). Lacking something that carries with it the idea of delight, the individual might understand "the impossibility or unattainableness of the good propos'd," in which case he would abandon hope of acquiring it; his uneasiness would probably disappear at this point. If, on the other hand, the proposed good is not out of one's reach, achieving it could well be the most reasonable way of dispelling uneasiness. In stimulating desire, "uneasiness" becomes, for Locke, "the chief if not the only spur to humane Industry and Action" (II.xx.6). Too "little uneasiness in the absence of any thing" can prove deleterious, if it "carries a Man no farther than some faint wishes for it, without any more effectual or vigorous use of the means to attain it" (II.xx.6). This rather cursory treatment of the passions is all Locke requires to demonstrate that the various passions are but variations of desire. Indeed, as he acknowledges in the following chapter, "wherever there is *uneasiness* there is *desire*" (II.xxi.39).[19]

A SINGULAR AGENCY

This redefinition of the passions prepares the unruly aspects of the early modern subject to enter into a new relationship with the individual will. Preferring to understand the will not as an independent faculty so much as a component of "volition," Locke rejects the traditional notion of the human will as a stern opponent and would-be master of the passions. From his claim that "the uneasiness of desire" is the source of all motivation, it follows that there can be no "voluntary action performed, without some *desire* accompanying it." This, he explains, "is the reason why the *will* and *desire* are so often confounded" (II.xxi.39). Operating in collaboration with the will, desire becomes a relatively aimless, if not passive force that seeks a cure for uneasiness and looks to will for direction. On its own, however, the will is similarly aimless, its chief purpose being to determine "which desire shall be next satisfied, which *uneasiness* first removed" (II.xxi.46). Once desire is part of the cure rather than the cause of uneasiness, it no longer makes sense to pit the will in a lifelong battle against desire. Indeed, after Locke, one cannot imagine life without desire. Instead of a battleground for contending forces, as it was for early modern intellectuals, the life of an individual can be understood as a "train of voluntary actions" (II.xxi.40). Within this distinctively modern framework, desire informs many different choices, the sum of which serves as the measure of an individual's worth. It is not whether one desires or even what variety of desire one has, but what one does with it that matters— and that depends largely on judgment.

As the keeper of the information that collects in the empty space of the mind, judgment provides a framework and container for desire, as well as the options among which the will has to choose before committing the individual to action. Any flaws in the train of voluntary actions that make up one's life are therefore attributable to flaws in that individual's judgment rather than to either the force of his desire or the weakness of his will. Locke notes, for example, how a "future pleasure, especially if of a sort which we are unacquainted with, seldom is able to counter-balance any uneasiness, either of pain or desire, which is present" (II.xxi.65). Having never tasted such pleasure, men are apt to conclude "that when it comes to trial, it may possibly not answer the report, or opinion, that generally passes of it . . . and therefore they see nothing in it, for which they should forego a present enjoyment" (II.xxi.65). On this "*false* way of *judging*," he observes, any number of men have traded in the possibility of heaven for a few transient pleasures (II.xxi.65). Burton's *Anatomy* argues that reason does not stand a chance against the various forces converging in the brain to stir the individual to action. Although reason's failures are at least as frequent as its successes, according to Locke, one can improve his faculty of judgment through more information, reflection, and education. It is indeed the individual's duty to do so. By putting reason in charge, Locke removes the shroud of determinism from individual decision-making.

To introduce desire and will into the field of reason, he is especially intent on maintaining the singular agency of the human mind. To this end, he reserves special contempt for authors who refer to the faculties as if they were "some real Beings in the Soul, that performed those Actions of Understanding and Volition." This tendency among his peers and predecessors has, Locke surmises, "misled many into a confused Notion of so many distinct Agents in us, which had their several Provinces and Authorities, and did command, obey, and perform several Actions, as so many distinct Beings" (II.xxi.6). Indeed, it is entirely reasonable to regard Locke's discussion of the passions in Book II of *An Essay Concerning Human Understanding* as an argument against the factionalized body dominated by the humors. To be free of the multiple forms of agency that direct the will each towards its local end, Locke renames the faculties in terms of what they do. Hence understanding becomes "the intellectual faculty" and will is "the elective faculty," or faculty of choice. Thus reconceived, the faculties cease to operate as agents each in its own right and come to resemble "abilities" or "powers," which, he says, "are but different names for the same thing" (II.xxi.20). Defined as powers rather than as agents, the faculties no longer need to compete for control of the individual. Each tends to its business within a rational system, where "Digestion is performed by something that is able to digest; Motion by something that is able to move, and understanding by something able to understand" (II.xxi.20). Separated from the body and yet enclosed within it, the mind can enjoy a new kind of reciprocity with the body, that of owner and caretaker.

Locke's theory of government requires a subject capable of voluntarily submitting to government. To imagine a state governed by its citizens, Locke has to transform the individual driven by the passions into one who would voluntarily renounce any actions that might encroach on the persons and properties of other individuals. Before an individual can, of his own volition, enter into the social contract as Locke describes it in his *Second Treatise of Government*, that individual has to undergo an internal version of that exchange. He has to understand negative rights as a positive good—the right not to be violated in one's person or property. He has to desire only those goods that are truly good, because they extend his person and property without violating the negative rights of his fellow citizens. To do so, he has to reject the fantasy supporting the early modern state, namely, the fantasy that one could rule himself only if entitled by lineage, wealth, force, or God to rule others. The social contract cultivates a radically different fantasy that appears to do away with the distinction between entitlement and subjection. If one's desire were to submit to reason, in the new scenario, then there would be no need for political coercion except, of course, in the cases of individuals who cannot subject their own desire to reason. Driven as they are by the impulses of the body, an activated imagination, or spiritual possession, to name but three external stimuli capable of overturning self-control, these people are hardly at liberty to subject themselves voluntarily to the laws protecting persons and property.[20] In effect, only those whose volition works in collaboration with judgment can be considered individuals.

If Locke's model of the state calls for a critical mass of such self-governing individuals, then his model of mind requires what can only be called a psychology: the articulation of multiple and potentially contending forces as a self-enclosed and purely mental system whose parts are interdependent and add up to much more than their sum.[21] As his successors were quick to point out, however, Locke did not provide that psychology. His model of the subject, like his model of the state, assumes that negative rights and a sense of uneasiness are sufficient inducement for men to agree to curtail their acquisitive desire. He neglected to explain why one would want others—not only their immediate dependents, but also potential competitors—to enjoy the same autonomy he had secured for himself, his dependents, and his property. Moral philosophy rose to the challenge of filling in the empty space that remained in Locke's mind, even after it had acquired reason. For lack of an external authority to compel them, there had to be some internal inducement for individuals to desire the general good.

Enter the Internal Senses

Francis Hutcheson is perhaps best known for arguing on behalf of the "internal senses," for which he is credited with influencing no less important figures than David Hume or Hutcheson's student Adam Smith. Overshadowed by the work of these successors, the four treatises contained in Hutcheson's *Inquiry into the Original of Our Ideas of Beauty and Virtue* (1725) and *An Essay on the Nature and Conduct of the Passions and Affections with Illustrations of the Moral Sense* (1728) lay out *the* argument that physicians and philosophers of the time had to address if they wanted to recuperate the irrational powers of the human mind. Thus it is to Hutcheson that we turn in support of our claim that the sentimental model of the subject that dominated eighteenth-century letters was not so much opposed to Locke as dependent on his assertion that the mind began as white paper "void of all characters." Hutcheson accepted the premise that all our knowledge begins only as sensations come into the mind through the physical senses. He says as much, when he opens his treatise "Concerning Beauty" with the Lockean proposition that "the proper Occasions of Perception by the external Senses, occur to us as soon as we come into the World," while "the Objects of the superior Senses of Beauty and Virtue generally do not."[22] Still agreeing with Locke, Hutcheson goes on to argue that once sensations have registered on the mind, they inevitably combine to form complex ideas.

But he takes a subtle and decisive step away from Locke in asking us to see these complex ideas as analogous to objects in the world, capable of generating sensations in their own right. When we contemplate such ideas, Hutcheson contends, they are "then present to our Minds, with all its Circumstances, altho' some of these Ideas have nothing of what we commonly call sensible Perception in them" (xiv). Even when these ideas do include information garnered from the physical senses, "the Pleasure [we receive] arises from some Uniformity, Order, Arrangement, Imitation; and not from the simple Ideas of Colour, or Sound, or Mode of Extension separately consider'd" (xiv). Hutcheson, in other words, gives Locke his due in order to launch an argument *against* the notion that held the rational operations of the human mind or some deficiency thereof chiefly responsible for human behavior. Hutcheson obviously found the ideas of pleasure and pain that we form on the basis of such sensations much too crude to explain many of the decisions we make and certainly not our proudest moments. How, for example, does reason account for the "far greater Pleasures" that we take "in those complex Ideas of Objects which obtain the Names of Beautiful, Regular, Harmonious" (4)? Such pleasures certainly differ from any empirical understanding "of Principles, Proportions, Causes, or of the Usefulness of the object" (8). Nor does education, custom, or example explain what appears to be an internal sense of beauty; witness the fact that the "Poor and Low" can enjoy the beauty of nature as well as "the Wealthy or Powerful" (62). If our knowledge of beauty is not in fact based on the ideas of pleasure and pain derived from physical sensations, if, further, our knowledge of beauty cannot be learned at second hand through education, then the five external senses cannot supply all the sensations an individual requires in order to become fully himself. There has to be another source of sensation. Hutcheson proceeds by analogy to argue that we possess a capacity for understanding beauty distinct from and yet parallel to our understanding of the physical properties of objects. He insists on this analogy in deciding "to call our Power of perceiving these Ideas an internal sense, were it only for the Convenience of distinguishing them from other Sensations of Seeing and Hearing, which Men may have without Perception of Beauty or Harmony" (6).

In turning from his essay on beauty to the one on morality in *An Inquiry into the Original of Our Ideas of Beauty and Virtue*, Hutcheson shifts his concern from the individual's relationship with objects to the individual's relationship to other subjects. This is clearly what he is after, when he sets up an analogy between the process by which one arrives at a judgment concerning the physical properties of an object and the process by which we come to regard that object as beautiful. He wants to provide a natural source within the mind for emotional responses, one that does not grant those responses the kind of tyranny over body and mind formerly exercised by the passions. Reason might prevent us from pursuing some goal in the heat of the moment, he insists, but reason alone will never yield a moral assessment of our actions. Reason cannot make men desire the well-being of people beyond their immediate families. To produce a model of the individual who would be naturally benevolent, Hutcheson begins by attacking Locke's claim that reason is chiefly responsible for individual agency. In addition to reasonableness, Hutcheson insists that human nature must include what he rather awkwardly calls "a disinterested ultimate Desire of the Happiness of others." He insists further "that our Moral Sense determines us to approve only such Actions as virtuous, which are apprehended to proceed partly at least from such Desire" (97). But it is one thing to declare the existence of a moral sense and quite another to argue into being a sense that operates distinct and apart from reason and may consequently pull desire and instruct the will to go in another direction. His treatise "On the Nature and Conduct of the Passions and Affections" tackles this problem head on. To make room in the mind for such a power, Hutcheson must prove reason insufficient to the task.

His treatise on beauty established that while some of our sensations of pleasure and pain enter the mind through the physical senses, others arise from complex ideas and elicit an aesthetic response distinct from our desire for that object. Having argued for the existence of internal senses by analogy to the physical senses, he can move on and repeat the process. Thus his treatise on the nature and origins of human virtue establishes an analogy between the way we recognize and respond to beauty, on the one hand, and the operations of our internal moral sense on the other. In order to elicit our approbation, he concluded, simple ideas form complex ideas as to whether an object is good or evil or else some combination of the two. But it was not until three years later, in 1728, that, in our estimation, Hutcheson actually made his signature move.

In his treatise on "The Nature and Conduct of the Passions and Affections," he abandons the Lockean formula of argument by analogy and seizes on the concept of "calm desire" as a true competitor and potential partner to Lockean reason for the role of prime mover of the human subject. He translates the difference between the internal and external senses into a distinction between calm and spontaneous desire. Locke insisted that reason modifies our ideas of pleasure and pain by making us take a hard look at the facts supporting those ideas, and so it may prevent us from acting on rash desires. Contending that much more is required of the citizen of a modern state than that, Hutcheson renders unto reason only what is owing to reason and goes on to address the thorny problem of how to make man benevolent. To curtail his own desires, according to Locke's own formula, the individual has to desire something well beyond anything that the idea of pleasure derived from the physical senses could make him want. There are, for Hutcheson, two different varieties of desire.

There are calm and spontaneous varieties of both selfish and public-spirited desire. Indeed, Hutcheson considers an individual's "*calm desire* of [his own] good" not only morally compatible with his "general calm desire of the *Happiness of others*" but also morally at odds with his "*particular Passions* toward objects immediately presented to some sense."[23] Such particular and immediate passions are, in Hutcheson's view, of a piece with the love, compassion, and other varieties of natural affection, which may indeed have nothing of evil in them and do not require moral approbation before they can exert a powerful influence over human behavior. When examined in moral terms, concern with whether or not our desires are selfish drops precipitously in importance relative to the question of whether the intention of such a desire is good and its consequences beneficial to all concerned. Only when the moral sense engages our ideas of pleasure and pain do we *feel* that our pursuit of that pleasure would be a good and worthy cause of action. And only when we give the moral sense a chance to inform our desires can a "calm desire for universal benevolence" prevail over particular passions and bring us the pleasure of "constant Self-Approbation" (25). With "calm desire," Hutcheson abandons the security of analogical reasoning, on which he depended in his *Inquiry into the Original of Our Ideas of Beauty and Virtue*, and sets out into historically new discursive territory.[24]

At least this is what we might infer from the fact that he follows his argument on behalf of calm desire with a sequence of logical maneuvers designed to give that notion a conceptual architecture comparable to Lockean reason. Hutchison provides a list of "definitions" for the various sensations received by the moral sense as well as for the ideas of good and evil we may form on that basis (26–27). He then uses those definitions to create "axioms" describing all possible relationships between these sensations, ideas, and the desires that might accompany them (28–30). These axioms, he claims—with less than the certainty his logic would imply—"seem to be the general laws, according to which our desires arise" (30). Awkward and tentative, this is hardly a move that could give rise to British sentimental discourse. Indeed, we could not consider Hutcheson so important a supplement to Locke had the Scotsman not abandoned the philosophical method associated with his predecessor and begun working the other side of the opposition between reason and emotion. To embark on this new discursive terrain, he poses the question of why we need the passions at all. Without them, after all, one could live a life of calm desire, never repeating bad decisions in the overdetermined manner of early modern individuals.

AFFECTIVE NORMATIVITY

To demonstrate the importance of the passions, Hutcheson selects a peculiarly modern example. Without ambition, he contends, man's natural aversion to labor and propensity for mirth would render him weak and lazy. What is more, "Without a great deal of human labor and many dangers, this earth could not support the tenth part of its inhabitants. Our nature therefore required a sensation, accompanying its desires of the *Means of Preservation*, capable to surmount the uneasiness of labor" (35). So, too, must we have intense affection for our offspring in order to give them "perpetual labor and care" beyond what can be expected from "the more general ties of benevolence" (35). Indeed, he continues, parents must experience the pain of such desire in order "to counterbalance the pains of labor and the sensations of the selfish appetites," as they "must often check and disappoint their own appetites to gratify those of their children" (35). Such "diversity of temper" is natural. It not only ensures the preservation of the individual body, according to Hutcheson, but also ultimately furthers the good of the human aggregate. Has he, in abandoning the philosophical procedures associated with Locke, opened the way for the return of the early modern passions?[25] His notion of diversity does indeed invite comparison with the seventeenth-century notion of "countervailing passions," whereby an individual achieved stability as the desires pulsing from one of his organs ran into conflict and reached accommodation with another, enacting within the body much the same relationship by which the great landowners of England neutralized one another in and around 1688.[26]

Hutcheson has opened a Pandora's box, however, so that he can continue reclassifying human desires on the basis of whether they arise from our calm reflection on ideas of pleasure and pain or from immediate sensations. He uses this framework to subordinate the passions to a distinctively modern combination of reason and morality that we now characterize as normative. He identifies desires and aversions that arise from the process of self-reflection as the "spiritual" or "pure" affections (39); through reflection we come to feel the uneasiness that accompanies some absent but anticipated pleasure or pain. Affection therefore remains for Hutcheson, as for Locke, purely a product of thought and at one step's remove from any physical source. Not all affection, however, is pure. "When more violent confused sensations arise with the affection, and are attended with, or prolonged by bodily motions," he acknowledges, "we call the whole by the name of *Passion*" (39). Thus we may want to be with a person whether or not it makes us happy. So, too, men will shriek and flee whether or not what they suppose to be dangerous can actually harm them. In Hutcheson's nomenclature, "These *propensities* . . . when they occur without rational desire, we may call *Passions*, and when they happen along with desires, denominate them *passionate*" (40–41). Let us consider what he has done to desire by splitting the "affections" off from those desires triggered by the presence of an object. Hutcheson has obviously set the stage for elevating those faculties that spring into action in response to sensations. At the same time, he has also set the stage for debasing the early modern body, home to "the passions" and therefore the source of impurities that adulterate not only the cognitive operations of reason but the affective operations that move us to act on the social virtues as well.

His reduction of "the *Passions*" to the adjective "*passionate*" encapsulates the argument to come. Hutcheson grants no validity to classical tragedy, where the passions choreograph individuals of high birth and great authority in scenes of spectacular self-destruction. "There is nothing in our nature leading us necessarily into the *fantastic Desires*," which, he insists, echoing Locke, "arise through our ignorance and negligence; when, through want of thought, we suffer foolish associations of ideas to be made, and imagine certain trifling circumstances to contain something honourable and excellent in them" (62–63). Obviously addressing a class very different from the one for whom tragedy was staged, he makes it clear what features of the old ruling class render the individual no better than a slave to passion:[27]

> We know how the inadvertences, negligences, infirmities, and even vices, either of great or ingenious men, have been affected, and imitated by those who were incapable of imitating their excellencies. This happens often to young gentlemen of plentiful fortunes, which set them above the employments necessary to others, when they have not cultivated any relish for the pleasures of the imagination, such as architecture, music, painting, poetry, natural philosophy, history. . . ; when their hearts are too gay to be entertained with the dull thoughts of increasing their wealth, and they have not ability enough to hope for power: such poor empty minds have nothing but trifles to pursue; anything becomes agreeable, which can supply the void of thought; or prevent the sullen discontent which must grow upon a mind conscious of no merit, and expecting the contempt of its fellows; as a pack of dogs, a horse, a jewel, an equipage, a pack of cards, a tavern; anything which has got any confused ideas of honour, dignity, liberality, or genteel enjoyment of life joined to it. (63)

After taking issue sharply with Locke on the adequacy of reason, Hutcheson's argument arcs around at this point to strike up a new relationship with its former opponent, a relationship that aims at "the best *Management* of all our desires" (88). A mind that remains empty even after it receives numerous sensations is a mind that has exercised neither the moral sense that bends desire to the general good, nor the reasoning ability to make an individual happy in strictly private terms. By the end of this passage, Hutcheson has put the two powers of mind to work on the same sensory data and made the parallel trajectories created by his earlier analogy of the moral sense to the operations of reason converge upon the common objective of a life of "honour, dignity, liberality, and genteel enjoyment" (63).

Such a life presupposes "a Desire of public Good" (65). Like the "fantastic Desire" that tormented tragic heroes of centuries past and impeached the reason even of ordinary men (62), the "Desire of public Good" is part of one's nature. Even before reason goes to work ordering our sensations, Hutcheson declares, our desires "are fixed for us by the Author of our Nature, subservient to the interest of the system; so that each individual is made, previously to his own choice, a member of a *great Body*, and affected with the fortunes of the whole" (65). If, as Locke argues, the rational faculties ensure that reasonable individuals understand the world outside the mind in much the same way, then the affective faculties, as Hutcheson describes them, ensure that each individual desires what is best for the human community, even when that desire conflicts with some rash or selfish desire. This formulation of the nature and conduct of the passions couldn't be farther from the early modern notion of the passions.

This formulation puts us squarely within a modern paradigm of normative desire—desire as natural as reason to each and every individual, desire whose deviation from the standard of "calm *Universal Benevolence*" present a threat to the entire community, desire, then, that must be "managed" for the good of the whole (89). Such a project requires a new relationship between reason and morality, as the passions thrive on ignorance and in the absence of clear and refined ideas of pleasure and pain. Reason shows us that violent passions, even those we may regard as tender and benign, do not bring lasting satisfaction, so that we may come to regard such passions as causes of pain. But even if we come to understand that "this Discipline of our passions is in general necessary," reason cannot make us desire what is most important to our personal happiness— namely, the subjection of both reason and affection to calm universal benevolence (88). To want what is most important, we must already desire it; we must by nature take pleasure in both self-approbation and the public good. Otherwise, there would be no inducement to discipline.[28]

Culture in the Field of Desire

Our account of the relationship between the passions and politics as conducted in and through Locke's model of the subject would be incomplete without some sense of what happened to his figure of the empty mind at the end of the eighteenth century. How did *An Essay Concerning Human Understanding*—specifically the chapter "Of Power" (II.xxi) —generate the questions that would preoccupy authors and intellectuals of various ideological stripes during the nineteenth century, as modern nationalism emerged and assumed the shape of empire in both theory and practice? To sketch the mere outline of an answer, we take a somewhat anomalous route and consider briefly an unlikely pair of texts published in 1798:

Thomas Malthus's *An Essay on the Principle of Population* and Joanna Baillie's "Introductory Discourse" to *A Series of Plays: in which it is attempted to delineate the stronger passions of the mind; each passion being the subject of a tragedy and a comedy*. Both authors define the individual as a mind void of characters, one that is inscribed through encounters with an external world on the basis of which it forms ideas of pleasure and pain. Both are concerned, as Hutcheson was, with how to direct human behavior toward socially beneficial ends. Neither, however, can assume that goal can be reached within and by the agency of the individual mind alone. This is the difference between eighteenth-century moral philosophy and the problematic within which Malthus and Baillie wrote. Locke's consolidation of agency within the individual mind effectively removed the body from consideration and gave the mind sole regulating power not only over itself but over the body as well. While Hutcheson acknowledged that external causes might influence the body, he also maintained that benevolence was the primary and only natural human desire, thus capable of shepherding all rash and immediate desires toward the larger collective good. Malthus and Baillie have to consider whether the force that regulates human behavior comes from within the human mind or from without in the form of some biological imperative. When understood in these terms, the problem was no longer one of how to bend the individual will to that of the aggregate but how to bend the desire of the aggregate to the will of a literate elite—one individual at a time.

Thomas Malthus writes from the perspective of the common good, or what he considers the relative happiness or misery of "the population." From this perspective, the human body plays an even more central role in human destiny than it had in early modern literature. The collective body is the source of the labor that produces all those objects that display the decision-making prowess of Locke's ideal citizen. The collective body also consumes. Hence the "two postulata" by means of which Malthus challenges the sufficiency of Locke's empty mind: "First, That food is necessary to the existence of man. Secondly, That the passion between the sexes is necessary and will remain nearly in its present state" notwithstanding human progress in every other respect.[29] Here, the passions have been whittled down to one all-powerful sex drive, which in evolutionary theory not only subsumes lust, ambition, hatred, envy, and all other rash or immediate impulses, but also displaces anything resembling benevolence as the mother of all desires. Once one understands the passion between the sexes as the body's natural equipment, then it becomes, as Malthus explains, "a palpable contradiction to all experience, to say that the corporal propensities of man do not act very powerfully, as disturbing forces" in "a decision of the mind" (163). Because these propensities "will urge men to actions, of the fatal consequences of which, to the general interests of society, they are perfectly well convinced," he concludes, starvation, war, and disease are inevitable (163–64). These forms of misery are the only natural checks on unbounded sexual desire. Does this mean that the individual no longer owns himself, as he did a century before?

We are too familiar with the rhetorical behavior of British culture at the moment of the emergence of industrial capitalism to believe that Malthus's formula for disaster would have caught hold as fast and widely as it did had it not set the stage for resolving the problem of sexual desire at the same time and in the same terms that it formulated that problem. Indeed, Malthus himself points the way to the solution that would put its stamp on all Victorian thought. Adversity improves us, he argues: "Had population and food increased in the same ratio, it is probable that man might never have emerged from the savage state" (206). Thus the problem of population offers up its own solution in that the human mind must grow vigorous and more intelligent in overcoming the passions: "When the mind has been awakened into activity by the passions, and the wants of the body, intellectual wants arise; and the desire of knowledge, and the impatience under ignorance, form a new and important class of excitements" (211). It is not in avoiding problems but in surmounting them, in other words, that both individual and collective are each enriched without any cost to the other.[30] If, on the other hand, a period were to arrive when there were no such problem-solving to be done, in Malthus's judgment, "one of the noblest stimulants to mental exertion would have ceased," and it would be "impossible that . . . any individuals could possess the same intellectual energies as were possessed by a Locke, a Newton, or a Shakespeare" (213). Within a framework where all desire is ultimately shaped by sexual desire, the subject comes into his own as he harnesses his sexual energy and transforms it into intellectual achievement. To put it in Lockean terms, the subject comes to own himself (and eventually herself) as he overcomes what is unruly, childish, and primitive within him.

Joanna Baillie's "Introductory Discourse" to her *Plays on the Passions* explains how culture brings about the transformation distinguishing modern individuals from those who remain slaves to their natural desires. Where Locke and Hutcheson allow us to observe the reflective powers of the mind and show how those powers shaped human behavior, Baillie asks us to observe the human body, as it sheds the invisibility afforded by cultural conformity and displays the natural passions animating behavior. Rather than dividing the human aggregate into those who develop reflective powers as opposed to their dependents who lack such powers of judgment, Baillie imagines a world composed of those who are spectators and those whose lack of culture dooms them to remain the object of the gaze.[31] We are naturally fascinated with theatrical displays and especially tragedy, she contends, because "any person harbours in his breast, concealed from the world's eye, some powerful rankling passion of what kind soever it may be."[32] What struts and frets its hour upon the modern stage is not some grand and noble human being, then, so much as a component of ourselves personified and enacted in the extreme. In witnessing such spectacles, we witness "those passions which conceal themselves from the observations of men." We do so, moreover, without ourselves becoming thrall to the passions (8). Indeed, we require the spectacle of deviance in order to learn the secrets of interiority, namely, the "powerful rankling passion" that we must continue to conceal (3). One's status as a modern subject henceforth depends on it. In such a cultural milieu, literature ceases to offer a normative model of character and begins to elicit in readers a desire to see what they could not be and still belong to respectable society.

The division of the population into spectators and objects of the gaze thus ushered in the form of self-government peculiar to the layered, internally divided, and self-conflicted individual associated with Victorian culture. The discovery of the sex drive as the ultimate source—however diverted and displaced—of every action revised Locke's empty mind for the age of imperialism, where each blank space on the map of Empire concealed, in the words of Conrad's Marlow, a native woman "savage and superb."

Rousseau's Quarrel with Gratitude

Patrick Coleman

ONE OF ROUSSEAU'S COMPLAINTS about modern society was that it stifled
the freedom of response that supposedly distinguished gratitude from
forced obligation. He got angry when friends reminded him about the
gratitude he owed to his patrons. But he was just as uncomfortable about
being a benefactor. In a memorable passage of his *Reveries*, Rousseau tells
the story of a young lame boy he used to see on the streets of Paris. The
first few times they met, he would cheerfully give the boy a coin, but "this
pleasure, having gradually become a habit, was inexplicably transformed
into a kind of duty I soon felt to be annoying."[1] So constrained did Rousseau feel that he finally avoided that street altogether. "I know," he writes,
"that there is a kind of contract, and even the holiest of all, between the
benefactor and the beneficiary" by which the latter commits himself to
be grateful and the former commits to renewing his generosity as much
as he can. To break this contract is unjust, but nonetheless it is "the effect
of an independence the heart loves and renounces only with effort."[2]

Rousseau's discomfort with gratitude (and other dispositions such as
trust that involve relationships where the emotional intersects with the
social, and in which the reciprocity of gift-giving shades off into contractual exchange)[3] points to a broader tension in early modern French discussions of civility. Is it possible to imagine a society in which gratitude was
wholly disentangled from an oppressive sense of dependence? In the classical discussions of the theme in Cicero's *On Duties* and Seneca's *On
Benefits*, that question did not arise. While the ancients emphasized that
gratitude must not be compelled, they were not concerned with drawing
a clear line between customary, political, and religious obligation. Their
focus was more on instilling in well-born souls the values of honor and
magnanimity. In early modern Europe, however, when with the rise of
nation-states political rule began to be defined around a new notion of
sovereignty, and when religious divisions were forcing theologians to rethink the role of both church and state in mediating humanity's relationship to God, clarifying the nature and forms of obligation became a matter of pressing cultural concern. One might say that the development of
polite sociability in the salons and other unofficial sites of social exchange
in seventeenth-century France reflected a desire to disentangle gratitude

from the domain of political obligation, where it was becoming superfluous, and to reconstitute it as part of a new dynamic of civil sociability distinct from the rationalized, absolutist politics of monarchy and court.[4]

Indeed, changing conceptions of human knowledge and interaction suggested that gratitude might no longer have a role to play in the acknowledgment of the authority of natural and political laws. In the area of epistemology, it is instructive to compare two famous texts of the early seventeenth century. In his *Introduction to the Devout Life*, François de Sales advances as a generally accepted principle, even a proverbial expression of obvious wisdom, that knowledge produces gratitude ("la connaissance engendre la reconnaissance").[5] Knowledge is a gift, and the more you know, the more aware you are that it is a gift. In Descartes's *Meditations*, the philosopher who has put everything in doubt, on the supposition that an evil genius might be fooling him, arrives at the idea of a God who anchors all knowledge in his infinite and perfect being. He takes a moment at the end of the third meditation to contemplate and adore this God, but says nothing about being grateful.[6] No doubt this is because Descartes himself has done the epistemological work. Gratitude has no place in a conception of knowledge based on clear and distinct ideas. Certainty comes from method, not from mercy, and the acquisition of knowledge diminishes rather than underscores man's dependence on things outside himself.

In political philosophy, too, gratitude was becoming an increasingly irrelevant concept. Hobbes and other natural right thinkers sought to develop an idea of obligation that, however absolute, was based on a conception of humanity as a collection of autonomous individuals. Obedience was to be ensured by reason and force, not by gratitude, since even in acknowledging the sovereign's authority the subjects must feel secure that their psychological independence is respected. Eighteenth-century French philosophes, especially those of materialist bent, carried this trend forward by exalting the rule of law in all areas of life. It might seem to us that grounding all human relationships in an impersonal system of laws implies a deterministic, or at least instrumental, view of human nature at odds with the Enlightenment emphasis on freedom, but we need to appreciate how this discourse could hold an emotional appeal for those who felt the oppression of arbitrary human will. It is in fact remarkable how much faith many writers of the French Enlightenment placed in "the laws" (the expression was sometimes used in an absolute sense) as a sufficient answer to the problems of social interaction.

This outlook stood in tension with the equally influential but deliberately antisystematic discourse of polite sociability inherited from the salons of the seventeenth century. The creation of an unofficial public sphere governed by personal *égards* also promised liberation from oppressive constraint. In different degrees and combinations, both currents of thought contributed to the Enlightenment's confidence about social reform, and yet neither could be adopted wholesale by the leading philosophes. The idealization and homogenization of law might offer relief from the chaos of conflicting arbitrary rules, but it might, as Montesquieu recognized, also appear dangerously reductive as a model of social interaction. Conversely, while the extension of the flexible rules of politeness to social life might provide an alternative to the rigidity of law, such a move could also be experienced as unduly personalizing obligation in domains better governed by abstract rights. Rousseau's story about the beggar reflects this uneasiness. If only everybody got what they deserved by right, then one could do away with the burden of gratitude. Yet, would a society in which gratitude has no place really be one in which freedom could flourish? Rousseau's persistent ambivalence on this point, expressed in different ways throughout his works, illustrates some profound and underappreciated tensions in early modern thinking about the ordering of human relationships.

Discourse on Inequality

A striking fact about humanity's natural state, as Rousseau depicts it in the *Discourse on Inequality*, is that emotion of any kind is entirely absent. Men (Rousseau refers only glancingly to women and children) are solitary and independent: they are strong enough to survive without assistance, and when they lose their strength, they die without fuss. Living entirely in the moment, without memory and reflection, they have no occasion to regret the past or worry about the future. While they are subject to sudden fright, they have no fear. Nor are they prone to what have been called the "vehement emotions."[7] Since nature provides for their physical needs, there is no need to compete for resources. Should a man steal another's apple, it is easier to pick another apple than to fight for the stolen one.[8] Rousseau agrees that "the more violent the passions, the more necessary are Laws to contain them: but . . . it would still be worth enquiring whether these disorders did not arise with the Laws themselves."[9]

It is well known that by conceptualizing the state of nature in this way, Rousseau was taking issue with modern natural law thinkers on the origins of political association. For Hobbes, for example, gratitude, along with benevolence or trust, is one of the "laws of nature" reason tells us we should follow to preserve the peace and ensure our self-preservation amidst the violence of the state of nature.[10] According to Rousseau, there is no need to develop such dispositions, let alone the reasoning required to arrive at any supposed laws of nature.

Rousseau is equally concerned to reject the argument that sociability finds its source in the natural weakness of human nature.[11] In his widely read compendium of natural law, Pufendorf writes: "Man is an animal with an intense concern for his own preservation, needy by himself, incapable of protection without the help of his fellows, and very well fitted for the mutual provision of benefits."[12] It follows that gratitude is one of the "common duties of humanity" underpinning the "common sociality."[13] For Pufendorf this duty is owed "by every man to every man": the system of favors recognizes and promotes the equal dignity of all men. It is not tied to a hierarchical, oppressive system of feudal obligation. According to James Tully, Pufendorf's discussion of gratitude is meant to show the reader how the performance of duties is "advantageous to each party."[14] Yet, the obsequious dedication of the work to "the most illustrious and exalted hero, Lord Gustavus Otto Steenbock," stresses the subservience of one to the other: "I might be rightly criticized for ingratitude if I neglected any opportunity, however slight it might be, at least to declare the extent of my obligation to you."[15]

The "Epistle Dedicatory" of the *Discourse on Inequality* also pays "public homage," in this case to the Republic of Geneva, but Rousseau's rhetoric stands in sharp contrast to Pufendorf's. Although he speaks of the duties he owes to his country, the emotion that informs them is not gratitude, but "zeal."[16] As a citizen, and thus as a member of the very General Council he is addressing, he need not legitimize his writing by referring to a patron, or to a relationship with any particular individual. Zeal is a response to ideas, in this case to republican political principles, rather than to persons. The city's patrician elite, which in practice ruled the republic, was quite aware of the difference. It rightly discerned the subversive potential of the work, for despite the extravagant praise Rousseau lavishes on the ruling "Magistrates," the *Discourse* implicitly encourages the citizenry to measure the government's conduct against those principles. Thus, while Rousseau's state of nature is radically presocial, the relationships between citizens evoked in the "Epistle Dedicatory" are not social ones either, in the sense that they are viewed as a result of the pattern of human development set out in the *Discourse* itself. Rather, they rest on a political foundation that, in Rousseau's presentation, seems to be immune to the corruption that comes with "progress." The republic fosters in its citizens a spirit of independence unknown to men living under other regimes.

Still, Rousseau is more than ready to acknowledge the personal dimension of his relationship to the city that nurtured him. Above all, he recalls the lessons in republican virtue he learned from his father, an independent craftsman proud of his status as a citizen equal (in theory, at least) to any other. Yet, although he writes wistfully about "the tender teachings of the best of Fathers,"[17] he does not say anything about being grateful to him. On the biographical level, this omission may be explained by the fact that the elder Rousseau left his ten-year-old son behind when, after a swordfight in the street, he exiled himself from Geneva rather than make amends to the authorities. Rousseau was torn between a need to idealize his father and a reluctant recognition that the man had abandoned him. On the textual level, this ambivalence takes the form of an apparently contradictory but all the more seductive portrayal of his homeland. In the happy world of the Genevan republic, the transmission of republican values is personalized but without creating any personal obligation, only a general zeal for the city's well-being.[18]

This zeal is not only compatible with a denial of personal debt, it may even be nourished by resistance to such an idea. This is another lesson Rousseau learned from his father. The latter, who liked to have his "Tacitus, Plutarch, and Grotius before him amidst the tools of his trade," was in fact, as his decision to leave Geneva would demonstrate, more a potential dissident than a submissive son of the republic himself.[19] The one and only mention of gratitude in the body of the Discourse confirms this idea in a different way. In part 2, Rousseau reminds the reader of the traditional principle that "gratitude is indeed a duty that ought to be performed, but it is not a right that can be exacted." He does so in order to refute the thesis that political authority derives from the model of paternal authority.[20]

The neediness of men abandoned to their own devices may not be a factor in the state of nature or in an idealized republic, but it certainly plays a role in the historical world. As Rousseau tells the story, once human population spread beyond the bounds of naturally fertile areas, people were forced to cooperate with each other. The institution of private property, however, necessarily favored the strong and the lucky over the rest. Like the political contract that eventually followed, it provided security for the weak only by allowing the powerful to oppress them in a more orderly way. Since the thrust of Rousseau's hypothetical history is to demystify social relationships by unmasking their origin in violence and trickery, any reference to the softer side of human reciprocity, including the notion of gratitude, would spoil the argument. There is, however, one place in the Discourse where neediness, instead of providing an opportunity for oppression, becomes the occasion for an emotional connection, one that Rousseau views as beneficial, and that he calls pity.

Pity for Rousseau creates sympathy for another human being through identification with his suffering. This imaginative bridge between one person and another lays the foundation for a first, fragile kind of social bond.[21] However, while pity introduces the idea of human vulnerability hitherto absent from Rousseau's analysis of human nature, it does so from the position of a spectator who is not needy himself. This spectator is vulnerable to the experience of the other's vulnerability, not of his own. One might explain this dissymmetry by arguing that Rousseau's aim in the *Discourse* is to restore to his readers a sense of power and initiative stifled by modern society. To focus on the subject's vulnerability would be counterproductive. Pierre Force suggests very plausibly that Rousseau wants to emphasize, in opposition to Augustinian and Epicurean traditions, that pity is not self-interested.[22] As Rousseau describes it, pity expects no return. And yet, the compassionate man is not presented as detached or disinterested. Even if it does not lead to an exchange of favors, pity does forge a kind of relationship—if it did not, then it could not function as a catalyst for sociability. At the same time, however, Rousseau says nothing about the other person's response to the spectator's compassion.[23]

What Rousseau is doing, I believe, is dramatizing neediness in such a way as to avoid provoking in his readers a feeling of dependence on others, whether they identify with the compassionate person, the sufferer, or with the sentiment that joins them. The description of the compassionate man, like Rousseau's description of the zealous citizen, models a mediated form of solidarity. The subject Rousseau dramatizes is not invulnerable, above the fray. He is vulnerable to others' vulnerability, but not in such a way as to create a relationship of dependence. He can imagine himself as the sufferer, who becomes an object of a spontaneous compassion that is all the more precious in that no gratitude is expected, just as he can imagine himself as compassionate without becoming bound, like Rousseau himself in the sixth "Walk," to the object of his compassion. If self-interest is what stifles pity, what triggers that self-interest is the feeling of being stifled by constraint.

Rousseau's reader is involved in the scene of pity, one might say, but not absorbed into it—and so less likely to recoil in a self-protective way from the spectacle Rousseau stages for him. It would be easy to criticize this strategy as endorsing a facile form of sentimentality. But Rousseau wants to prevent the self from scrutinizing its own compassion, since reflection (with the attendant activity of self-judgment) is another form of constraint generating the self-interest that causes one person to be alienated from another. Rousseau's critique of tragedy in the *Letter to d'Alembert* for encouraging spectators to congratulate themselves for shedding tears over imaginary victims, and so to excuse themselves from helping victims in the real world, shows him to be aware that any attempt to balance involvement and detachment can easily be distorted by the ruses of self-love.[24]

It is precisely the ease with which compassion can be distorted that makes it impossible for Rousseau to make sympathy the basis of an ethical system, in the manner of his contemporaries Hume and Smith. The figure of the impartial but sympathetic spectator offers those philosophers another way of reconciling personal connection with a salutary distance. For Rousseau, however, a restless will and a vivid imagination are more fundamental to human nature than reason, and so the dynamic of sympathy can never be kept free from corruption. In any case, these British thinkers do not appear on the intellectual horizon of the *Discourse on Inequality*. In the foreground instead are those rationalist philosophes who integrate relationships of gratitude all too smoothly into their "codes" or "systems" of nature.[25] The major French works in this tradition postdate the *Discourse*, but Rousseau was already acquainted with this line of thinking through writers such as Mandeville. Through his friendship with Diderot, he was also acquainted with some of the more radical thinkers such as Helvétius and Holbach. A brief look at the latter's *Système social* will illustrate the kind of thinking Rousseau has in mind.

For Holbach, "justice wills that man make himself useful to Society, because it is useful and necessary to himself. Gratitude is an act of justice."[26] Justice and utility are conflated, and from this perspective there is no difference between the traditionally free obligation of gratitude and enforceable obligations as defined by law. Moreover, Holbach takes a view of compassion that, while superficially similar to Rousseau's, is in fact decisively different. He tells us, for example, that misanthropy is bad, but not because it is a denial of fellow feeling. Rather, "the interest we take in the beings of our species increases [*multiplie*] our own well-being by exercising our sensibility, and allows us to make a claim on their gratitude."[27] Holbach and Rousseau both start from the self's own expansiveness rather than from a reciprocal relationship, but the element of vulnerability is entirely missing from Holbach's text. On the contrary, in the light of Holbach's remark that "man is a lump of wax that we fashion as we will,"[28] the notion that our interest makes a claim on the other's gratitude not only returns us to the self-interested notion of compassion Rousseau was at pains to avoid in the *Discourse*. It transforms the sociable commerce of favors into a one-way form of manipulation, for it never occurs to Holbach to make himself the object of another's gaze. He speaks only from outside the system he describes, as a subject whose own position is free and secure.

It may be objected, however, that this is also true of Rousseau's *Social Contract*, which in contrast with the *Discourse on Inequality* is cast in impersonal, even mathematical language. Moreover, Rousseau's invocation of the quasi-divine figure of the Legislator seems to suggest that manipulation and mystification are a necessity of political life. To answer these objections, we need to ask whether gratitude has a role to play in Rousseau's political theory.

SOCIAL CONTRACT

Rousseau's demystification of sociability in the *Discourse* makes it understandable that the *Social Contract* should not appeal to the language of benefits and gratitude in laying the foundation of political right. Such language is also foreign to the republican tradition to which Rousseau appeals. Machiavelli's *Discourses*, several times cited by Rousseau, warn rulers against the "vice of ingratitude" when it comes to rewarding military heroes, because these heroes may turn against the state,[29] but they ascribe no role to gratitude itself in the political order. More important are the energy of *virtù* and the controlled strife of contending parties. While Rousseau differed from his Florentine predecessor in condemning factional strife, he, too, defined political virtue in terms of force of will rather than mutual dependence and reciprocity. He was not alone in this view, as we can see by comparing the *Social Contract* with another contemporary expression of the renewed vitality of the republican tradition in France, the abbé de Mably's influential *Entretiens de Phocion*. Although its subtitle is "on the relationship between morality and politics," it makes almost no mention of the emotions, and says nothing about gratitude. Its emphasis is all on the austerity and vigilance of an undifferentiated *vertu*.[30]

Not all republicanism, however, repudiated the language of favor and gratitude. A Christian thinker like Calvin, who played a key role in the newly independent republic of Geneva, made gratitude a foundational theme in his *Institutes of the Christian Religion*.[31] The social contract could be cast in the covenant language of the Bible, with thanksgiving as the people's primary response to the ultimate sovereignty of God. There were a number of reasons, however, why despite his Genevan background Rousseau did not appeal to this tradition. In theology, the hardening of the doctrine of predestination in seventeenth-century Reformed orthodoxy, and then the movement of the Genevan clergy in the eighteenth century towards a more rationalistic form of theology verging on deism, had largely drained the notion of gratitude of its vitality and point. Neither the harsh nor the impersonally benevolent God was likely to inspire much gratitude.[32] On the political level, Rousseau was all too aware of Calvin's intolerance of dissent, and of the way Geneva's patrician families in his lifetime controlled the city behind a veil of republican rule. Thus, it is no surprise that the social contract as he presents it is a purely impersonal affair: the people contract with each other as equals without regard to their relative economic or other circumstances. It would seem that in a society founded on a will that is truly general, gratitude would have no place.

Yet the polity formed by the social contract cannot do without benefaction altogether. Something is needed to motivate obedience to the laws even when no one is looking, and so Rousseau advocates the institution of a "civil" religion. Rousseau speaks of religion in terms more like Machiavelli's than Calvin's, but he does not treat religious belief as merely a useful illusion to be controlled by secular authority. True, Rousseau's list of the civil religion's dogmas has a utilitarian ring: "The existence of the powerful, intelligent, beneficent, prescient, and provident Divinity, the life to come, the happiness of the just, the punishment of the wicked, the sanctity of the social Contract and the Laws; these are the positive dogmas."[33] But religion must do more than prevent actions contrary to law. It must generate what Rousseau calls the "sentiments of sociability" that motivate good behavior in the absence of sanctions.[34]

It is not clear how hope of reward and fear of punishment by themselves can serve this less immediate function. Calvin, who grounds obedience in a prior sense of gratitude, can show how the calculus of reward and punishment is to be subordinated to a wider appreciation of divine charity, based on the Christian idea of God.[35] But for Rousseau, Christianity is too narrowly dogmatic in its institutional forms, and too otherworldly in its primitive essence, to serve as the civil religion. In Hobbes, hope and fear are focused on sanctions in this world, but they also have a motivating context. His sentiments of sociability are grounded in a constant and pervasive awareness of the potential for violence in human life. Rousseau, on the other hand, believes men are not naturally disposed to aggression. Even more important, the institution of the social contract is predicated on each citizen's willingness to overlook the differences of money and power among them and to give everything over to the people as a whole. For Rousseau, the political equality and solidarity that results from this is a sufficient guarantee against serious violence among fellow citizens.

It might be more accurate to say that the real guarantee is that the imaginative world of the society created by the contract leaves no room for the possibility of such conflict to be entertained. Here again, the contrast with Hobbes is instructive. The laws of nature that according to *Leviathan* generate sociability are also mediated through an exercise of reason that leads to clear and compelling conclusions. Rousseau's civil religion is also reasonable (in the sense that its dogmas do not offend reason), but it is not, indeed cannot be, the product of deliberation or debate.[36] For Rousseau, arguments over religion lead either to sectarian conflict (if they stem from unreflective conviction) or to the disenchantment that follows from adopting a self-conscious, critical attitude toward belief—that is to say, the enlightened approach of the philosophes. Where there are solid guarantees against sectarian conflict, as in a society grounded in a truly general will (and in Geneva as Rousseau portrays it in his *Letter to d'Alembert*), the latter presents the greater danger. In a context of peace and security, when most people unreflectively obey the law, the exercise of critical reason can only serve to alienate the citizen from the community by encouraging him to give priority to the interests of his private self and avoid the burden of obligation. Thus, Rousseau presents the civil religion as something to be taken on faith. Sentiments of sociability can only emerge through a consciousness that is active but unreflective, in other words through the imagination.

Rousseau's discussion of the civil religion does not, however, tell us *how* it is imagined, what it feels like from the inside. In one sense, this is to be expected, since the "religion of the citizen" (as opposed to the individual "religion of man" we will read about in *Emile*) is concerned only with external behavior, not with belief. The hearts of the people are not to be policed.[37] It should not matter to the government what emotion motivates obedience to the laws. However, once religious feelings start to be nurtured, it might not be possible to contain the results within the framework of the political order. Since by definition gratitude is not governed by legal obligation, its scope may exceed the limits defined by the social contract and thereby subvert them. Precisely because self-interested reason is absent, gratitude might blur the boundaries between citizens and outsiders (by appealing to the idea of universal Christian fraternity, for example). It might foster a desire for an intensity of emotional connection with others that competes with the requirements of orderly sociability by creating unrealistic, and potentially oppressive, expectations of intimacy.[38] And yet, the God of the *Social Contract* is not merely an impersonal and all-seeing judge. Such a God could not inspire sentiments of sociability. It is noteworthy that Rousseau speaks, not of "a" but "the" Divinity, one who is "beneficent, prescient, and provident." These qualities evoke a more personal kind of relationship than one defined by self-interested hope and fear. One might say that Rousseau creates a space for gratitude in his civil religion—but leaves it vacant.

To understand the meaning of this gesture, we must attend to the way Rousseau presents his argument as well as to the content of what he says. For this space is located at the intersection of two different authorial perspectives. In much of the *Social Contract*, Rousseau speaks of religion from outside, looking at it in purely functional terms as something to be manipulated for the common good. When he writes matter-of-factly that the peoples of the past identified their kings with gods, each people having its own national deity (the ancient Israelites being no different in this respect from any other nation); and when he dismisses Christianity as undermining the citizens' wholehearted allegiance to the state, Rousseau seems to be addressing a reader—a Machiavellian prince in waiting, perhaps—who will accept such a disenchanted point of view with equanimity.[39] But Rousseau does not always speak from outside the belief system he advocates, to readers who likewise see themselves as too enlightened to need the civil religion themselves. In the opening paragraph of the chapter on civil religion, Rousseau cites "the reasoning of Caligula" he had reported in the second chapter of Book I, to the effect that, just as the shepherd is superior in nature to the sheep, the rulers of men are superior in nature to their peoples. According to Caligula, either kings are gods, or subjects are beasts.[40] The tone of this earlier passage was one of indignation at the exploitation of religious feeling (directed, as in the *Discourse on Inequality*, at the natural law arguments of Grotius and Hobbes), not cynical acceptance. The chapter on civil religion echoes this protest with an ironic comment on those early peoples who took their kings for gods. "It takes a long degradation of sentiments and ideas before one can bring oneself to accept a being like oneself as master, and flatter oneself [into believing] that one will be well off as a result."[41]

In this comment Rousseau identifies with the subjects, not the prince, and the reader is clearly meant to share Rousseau's indignation that things should come to such a pass. Consequently, the reader cannot wholly adopt the Machiavellian point of view on religion that dominates the rest of the chapter. Rousseau has reopened, from below as it were, a critical space between human and divine authority that national religions had collapsed. While the civil religion supports the social contract by giving it a sacred underpinning, it is crucial that critical space be preserved if the sentiments of sociability fostered by religion are not to lead—as, according to the *Discourse on Inequality*, sociability ultimately does—to despotism, that is, to the fusion of personal and legal authority in the hands of an absolute ruler. If not held in check, the dynamic of sociability, with its personalizing of relationships, including that between the citizens and God, will corrupt the generality and impersonality of law. This nightmare would be the modern, "enlightened" version of the archaic theo-political synthesis Rousseau denounces in his disenchanted history of religion.

It is precisely for this reason that Rousseau imagines the God of the civil religion in terms at once personal and general, as a purely potential object of gratitude. Religion thus provides a background matrix rather than a foundation for "sentiments of sociability." Not only does gratitude remain outside the realm of legal obligation (this is true in the discourse of sociability also), it is not entirely determined as to its object or content. One might describe the dynamic of gratitude in the terms of Kantian aesthetics and say it has purposiveness without specific purpose. Gratitude supplements the general will, not by completing it through the addition of an affective element (which, once again, would be to corrupt its generality) but by forestalling the collapse of the political community into a system enclosed upon itself. Whether or not Rousseau's God "really" exists (and the question remains a subject of scholarly debate), his most important function in the civil religion is to prevent citizens from taking any person—human or divine—as their political master. For this, they should be thankful—even though, in Rousseau's paradoxical logic, the thanksgiving cannot itself be made an object of understanding without spoiling the thanks.

A similar distancing can be found in the chapter devoted to another figure who illustrates the movement between the "inside" and "outside" of Rousseau's political system: the Legislator. In the seventh chapter of Book II, Rousseau addresses what he sees as a fundamental problem in the creation of any political community. The people's will is only truly general if it transcends their socioeconomic, demographic, and other circumstances. Individuals, who can see clearly what their situation is, are liable to prefer self-interest to the general welfare. "Individuals see the good they reject, the public wills the good it does not see."[42] Someone from outside is needed in order to bridge the gap between understanding and will, and thereby devise the system of positive laws most appropriate to a specific political body. So difficult is the task, Rousseau says, that "it would require gods to give men laws."[43] Absent any actual divine intervention, legislators must make the gods speak through their mouths. Moses and Mohammed are thus not to be condemned as "impostors" for presenting themselves as prophets of a divine lawgiver. They should be judged by their results. And Rousseau's criterion is a purely practical one. The survival over time of the peoples they shaped provides the only real, that is, empirically verifiable, evidence that understanding and will have been harmoniously combined.[44]

Similarly, Rousseau claims that only if people believe they are submitting to the laws of nature (in the sense of rules independent of human desires) and not to the arbitrary will of any individual will they accept "the yoke of public felicity."[45] As with the civil religion, the perspective Rousseau adopts is that of the disenchanted and knowing observer, and his idealizing rhetoric about the superhuman qualities of the Legislator can be read as an endorsement of religious trickery. The problem with this interpretation is that Rousseau's artfulness is too transparent. His text highlights the gap between understanding and will it was the mission of Moses and Mohammed to fill (or at least to paper over).

There are two possible inferences from this paradoxical feature of the text. Rousseau may want the ordinary reader to become as shrewd as the political philosopher, or he may want the philosophical reader to share some of the awe lesser mortals feel when they consider the legislator. That both intentions may be at work here is suggested by the author's shifting position with respect to his argument. Rousseau tells us neutrally the legislator must see all "the passions of men" without experiencing any of them, but then he shifts to the first person: the legislator must have no connection to "our nature" while understanding it thoroughly; his happiness must be independent "of us" and yet he must be willing to concern himself with "our" happiness.[46] Here Rousseau identifies with humanity's lowly condition rather than analyzing it from the outside.

Yet, having once again prepared the ground for a subjective response to the legislator, Rousseau says nothing about what the response should be. The "true politician" will admire the "genius" of Moses and Mohammed,[47] but how are the citizens to react to their ("our") own legislator? Are they ("we") to be grateful to the one who mediates understanding and will for us? One might expect so, but while Rousseau has brought us to the brink of gratitude, he leaves us there. For the legislator's gift the citizens of the *Social Contract* give no thanks. Rousseau may not want to encourage the credulity that goes with idealizing a person rather than the laws themselves. On the other hand, the absence of any commemoration of the legislator's initiative may suggest it is dangerous to be reminded of it too often. The prestige of the laws may be undermined by "enlightened" understanding of their origin. Recalling the legislator's initiative may encourage the citizens to become more politically assertive than is good for the stability of the state.[48]

Thus, "we" cannot be like the credulous believers Rousseau talks about, but we cannot *not* be like them. We, too, must look outside ourselves for an agent possessing that combination of knowledge and will needed to set our (or any) community on a firm foundation. Rousseau does not resolve the contradiction, and perhaps he simply has no answer. Another possibility is that his aim is not so much to propose a solution (he stresses he is not himself a legislator) than to prevent our imagination of politics from closing in upon itself even as he stresses the need for unity of will. He does not do this by fostering an explicit awareness of conflicting values; that would be too risky. Instead, he moves the reader from a self-congratulatory position of detachment to a place within the community of those looking for help, so that their neediness can be shared and appreciated. From there he directs our imagination beyond the boundaries of the political order, precisely by emphasizing that the possibility of its existence has been *given* by an agent outside it. This is the place of gratitude. At the same time, there is no place *for* gratitude in the *Social Contract*. The premise of the book, after all, its promise to readers suffering under arbitrary regimes, was liberation from personal dependence on gifts and favors into the impersonal space of contractual law.

Yet, despite the ingenious way Rousseau conceptualizes the contract as a process through which the individual gives everything over to the whole and receives it all back as a citizen—that is, as a process in which nothing has changed materially but yet everything has changed in the mode of possession—the genre of the political treatise does not accommodate the play between givenness as reality to be acknowledged and givenness as a gift to be received with thanks. It is here that fiction, for all Rousseau's condemnation of the dangers of artifice and make-believe, can play an important epistemological as well as existential role. In his epistolary novel, *Julie*, Rousseau's characters discuss gratitude in the letters they write, but they also dramatize it in their relationships with each other. Thus for the reader gratitude becomes at once an object of analysis and an occasion for feeling in a way that is not possible even in philosophical writing as complexly orchestrated as either the *Discourse on Inequality* or the *Social Contract*.

JULIE, OR THE NEW HELOISE

Rousseau's novel offers a utopian vision of harmony on the estate of Clarens but never loses sight of the real world of power.[49] Gratitude for favors is proof of moral refinement, but we are also shown how the sense of obligation can be manipulated to advance the benefactor's self-interest. This is especially true where sexual desire is involved. At the very beginning of the story, St. Preux tells his pupil Julie that he cannot accept payment for his lessons. If he were obliged to her family, indulging his passion for her would be a violation of trust. The "editor" of the letters comments moralistically that being paid in gratitude makes the fault even greater.[50] Later, Julie tells St. Preux it would be wrong to use the peasant girl Fanchon as an intermediary for their secret letters. They have helped Fanchon in the past, but it would be an abuse of gratitude to ask her to become complicit in their forbidden correspondence.[51]

The imagined exploitation of gratitude for erotic ends takes increasingly lurid forms when the temporary stability of the Clarens *ménage* starts to break down. Julie, ostensibly happy in her marriage to M. de Wolmar, exhorts her former lover St. Preux to marry her cousin Claire. If he remains single and celibate, she argues, he might take sexual advantage of Fanchon's continuing gratitude to him as her benefactor. Of course, the reader understands that Julie's moralizing is a way defending against her own love for St. Preux, but the way she seizes on a possible abuse of gratitude is significant.[52] And in the "Loves of Milord Edward Bomston," an episode Rousseau left out of the published novel, we find this supposedly phlegmatic Englishman entangled with a worldly and married Roman marquise. She will not grant him her favors, but in order to keep him attached she procures for him a courtesan named Laura. Edouard's gratitude, we are told, was harder for him to contain than his love.[53]

In other contexts, gratitude can prove equally corrosive of human dignity. Julie was engaged to Wolmar because he saved her father's life when they were serving together as officers in the Dutch army. M. d'Étange decided to repay his obligation by giving Wolmar his daughter for a wife. We are told it would be ungrateful of him to go back on his word simply because Julie was not consulted and has fallen in love with someone else. Rousseau clearly intends the reader to view the father's action as another perversion of gratitude.[54] The dutiful Julie herself believes it would be a sin even to think that the gratitude she owes her parents might have limits.[55] Rousseau avoids a direct confrontation of the issue by introducing a new factor into the story. Wolmar loses his fortune in the turmoil of Russian politics. Canceling the marriage now would suggest that money took precedence over loyalty. The implication is that while the free ideal of gratitude may be distorted by custom or prejudice, the characters cannot escape the larger social system of obligations in which they live.

In his portrait of Wolmar, however, Rousseau puts gratitude in a different kind of context. He initially presents Wolmar to the reader as a man of rational and utilitarian outlook, a man who likes to observe humanity from above. In his detachment, Wolmar resembles the French philosophers Rousseau criticized in the *Discourse* for their lack of sensibility. After rescuing Julie's father, however, Wolmar began to change. He did not expect any gratitude, but the "sensible and grateful heart" of Julie's father began to give him "a better opinion of mankind."[56] He became more involved with his fellow men, and although he claimed that in doing so he only becomes a better spectator,[57] closer contact with people makes this confirmed bachelor want to get married. The spectacle of another person's gratitude breaches his self-sufficiency just enough that he eagerly agrees to be Julie's husband and master of the Clarens estate.

Wolmar does not hesitate to exploit his servants' personal loyalty to Julie to ensure the running of his household, but there is one important exception to his patriarchal attitude: he does not expect gratitude from his servants. He has trained them and given them work they enjoy, yet the very egotism by which he sets himself above them acts as a barrier to obligation. "Intention alone creates obligations, and a person who takes advantage of something I want only for myself owes me no gratitude."[58] Of course, the servants do feel obliged to him, but the relationship retains an impersonal quality that prevents it from becoming oppressive. In this respect it is very much like Rousseau's conception of the relationship between God and human beings. St. Preux makes the reference explicit when he freely expresses his own gratitude to Wolmar for helping him return to virtue by sublimating his love for Julie. Since St. Preux is not Wolmar's employee, gratitude is an appropriate response. The young man's "grateful and sensible soul" inspires him to say: "I can offer you, as to God himself, only the gifts I have received from you."[59] His feeling of dependence is not a burden, precisely because Wolmar does not need to be repaid.

The other side of the coin is that although Wolmar appreciates the advantages he enjoys as Julie's husband and master of a vast estate, he does not himself express any gratitude for his good fortune. Like the Legislator of the *Social Contract*, his role is to be concerned with others' happiness while remaining independent. His role in the book is somewhat God-like, but he himself is an atheist. Yet, while Rousseau wants to echo Bayle in showing that an atheist can be moral, Wolmar's unbelief is presented as a flaw. The more vulnerable characters, Julie, St. Preux, and Claire, need a strong mentor figure like Wolmar, but their dependence is offset by their delight in a capacity for sensibility that allows them to feel superior to the "cold" Wolmar. At first, this division of qualities gives stability to the small circle of "beautiful souls." But Julie soon becomes dissatisfied. She secretly wishes for her husband's conversion, so that he, too, may discover the sweetness of gratitude. Whether her wish arises from concern about his salvation or from resentment at his lack of neediness, it is a sign the emotional equilibrium of Clarens cannot be sustained. Julie is increasingly torn between her never-extinguished passion for St. Preux and her wifely loyalty, and only the fatal illness that befalls her after saving her son from drowning allows her to give each of these ties its due in her deathbed confession.

Milord Edouard's behavior illustrates the novel's ambivalent attitude toward gratitude in a different way. In the early part of the story this wealthy English peer offers Julie and St. Preux one of his English estates as a refuge from the wrath of Julie's father. Loyalty prevents the lovers from accepting his proposal, but they are deeply grateful for it, especially since Edouard is not bound to them by blood or social obligation. Indeed, when the discovery of St. Preux's correspondence with Julie forces him to leave with Edouard for Paris, only his obligation to his benefactor enables him to part from his mistress. Later, after St. Preux has been living at Clarens with Wolmar and Julie for some time, it is Edouard's turn to ask his friend to leave with him, this time for Italy. Edouard has fallen in love with Laura, the courtesan procured for him by the marquise, and he is debating whether to marry her. He relies on St. Preux to decide whether her character justifies this irregular match. Edouard writes: "I take pleasure in making everything common between us, gratitude as well as attachment."[60] In a letter to Wolmar, however, Edouard belies this idea of a reciprocal gratitude. "You know that in order to satisfy his gratitude and fill his heart with new objects, I affected to lend this journey more importance than it really had."[61] Here is another form of that manipulation of gratitude about which the novel is so uneasy. Given what we know about Edouard's own susceptibility to gratitude, however, it may be that what he is really affecting is detachment. Whatever the case, the incident underscores just how exceptional it is for gratitude not to be abused, either by being exploited in the interest of domination or by being idealized as an escape from the stress of autonomy.

Can gratitude, then, ever enhance the self and its agency? Two incidents suggest it can, although, significantly, neither involves an obligation to other human beings. The first occurs during St. Preux's stay in Paris, where he composes a lengthy critique of life in the French capital. In reply to Julie's suggestion that Parisian hospitality should make him more indulgent, he replies: "The esteem and gratitude their kindnesses inspire in me only increase my candor."[62] The notion of an empowering gratitude is a striking one. Rousseau is clearly alluding to his own relationship with the Parisian public.[63] Yet it is interesting that St. Preux names no actual Parisians and indeed describes no personal acquaintants. The only exception is an ironic one, when he mistakes the seductions of prostitutes in a brothel for the civil hospitality of urban hostesses—another illustration of the dangers of confusing ethical attachments with erotic ones. Otherwise, the French politeness that empowers St. Preux has an impersonal quality that prevents it from fostering dependence. Looking back at Wolmar, we may wonder whether his own privileged position, at once inside and outside the Clarens circle, is only tenable to the extent that he relates to the little society as a whole more than he does to any individual, even Julie. When she dies, it is suggested that his love and grief are pushing him toward religious belief, but this triumph over insensibility also marks the end of his role as legislator for others. It is St. Preux who will be entrusted with the education of Julie's children.

The empowering gratitude St. Preux enjoys as a thinker and writer in Paris is not, however, available to ordinary people. The second kind of self-enhancing gratitude is one to which anyone may have access, since it involves the cultivation of a relationship with God. It begins negatively, with Julie worrying that her gratitude to God for the happy life she enjoys at Clarens is too self-regarding, that it is "a self-interested gratitude."[64] The assumption here, inherited from seventeenth-century Augustinian *moralistes*, is that self-interest robs sentiment of all moral worth. In one of his *maximes*, La Rochefoucauld had declared: "Gratitude is like the good faith of merchants: it keeps commerce going; and we do not pay because it is just to return what was loaned, but in order to more easily find people who will lend."[65] The difficulty of discerning genuine motivation led many eighteenth-century thinkers to define virtue in terms of practical results rather than of an unattainable (and unascertainable) purity of intention. Rousseau's insistence in the *Social Contract* that the citizen's motives should not be scrutinized is informed by this tradition.

The premise of *Julie* is that the heroine can become a virtuous wife and mother even though she had a sexual relationship before marriage and continues to love someone other than her husband all her life. Thus St.

Preux, who reports the discussion to us, seeks to calm Julie's scruples about her motives. Self-interest (in the legitimate primary sense of *amour de soi*), he claims, is what anchors us in the real world. Julie's gratitude to God, which arises from and nourishes her attachment to those around her, is right and good, precisely because it enhances her earthly life while preventing her from taking it for granted. He contrasts her gratitude with the misguided devotion of the "mystics" whose lack of self-interest does not prove purity of will, but only empty-headedness. They rise up to God and no longer know where they are.[66]

What St. Preux does not realize is that Julie's anxiety about the relation between this world and the next stems from her enduring passion for him. A creature of passion, she cannot bear the tension of being a model of virtuous conduct. She longs to escape. St. Preux feels some of the same stress, but the difference is that Julie cannot relate to anything—to domestic society, or to the wider world of Paris, or to God—in general terms. As a woman, her relationships are all particular and personal.[67] They have a self-involving quality envied by the men, but by the same token she cannot bridge the gap between dependence and autonomy through a self-enhancing, because impersonal, gratitude. Indeed, her reaction to life at Clarens is that she is "too happy." She cannot live both inside and outside her own world, and she feels most self-interested when she is most selfless. Her dilemma cannot be resolved, and so her death, and with it the end of the Clarens experiment, becomes inevitable. Unlike the peoples founded by Moses and Mohammed, the Clarens community cannot survive the loss, not of its legislator, but of its presiding spirit. In the absence of Julie, the dream of reconciling reciprocity and authority, attachment and autonomy, is exposed as an illusion.

On the other hand, Julie's death does unite the novel's characters, and along with them Rousseau's readers, in a solidarity of grief. That readers of both sexes and of various social conditions wept for Julie suggests that they, too, felt oppressed by social structures unable to accommodate their emotions.[68] As author, Rousseau plays the role of a different kind of legislator, who instead of a system of laws offers the public an imaginative framework in which his readers' inchoate feelings could take articulate form. The outpouring of appreciative letters Rousseau received shows how grateful readers were for the gift.[69]

EMILE AND THE SAVOYARD VICAR'S "PROFESSION OF FAITH"

Is it possible to say something more encouraging about how individuals can live successfully in society, connected to others by gratitude yet autonomous and self-possessed? This is one of the tasks Rousseau sets for himself in *Emile*. Whereas the *Discourse on Inequality* emphasized the independence and self-sufficiency of man in the state of nature, *Emile* acknowledges that man is by nature weak and therefore destined to be sociable.[70] The contradiction between the two texts may be explained by the difference in their purpose. The *Discourse*, even in its evocation of pity, was intended to provide a critical perspective on social life, while *Emile* moves toward a more constructive vision, in which positive emotional attachment plays a major role. In the state of nature, there is no room for love; human couplings are random, instinctual, and short-lived.[71] In the first part of *Emile*, which focuses on the negative education of nature, there is no question of love either, but in book 4, the tutor starts preparing Emile for the lifelong partnership of marriage. It is still true that "every attachment is a sign of insufficiency. If each of us had no need of others, he would hardly think of uniting himself with them." But now Rousseau adds, "from our very infirmity is born our frail happiness."[72] Only God, who is omnipotent, is truly self-sufficient and can therefore be happy in solitude. Because human beings are weak, they can only love if they need someone else, and a person who does not love cannot enjoy such happiness as is available on earth.[73]

It is at the point where Emile's sexual desires begin to stir, and his need for a partner becomes acute, that Rousseau introduces the idea of attachment to other people and the notion of gratitude in particular. This does not mean the ideal of self-sufficiency is abandoned altogether, but because erotic desire is so powerful Emile needs both human and divine support to help defend his autonomy even as he opens himself to the vulnerability of love. Before he meets the woman of his dreams, therefore, Emile must be initiated into social relationships in a manner that recognizes his need for support without undermining his feeling of self-possession. Emile's education in sociability will cultivate in him sentiments of friendship and gratitude that his tutor can call upon in order to bind Emile to himself (as Edouard did with St. Preux), but not for the tutor's benefit. The latter's only goal is to help Emile contain the wayward force of his desires.

Rousseau's concern here is not primarily with morality in the conventional sense. If sexual love is dangerous, it is because it can result in excessive attachment to a particular person at the expense of commitment to a general ideal or principle. In this respect, the problem is analogous to that of loyalty to a national leader, a national god, or even to the national community itself, considered as an empirical entity and not as a contractual structure.[74] Thus, before meeting and marrying Sophie, Emile will be encouraged by the tutor to picture an ideal woman who can provide a standard by which the merits of real women can be judged. As always with Rousseau, an element of distance and impersonality in emotion is necessary to give the self some room for maneuver.

Realistically, however, Emile cannot become emotionally attached without investing in the particularity of another person. The function of gratitude, as Rousseau conceives it, is to help deal with this problem. Rousseau begins by postulating a basic reciprocity in the development of attachment. "In becoming capable of attachment, [Emile] becomes sensitive to that of others . . . We like what does us good. It is so natural a sentiment!"[75] What makes the feeling natural is that it responds to a "what" rather than a "who." That is to say, it is not burdened by reflection on what the other's intentions might really be. Because the evidence is necessarily uncertain, such an examination may well generate anxiety and thus uncomfortable feelings of dependence on the object. Rather, the natural response is to the effect itself, and it is immediate and unreflective. A side benefit is that Emile's gratitude gives the tutor a potential "empire" over him, provided the tutor not demand Emile be grateful but instead allow him to arrive at gratitude on his own.

The tutor's relationship with Emile includes an element of control because attachment, and the sociability that derives from it, is the source of other feelings in addition to love. In seeking out "what does us good," men may look on other people as instruments of their own well-being. As in the *Discourse on Inequality*, awareness of other people leads to reflection and comparison, activities that inevitably pervert legitimate self-interest into vanity. As soon as Emile begins to compare himself to other people, he wants to occupy "the first position."[76] He makes himself the center of his world. Rousseau warns his readers that Emile's education into sociability should not begin with courts and salons. The brilliance of these assemblies can only provoke vanity or envy, while social success will give Emile a taste for power.

Instead, education in sociability should focus on the suffering that is the common lot of humanity. Picking up another theme of the *Discourse*, Rousseau shows how the emotion of pity allows Emile to exercise his imagination and sensibility in a way that allows him to feel his own power, but only through identification with, and appreciation for, the weakness of others. By putting himself imaginatively in their place, he no longer makes himself at the center of his own world, but without actually giving up anything of his own. Of course, Emile must learn about more positive forms of power, but he will not do so through direct contact with men who rule others and whose place he would then want to occupy. Instead, he will read Thucydides and Plutarch, who will inspire him to be brave and bold, but who will also inoculate him against delusions of invincibility.

Similarly, when Rousseau wants to show gratitude in action, he surprises us by adopting the same indirect approach, as if gratitude were as dangerous to handle as power. And indeed, we have just seen how the tutor's control over Emile is based on his pupil's sense of obligation.[77]

Emile himself will not witness actual displays of gratitude. He might be tempted to bestow favors himself just for the pleasure of putting people in his debt. Worse, he might feel resentment at his inability, for lack of resources, to become a benefactor. Nor is Emile made to reflect on his own gratitude to the tutor until he is able to see him as a fellow sufferer. The tutor, he comes to realize, has sacrificed his own career and social life (including the possibility of marriage) to devote himself to his pupil's upbringing. The relationship between tutor and pupil, however, is too limited in scope to illustrate the socially constructive and self-enhancing role of gratitude in a paradigmatic way. As a contemporary analogy to one of Plutarch's *Lives*, therefore, Rousseau tells the story of the Savoyard vicar and the boy he rescued from degradation.

The vicar's "Profession of Faith" is not directly tied to the narrative of Emile's development, and so it is often read as a detachable set piece in which Rousseau presents his religious convictions. In fact it is the culmination of Rousseau's thoughts about gratitude and its role in human flourishing. The fact that the vicar does not speak in Rousseau's name, and that the boy of the story, who listens to the vicar's speech, is not supposed to be the future author of *Emile* either, but only a fellow citizen who passes the speech on to him, does not mean that Rousseau disagrees with the vicar or that his ideas bear only a contingent relation to the rest of the text. Rather, in addition to serving as a defense against the French censor, this relay of voices is designed to prevent the exploitation of the gratitude expressed in the "Profession of Faith" by any power, political, ecclesiastical, or even authorial. It is just because what the vicar says is vitally important and an integral part of the book that Rousseau does his best to present it as a "sentiment . . . for examination," not a rule to follow.[78]

The vicar's "Profession of Faith" is set in a context that blends fact and fiction, personal voice and discursive generality. The confident authorial first-person of the main text gives way to the more vulnerable "I" of someone who as a boy had been made angry and bitter by mistreatment. He would have fallen into vice had not he met a kindly priest who helped him escape from the hospice where he was confined. The boy forgets his benefactor and is soon punished for his "ingratitude" by falling again into distress. The prodigal returns, however, and is welcomed back. Like Emile's tutor, the priest does not boast of the help he gives the boy, and like Milord Edouard he pretends to need the boy's help in his research, and thus "he fed the noble sentiment of gratitude in him."[79] What attaches the boy even more to the priest is that the benefactor deserves compassion himself: a youthful love affair with a parishioner has spoiled his chances for advancement in the church. But while conforming outwardly to the dogmas and rituals of the Catholic Church, the vicar holds to his own unorthdox theological system. This system he imparts to his protégé with a mixture of humility and pride designed to foster in the boy a similar mixture of gratitude to a higher power and confidence in his own.

Against the materialist philosophes, the vicar argues that the universe must have been created by an intelligent will external to it. Man, who shares the ability to act by free will and not by determined motion alone, is the king of creation. Not only does he have power to master the animals, his capacity for wonder proves his superiority over the whole world of matter. It takes little reflection to realize, however, that man did not earn this position through any merit of his own. Thus gratitude is a natural response to the Creator. "From my first return to myself there is born in my heart a sentiment of gratitude and benediction for the Author of my species; and from this sentiment my first homage to the beneficent divinity."[80]

When the vicar then turns to the human world around him, he sees a different picture. Disorder reigns; people do not occupy the social position they deserve. God himself is not to blame, because an omnipotent God can only will the good.[81] Man creates his own misery by taking the human tendency to think of oneself first as evidence that he really is the center of the universe. He should instead look to God, who as creator is the true center of a cosmic order obscured by humanity's errors and perverted by its wayward will.

Overcoming one's attachment to the things of this world and contemplating the majestic order of the universe leads to a second, higher response of gratitude. The divine favor involved here is not the power to rule the earth, but the prospect of eventual liberation from the burden of earthly existence, including all relationships of dependence and power. It follows from this that the vicar will not ask anything specific of God: petitionary prayer would betray a misunderstanding of what divine providence is all about. The vicar's confidence in ultimate release is not, however, the selfless mysticism Rousseau condemned in *Julie*. On the contrary, the vicar never stops focusing on the needs of the self here below for reassurance and stability of self. And yet, the vicar's faith is not for Rousseau merely a projection of the self's desire for order onto the cosmos. The voice of conscience, which expresses an innate love of order and leads us to look beyond ourselves, is for Rousseau independent of all self-interest.[82] As in the *Social Contract*, Rousseau wants to define a place for the self at once within and outside the system of mutual obligations, which allows the self to flourish only by destroying its independence. Because the vicar's gratitude is not tied to any concrete earthly benefit or to a benefactor who needs any favor in return, it allows him, albeit by anticipation, to be more wholly who he is: "*me* without contradiction or division."[83] In the end, the vicar will feel grateful, not for having his needs met, but for no longer having needs at all. Here at last is the gratitude vital to human happiness without the dependence that spoils it.

If we ask how the gratitude fostered by faith can protect the vicar's protégé from delinquency, the answer does not lie in any religious prohibition. The vicar ends his speech with a general warning against bad habits, but he says nothing about specific rules of behavior. This is because the "vice" against which he warns the boy is psychological rather than moral in origin. Social oppression had made the boy feel depressed and unworthy, and so the primary function of gratitude is to restore him to himself. As an attachment based on the contemplation of an attractive and order-creating Other, it involves no self-alienating desire and seeks no reward other than a heightened sense of integration.

Whether the lessons of the "Profession of Faith" will be of any use to Emile is another question. In his political education, Emile was a spectator who contemplated the great men of history from a distance, the better to appreciate their courage without losing sight of their vulnerability. He is not being educated to be a ruler himself. The "Profession of Faith" is also focused on the value for the anonymous boy of sympathetic contemplation. The vicar himself gives his speech against the backdrop of a beautiful landscape—but one in which no people can be seen. He tells us that he now fulfills his ritual and pastoral duties as priest with wholehearted care, but he accepts that these duties exclude intimate involvement with individuals. Nor is his protégé's gratitude said to spill over into other relationships. Despite the warmth of its theistic overtones, the vicar's faith has no interpersonal concreteness. This did not matter to the readers of Rousseau's day. If the charms of "natural religion" are now hard to see, the enthusiastic response of Rousseau's readers reminds us that for Rousseau's contemporaries the attraction of religion that seemed to combine personal validation with a saving sense of distance and impersonality should not be underestimated.

But while in politics and religion Emile can preserve a measure of detachment, it is difficult to see how this could be true in love. Emile is raised so as to be able to live productively in any country and to adopt any reasonable expression of faith, but his marriage implies a lasting bond with a specific woman. Thus the prospect for success in love is not encouraging. While *Emile* does end with the hero happily united with his bride, its abortive sequel, *Emile and Sophie, or the Solitary Ones*, shows the marriage breaking down very quickly once the lovers have to deal with each other as real people. Even the original *Emile* ends in a kind of palinode. Instead of Emile bidding his tutor farewell as he sets off with Sophie, Rousseau has the young man beg the tutor to stay on, complaining that he cannot do without his guidance. In neither case can the gift of self-possession be received, acknowledged, and shared without something going wrong.

Perhaps in the end the only exception to this rule is to be found in the relationship between the author and his readers, but even there the process is a risky one. If *Julie* provided an imaginative context in which dreams of psychological and social integration could be contained, *Emile* underscores what is problematic in trying to apply imaginative paradigms to particular real-life contexts. Rousseau's writings continue to be relevant today because they never cease wrestling with the tension between imagination and application, both in their arguments and in the complex seductiveness of their modes of address. In accepting Rousseau's invitation to "examine his sentiments," therefore, responsive readers will find reasons to be grateful for the opportunity, but that gratitude will include some ambivalence of their own about the favor Rousseau has done them.

Parting with Prejudice

HUME, IDENTITY, AND AESTHETIC UNIVERSALITY

Neil Saccamano

> Nothing can oppose or retard the impulse of passion, but a contrary impulse. . . . We speak not strictly and philosophically when we talk of the combat of passion and of reason. Reason is, and ought only to be the slave of the passions, and can never pretend to any other office than to serve and obey them. As this opinion may appear somewhat extraordinary, it may not be improper to confirm it by some other considerations.[1]

David Hume's well-known critique of the sovereignty of reason in human life is "extraordinary" not only because he reverses the positions of master and slave by bestowing authority on the passions, but also because he declares the traditional discourse of the passions to be unphilosophical in its use of the metaphor of combat. " '[T]is impossible that reason and passion can ever oppose each other, or dispute for the government of the will and actions," since emotions, feelings, sentiments, or affections—the passions, in Hume's broad sense of the term—have unquestionable jurisdiction over praxis (*T*, 416). Hume develops his critique of the misleading figure of dispute in this tradition by rather dramatically exemplifying the social implications of his novel opinion: "'Tis not contrary to reason to prefer the destruction of the whole world to the scratching of my finger" or "for me to chuse my total ruin, to prevent the least uneasiness of an *Indian* or person wholly unknown to me. . . . 'tis not the passion, properly speaking, which is unreasonable, but the judgment [accompanying it]" (*T*, 416). There can be no contradiction between reason and passion for Hume because the passions, which alone produce actions arising from a propensity to pleasure and avoidance of pain, have nothing to say to the discourse of reason, which addresses the truth and falsehood of judgments. What Hume understands to be his extraordinary contribution to moral philosophy consists, somewhat paradoxically, in speaking to the sovereignty of unspeakable passions in common life.

Of course, as many philosophical studies of Hume have pointed out at least since Norman Kemp Smith and as we shall also have occasion to investigate in this essay, Hume's maxim here concerning the proper enslavement of reason is polemical and needs to be qualified by his more intricate analyses of the role of critical reflection in the domain of praxis.[2] But this famous passage bears reciting to remind ourselves that what is at stake in the passions for Hume is a matter of life and death—my own as well as that of others, particularly strangers, the world of persons "wholly unknown to me." For Hume, we should recall, moral philosophy is another name for the science of human nature and comprehends the sciences of logic, which explains our "reasoning faculty and the nature of our ideas"; morals (in the sense of ethics) and criticism, both of which "regard our tastes and sentiments"; and politics, which considers "men as united in society and dependent on each other."[3] In the "Abstract" of the *Treatise*, Hume comments that this work contains his complete presentation of the science of logic, and that he has "laid the foundations for the other parts in his account of the passions" (*T*, 646). As evinced by the range of issues treated in Books 2 and 3—from the nature of vice and virtue, beauty and deformity, sympathy, and benevolence, to the origins of justice, property, society, and government—Hume's account of the passions links together ethics, aesthetics, and politics. In fact, despite the great attention paid to Hume's "logic" and skeptical epistemology by subsequent philosophers, Hume considered the sciences founded on the passions to be at the core of his philosophical project, at least according to a letter from 1734 in which he explains his goal in writing the *Treatise*: by "throw[ing] off all Prejudices either for his own opinions or for this [*sic*] of others" and by taking human nature as his principal object of study, he would "derive every Truth in Criticism as well as Morality."[4] Not the critique of personal identity or causation but the study of taste and sentiment is here accorded priority.

The linkage of aesthetics and ethics through a shared origin in sentiment is apparent in the way Hume frequently parallels the two sciences, usually by citing a common sense of beauty as analogous to a common sense of morality. My essay will proceed from the premise, however, that aesthetics is not simply a parallel field of investigation in Hume. To the extent that aesthetics concerns itself predominately with the force or liveliness of sensations, particularly of pleasure and displeasure, as the basis of judgment, the study of taste conditions or models the other sciences founded on the passions and even, perhaps, the entire science of human nature, as Hume sometimes suggests: "Thus all probable reasoning is nothing but a species of sensation. 'Tis not solely in poetry and music, we must follow our taste and sentiment, but likewise in philosophy. When I am convinc'd of any principle, 'tis only an idea, which strikes more strongly upon me" (*T*, 103). In this respect, that Hume did not compose a separate enquiry concerning beauty or criticism might signal just how difficult it is to extricate questions of taste from epistemological, moral, and political issues in his philosophy. But that speculation aside, the few

essays Hume did publish on taste and the arts are more productively ap-
proached with their broader import kept to the fore, so that they might be
read as elaborating problems of sentiment in which (to stay with Hume's
examples of indisputable passions) self-love and self-sacrifice, universal
indifference and universal humanity, are at stake.

In recognition of the links among Hume's passional sciences, I will be
concerned with margins or limits in a couple of ways. Devoted primarily
to a reading Hume's "Of the Standard of Taste," my essay is oriented
toward passages located at the borders of Hume's discussion of taste in
that piece; these passages also mark the limit of aesthetics for Hume and
hence a place where aesthetics, ethics, and politics are complexly linked.
There, Hume turns his attention away from the sentiment of pleasure
characteristic of aesthetic experience and toward sensations of pain, displeasure, or affective violence felt in response to certain tragic representations. These moments of pain not only signal the aesthetic failure of certain representations but also indicate the condition and limit of aesthetics
as, specifically, a movement toward universality. For what is central to
aesthetics in Hume is the possibility or necessity of departing from our
particularized and contingent positions of identity that, for him, constitute prejudice. Insofar as aesthetic judgment entails the displacement of
particular selves and a movement toward a general or universal point of
view, we can understand the centrality of aesthetics to the science of
human nature, successfully to attain which the young Hume believed little
more was required than "to throw off all Prejudices." By focusing on the
pains of aesthetic failure, then, I want to elaborate the ethical and political
interest of Hume's theory of taste and to provide a somewhat sympathetic
reading of this skeptical philosopher's invocation of universality in relation to what he considers the prejudice of identity.[5]

At stake in taste and sentiment for Hume is the possibility of human
community, "a party of humankind," that in principle includes all strangers and cuts across social and national divisions—"a sentimental *we* of
art," as Jean-François Lyotard calls it, a community that can stipulate
"no determinate conditions for membership."[6] Given this interest in
human *qua* sentimental community, it should come as no surprise that the
distinction on which Hume's discussion of aesthetic universality pivots (in
moments of forgetting or recollection) is that of friendship and enmity. If
we accept the terms of Carl Schmitt's political theory and take the category of the concrete public enemy to be the decisive concept of the political, we could understand Hume's appeal to aesthetic universality in terms
of the familiar Enlightenment notion of humanity as issuing in a depoliticized cosmopolitanism: "The concept of humanity excludes the concept
of the enemy" and, as a universal category overriding nations as political
entities, "would necessarily have to mean total depoliticization."[7] More-

over, for Schmitt, to think the political as derived in some manner from the aesthetic or the moral is not only to deny its autonomy, but also to fall prey to ideology by ignoring the fundamental status of the political—and especially the possibility of war—as the essence of the human.[8]

In the reading that follows, however, I aim to show that the appeal to humanity as a universal category consisting of freely self-relating individuals in Hume neither eliminates the concept of the enemy in the name of some affective cultural community nor functions solely as an ideological ploy that normativizes those who recognize themselves as human subjects. On the one hand, Hume bases aesthetic and moral judgment on an impartiality that makes possible a just sympathetic response to the sentiments of others and that thus affirms a potentially universal humanity. To the extent that sympathy extends beyond particular national and historical positions, it involves the possibility of cross-cultural encounters that suspend political relations. On the other hand, Hume does argue for something like the autonomy of the political in Schmitt's sense—in the sense that we may kill those who might be good and beautiful to affirm our political essence. For instance, against Cicero's claim that the double meaning of the word *hostis* (stranger and enemy) can be ascribed to the "humanity" of the ancient Romans, who sought to "soften" the name of enemy, Hume judges it more probable that the "ferocity of those people" in particular led them, on the contrary, to consider "all strangers as enemies"; moreover, a sentiment of humanity that would regard "public enemies with a friendly eye" is generally not "consistent with the most common maxim of [state] policy or of nature."[9] In fact, aesthetic, moral, and political sentiments "are apt to be confounded" so that we seldom "do not think an enemy vicious" and often find it difficult to allow "the voice of an enemy" to be "musical"; yet, Hume insists, "this hinders not, but that the sentiments are, in themselves, distinct; and a man of temper and judgment may preserve himself from these illusions" (T, 472). This man of judgment is a man of taste but also a man of war, for whom "the fortifications of a city belonging to an enemy are esteem'd beautiful" and who, all the same, "wish[es] that they were entirely destroy'd" (T, 586–87). Although, as we shall see, the communicability of passion in aesthetic experience might work to displace the prejudice of identity, sympathy has a limit defined by putatively independent moral and political imperatives.

Hume's insistence on an affective limit in cross-cultural aesthetic encounters suggests, however, that the notion of universality has all along had potential political effectivity. The possibility of an aesthetic experience of works from other times, places, and peoples seems to figure the promise of a universality that does not threaten "total depoliticization" in Hume but that might very well alter historical-political arrangements. In this respect, Hume might be productively read in relation to recent critical reevaluations of Enlightenment notions of universal humanity not in terms of an apolitical cosmopolitanism that no longer recognizes national borders, but in terms of a "cosmopolitics" that emphasizes the multiple interconnections among nationally identified individuals and does not transcend such particularities of identity in the name of an abstract global citizenship.[10] "A cosmopolitanism worthy of its name," one critic has recently objected, would contradictorily "have to give space to the very nationalism that the term is invoked to counter."[11] Yet before consigning cosmopolitics and its universalist promise to an imperialist ideology and history that totally determine it, we might consider whether an emancipatory politics must be persistently haunted by these terms with their potential for unsettling or dislodging established national and international relations. Kant compared skeptical philosophers to "a species of nomads [who], despising all settled modes of life [cultivation or settlement of grounds], broke up from time to time all civil society."[12] In Hume, however, skepticism does not in practice produce nomadic subjects as much as it induces a displacement whose political consequences he hopes to manage.

As James Noxon and other philosophers have noted, a distinctive feature of Hume's aesthetics is his insistence on critical reflection to regulate judgments of taste.[13] Despite the readings of those who stress the primacy of *aesthesis* as sheer sentiment in Hume and other British empirical philosophers, Hume continually argues for the necessity of "universal propositions" and "general laws" of reason to condition and reorient sentiment in both ethics and aesthetics.[14] In the *Enquiry Concerning the Principles of Morals*, for instance, Hume mediates the competing claims of reason and sentiment to authority in ethical judgment by positing for both morality and criticism "an internal sense or feeling, which nature has made universal in the whole species," and, at the same time, by insisting that "it is often necessary . . . that much reasoning should precede" and "pave the way for such a sentiment" (*EM*, 173). Although the need for reasoning to condition sentiment becomes especially urgent in Hume with regard to justice, at this moment in the second *Enquiry* he proceeds to make his case by distinguishing between natural and artistic beauty: "Some species of beauty, especially the natural kinds, on their first appearance, command our affection and approbation; and where they fail of this effect, it is impossible for any reasoning to redress their influence, or adapt them better to our taste and sentiment. But in many orders of beauty, particularly those of the finer arts, it is requisite to employ much reasoning, in order to feel the proper sentiment; and a false relish may frequently be corrected by argument and reflection" (*EM*, 173). As Hegel will also do, Hume excludes natural beauty from the science of aesthetics and concentrates, instead, on the "finer arts" because natural forms evidently elicit pleasurable sentiments that cannot be "adapted" through reflection so as to become aligned with affective propriety. Since Hume supposes aesthetic discourse as the criticism of exclusively cultural productions to have the power to enable subjects of sentiment to feel what they ought to feel and thus to reconcile passion and obligation, he can then claim that there is a "moral beauty" that "partakes" of this same corrigible quality and "demands the assistance of our intellectual faculties in order to give it a suitable influence on the human mind" (*EM*, 173).

That the passions in Hume frequently require the intervention of critical reflection to both condition and regulate them is not surprising.[15] This requirement is consistent with Hume's repeated emphasis on general law as the probabilistic knowledge based on, but not identical with, particulars in every instance (an empirical universality, for Kant, lacks a priori necessity and thus cannot be a "true or strict, but only [an] assumed or comparative universality").[16] In his essay "Of Commerce," for instance, Hume differentiates the "common man" from philosophers and politicians in terms of adeptness at generalization: "Every judgment or conclusion, with the [bulk of mankind] is particular," he insists; "[t]hey cannot enlarge their view to those universal propositions, which comprehend under them an infinite number of individuals," whereas "it is the chief business of philosophers to regard the general course of things," for "general principles, if just and sound, must always prevail in the general course of things, though they may fail in particular cases" (*E*, 254). The failure of general principles to "comprehend" all "individuals" at any moment is not, for Hume, only a provisional limitation of universality on the way toward realizing total inclusion. The divergence of general principle and particular case is irreducible. At the same time, however, this gap signifies the unreliability not of general laws but, on the contrary, of particular instances and, by extension, of the immediacy—the "firstness" or sheer givenness—of an individual experience. The recourse to the facticity of sentiment, the feeling of beauty as well as morality, would also fall under this suspicion; otherwise, "what each man feels within himself [would always be] the standard of sentiment," as he puts it in the second *Enquiry* (*EM*, 171).

In the *Treatise*, Hume had already stressed the regulative function of generality with regard to sympathy as a medium of communication that allows us to feel the pains and pleasures of others. Sympathy lies at the origin of aesthetic and moral judgment as well as, more broadly, of a sentiment of humanity. Hume insists in this early work (if not afterwards) that "there is no such passion in human minds, as the love of mankind, merely as such"; the happiness or misery of others may, "in some measure, affect us, when brought near to us, and represented in lively colours," but "this proceeds merely from sympathy, and is no proof of such an universal affection to mankind" (T, 481–82).[17] "The nature and force of sympathy" depends on "the minds of men [being] similar in their feelings and operations" so that "all the affections pass readily from one person to another, and beget correspondent movements in every human creature" (T, 575). And in the case of both aesthetics and ethics, this possibility of a sympathetic response to the feelings of a beautiful or virtuous character entails a sentiment of humanity that displaces individuals from their particular position and interests. In arguing for the generalizing operation of sympathy, Hume claims that individuals respond not only, for instance, to a tragic character in a play or a virtuous character in society, but also to those others potentially affected by a character's beauty or virtue. A tragedy might well bring the passions of a foreign character near to us through forceful representation, but Hume goes out of his way to argue that an aesthetic object deemed beautiful "pleases only by its tendency to produce . . . the pleasure or advantage of some other person," some other spectator or reader or possessor, and the "pleasure of a stranger, for whom we have no friendship, pleases us only by sympathy" (T, 576). Similarly, justice is a moral virtue because it has a "tendency to the good of mankind" and the "interests of society"—a social and extensively human interest that is neither our own "nor that of our friends" and that therefore "pleases only by sympathy" (T, 577). Our proper aesthetic and moral pleasure is the pleasure we sympathetically infer that beauty and virtue give to strangers.

Yet, since sympathy in Hume acts primarily as a medium of affective communication—and thus transmits happiness or misery in a kind of involuntary way that Philip Mercer considers an "infection" or "contagion"—he must also introduce reflection to regulate the variability in the force of sentiment that results from the contingencies of proximity and distance, familiarity and foreignness.[18] For "every particular man has a peculiar position with regard to others," he observes, and if "each of us [were] to consider characters and persons only as they appear from his peculiar point of view," we would experience "continual *contradictions*" and could never "converse together on any reasonable terms." Hume assumes we want to correct for these variations in sentiment by arriving at a "more *stable* judgment" in morality, as we do in aesthetics: "we fix on some *steady* and *general* points of view; and always, in our thoughts, place ourselves in them, whatever may be our present situation. In like manner, external beauty is determin'd merely by pleasure; and 'tis evident, a beautiful countenance cannot give so much pleasure, when seen at the distance of twenty paces, as when it is brought nearer to us. We say not, however, that it appears to us less beautiful: Because we know what effect it will have in such a position, and by that reflexion we correct its momentary appearance" (*T*, 581–82). Through reflection we displace ourselves from our presumed "peculiar position" with regard to others and unsettle the self-evidence of the present. Such acts of self-adjustment as self-displacement are not, for Hume, the effect of reflection as an intrusive social instrument of calibration, but the necessary consequence of the repetition of experience itself; as he remarks, "Experience soon teaches us this method of correcting our sentiments" (*T*, 582). By recalling not only specific past experiences in which we remember that our perceptions varied but the principle of generality itself—by which we know that our pleasure in beauty varies invariably according to the law of proximity and distance—we always have the possibility of placing ourselves "in our thoughts" in a general point of view.

To identify with this general position of knowledge based on self-correcting experience as a law is, for Hume, to place oneself in the perspective of language, in a number of ways. The general view, or the perspective of knowledge, regards what we can and ought to *say*: "we say not," Hume writes, that a beautiful person is less beautiful from a distance; we seek the stability of the general not to avoid experiential fluctuations as such but to prevent continual "contradictions." In fact, the *theoretical* uniformity of experience is to be found in the general terms of language itself, "terms expressive of our liking or dislike . . . as if we remain'd in one point of view" (*T*, 582). Critical self-reflection is either what language makes possible or what makes language possible. Indeed, he notes, "'twere impossible we cou'd ever make use of language, or communicate our sentiments to one another, did we not correct the momentary appearances of things, and overlook our present situation" (*T*, 582). With language comes the possibility of knowledge, the general communicability of sentiment, and thus sociality.

Moreover, when Hume broaches the issue of taste in his essay devoted to seeking its standard, he frames the difficulties of aesthetic experience as precisely a problematic of language and the peculiarities of reference.[19] Critical of a philosophy that rests on the proposition that "[a]ll sentiment is right; because sentiment [unlike understanding] has a reference to nothing beyond itself" (*E*, 230), Hume aims for a standard that would align the sentiments of persons, elicited by particular objects, with the sentiments of praise or blame belonging to "the very nature of language" and accounting in part for social "harmony" (*E*, 228). Although Hume represents the search for a standard as a means to perform "at least" an act of "decision . . . confirming one sentiment and condemning another," he clearly gives priority to constituting an aesthetic community through a "rule" by which sentiments "may be reconciled" (*E*, 229). Yet in the opening section of this essay, Hume's censure of Homer's epics and the Koran for lacking a "steady rule of right"—the Koran, especially, remains caught in the mirror of self-reference insofar as "every action is blamed or praised, so far only as it is beneficial or hurtful to the true believers" (*E*, 229)—already suggests the crucial function of critical decision (literally, a cutting off or severing) at the limit of reconciliation. As we shall see, Hume's resort to decision indicates the irreducibility of national identity and the enemy.

In quest of reconciliation, Hume moves quickly in this essay from some aesthetic criteria of works to the standards of the true critic and what he calls their "faculties": delicacy of taste, practice, and impartiality. One of these obstacles to just taste—prejudice—names the problem of particularity that Hume seeks to conciliate with generality and sociality. However, just before the last section of the essay, Hume concedes that a "certain degree of diversity in judgment is unavoidable" and cannot be accounted for by "some defect or perversion in the faculties" he has enumerated (*E*, 243–44). These apparently irreconcilable differences derive from three kinds of particularized identity: psychological ("different humours of particular men"), historical, and national-cultural ("particular manners and opinions of our age and country"). Yet in Hume's probabilistic accounting, the differences made by these forms of identity do not go as far as to "confound" the standard of taste because they remain only contingent cases or isolated points located at a somewhat greater distance from what he recalls to be the regularities or norms of taste. "The general principles of taste are uniform in human nature," he insists (*E*, 244).

Although Hume presents these psychological and national-historical peculiarities here as relatively inconsequential excess, he had previously held prejudice responsible for a perversion of taste in regard to precisely these particularities of identity. Freedom from prejudice, Hume had argued, is a necessary condition for aesthetic experience to be able to correct itself through reflection. And freedom from prejudice means the suspension of local differences assumed to be naturally determinant. As Hume elaborates both the given place of identity and the imperative to displace it as a condition of taste, we also come upon an act of violence at the heart of aesthetic pleasure. He remarks:

> [W]hen any work is addressed to the public, though I should have a friendship or enmity with the author, I must depart from this situation; and considering myself as a man in general, forget, if possible, my individual being and my peculiar circumstances. A person influenced by prejudice, complies not with this condition; but obstinately maintains his natural position, without placing himself in that point of view which the performance supposes. If the work be addressed to persons of a different age or nation, he makes no allowance for their peculiar views and prejudices; but, full of the manners of his own age and country,

rashly condemns what seemed admirable in the eyes of those for whom alone the discourse was calculated. . . . By this means, his sentiments are perverted; nor have the same beauties and blemishes the same influence upon him, as if he had imposed a proper violence on his imagination, and had forgotten himself for a moment. So far his taste evidently departs from the true standard. (*E*, 239–40)

This passage relies on a chain of figures of motion and rest that organizes Hume's scientific discourse of human nature and especially of the passions as a moral mechanics: sentiments depart or remain in place, impart and communicate their force, enter into, resist, counterbalance, or overpower and convert each other, and so on. Here, the dynamics of affective force structures a complicated analysis of aesthetic deviation according to which the departure from the standard of taste results from the failure to depart from what Hume calls the "natural position" of prejudice. That Hume ascribes the perversion of taste to an obstinacy of position—"obstinacy" meaning a resolve, literally, to stand against—makes clear how the notion of prejudice straddles psychology or pathology and morality. As if he were looking back from a vantage point offered by reflection, Hume sees an identity in place but also something like a choice to stand still or to part with it. In other words, this given or "natural position" has already been effectively displaced by his supposition that the individual has always had the ability to move, or capability to have been moved, toward other times, places, and nations. Identities, in this sense, do not have the existential primacy of an "ontopology" but are secondary in Hume; a "natural position" is a taking-stand that, as an act or event, already implies a pre-positive notion of subjectivity, a prepositional self already parted from itself and departed toward others before (as it were) the position designated by the proper name is taken up. "Before" obstinately itself, "I" is already moved toward others. Hume issues a call to depart from oneself as if a particular identity were an empirical given that might or might not be left behind because the possibility itself of this movement is only contingent or empirical. However, we could also understand the possible performance of empirical acts of self-departing as conditional upon a self-parting that must be presumed to have opened out individuals to others. Indeed, the priority of this self-parting movement is akin to what Étienne Balibar deems the "true universalistic element [that] lies in the *internal* process of individualization: the virtual deconstruction and reconstruction of primary identities."[20] To be a particular person is to be moved toward others in a way that both supports and unsettles the presumption of autonomous identity.

In presuming prejudice to be obstinacy, Hume not only can diagnose the vitiated sentiments of such a pathological condition but can implicitly reproach those who refuse to let slip their peculiar views and let fall the distinctions between friend and enemy, modern and ancient, native and foreigner. Such oppositional identity-formations, then, only contingently define individual and collective subjects for Hume; from the vantage of reflection, he implies that a decision has already been made to remain in place with them. In this enlightened account, prejudice is perverse because it stubbornly and even unjustly resists the denaturalizing movement of identity that also conditions aesthetics and ethics. Hence Hume asserts the necessity of leaving: "I must depart from this situation." Here, too, we come upon the nuances of agency related to the tension between psychopathological processes and moral-aesthetic choice. First of all, the necessity signified by "I must depart" may remind us of the kind of involuntary affective motion to which Hume often resorts when characterizing the familiar dynamics of experience. Of course, Hume's most famous example of such affective necessity occurs at the end of Book 1 of the *Treatise*, where nature's sudden impulsion "cures" him of the paralyzing "philosophical melancholy" into which his skeptical critique of reason has plunged him: "Most fortunately it happens . . . [that] I find myself absolutely and necessarily determin'd to live, talk, and act like other people in the common affairs of life. . . . I may, nay I must yield to the current of nature . . . [in] blind submission" (*T*, 269). Just as in this instance of passional necessity, the submission to which Hume calls the perfect example of his skeptical disposition and the basis of his entire philosophy, mistakes in taste should be understood as misplaced affections that result from prejudice holding sway in the present but that will fortunately and inevitably cede to the natural force of sentiment in its ultimate truth.

Secondly, however, the necessity in Hume's statement might signify an ethical imperative. To part from ourselves here and now in aesthetic experience is not just a matter of an inevitable affective impetus but a moral obligation, a call to respond and assume responsibility for our positions. All works of art are naturally conditioned by the particularities of their time and place, and impartiality is required to take account of such contingent norms by recognizing our own so that we do not simply oppose prejudice to prejudice, identity to identity, and—most importantly—so that we can sympathetically place ourselves in the "point of view which the performance supposes" and see with the "eyes" of those strangers "for whom alone the discourse was calculated." One must become impartial in the sense of ethically imparting oneself toward others. Or, rather, if we regard "natural positions" of identity as derivative for Hume, one must recognize that one has already been imparted toward others and must therefore act accordingly by not actively maintaining one's given position and standing against others. As Theodor Adorno remarked, "it belongs to morality not to be at home in one's home."[21] Hence to forget even becomes a moral command: "considering myself as a man in general, [I must] forget, if possible, my individual being and my peculiar circumstances." From this perspective, forgetting is not just an event that befalls a passive subject who suffers it: to part with oneself for Hume is also actively to forget oneself a moment as a moral and aesthetic imperative.

The nuances of this account of self-parting as the condition of taste follow, I believe, from Hume's sense that language offers the possibility of a general position that, however, cannot be occupied. As a memory aide for active self-forgetting, the category of "humanity" might provide the impetus to displace identity-positions in Hume without, however, immediately "subjecting" or disciplining individuals by soliciting their identification with positive norms. Hence to "consider" oneself in terms of such a category does not mean to assert one *knows* and *is* normatively human. To depart from oneself is to be willingly imparted toward others but not necessarily to have arrived once and for all at other determinate positions or at the place of a generalized other ("humanity") from which one can normatively identify oneself and others as being the same. Self-parting functions negatively: it works to "empty" (as it were) natural persons who by definition are "full of the manners of [their] own age and country." In fact, when Hume describes in the *Treatise* how variations in particular experiences of beauty do not alter the "general decisions" that language allows us to communicate, he specifies this generality as conditional— "*as if* we remain'd in one [general] point of view" (*T*, 582). Aesthetic experience moves us to imagine ourselves as figuring a universal humanity whose (linguistic) perspective we can never embody, fulfill, or realize here and now.[22]

On the other side, Hume (the Scot) does not minimize the affective bonds with naturalized identities no doubt habitually strengthened over time. His philosophical psychology acknowledges the force that place impresses on subjectivity; the recognition of a displacement or movement at the origin of the self does not necessarily, immediately, or completely transform the identifications that structure the affective life of subjects. If the invocation of humanity does not necessarily entail a cosmopolitanism in which we are at home everywhere, neither does it entail a nomadic transcendence or diasporic ideal of detachment. As Adorno's aphorism dialectically implies, morality involves not being at home precisely *in* our homes. In fact, self-parting is also presented by Hume as an act of affective violence. For a shared or impartable aesthetic pleasure to be possible, we must take pains to denaturalize our peculiar selves by "impos[ing] a proper violence" on ourselves so that the same beauties can generally have the same effects. From the perspective of obstinate particularity, a movement toward others might well feel like expropriation or dispossession. Yet that Hume also calls this violence "proper" testifies not only to the self-imposition, but also to the justness, of this wrenching act: a willing self-violation—or willingness to acknowledge the self's prior violability—becomes necessary for aesthetic pleasure to be considered generally impartable in Hume once historical and national identities have been supposed as the natural point of departure.[23]

In emphasizing the negative dimension of Hume's aesthetics, I want to forestall the critique of Enlightenment notions of aesthetics and ethics, and the claim to humanity that they presuppose or produce, as ideological—a critique in which political theorists on the right and left might agree.[24] Even assuming the ruse of universal humanity in aesthetics and ethics, a dialectician would still question whether there might be some "truth" in this "false" moment. As Chantal Mouffe has remarked on the tension between freedom and equality in liberal-democratic regimes: "[I]t is the idea of equality which provides the backbone of the left vision while the right—in the name of liberty—has always condoned diverse forms of inequality. The fact that a certain type of egalitarian ideology has been used to justify totalitarian forms of politics in no way forces us to relinquish this struggle for equality."[25] In ways that I find quite pertinent to rereading the history of aesthetic theory in relation to politics, recent debates among Judith Butler, Ernesto Laclau, and Slavoj Žižek, for instance, have attempted to underscore not only the inevitability but the necessity of the claim to universality for a progressive politics: as Laclau puts it, "an emancipatory discourse . . . does not dissolve into mere particularism but keeps a universal dimension alive."[26] Their discussions also proceed with full knowledge that universality has been invoked historically to sanction imperialist and other unjust practices and that the category itself may be considered impossible insofar as it is always "contaminated" by the exclusive norms and identities that it claims to supersede (*CHU*, 15). As such a contradictory category, universality is a promise that cannot be fulfilled and will never coincide with any present but can only be repeatedly performed here and now *as* a promise—as a call to come to a place or moment that always remains in the future—or repeatedly cited as the name of an empty place that can never be occupied. But, as Butler and Laclau too insist, albeit it in different ways: "the exclusionary character of those conventional norms of universality does not preclude further recourse to the term," although the affirmation of universality must be met with critical vigilance (*CHU*, 39). Since "no universal is freed from its contamination by the particular contexts from which it emerges and in which it travels" and "this contamination will always end in hybrids in which particularism and universalism become indissociable," as Butler notes, a crucial task is to expose the exclusions attending every claim of universality (*CHU*, 40, 193). Yet the appeal to universality as a promise or an empty place nonetheless retains emancipatory potential—and affirmatively opens up to a future—because of the political-historical effects it makes possible here and now. As Jacques Derrida has remarked, for example, the conjuring up of a "democracy to come," which "will never present itself in the form of full presence, is the opening of [a] gap between an infinite promise . . . and the determined, necessary, but also necessarily inadequate forms of what has to be measured against this promise"; and "this memory of a hope" irreducible to the present leaves "an empty place" for to what is to come.[27] Recurring to the interval or gap that conditions acts of identification, the claim to universality (re)enables particular subjects to disidentify with social and cultural positions given here and now, to attempt to translate their interests or find equivalences among them, and thus, perhaps, to remobilize the terms of a prevailing hegemony in the social field so as to provide ("with luck," qualifies Butler) a discursive "site for disidentificatory resistance" (*CHU*, 151).

To return specifically to Hume's recourse to universality, we should remember that he puts it polemically to work against political absolutism and the social stratifications the latter upholds. In defining individuals by abstracting them from their contingent circumstances and moving them to consider themselves in relation to a general humanity, Hume, too, attempts to remind subjects of the possibility of displacing themselves from the social positions based on their birthright and of altering a given social structure. And to the extent that such a moment of critical self-parting is constitutive of the aesthetic encounter, we might rethink the political potential of art in this project. However, we cannot do so without at the same time critically marking the limits of Hume's invocation of aesthetic universality. The different hegemonic formation toward which universality moves in Hume is, in my reading, liberalism, for which mobility is itself a requirement of the market and in which individuals are no longer positioned solely by birth but by their capacity for economic exchange.[28] As Howard Caygill has demonstrated: "The British theory of taste is inseparable from the justification of civil society" and its "virtuous circulation" of "goods."[29] To argue, however, that universality could only have been the alibi of liberalism from the beginning would be to construe such acts of disidentification as necessarily determined by the historical conditions of their occurrence—as if to consider oneself as not-quite-identical with one's given social position is always and only to live on the grounds and within the horizon of the liberal nation-state and capitalist hegemony. Even Balibar, in his account of the hegemonic or integrative function of a certain universality in constructing subjectivity, concedes that "there is undoubtedly a meaning of universality which is intrinsically linked with the notion of *insurrection*"—what he calls an "ideal universality" that recalls Enlightenment hopes of emancipatory progress and haunts any determinate hegemony by "introduc[ing] the *unconditional* in the realm of politics."[30] So, although we will now reconsider the appeal to universality in Hume—to elaborate how a particular social formation belies (as always) universality, how the act of forgetting one's national-cultural identity may be itself prompted by cultural norms, and how, in fact, "contamination" itself becomes a concern at the end of the essay on taste—we should not simply dismiss the social and political potential of aesthetic universality in his work.

If we turn to the second, apparently negligible, discussion of these particularities of identity in the essay, we may note the limits of self-parting as the condition of taste—marked, once more, with violence. On the one hand, in insisting on impartiality, Hume offers something like a critique of specular reflection. The pleasures of taste require a self-displacement that, at the least, ought to suspend the practice of evaluating cultural works on the basis of whether they mirror our own particular, naturalized norms, as if ours are the eyes for whom every work must have been calculated. Yet in returning to this issue Hume, on the other hand, lingers with perversity and halts a potentially unlimited movement toward others. At first he seems merely to concede that there are some pathological investments with which one ought to, but unfortunately cannot, part. Just as our psychological differences give us "a peculiar sympathy with the writer who resembles us," so too "we are more pleased, in the course of our reading, with pictures and characters, that resemble objects which are found in our own age and country." Since "it is almost impossible not to feel a predilection for that which suits our particular turn and disposition," Hume concludes, it would be vain to "endeavour to enter into the sentiments of others, and divest ourselves of those propensities, which are natural to us" (E, 243–44). In "The Rise of Arts and Sciences," in fact, he reassuringly points to the "mutual jealousy" that persists between states having a "great intercourse of arts and commerce" and that prevents one nation from laying down the "law . . . in matters of taste and reasoning": "The contagion of popular opinion spreads not so easily from one place to another. It readily receives a check . . . where it concurs not with prevailing prejudices" (E, 120). Hume, then, does not merely concede the vanity of certain efforts at self-parting in the face of the virtually irresistible pleasures of aesthetic perversity: he takes a stand against such sympathetic communication as spreading "contagion" and thereby as potentially transforming our prejudices. He counts on some irreducible and resistant "naturalization" of identity—especially national-historical identity—for a social order to function in the wake of displaced positions or departing traditions accompanying the global diffusion of arts and commerce.

Hume's reaffirmation of the particularities of identity and the aesthetics of specular reflection brings him back closer to Rousseau. As if directly responding to Hume as well as d'Alembert, Rousseau remarks in the *Let-*

ter to M. d'Alembert: "Man is one; I admit it! But man modified by religions, governments, laws, customs, prejudices, and climates becomes so different from himself that one ought not to seek among us for what is good for men in general, but only what is good for them in this time or that country."[31] Rousseau's assessment of theater and, more broadly, spectacle never leaves or returns to such particularized identities as if they were a point of departure. Rather, aesthetic pleasure is always a pleasure destined for and experienced by a particular national public that alone, therefore, will evaluate all cultural productions as always oriented toward it. Logically enough, the political priority of national identity in Rousseau's account demands public spectacles of national self-presentation.

When Hume returns to prejudice, he approaches Rousseau's argument without, however, following it to the end of the line where taste itself would be reduced to merely "the art of being knowing about petty things" [L'art de se connaître en petites choses] and where theater would need to disappear in deference to the *moeurs* of a community.[32] In Hume, morality does not foreclose taste from the outset but comes to interrupt a requisite movement of aesthetic self-displacement that, if let run its course, might break the particularized bonds of national-cultural identity. Hence a reversal occurs. Rather than attempting to reconcile all sentiments, Hume now in effect posits deviation from the beginning—certain identity-positions must necessarily be discordant. Moreover, these so-called "natural positions" must be retained and fortified—not imparted toward universal reconciliation—for Hume to claim that morality has predetermined the limits of taste. Occasionally in Homer and the Greek tragedians, he writes, "we are displeased to find the limits of vice and virtue so much confounded" that we "cannot, nor is it proper [we] should, enter into such sentiments" (*E*, 246). "Displeasure" as both disapproval and a feeling of pain marks the limit of impartiality as the condition of taste. *This* feeling of displeasure has the status of a sheer contingent fact of experience that, however, remains justly unimpartable. We might suspect here a temporal sleight of hand: perhaps *because* Hume wants to resist the movement toward others that could challenge the moral authority of certain national-cultural norms, he posits the priority of displeasure as sheer immovable fact of experience. In the essay "Of Moral Prejudices," for example, he objects to those critics who treat "public Spirit, and a Regard to our Country ... as chimerical and romantic" because, if their "Schemes" were "to take Place, all the Bonds of Society must be broke" (*E*, 538). In any case, Hume at this moment in the essay on taste resists the self-displacement that he had previously called for as a violence proper to counter prejudice:

But a very violent effort is requisite to change our judgment of manners, and excite sentiments of approbation or blame, love or hatred, different from those to which the mind from long custom has been familiarized. And where a man is confident of the rectitude of that moral standard, by which he judges, he is justly jealous of it, and will not pervert the sentiments of his heart for a moment, in complaisance to any writer whatsoever. (*E*, 247)

Hume sounds like the republican Rousseau once the polite arts threaten the *moeurs* of a people: Unlike in republics, he observes elsewhere, in "civilized monarchy" we develop a refined taste that cultivates our "wit, complaisance, or civility" and leads us "to resign our inclinations to those of our companion, and to curb and conceal that presumption and arrogance, so natural to the human mind" (*E*, 126). Yet there is a righteousness about one's national-cultural identity that cannot be changed without "a very violent effort." An affective marker of the limits of disidentification, the violence committed in displacing national conventions is regarded as improper. If standing with "natural positions" was previously responsible for the perversion of sentiment, here the imperative to part with these positions becomes an illegitimate command to "pervert the sentiments of the heart" in the name of a morally corrupt politeness. Hume makes an effort now to remind us not to forget that there are— that there ought to be—moral limits to crossing the borders between friend and enemy, native and foreigner.

The failure of the aesthetic in Hume marks the limits of universality as a claim of aesthetics itself. When certain cultural representations elicit displeasure rather than pleasure, they do not simply fall short of imparting the sentiment that aesthetically defines them as "good art" or that signals the "good taste" of the spectators. The inability of a tragedy, for instance, to aestheticize suffering might devalue the work for Hume, but it also signifies a failure to distinguish between the representation of suffering and the experience of suffering. The failure of a literary work to represent violence or pain aesthetically, with pleasure, is the failure of art and reality sufficiently to differentiate themselves from each other so that one might mimic the other: what fails is the affective difference between them and thus the possibility of an aesthetic mimesis. In this respect, the failure of the aesthetic relation to (the representation of) suffering or violence discloses the extent to which the naturalization of identity has already taken place and cannot be left behind through the movement toward universality. In the pain we feel at the representation of tragedy, we affectively find the selves we have already become. I phrase it this way to stress that aesthetic failure is the experience by which we come to this recognition of our self-identity and, for Hume, its "natural," pre-judicial constitution. We arrive at the limits of self-parting in experiencing the failure of cultural representations to become aesthetic. We do not necessarily know the "natural position" of our identity in advance of an encounter with (failed) cultural works, as if we are willing to depart from what we already know to be ourselves for a moment, but only up to a certain moral point. Rather, in the failure of the aesthetic we discover what identity we have naturally become at that moment in time and thus the self with which we cannot immediately part as merely a symbolic or discursive position.

The object of poetry, Hume had earlier declared in the essay on taste, is "to please by means of the passions and the imagination"; when he turns at the end to flawed examples of tragedy that displease instead, he refers to Corneille's *Polyeucte* and Racine's *Athalie* as plays in which religious opinions do not appear as negligible national-historical differences and thus have "disfigured two very fine tragedies" (*E*, 240, 248). In one respect, Hume's account of the aesthetic failure of these French tragedies might appear inconsistent. For what mars this drama is precisely that religion has been habituated into an identity-position that cannot be parted with: those religious principles take "strong possession of the heart" and do not comprise merely a "prevailing fashion" (*E*, 246–47)— as with Greek and Roman paganism, which, Hume claims elsewhere, "happily makes no . . . deep impression on the affections and understanding."[33] One could certainly imagine that religious sentiments would fall in the category of norms of judgment of which individuals are justly jealous and which they will not pervert even for a moment. On the other hand, the displeasure or pain elicited by such tragedy for Hume becomes the means to dissociate morality and religion: religious identities taken to heart "alter the natural boundaries of virtue and vice" because they "inspire a violent hatred of every other worship," instead of reconciliation (*E*, 247). Hence, as with the Koran, Hume finds it painful to read or attend a tragedy that endorses what he calls the "bigotry" of French Roman Catholicism, that "represent[s] all pagans, mahometans, and heretics as the objects of divine wrath and vengeance" (*E*, 247) and solicits the exclusive religious-political identification of the particular audience it mirrors. Unlike the plays of Shakespeare, which supply Laurence Sterne's sentimental Yorick with his passport to France in time of war, these tragedies cannot depart the shores of France and successfully cross the channel: "Such sentiments are received with great applause on the theatre of Paris," Hume notes, but not at London (*E*, 248). For Hume, then, we cannot move toward others, those strangers on stage or in the hypothetical audience, who refuse to relinquish the friend-enemy distinction, who refuse, in this respect, to be (human) like us.

The alignment of a moral critique of religion with the conditions of taste indicates the social work Hume looks to aesthetics to perform. In this civil society, national-cultural differences derived from sectarian identity-politics must be placed out of bounds. In this limit condition of aesthetics—the displeasure or pain of moral confusion that *cannot* and *ought not* be converted to pleasure through the pain or violence of self-displacement—we might read Hume's attempt to suspend political conflict via an aesthetic impartiality that must, however, exclude (certain) religious subjects as uncivil and inhuman. For Hume, the claim to universality entails the forgetting of religious identity as a political subject-position, and only religions compatible with such a demand—only those religions whose credo includes the forgetting of politics and whose faith is not taken politically to heart—may find inclusion in humanity. Put somewhat differently, to make a politics of religious subjectivity—or a religion of political and social subjectivity—is to emphasize the fundamentally antagonistic or conflictual claims of universality indissociable from these positions that Hume would prefer to relegate to mere particularisms. As Žižek has remarked of Judaism, Christianity, and Islam as equally religions of the book whose differences, however, cannot be reconciled without eliminating their identities: "each particularity involves *its own* universality, its own notion of the Whole and its own part within it; there is no 'neutral' universality which would serve as the medium for these particular positions" (*CHU*, 316). To impart them toward each other, to let them communicate sympathetically or through translations, would be potentially to infect them with a sickness unto death.

If the lines Hume cites from Racine's *Athalie* may be taken to indicate how this play and others fail aesthetically, we can say that what pains Hume is not only that the play seems to endorse the position that, for certain religions, political authority must be legitimated by a sectarian identification that (pre)judges all other religious subjects as enemies of the state. Although Hume's attack on the politics of "intemperate zeal" is one commonly mounted by British Protestantism in the period, the lines he singles out from *Athalie* stress, more interestingly, the pathology that zealotry ascribes to acts of speech that cross religious-political borders. What this play seems thereby to figure is not so much the refusal to anaesthetize or quarantine the political sentiment of hostility but the potential of sympathy to spread this sentiment and to transform and convert others. If the notion of humanity in aesthetics impels us to move toward the position of others to whom a play is addressed, we might enter into the sentiments of those for whom we and our friends are the enemies and possibly alter our "natural" but historically variable political affections. In light of this possibility, we can better understand why Hume refers to a scene in which Joad, the high priest of the Jews, denounces both his wife Josabet and Mathan, the emissary of Queen Athalia and the high priest of Baal, for engaging in conversation. Hume writes: " 'What is this,' says the sublime Joad to Josabet, finding her in discourse with Mathan, the priest of Baal, 'Does the daughter of David speak to this traitor? Are you not afraid, lest the earth should open and pour forth flames to devour you both? Or lest these holy walls should fall and crush you together? What is his purpose? Why comes that enemy of God hither to poison the air, which we breathe, with his horrid presence?' " [Vient-il infecter l'air qu'on respire en ce lieu?]' " (E, 248).[34]

Joad is "sublime" for Hume, we may surmise, insofar as he deploys the power of horror. The spectacle of Josabet and Mathan breathing the same air in conversation presents to Joad a threat of "infection" that might annihilate their different positions. Mere proximity to the enemy ought to elicit the recoil of horror. For God, according to his sublime priest, has friends and enemies, but the righteous run the risk of being devoured as sinners through the contagion of sympathetic communication—a risk Joad seeks to prevent by producing a horror that once again compels differentiation. However, Mathan responds to the spectacle that Joad stages to denounce his wife's transgression by remarking, as Hume himself might: "On reconnaît Joad à cette violence" [One recognizes Joad in this violence]. Racine, in fact, stresses at various moments in the play that horror is itself a kind of violence. Racine stages this recourse to the violence of difference as a desperate response to the doublings in the play— two high priests, two religions, and two monarchs, two nations that recoil in horror to preserve their preexisting antagonism despite, or because of, their shared lineage: this violence is all in the family. For instance, in the course of recounting her own "juste fureur" against the Jews in response to what she calls the "spectacle d'horreur" of seeing her mother, father, and numerous royal children killed, Athalia herself remarks to Josabet: "Enfin de votre Dieu l'implacable vengeance / Entre nos deux maisons rompit toute alliance: / David m'est en horreur et les fils de ce roi, / Quoique nés de mon sang, sont étrangers pour moi" [Finally, the implacable vengeance of your God broke every alliance between our two houses: David abhors me and the sons of this king, although born of my blood, are strangers for me] (2.7). And Athalia offers one reason why the royal race of David, although of her own blood, loathes her: Josabet and Joad transmit hate to their children by repeating the history of the Jews' suffering in which, she tells them, "Vous ne leur prononcez mon nom qu'avec horreur." Athalia and presumably Racine know that the historical representation of "malheurs" as a "spectacle d'horreur" can repeat violence by refusing to allow the moment of hostility to be imparted as a collective and recollected past.

In his essay on tragedy, Hume had also marked the limits of the pleasure taken in the representation of pain with regard to a moment of violence in another national conflict: the execution of Charles I. In Clarendon's narrative of the civil wars, Hume approvingly notes the historian's refusal to stage the king's death, the "catastrophe of the royal party," as "too horrid a scene to be contemplated . . . without the utmost pain and aversion" by the contemporary reader (*E*, 223). What resists aestheticization is not merely an action that might be "too bloody" and "excite movements of horror as will not soften into pleasure," as Hume explains with reference to tragedy and especially to paintings made "for churches and convents," which depict "such horrible subjects as crucifixions and martyrdoms, where nothing appears but tortures, wounds, executions, and passive suffering without any action or affection" (*E*, 224). It is not, I would suggest, the violence per se of "passive suffering" that cannot be aesthetically pleasurable; it is, rather, that this violence consecrates acts of sacrifice with political consequences. For "passive suffering" is associated by Hume in the *Natural History of Religion* with Catholicism as the religion that sanctifies absolute subjection instead of the subjugation of tyrants and the defense of one's native country, and it also names the central problematic in Corneille's *Polyeucte*: the possibility of conversion to Christianity that produces martyrs who take pleasure in suffering: "Tourmentés, déchirés, assasinés, n'importe, / Les supplices leur sont ce qu'à nous les plaisirs" [Tortured, mangled, murdered, whatever: agonies are to them (Christians) what pleasures are to us (Romans)].[35] In Hume's account of the conditions under which such violence would be aesthetically pleasing, we can, finally, see the projected community of taste as Hume's hope to manage political divisions associated not only with the religious enemy France but also, of course, with England's obstinate internecine conflicts, which belie the premise that enemies are other than friends or family and reside in some other place. The author and contemporary readers of the catastrophe of civil war in Clarendon's narrative, Hume explains, "were too deeply concerned in the events, and felt a pain from subjects, which an historian and a reader of another age would regard as the most . . . agreeable" (*E*, 224). Here, historical displacement allows the distinction between friend and enemy to be constituted in an act of memory by which we British (now) exist as such and are not (any longer) our own enemies. And in so doing, it turns civil war into a no-longer-present spectacle for a community of readers who can and ought to share in its pleasures. Aesthetics in Hume requires the present moment of political and social hostility to become a pleasing recollection of the past.

Vico, "Tenderness," and "Barbarism"

Riccardo Caporali

AFTER THE BRIEF PERIOD of Jacobin interpretations at the end of the eighteenth century,[1] all the elucidations of the nineteenth century and the first half of the twentieth explicitly denied the possibility of tracing a political intention or even, more simply, intonation in Vico's philosophy. For Croce, Vico was a beautiful spirit, "impartial and innocent," and politics was "above his head, like the heavens and the stars."[2] And even earlier Giuseppe Ferrari, the scrupulous editor of a complete edition of the works of the Neapolitan philosopher, had delivered his own judgment: "And of what use is the preciseness of the *Scienza Nuova* and the flight of its creator if it refuses to make any response to the questions of the century? So it behooves us to continue on our way with men who are less refined, but indubitably more illustrious."[3]

The acceptance that there is a political aspect to Vico's thinking has been relatively recent, emerging over the last few decades. Based essentially on the relationship between the development of his theoretical research and the historical vicissitudes of the time in which he lived (the tribulations of the Viceroyalty of Naples in the seventeenth and eighteenth centuries, with the passage from Spanish to Austrian rule), this new historiography has produced some brilliant analyses, especially of the early works, which are most amenable to such an approach: the seven *Orationes*, the lectures that Vico, as professor of rhetoric at Naples University, was required to give at the beginning of the academic year.[4] However, this method of research has proved less fruitful with respect to his main writings (the *Diritto Universale*, the three versions of the *Scienza Nuova*), where the echoes of the historical period grow more distant and blurred, and any role played by politics has to be sought independently, within the more general structures of Vico's philosophy. Indeed there have been attempts, in recent times, to respond to this need as well, with some important and commendable results, although these have been divergent and in certain cases even contradictory. A few have represented Vico as a realist and a disenchanted follower of Machiavelli (barely veiled by the prudence demanded by the place and time in which he lived), while the majority have painted him as an orthodox Catholic, hostile to any form of modernity.[5] This work sets out to investigate the connections between "politics and sentiments" in the *Scienza Nuova*. The hypothesis on which this exploration is based is that it is precisely through such connections—which have almost always been ignored by scholars[6]—that light can be thrown on the actual nature of Vico's *philosophia civilis*.

If we were to judge purely by the frequency with which the terms are used, there would certainly be no way to make a comparison between *tenerezza* ("tenderness")[7] and *barbarie* ("barbarism") in the *Scienza Nuova*. Sticking to the definitive version of Vico's masterpiece (that of 1744), the first word appears four times, the second fifty-six.[8] This fact, this evident quantitative discrepancy, would be enough to underline the sporadic and secondary presence of the one with respect to the conceptual prominence assigned to the other, intended to indicate the central problem of the work: the problem of an ideal "course," starting out from the "common nature of nations," that unfolds from the crude and primitive—but positive and constructive—origins of a "primitive" or "greater barbarism" only to end in decline and crisis, in the far more negative and destructive "return of barbarism" (or also, as it is put repeatedly, the "second" or "last" barbarism). And yet—this is the hypothesis that is going to be presented here—it is precisely in "tenderness" that it may be possible to identify a goal, an objective and point of arrival, in Vico's long research into the emotional and passionate dimension of human nature: an investigation that, coming in its turn at the conclusion of the Neapolitan philosopher's entire reflection on "civilization," ends emblematically with "tenderness" in order to embrace an alternative, a positive and appositive pole to "barbarism."

TENDERNESS

Tenderness makes its first appearance in the second edition of the *Scienza Nuova*, that of 1730: "Once sovereignty had passed from the nobles to the people, the plebeians began to measure their strength, wealth, and power by the number of their offspring, who, until they were married, were considered the fruit and benefit of their fathers, and the laws began to instill in them a tenderness for their own blood, and the praetors began to regard it as *bonorum possessio*, starting to remedy faults, or defects of testaments in order to spread abroad wealth, which is the only thing the common people admire."[9] The passage—like the other three added in the last edition—is inserted in book 4, dedicated to the "Corso che fanno le nazioni" ("The Course of Nations"), and specifically the chapter in which Vico deals with the "Custodia degli ordini" ("The Guarding of Social Orders"): with the fierce, unyielding defense of the aristocratic regime by the "father-heroes" against the "men" (the *famuli*, the "servant-foreigners"). It is an armed defense, founded on the conviction of the natural superiority of the nobles (who considered themselves of divine origin since they were the offspring of solemn marriages, sanctified by the augurs, rather than of the bestial couplings reserved for plebeians), of the prerogatives and privileges of the *patres*: marriages, as we were saying, and then the right to be judge or priest, and thus the laws themselves, considered sacred, an expression-command of the divine will. In this specific case, the subject is the "testamentary laws": something that immediately excludes any "lyrical" interpretation of the theme of tenderness, setting it instead, as always happens in Vico, in an ethical and political dimension. Drawing very freely on his sources—in this case Roman law—he argues that the heroic republics only provided for "legitimate successions," for bequests rigidly regulated within the order of the fathers, excluding "testamentary" ones, expressions of an individual will that permitted dispersion and, above all, "inheritance" even by nonnobles. This was done to prevent the distribution of wealth (the "hallowed" possession of land), by its fragmentation among the "masses," and through this the dispersion of "power" (985).[10] Free inheritance was, in a manner of speaking, a threat to the property ("ownership"), family ties ("kinship"), and nobility ("clanship") of the aristocracy (987). And anyone who sought to introduce it was immediately and ruthlessly eliminated. The "magnanimous" Spartan king Agis, who attempted to "free" the "poor plebeians of Lacedaemon" with a law that allowed bequests to be made outside the circle of the *patres*, met a sad fate: "the ephors had him strangled" (668).[11] The origins of the nation were clearly based on a utilitarian process, although—it must be pointed out straightaway—they were not shaped and concluded by that process alone. The "public good" was originally literally the "patria," that is, the "concern of a few fathers" (677): born out of the alliance of the "lords" in defense of their "family monarchies" and against rebellious servants, the first *universal*, the first form of political authority, was the determined preservation of an advantage ("wealth and power") that did not allow departures from or attacks on its own proud solidarity: to the point where this pervaded—as we shall see shortly—the whole identity, the entire emotional world of the heroes.

Even the plebeians spoke the language of advantage. It was, at the beginning, little more than a growl, and then a roar: the rebellion against "labor," repressed by the fathers united for the purpose in a "republic." Servants had no legal standing, and were therefore strictly barred from any form of ownership or civil protection; not even their offspring were "legally" recognized as theirs. Once "sovereignty" had passed "from the nobles to the people," however, the labor of their children became their "fruit and benefit": that is, profit not yet positively "disciplined," a natural and spontaneous benefit, not yet prescribed and guaranteed by "law"; and one that for this very reason opened the way to something unprecedented, not envisaged and not established, something that was not "required." It led to "tenderness for their own blood," a changeable and indefinite feeling, that in turn was immediately translated into desire for "form," into the aspiration to a recognition of "principle." Among the fathers, "legitimate" succession, the rule of "inheritance," responded to the passion for the wealth-power of the "whole," to the absolute priority of the collective power of the class; among the plebeians, the demand for the "testament" came in dribs and drabs, out of their love for their children.

Now we come to the addition made in 1744, to the paragraph in question: ". . . and so began to feel tenderness for their own blood. By contrast, the plebeians of heroic cities had not felt such affection. Plebeian fathers had only begotten children into slavery; indeed, the nobles forced them to mate so that the offspring were born in the springtime, when they would be more healthy and even robust. . . . Plebeian mothers in turn must have hated rather than loved children who occasioned the pains of childbirth and inconveniences of nursing without offering them any joy or benefit in life" (994).[12] It is worth pointing out, in this connection, the further, marked accentuation of the material sources of the feelings. In the 1730 version, the phrase "the laws began to instill in them a tenderness for blood" might have given rise to the misunderstanding that a structured emotionality already existed among servants in the aristocratic state, but was only legally recognized with the subsequent advent of the popular republic. The definitive reading of 1744 eliminates this potential ambiguity by resorting to a more immediate and explicit "began to feel the tenderness for blood." Above all, this follows the bleak reference to the hatred of plebeian mothers for offspring generated under conditions of alienation and coercion, who brought them nothing but "pain" and "inconvenience." Love for children arose from the moment their mothers began to derive from them "any joy or benefit in life." There was a benefit that produced, that prompted pleasure and tenderness. It was not, however, the benefit of the heroes. In the world of the fathers there was no tenderness. Not for the plebeians. But not even for themselves, for the "lords": "Indeed, there is no reason to believe that heroic fathers felt any familial tenderness, since all the evidence points to the contrary" (991).[13] Tenderness was an achievement of the age of men.

After losing Briseis, Achilles "makes outcries which both fill heaven and earth, and provide the entire plot of the *Iliad*"; and yet he never shows "the slightest feeling of amorous passion at losing her." And Menelaus, "who mobilizes all of Greece against Troy on Helen's account," never displays "even the smallest sign of a lover's anguish or jealousy of Paris, who has stolen Helen and enjoys her" (708). There is no love in the first two ages of the nations—an absence that takes on the significance of a limit beyond which the time of the "fathers-heroes" could not go, in the "accomplishment" of *humanitas*, of the nature of men. Nor was it the only thing missing.

It goes without saying that the extraordinary regenerative function of this age, the indispensable creative action of the age of consciousness and imagination, is not in question. Without the reaction to the frightening burst of thunder, no escape from the "bestial wandering": no remedy for that savage condition into which the "pagans" rapidly descended, scattering through the "great forest" of the earth after the Flood. Without that paralyzing terror, no awakening from the primitive torpor in which such early men, "stupid, insensate, and horrid beasts" were steeped (374). An instinctive attempt to give meaning to fear, to contain the excruciating pangs of *timor*, the imagined god of lightning, the deafening and booming command of Jupiter, corresponds to "nature," to the beginning-nascence (147) of humanity, beyond the blind wandering of the beast, which in search of grazing and water has lost its upright condition and its view of the sky. Without the fiction of this crude and superstitious *religio* of the fathers and the heroes, there was no redemption from the "abominable state": no principle of "order," no morality and virtue, no possibility of civil aggregation. The passage from brutish wandering to the first barbarism of consciousness is not, really, even that, it is not a true *passage*: not a transition (a transfer and a point of arrival, an outcome) but a clean break, a radical transformation, a new start. A great and crucial experience, and yet—and here is an invalidating point—transitory, marked from the outset by the necessity-inevitability of its own surmounting. The reconstruction of the common nature of the nations requires "the mighty effort to summon up a form of society and of humanity."[14] It means sinking into the dawn of civilization—precisely where Vico, in addition to philosopher and metaphysician, becomes a brilliant "anthropologist."[15] The excavation into the "dark mythical age" does not lead, however, to the celebration of its primacy. The decoding of myth does not end up in the mythical exaltation of myth itself. The eulogy of primitive barbarism is also, at the same time, its obituary.[16]

BARBARISM

> The founders of pagan antiquity must have descended from the races of Ham, Japheth, and Shem, who one by one gradually renounced the true religion of their common father Noah. This religion was the only bond which kept them within human society, both in the union of marriage and hence in their family groups. When they renounced it and began to couple promiscuously, they dissolved their marriages and dis-

persed their families. In this way, they began to wander like brutes through the earth's great forest. . . . They were scattered widely as they fled from the wild beasts which abounded in the great forest, and as they pursued women who in that state were wild, timid, and intractable. And they were further separated as they sought pasture and water. (369)

To describe the bestial regression of the "pagan" races after the Flood, Vico resorts to terms that can essentially be traced back to three main semantic areas: "movement," "solitude," and "disorder." "Brutish wandering" (17), "with brutish wandering or migration" (13), "wandering in brutish and abominable error" (336), "to survive by fleeing" (1098), "drifting" (1099): for moving he uses the words *errare* (meaning both to wander and to err), *vagabondare*, to roam (*empi vagabondi*, "impious nomads") (561) and *sbandare* (to scatter). It is a blind and instinctive instability in which they lose themselves and their goal: "the brutish wandering . . . had scattered and dispersed them through the earth's great forest" (22).[17] Whence the isolation, the loss of all *societas*: "mothers abandoned their children, they grew up without hearing any human speech, or learning any human behavior" (369); the primitive brutes are "solitary and aimless" (62), "weak, drifting, and solitary people" (§1099), all alone, and therefore "weak, and hence miserable and unhappy" (17). Far from leading to the Cartesian cogito, solitude produces bestial regression. The absence of relations results in a loss of identity and certainty, inducing silence ("mute beasts," "lacking human customs and speech" [230 and 62]), in the dark ("obscure because it lacked the civil light," "civil night, night of names" [688]), in oblivion: "for such men left no name of themselves to their posterity" [717]). Anonymous, devoid of sure references and genuine awareness, the brutish wandering is what the poetic wisdom of the fathers-heroes would later call Chaos ("confusion of human seeds in the abominable age when women were shared promiscuously"), or the Orcus: "a formless monster that devoured all things. For people born in this abominable promiscuity lacked the proper form of human beings; and without any certain offspring, they were 'swallowed up' by the void, leaving no trace of themselves." Brutish wandering is the liquid state of Proteus, whom Ulysses fights without being able to seize hold of him, because he "keeps changing shape." Humanity sinks into a "formless" state, "greedy for forms": such as to consume—in its unceasing instability, in its continual mutability—"all forms" (688).[18]

The abrupt, immediate interruption of the "wandering" was the first effect produced by the terror of the thunder god. An instantaneous effect, enforced, violent, and irresistible. The trembling sense of wonder aroused by the horrible spectacle of lightning annihilated the primitive: it restrained it, concealed it: "Moral virtue began, as it must, from a conscious effort. Chained under the mountains by their frightful religion of thunder-bolts, the giants checked their bestial habit of wandering wild through the earth's great forest. Completely reversing their customs, they now settled down" (504). To "humble themselves" to a deity was the only way "to end their bestial wandering through the earth's forests" (1097). It was the only way of "casting them down" (387), of "sending them under-ground" (399), of binding them to the "immobility" of the earth. Fear produced the first religion: not someone's conscious deception of some-one else, but the spontaneous, naturally "providential" capacity to believe and imagine. "Primos in orbe deos fecit timor": drawing on Statius (and Lucretius), Vico appropriates a classical argument used by freethinking critics of religion, although with the objective of using it in favor of reli-gion itself, but only on the front of its indispensable civil function: a sort of twofold "movement" that conveys the complexity, perhaps even the deviousness, of the concept. Atheism, in any case, was "stupidity and folly"; without the binding power of *religio*, there would never be any humanization. Jupiter "ordered": he commanded by putting in order. The "pauci quos aequus amavit Iupiter" were placed "in conatus": not—in Hobbesian, Spinozistic terms—in the open and spontaneous condition of effort, of potentially inertial energy aimed at its own conservation, but in control of themselves, in a position to check the immediate drives of the body, first of all "their urge to sexual intercourse" (§1098): "At first, a small number of the hardiest people withdrew from the abominable state of the lawless world and founded families, with whom and for whom they placed fields under cultivation" (248). Thus the early fathers were "prudent" ("in making sacrifices in order to 'procure' omens, that is, to interpret them properly"), "temperate" ("by virtue of their marriages") and "also possessed fortitude," owing to their habit of cultivating the fields (14).[19] It was a crude and primitive virtue, very different from that of philosophers and "authors of romances"; a "savage and superstitious" morality, produced by the senses, "which combined religion and cruel savagery"—although the only one, unlike the sterility of atheism, capable of showing the way out of the forest, toward the "most brilliant nations" (§438, 516–18). Nothing to do, in short, with the "innocence" of the "golden age," with the "gallant heroism" haughtily fantasized by the learned of later times (§708 and 1079): that virtue was the religion of the Scythians, who planted a knife in the ground and worshiped it as a god; it was a "fanatical superstition which, by means of the powerful terror their imagined deity inspired, held in moral check the savage, proud, and ferocious men of the early pagan world" (518). "Settled," "hidden and settled," "kept and settled." In contrast to the transient motility of the brutish, the virtue of the fathers was condensed in "fixity": in aggrega-tion, in conservation, in the defense of the "certain" and the "closed" in order to overcome the isolation and the dispersion of the uncertain, of the open. The danger of the relapse into the disorder of brutish wandering was the hero's obsession: "As political thinkers point out, this form of state [i.e., the aristocratic-heroic republic] consists entirely in safeguarding its boundaries and orders. In this way, the very form of government induces newly civilized peoples to continue to live within these restrictions, and thus to forget the infamous and abominable promiscuity of their bestial and brutish state" (629). The ungraspable mutability of the formless gave way to the order of "grasping," of forcing. The lands were conquered, "physically occupied by the giants," and then defended with arms from the incursion of the brutes still living in the abominable state. Similarly wives were "manucaptae" by the violence with which the giants "dragged [them] into their caves": kept "as a necessity of nature for bearing children" and, "in other respects," treated as slaves (510 and 671). Finally, this physical oppression also produced "despotic dominion," absolute "sovereign power" over offspring and *famuli*, the weakest of the still wandering primitives, who had taken refuge in the lands of the fathers in search of protection and were accepted on the proviso that they "serve the heroes as journeymen" (555 and 556). This force was legitimized through patronage and, above all, through the very exercise of supremacy and command. However, the final, irreversible guarantee of the "grasping," of the ordering "grip," was, in the last resort, only death: "Later, the pious giants who settled in the mountains must have noticed the stench which arose from the corpses of their dead as they rotted on the ground nearby, and must have begun to bury their dead . . . The pious giants imbued their tombs with such great religious awe, or fear of the divine, that the Latin expression *locus religiosus*, hallowed ground, came primarily to mean a cemetery" (529). "Fixed" as a mark of burial, the tomb "slabs" were "the trunk of a genealogical tree" (530). The tombs assured (ascertained, made fixed and certain) the identity of the giants: "'sons of the earth,' or descendants of the buried dead," and "nobles," because they were "humanely engendered in fear of divinity" (13).[20] "Humanitas" from *humare* ("to bury"), according to one of Vico's many fanciful but ingenious etymologies: mixed forever with the earth, finally transformed "into earth," the bodies of the ancestors are presented as the first "shields," the first "arms," the first line of defense of lineage and of the fields (12 and 529). The frightening liquidity, the insidious sliminess of life is given shape by death. The inexorable stillness, the inescapable immutability of death founds and protects the order of life.[21] An unyielding order, incessantly evoked, continually nurtured by exigencies of death. The "certain," the definite, requires mutilation and sacrifice: here Vico turns to Livy's examples of Scaevola, who "places his right hand in the fire for failing to kill Porsena, which so unnerves the Etruscan king that he is put to flight"; or of people like Marcus Curtius, who throw themselves "mounted and armed, into fatal chasms"; or of the Decii, "father and son, [who] sacrifice themselves to save their armies"; or of Atilius Regulus, who "returns to certain and cruel death in Carthage in order to preserve the sanctity of Roman oaths" (668). Often the violation of order required renunciation of the most precious thing of all, of the greatest investment in the continuity of life and form. The flouting of order demanded the sacrifice of one's children: when "the ancient Phoenicians were threatened by some great disaster like war, famine, or plague, the kings sacrificed their own children to placate the anger of heaven." And the Carthaginians, their descendants, "after their defeat by Agathocles of Syracuse, . . . sacrificed 200 noble children to placate their gods," while "Agamemnon's votive sacrifice of his daughter Iphigeneia" testifies to the existence of "this impious piety" even among the Greeks: "This will surprise no one who considers the Cyclopean paternal power of the first fathers of the pagan world, which was practiced by the Greeks, who were the wisest. In both nations, fathers had the right to kill their new-born children" (517). "To disdain and risk their lives" was the objective at which the education of boys was aimed among the Spartans, who "in order to teach their sons to fear neither pain nor death, . . . caned them in the temple of Diana, often so severely that they fell dead, convulsed with pain under their fathers' blows" (670 and 673). "Possessing limited intelligence, but endowed with vast imaginations and violent passions" (708): the primitive perception of the fathers "with inner distress and disturbance" (218), their vague and confused ability to feel and suffer, desire and think, is subsumed within the "whole" of the divine order from which it stems. It is a sort of holism with its roots in theology and the imagination that pulls the strings of the "hero," that sums up his whole nature in the demands of the "part," of his role as "hero." Terrible, ruthless demands: no hesitation in Brutus, who "beheaded his two sons for plotting to restore Tarquinius as king of Rome"; no vacillation in Manlius, "nicknamed the Imperious," who "beheaded his valiant son for fighting and winning a battle against his father's orders" (517). There is no difference between the "role" and the "actor," no gap (distinction, break) between the "function" and the "person," just the exigencies of an ethics dictated by seizing, by occupying. Achilles represents the prototype of this virtue. To the dying Hector who wanted to negotiate his own burial, the Greek hero replies contemptuously that wolves and lions do not come to terms with lambs: leaving unburied the corpses of enemies killed in battle would be like canceling them out forever, consigning their descendants to the "night of names." When Briseis is taken away from him, the Achaean prince abandons the war, wishing for the ruin of both Greeks and Trojans, rejoicing in the slaughter of his companions by Hector, mourning the slave girl even after his death and finding peace only when Priam's daughter Polyxena is sacrificed on his tomb: sacrifice and death, once again, are the characteristics of a "punctilious and haughty" code, which recognizes honor but knows nothing of tenderness and love: "Since such behavior can only be found in people who have the mental weakness of children, the vigorous imagination of women, and the seething passions of violent youth, we must deny that Homer possessed any esoteric wisdom" (787). "Children," "the young," "women": in the semantic universe of Vico, transitory (or at least partial, imperfect) states, foreshadowing or implying further advances, more definitive "accomplishments." The barbarism of the senses, the age of the heroes, is not the culmination of the course of the nation.

HUMANITY

The "fixity" of primitive barbarism made it possible to emerge from "abominable confusion," but in the long term became an obstacle to be overcome in order to move on to other developments, further spreading of the "human seeds" (388). The impetus for change, the mainspring of transformation, is always advantage: "Because of their corrupt nature, people are tyrannized by self-love, and so pursue their own advantage above all else. Seeking everything that is useful for themselves and nothing for their companions, they cannot subject their passions to the conscious impulse that directs them to just ends" (341). No possibility of control, no capacity for order and restraint of the "passions," except by starting out from the still myopic horizon, the still narrow prospect—in its turn passionate—of immediate advantage, of a profit that is all the more impelling, all the more pressing, the easier it is to perceive and experience: "People naturally enter a feudal system of benefices, *benefizi*, when they see that it maintains or increases their personal advantages: for these are the benefits, *benefizi*, one hopes to derive from civil life" (260). On the other hand, this spontaneous inclination toward advantage ends up becoming a particular "means," a "limited goal" at the service of a broader and "greater" purpose (1108): "In his bestial state, a man loves only his own well-being. After he takes a wife and has children, he continues to love his own well-being, and comes to love the well-being of his family as well. After he enters civil life, he comes to love the well-being of his city. After his city extends its rule over other peoples, he comes to love the well-being of his nation. And after such nations are united through war, peace, alliances, and trade, he comes to love the well-being of the entire human race. In all these contexts, the individual continues to love his own advantage above all else" (341).[22] The direct pursuit of advantage turns out teleologically to be at the service of those potentialities, of those natural propensities for expansion that, providentially instilled into human nature by God, are not contained in that direct pursuit. Vico clearly distinguishes and separates the "extraordinary help" that divine providence reserves for "sacred history" (for the Jewish people, continually and directly guided and "guarded" by the hand of God), from the "natural" and "ordinary help" given to profane history (313), to that progress of the "pagan" nations which in reality constitutes the true and principal subject of his masterpiece.[23] So the new science is, from this perspective, "a rational civil theology of divine providence" (2): "civil," insofar as it is concerned with the function of civilization that *religio* performs in the development of *humanitas*; and "rational," insofar as it is extraneous to the extemporaneous, exceptional character of the "miracle" (well-nigh absent, in the "course of nations") and capable of reflecting the regularity, the constancy of a *natural* action of Providence: capable, in fact, of explaining the dynamics of "ordinary" help in terms of "logic," of the rules of "science."[24]

Not "like a tyrant," or by "counsel of superhuman wisdom," but as a "queen," which "instead followed human customs," Providence always "arranged human institutions so that this same self-interest led people, even through these different and contrary ways, to live with justice like *human beings* and to remain in society" (2, 525, 1107). From the confused and scattered individual to the ordered world of the nations, from the poetic superstition of the oracles to the "truth" of philosophy: "natural" Providence—ultimately the power of expansion and transformation given by God to men—takes their passions beyond their own, limited designs: "Thus, people seek to satisfy their bestial lust and abandon their offspring, but they establish the chastity of marriage, from which families arise. Fathers seek to exercise immoderate paternal authority over their clients, but they subject them to the civil powers which create cities" (1108). This is a perspective focusing entirely on the "profane," and thus excluding from the course of the nations any eschatological or millenarian dimension. The "ordinary help" of Providence was aimed exclusively at the "survival" of nations: Providence endowed men "fallen into the condition of beasts" with the "acutest senses," "for their survival"; it "created a new civil order together with the cities" from the uprisings of the clients, "for the survival of the human race." Providence spread to ever broader spheres of sociality and rationality in order "to preserve human society," "to preserve the human race on the earth" (341, 707, 1100, 1108).[25]

An expression of fear, heroism arises from the imagination of the universal: from the command of Jupiter, who "fills" everything. *Iovis omnia plena*: everything exists inasmuch as it is impregnated, as it is "filled" by Jupiter. The "perfect civilization," on the other hand, has its distant origins in the characteristics of a restricted utility, of a particular, material aspiration: during the age of the gods (the age of families), "the family servants were barred from owning land, and [since] all the estates were in the hands of the nobles, they grew tired of constantly serving their lords. After many years, they finally rose up in rebellion" (20). Forced by the father "to perform a long and arduous labor" (583), the servants in the end resisted him, breaking away from his unique order. From "labor" to "rebellion": the immediate urgency, the impelling need to alleviate the physical suffering of the servant's toil served as a first kernel of identity of the *famuli*, an autonomous point of coagulation irreducible to their original state of being nothing but a "thing," to the initial not being other than "part" of the father. The result was twofold: the birth, on the one hand, of the aristocratic republics, created out of the union of the heroes to deal with "the masses of rebellious family servants," forcing them into obedience again; and the concession to the servants of a "bonitary owner-ship" of land, the recognition of a limited and temporary possession of their fields, "under the burden of the census and under the obligation of serving the patricians in wartime at their own expense" (107). Above all, it was an ownership that remained theirs only "at the pleasure of the heroes" (25, 264, 584, 597). The heroic republic, the city-state, was born "by force of arms" (25) out of the conflict of the fathers-gods and the masses: the first war, the first *polemos* in the history of the world. "The first cities, then, were composed solely of the nobles who governed them," and so "the servants merged to form the first plebeians of the heroic cities, in which they had none of the privileges of citizenship" (597). The order of the few who commanded and the multitude of the many, subordinate, who obeyed: these are the two parts that comprise "the subject of political studies"; and they are, above all, the "two invariable and opposite princi-ples which spring from the nature of human civil institutions. (1) The plebeians always wish to change the form of government, and are in fact the ones who change it. (2) By contrast, the nobles always wish to main-tain the *status quo*" (264 and 609). "And are in fact the ones who change it": the destiny of the heroic state is written in its very nature, charted by its very nascence: "almost every nation underwent this political process [the fall of the heroic republics]" (55).

Dictated by "benefits and needs," the aspirations and acquisitions of the plebeians consolidated a new reality, a partial and nuclear sphere that clashed with the cohesive universal of the fathers, and that eventually destroyed it. With the second agrarian law the *famuli* were granted "quiri-tary ownership" of their fields, that is, full dominion over them, protected from the arbitrary will of the nobles and sanctioned by a written law (in Rome—the paradigmatic example for Vico—the so-called law of the "Twelve Tables"). A further and decisive step came with the attainment of the right to "marriage," claimed by the plebeians in order to be able to hand down those possessions that, although now recognized as their property, could not be bequeathed to their children: "When plebeians died, they could not leave their fields intestate to their kin. For they had no direct heirs and no relatives on either the father's or mother's side, since all these relations depend on solemn nuptials. Nor could they dispose of their fields by testament, since they lacked citizenship" (598). Originating from aspirations like these, in matters of "private" law, the recognition of marriages, the concession of the unions hitherto reserved solely for patricians, corresponded in reality to the extension of citizenship to plebeians. From the census of Servius Tullius to the Twelve Tables and the *lex Canuleia*, the struggle of the plebs was a contest for "wealth," for land, for the possession of fields. Likewise, the subsequent battles for the right to become consuls and priests did not stem from political aspirations, for example—as Vico himself had postulated, in his *Diritto Universale* ("Universal Law"), following in the footsteps of Machiavelli[26]—from the manifest and lofty ambition of attaining the post of magistrate, but from the need to cancel out the last vestiges of the *jus nexi*, of the ancient personal and physical bondage.[27] The struggle for public "honors" was a titanic battle, a hard and bitter clash over labor, its ownership and freedom from subjugation. It was precisely through these immediate exigencies of interest (first the natural and then the legal possession of fields, its inheritability, debt, and the freedom of the body) that the plebeians succeeded in conquering and destroying the heroic state.

"As many years passed and the human mind advanced, the plebeians eventually had second thoughts about the vain claims of nobility" (1101). The growth of the "part" consumed the "whole." The consolidation of an unprecedented "private" shattered the "public." The spilling over of the particular well beyond the functions initially reserved for it by the universal swept away its essence and existence: "The plebeians of the heroic cities now grew numerous and warlike besides, which frightened the fathers, who must have been very few in a commonwealth comprising so few citizens. By the force of their numbers, the plebeians began to enact laws without senate authority, so that the commonwealths changed from aristocratic to democratic" (1006). This was not a merely *quantitative* change, with the entry of "all" or the "majority" into the former government of the "few." Born out of the particular, it was in fact a new form of the universal, a new distribution of relations and functions between the universal and the particular: "Under this popular liberty, the whole Roman people now constituted the city. As a result, civil ownership lost its proper meaning of public ownership, which had been called civil from the word city, and was instead divided and distributed among the private ownerships of all the Roman citizens now making up the city of Rome"

(621). A dismembering and reassembly of the "public" through the "private." In contrast with the single (holistic, organicist) track of the heroic republic, popular liberty ran on the double track of a "public wealth" that, on the one hand, "is divided into small shares according to the number of citizens," but on the other is re-formed into a unity (a *res-publica*), precisely and solely through them, precisely and solely through the spontaneous fitting together, the ever-shifting intermingling, the actual convergence of the "small shares" (951). The free republic was a direct, nonrepresentative democracy. It was a full, immediate recognition of natural equality and, at the same time, of the inevitably relational character of every advantage and necessity (of every *inter-esse*): "natural equity," which expanded "in free commonwealths. In these, each person seeks his own particular good, which is in fact the same for all, so that the people are inadvertently led to enact universal laws. Hence, they naturally desire laws which are generously flexible when applied to specific circumstances that call for the distribution of equal benefits" (39). This peculiar meeting of advantage, individuality, and universality gave rise to "logic" and "sentiments," broadening the horizons of both passion and reason. And so, on the one hand, "democracies love children" (996), completing the emergence of a now free and "benign" affectivity that went well beyond the seething automatisms, the conditioned and violent reflexes of heroism. And so, on the other, the plebeians dismantled poetic knowledge, dismembered theological myth under the blows of a reason whose critical and causative force grew in step with its "prosaic" requirements, with its "vernacular" demands. This process acquired a complete consciousness of itself through "philosophy." "In order for Socrates to sketch his intelligible general categories or abstract universals, he must have observed how the citizens of Athens passed laws by agreeing on a common notion of equal benefit to all." And "it was by observing" how "in civic assemblies, individuals passionately pursue their own private advantage, but they all dispassionately agree on a notion of their common advantage" that "Plato raised himself to contemplate the highest intelligible ideas of created minds" (1040 and 1041). And the Solonian *nosce te ipsum* ("know thyself") was finally transformed from the battle cry of the plebeians in their conquest of the heroic state into a universal principle of equality of the "rational humanity which is the true and proper nature of mankind" (973). Philosophy was born "in the public square in Athens" (1043) and at once assumed great importance owing to the power of that "square," its possibilities of persistence. Democracy was built on the death of Jupiter: on the definitive revelation of the arcanum, on the dismemberment of any theological foundation, external to the human, of political power. The extraordinary power of "popular liberty" was fostered by a functional (no longer metaphysical, no longer substantial) convergence of the particular and the universal, of the individual and the state. Vico's "age of men" spoke the language of modernity. Emancipated from theological myth, this spontaneous mechanism, this immediate combination brought to light the abstract "universal" of philosophy, which in turn explained and justified it, revealed it to be "true" and "just," insofar as it was more consonant with the "accomplishment" of human nature: "For since virtuous actions no longer sprang from religious feelings, philosophy had to make virtues intelligible in ideal form" (1101). The effect of "citizenship," through philosophy. The "dispassionateness," the "rationality" of the public was continually fostered by the recognition, by the admission of the equal insurmountability of all "private" passions. No intellectualism. And no moralism: no superimposition of culture (or "value") on the mechanism of public convergence. Less a government of philosophers than ever. Rather it was the mechanism itself that, at the height of its power, broadened the civil truths of philosophy, popularized them, translating them into "common sense," into "an unreflecting judgment shared" by a whole nation (260). Morality, if anything: ethics and culture as a shared commitment that, insofar as it was universal, was fostered by differences (emblematically, "the love for children"), accumulating them and diffusing them.

The whole of book 4 of the *Scienza Nuova* makes explicit this system, in which the first two periods are the preparation and anticipation of the third, the culminating moment, the true zenith in the history of the "nation." Vico proceeds in the sociological manner, using tripartite thematic juxtapositions: three sorts of nature, three sorts of costume, law, government, language, and so on. But it is, quite clearly, an *ironic*, shrewd and deliberate approach, which *evaluates* at the same time as it *recounts*. As a professor of rhetoric, he is well aware (before all those bloodless, analytical enervations) how *prescriptive* the apparent objectivity of a *descriptive* exposition can be. Let us look at some of the most significant examples. Nature: if "the first human nature was a poetic or creative nature produced by the powerful illusions of the imagination, which is most vigorous in people whose powers of reasoning are weakest," the second "was a heroic nature, based on the heroes' belief in their own divine origin. Since they considered the gods responsible for all things, the heroes regarded themselves as sons of Jupiter, under whose auspices they had been begotten." The third, however, is "truly human or civilized nature, which is intelligent, and hence moderate, benign, and reasonable. This nature is guided by the laws of conscience, reason, and duty" (916–18). Law: if the first law was "divine, by which people believed that their lives and affairs depended on the gods," and the second that of "force . . . tempered by religion," the third is "human law which is dictated by fully developed human reason" (922–24). Language: "the first was the divine and conceptual language expressed by wordless religious acts, or divine ceremonies," and the "second language used heroic emblems, in which arms are expressive." They were followed by the "third language [using] articulate speech, which is employed by all of today's nations" (929–31). Customs: "imbued with religion"; "punctilious, like those described in Achilles"; "dutiful, taught us by our sense of civil duty" (919–21). Jurisprudence: the first was "divine wisdom," a "mystical theology . . . whose sages were the theological poets, the first sages of the pagan world"; the second, "heroic jurisprudence," "taking precautions by the use of certain proper words." This second type of jurisprudence is "the wisdom of Homer's Ulysses, who always speaks so cleverly that he gets what he wants without breaking his word." The third is "human jurisprudence," which "examines the truth of the bare facts and which generously bends the strict principles of laws as equity dictates" (938–40). And finally "government": the first governments were "divine," in which "people believed that the gods ordained all things"; the second were "heroic," that is, "civil rights were all restricted to the ruling orders of the heroes, because their birth, regarded as divine in origin, gave them a noble nature"; the third "human," in which "the equality of our intelligent human nature makes everyone equal under the law" (925–27). "To believe" and "to be" are the antitheses around which the whole structure of this book is built, indicating the progress of the nations from a close-knit and heteronomous order, founded essentially on superstitious and authoritarian subordination (on the belief that people were in Jupiter's hands, on the force-superiority that derived from considering themselves commanded by Zeus the Thunderer), to one autonomously based on human power, through the full and rational manifestation of liberty and equality, "the true and proper nature of mankind." "Barbarism" is "ferocious," "monstrous," "prideful," and "punctilious." "Perfect civilization" (but this is too loose a translation of Vico's expression "compiuta umanità": it does not convey fully the idea of "completion" or "fulfillment," of the "humanity" that is "fulfilled," that reaches its highest level of development) is "generous," "moderate," "benign," and "reasonable" (7, 38, 338, 517, 584, 636, 918).[28] Vico contrasts the fear, exclusiveness, and secrecy of barbarism with the "candor" (769), "generosity," and "magnanimity" of the popular republics; the immutable fixity of the fathers ("kept and settled," tied to the overwhelming power of Zeus and the earth) with the versatile acuity of democracy, which ventures into the unknown of the "sea," into the uncertain but hopeful mobility of "commerce"; the proud virtue of heroism, dominated by sacrifice and death, with the conquest of new sentiments, which exalt life.

Of course, not even the free republics are immune from crisis. Unity and multiplicity, part and whole, advantage and "dispassionateness": the mechanism of reciprocity *works for as long as it works*. As long as it spontaneously retains the effectiveness of that equally spontaneous convergence that characterizes it and that—in its continual, unexhausted impetus from force to *ratio*, from passion to science, from differences to equality—makes it extraordinarily, immensely powerful. There is the maximum of potency, the maximum of danger, in that immediacy. And the danger is new, radically different from any earlier phase. The age of the gods and the age of the heroes contain within them the invincible "necessity" of their end. In their restricted forms of sociality and domination lurk the forces and the seeds of their necessary overcoming-outstripping.[29] At the zenith of the course, however, the liberty of the people coexists with the "risk" of crisis. A constituent risk, to be sure, which cannot be eliminated from the "constitution" (from the continual and ever-changing formation) of that "liberty." But no longer necessity, inevitability. It is the *Aufhebung* of heroism that is inescapable, not the end of *humanitas*. The crisis in democracy is open to various solutions: "recurrence" (which certainly implies the "late stage of decadence" [727] and the collapse of the nation), but also foreign conquest (which paradoxically saves it instead), and above all "monarchy," an equally "human" variant susceptible to continual, reciprocal conversions into popular freedom. The unilinear and openly teleological course of development that characterized the early stages of the cycle gives way, at the *upper* levels of the "course," to the polysemous logic of the developed world. The decadence of democracy is not inevitable: it is a permanent horizon of possibility.[30]

CRISIS

"The people's unbridled liberty"; "anarchy, or the unbridled liberty of free peoples" (737 and 1102). This is how the crisis starts, when the precious, extremely delicate circulation of advantage and rationality, of necessity and citizenship, dwindles and then comes to a stop. At this point the expansion of the particular eats into the universal on which it depends. The constituent and extraordinarily productive horizon of reciprocity as the true source of advantage recedes. The wells of community and its awareness are poisoned. The "small shares" no longer sustain the unity of the "whole." Now the masses that command are "greedy," tumultuously "slow to profit from rational precepts" (808), neurotically intent on promoting laws that benefit special interests, concerned, above all, with investing their wealth directly in politics (in power, in public dominance" [288 and 1102]).[31] A crisis in equality and new particular domains, new forms of personal subservience: factions, civil wars. There is no rule to explain this turnaround. It happens when it happens. Nor can any theory truly predict it, let alone avert it. Prevented from gaining a firm grip on civil life, even philosophy is caught up in the decadence. The breakdown of common sense robs philosophy of its ethos, its dwelling place and its language. And so what prevails, on a purely negative front, is the skepticism of the "learned fools" who, misusing their eloquence, devote themselves to "maligning the truth" (1102); or an edifying philosophical version of the crisis, its false conscience, gains ground: systematic doubt, the jaded withdrawal of the particular (of the individual, the "subject") into itself, which ends up assuming a foolish and impoverished view of itself, a wizened rationalistic transparency, vainly intent on deducing itself and its political subjugation. Two sides of the same problem, Vico's anti-Cartesianism and rejection of contract theory go together.[32]

But the crisis in popular liberty is not a necessity. Nor does it lead automatically (by an organicist-naturalistic perspective, or through idealistic dialectical contradiction) to the downward slope of the "course" of the nation. Of course, these periods of the "late stage of decadence" and of the "end" are generally the ones on which most emphasis is placed, as they are closely linked and subject to the weighty, dominant prospect of the "recurrence," which takes up the last book and the conclusion of the *Scienza Nuova*, with its potent images of sociality giving way to solitude ("they live like monstrous beasts in the utter solitude of their private wills and desires"), speech to silence ("stunned and stupefied"), *settling* to *wandering* (they go "to turn their cities into forests and their forests into human lairs"), tenderness and love to pride and resentment ("and in their extreme fastidiousness, or rather pride, they are filled with bestial rage and resentment at the least provocation"), and generosity to an "ignoble savagery" that leads them to "use flattery and embraces to plot against the life" (1106). Recurrence is often seen exclusively as a new beginning, as return: a view that can undoubtedly be abstracted from Vico's writings and that is easily exposed to the charge of historical and philological schematism (the Middle Ages as new state of nature) and philosophical quietism (the guarantee of humanity's survival through and beyond any crisis). Preserving someone or something of mankind, recurrence brings it back to the nonsettlement of the bestial state, a necessary presupposition, an indispensable condition for another "stroke of lightning," for another operation of consciousness and advantage. But the collapse of developed humanity—it should never be forgotten—marks in any case the end of the nation: catastrophe (breakdown of form), not apocatastasis (regeneration, restoration). The individualism, the exaggerated and withdrawn subjectivity in that "barbarism of reflection" which in its "calculated malice" (1106) shatters the powerful but delicate equilibrium on which stands the free republic, is not at all a "criticism of modernity," an antimodern denunciation of the modern: it comprises, at the most, a possible outcome, identifying a prospect of crisis that is never definitively obscured or liable to be obscured. If anything, "recurrence" is a warning, if we can put it like this, of the dangers of the postmodern.[33] Nor is it—it is worth repeating—a necessary outcome. Other "solutions" exist as well.

Monarchies arose "after long and great civil wars between peoples,"[34] caused by "the factions of the powerful" (29),[35] which dismembered the public *vis* in pursuit of their "private interests": "Eventually, the powerful persons in the democracy directed public counsel towards the private interests of their power. By pursuing their own private interests, free peoples let themselves be seduced by the powerful into subjecting their own public freedom to the ambition of others. This led to factions, acts of sedition, and civil wars, which proved ruinous to their nations and introduced the monarchical form into the state" (1006). A structure "which is the second human form of government," so that "in the present civilized age, these two forms of human government, democracy and monarchy, alternate one with the other; but neither of them naturally passes into an aristocracy, in which the nobility alone commands and all others obey" (29).[36] What is striking, at first sight, is this rigid division between heroism and the monarchic form, even though they appear to share the decisive element of the "narrowness" of rule. Monarchy, in fact, represents the maximum concentration of political power, total control of the "laws" and "arms." The first solution to the crisis in the popular republic is for an Augustus to emerge: "when all the orders and laws devised to safeguard liberty are now powerless to regulate it and hold it in check, this leader takes control of them all by force of arms" (1104). And yet Vico argues with pride—and with lucid understanding—in defense of this arrangement. The concentration of power in the hands of the king, the "infinite authority" of monarchs, who "show that, being above the laws, they are subject only to their conscience and to God" (974 and 1104), in reality responds to a logic completely different from that of the heroic republics: "In a free commonwealth, a powerful man can become monarch only when the people support his party. This is why monarchies must by nature be popularly governed" (1008). The monarchy has nothing to do with the joint government of the fathers because in it the maximum accumulation of public power is necessarily accompanied by the maximum deployment of the private, of "natural equality": "all the subjects are made equal under the monarch's laws . . . monarchs have a superior civil nature, because they alone possess the force of arms"; "the monarchs sought to make all the subjects equal before the law" (927 and 1023). An equality that places the powerful on the "same footing" as the weak, leaving the field clear for all, leaving them with the "natural" right to compete and diverge: "monarchs have accustomed their subjects to attend to their own private interests, while they themselves have taken charge of all public

affairs. And monarchs want all their subject nations made equal by laws"
(39). If the popular republics "love children," the monarchies "encourage
parents to love them"; to put it in a better way: monarchs do not limit
themselves to encouraging the love for children in their subjects, but want
them to be absorbed in that love, and therefore distracted from public
affairs (996). The power of "natural liberty" is depoliticized: the free circulation of interests (of passions) is circumscribed, blocked, driven outside the armed walls of the political sphere. Not just a particular form of
government (and even less a celebration of the ancien régime and the
division into classes),[37] the monarchy became a symbol, a substantial metaphor for a mechanism with a very capacity of "power." A variant within
humanitas, the variant that is representative of modernity and the one
that wins out in the end: "perfect monarchies" (1086).

Condensation of the public, expansion of the private: this is the gist
of Vico's image of the *imperium monarchicum*.[38] There is no external
foundation for this intrinsic interchange, for this intense, reciprocal reference. The sovereign tries to make "common sense" of civil difference
through the use of the old cement of *religio*, the last and most reliable
"shield of rulers" (1109). But that glue holds only within the system, as
part of the bond that holds the monarch and the masses together far more
directly. Here too, as in popular liberty, the "foundation" is in fact the
"function," the "principle" is the "process." On the one hand, therefore,
"as citizens become a sort of foreigners in their own nations, it proves
necessary for monarchs to rule and represent them in their own persons"
(1008).[39] The public sustains the unity that permits natural liberty. There
is no liberty without "government," without a sphere of political power
that is now untouched, unattainable by the "natural." But on the other
hand, "the masters of princes are peoples," "For the school of princes is
the morality of the age, or *saeculum*" (979).[40] Political power has no other
basis, no other legitimization than its own function as political power.
The king "must" guarantee the continual production and reproduction
of "natural liberty," in the "satisfaction" and "contentment" of life, otherwise his very survival is at stake: "The monarch must keep the people
content and satisfied with their religion and natural liberty. For without
the people's universal satisfaction and contentment, monarchies are neither long-lived nor secure" (1104). The difference in the "civil nature" of
the *rex* holds for as long as he is able to maintain the universal uniformity
of the laws, laws that—wrested with democracy from the arcanum of the
nobles and expressed in the "human or civilized language which used
vocabulary agreed on by popular convention, and of which the people
are the absolute lords"—"establish the equality of all their subjects"; so
long as he is able to "humble the powerful" and "keep the masses free
and secure from oppression" as well as "satisfied and their enjoyment of

natural liberty assured" (32 and 1008). When this reciprocity breaks down, when the mechanism of this functionality jams, the power of the masses storms the stronghold of *auctoritas* and reestablishes the direct democratic circulation between the "political" and the "natural": here— in all probability, as Vico does not say so explicitly—lies the key to the interchangeability of "human forms," those forms that in different ways keep the nation at its peak, preserving it from a crisis that always remains possible, a threat that can never be definitively excluded. This inter- changeability is, in any case, an indication of the highly communal charac- ter of the political forms of the age of men in that practice of "life" against "death." A practice that with the image of "tenderness" perhaps finds, in the late Vico, its most emblematic, incisive representation, as an alterna- tive to barbarism: "The situation is quite different in the more civilized states of democracy and monarchy. In a democracy, the citizens control the public wealth . . . In a monarchy, the subjects are commanded to look to their own private interests and to leave public matters to the sovereign ruler. We must also bear in mind that both democracy and monarchy spring naturally from causes which are quite unheroic: a love of comfort, affection for one's wife, tenderness for children,[41] and desire for survival. As a result, people today naturally pay most attention to those minor details that ensure equal benefit to all" (951).

Kant and the Relegation of the Passions

Howard Caygill

> Nobody on the other hand wants passion. For who would let
> themselves lie in chains when they could be free?
> —Immanuel Kant, *Anthropology from*
> *a Pragmatic Point of View*

KANT'S ACCOUNT of the passions occupies a surprisingly marginal place
in his philosophy. His few discussions of the passions (*Leidenschaften*)
are dedicated almost exclusively to their role in the pathologies of the
will. A sustained analysis of the passions is conspicuously absent from the
three critiques, as well as from critical works on physics and practical
philosophy such as the *Metaphysical Foundations of Natural Science*
(1786) and the *Grounding for the Metaphysics of Morals*. Although they
appear as a marginal theme in the *Critique of Judgement* and in postcritical works such as *Religion Within the Limits of Reason Alone* and the
Metaphysics of Morals (1797), the discussion is directed to relegating the
passions to a minor role in a larger account of action. The only extended
discussion of the passions in Kant's work is in a section of the lectures on
anthropology, *Anthropology from a Pragmatic Point of View* (1798), and
here too the approach is focused firmly on the pathology of the passions.
Only in the *Opus Postumum* might Kant be said to begin to return to the
wider scope of classical and early modern contributions to the theory of
the passions.

Kant's relegation of the discourse of the passions to a detail in his theory
of physical and ethical action is striking, especially given the overwhelming significance and richness of this discourse both before and after him—
so striking indeed that it raises the historical and philosophical question
of how it was possible for the discourse of the passions to have been so
reduced less than a century after the rich and complex contributions of
Descartes and Spinoza. The beginnings of an answer can be sought in the
impact of Newton's revolution in the understanding of physical action
upon the classical and early modern physico-ethical discourse of the passions. Not only was Kant heir to Newton's reduction of physical action
to the play of opposite and opposed forces, but he also pursued its consequences for moral action. His case for a rigorous distinction between

physical and moral action, with the latter governed by an intelligible freedom, denied the passions any constructive role in practical philosophy. They were demoted from their role as a chief source of ethical action and relegated to a role in the pathology of the free will.

The implications of Kant's relegation of passions become clearer when compared even summarily to the physico-ethical account of the passions that it succeeded. In the latter, passion is given conceptual significance in both ethical and physical discourse; indeed, its argumentative force depended upon the close relationship between physics and ethics. In one of the early and influential contributions to this tradition—Plato's *Timaeus*—*aesthesis* or sensible affect is closely related to *pathe*. The *Timaeus* relates how necessity dictated that in man there should be:

> First, sensation, the same for all, arising from violent impressions; second, desire blended with pleasure and pain, and besides these fear and anger and all the feelings that accompany these and all that are of a contrary nature: and if they would master these passions they would live in righteousness; if they were mastered by them, in unrighteousness.[1]

Plato first relates physical affect and passion by means the soul's response to pleasurable or painful feelings and then links the mastery of these passions to righteousness and unrighteousness. His intuition concerning the close relationship between the perception of the physical world and the passions is refined by Aristotle in his analysis of the workings of the soul in terms of the characteristics of "movement and sensation."[2] Passion is here understood physically as passive sensation and ethically as an expressive movement of the soul.[3] In both Plato and Aristotle, what will become known as *affect*—or the "impression" of the world on the soul—is joined by the emotions of pleasure and pain to *passion* or the "expression" of the soul in the world. Affect and passion are thus closely related, a relation that is carried over into that of the cognate disciplines of physics and ethics.

The persistence of the relationship between affect and passion is evident in two of the monumental expressions of the early modern philosophy of the passions: Descartes's *The Passions of the Soul* (1649) and Spinoza's *Ethics* (1677). In spite of Descartes's opening claim about the "defectiveness" of the ancient philosophy of the passions and his wish to begin anew and to "forsake the paths they followed," *The Passions of the Soul* does not abandon the basic premises of the ancient theory. In spite of his use of the revolutionary physiological discoveries of the early seventeenth century, the definition of passion is conducted in terms of the familiar combination of affect with passion or "impression" with "expression." His preliminary discussion ends in Article 27 with a definition of the passions of the soul as "perceptions or sensations or excitations of the soul which are referred to it in particular and which are caused, maintained, and strengthened by some movement of the spirits."[4] The passions, as in Plato and Aristotle, still involve a combination of sensation and movement. While Descartes's account of this relationship is cast in terms of the mechanical agitation of heart, brain, and nervous system, his point of departure is classical. The body experiences a passion insofar as it receives or "suffers" perceptions from the world, and responds to these with the active passions that originate in the soul.

The same might also be said of Spinoza's *Ethics*, which like Descartes but using a more intricate and subtle combination of metaphysics and physiology unfolds a complex variation on the classical concept of the passions. The definition of action in Book III of the *Ethics* respects the classical distinction between action and passion: "we act when something happens, in us or outside us, of which we are the adequate cause . . . we are acted on when something happens in us, or something follows from our nature, of which we are only a partial cause."[5] There follows a definition of the "affections of the body" distributed according to whether "the Body's power of acting is increased or diminished": if we are the adequate cause of these affections, then the affect is an action, if we are not, then it is a passion.[6] The increase in the body's power of acting—the expression of its desire to act—is a joyful passion or, according to Spinoza's definition of joy "a man's passage from a lesser to a greater perfection" while a decrease in the same is a sad passion or "man's passage from a greater to a less perfection."[7] The analysis departs from the opposition of action and passion in both nature and human nature: the movement between joyful and sad passions depends on whether one is the subject of action or subjected to it.

The account of physical action in terms of action and passion was fundamentally challenged by Newton's "Axioms or Laws of Motion" stated at the outset of the *Mathematical Principles of Natural Philosophy* (1687). In Newton's physics of force, the distinction between action and passion no longer holds; the opposition between being the subject of and being subjected to action is succeeded by a complex balance of reciprocal forces. The third law of motion, "To every action there is always opposed an equal reaction," regards what was traditionally understood as a passion in terms of a counterforce. Both acting and resisting forces are of equal dignity—one is no longer considered active, the other passive. The physical account of action in terms of action and passion was seriously undermined by Newton, and with it the link between affects and passions, or Aristotle's "motion and sensation."

While Leibniz would attempt to retrieve the distinction between action and passion metaphysically—notably in section 52 of the *Monadology*—followers of Newton, including Kant (albeit after an early Leibnizian phase) largely abandoned the physical distinction of action and passion.

The implications of the obsolescence of this distinction in physical explanation for the ethical discourse of the passions was considerable, especially given the close links between the physical and the ethical views of action and passion. One solution was to equate the ethical passions with physical force, as was attempted by early-eighteenth-century libertine writers such as Mandeville in the *Fable of the Bees*. Another response, prompted by a reaction to the work of Mandeville, was to elevate moral action above the play of natural force as an expression of a providential cosmology, as in Hutcheson's argument for a "moral sense." Kant's own practical philosophy represents an extreme case of the latter. While consigning physical nature to the play of the Newtonian equal and opposed forces of action and reaction, he elevated human free action above natural force. One consequence of this elevation of freedom beyond nature was to reduce the constructive role of the passions in the governance of human action, and to restrict them to serving as pathological influences compromising the freedom of the will.

This pattern of argument is already evident in one of Kant's rare, precritical discussions of the passions or *Leidenschaften* in the Rousseau-influenced medical text *Enquiry into Mental Illnesses* (1764). There Kant mobilizes the passions to contribute to a gnoseology of mental illness, using them to distinguish between *Torheit* (stupidity) and *Narrheit* (foolishness). This derivation of the two mental disturbances forms the central part of a discourse dedicated to the classification of mental pathologies. Already Kant's view of the passions possessed a number of definite characteristics that distinguished it from the broader physico-ethical tradition, although his position was by no means stable. The impact of Rousseau on his thought in the early 1760s led him to regard the passions not as an original part of human nature, but the product of civilization. At the same time, however, they are identified, in an analogy with Newtonian force, with "the drives (*Triebe*) of human nature." Like natural forces they possess differences of degree and are described literally as *Bewegkraefte* or "motivating forces of the will" [die Bewegkraefte des Willens].[8]

Kant immediately relaxes the Newtonian view of the passions as "motive forces" possessing only differences of degree by claiming that they also differ in kind, depending on whether they are morally good or indifferent or "worthy of hate."[9] Another property possessed by the passions (*Leidenschaften*) is their tension with the understanding (*Verstand*), with the degree of tension providing the etiology of particular mental illness. The degree of tension is determined less by the distinction between the passions and the understanding than by the balance or imbalance of their opposed forces. In *Torheit* the passion—even if benign—is so strong that it "binds" the reason in those cases and actions that interest it, but without totally incapacitating rational judgment. It applies a selective and par-

ticular force to the understanding, neutralizing a part of it but not compromising its overall function. The condition of *Narrheit*, by contrast, is
provoked by an onslaught of passions or "motive forces" that wholly
incapacitates the understanding. In this mental illness, the reason is
wholly disoriented by an alliance of the forces of the passions of pride
(*Hochmut*) and avarice (*Geiz*). The *verkehrten Vernunft*, or "disoriented
reason," is overcome by their superior force and left devoid of the possibility of reflection and judgment.

Kant's view of the passions at this stage has a number of general characteristics that will survive into his critical and postcritical understanding,
although many details will be refined and inconsistencies resolved. The
Enquiry into Mental Illnesses is characterized by an anthropological understanding of the passions—they are considered to be features of human
psychology. This departs considerably from the broader physico-ethical
discourse of the passions sketched above that combined human and physical nature. Yet in spite of his exclusive focus on the psychological features
of the passions, Kant cannot entirely free his discourse from the broader
entailments of the physico-ethical tradition of the passions.

Not only is the debt marked by the introduction of the discourse of
active and reactive force into the psyche, but also by the pronounced Rousseauian features of Kant's text. Insofar as his account of mental illness is
indebted to Rousseau's distinction between—in Kant's own words—"The
simplicity and contentment of nature" and "artificial compulsion," then
some relation between affect and passion has to be assumed. This relation
is largely understood in terms of corruption, with a natural "healthy understanding" (*gesunde Verstand*) being corrupted by the artificial passions
provoked by the world of civil society. Mental illnesses are indeed defined
in terms of this corruption of the "healthy understanding," with Kant
noting towards the end of his text that "Humans in the state of nature can
be subjected to stupidity hardly at all and only with difficulty to folly."[10]
Stupidity in the civilized state depends on "sensitivity" or *Empfindlichkeit*,
that is, an affectual relation to the social and physical world; without
sensitivity stupidity is not possible, leaving Kant to conclude ironically
that "The insensitive one is the wise person of Pyrrho."

While there is clearly a constitutive relationship at work in this text
between sensation and the drives that make up the passions, Kant does
not subject it to extended scrutiny. While he notes how the "rank and
false slogans of civil society gradually become general maxims that tangle
the play of all human actions,"[11] he does not make any link between the
slogans and passions as "motivating forces of the will." They are in some
way related, but Kant does not at this point discuss the relation any further; he does, however, intimate that the relationship can only be understood in terms of corruption. He will subsequently refine his understand-

ing of this relation, but at the cost of breaking the physico-ethical link by means of a radical distinction between affect and passion.

Another survival of the traditional discourse of the passions is the distinction between their benign and malign forms. The passions that produce *Torheit* are not intrinsically bad, and the person possessed by them can understand the objections that the understanding might raise against them. The victim of such passions is distracted, but not consumed by them. On the other hand, the exclusive passions that tend towards *Narrheit* overcome their victims who are unconscious of their hateful and tasteless qualities. The former, benign passions faintly echo the agreeable sensations and passions of the physico-ethical tradition, while the latter echo the painful sensations and passions. Nevertheless, this aspect of the passions is not developed further by Kant, and subsequently he will rigorously separate his understanding of the passions from the influence of agreeable and painful affects.

The *Enquiry into Mental Illnesses* anticipates many of the characteristics of Kant's later theory of the passions. It is also important for its links with a near contemporary text, *The Observations on the Feelings of the Beautiful and Sublime*. Both texts, under the stimulus of Rousseau, assign the analysis of feelings and passions to the branch of metaphysics then known as "empirical psychology": the feelings and passions have no longer any ontological or cosmological pretensions. This marks a departure from the position held in the Wolffian textbooks of the mid–eighteenth century, where passion still featured both in ontology and psychology as a physico-ethical phenomenon.[12] Kant, although still teaching metaphysics and ethics according to these officially prescribed textbooks, assigns passion firmly to empirical psychology, the same part of metaphysics that he was in the course of transforming into the new discipline of anthropology. Within this, the passions are assigned to the "higher faculty" and distinguished from the "lower faculty" of sensibility that is the home of the affects: the passions, in terms of Kant's definition of the "higher faculty," are the outcome of spontaneity, they "arise from ourselves."[13] They do not depend on the properties of objects disclosed in sensibility, but arise from our reflections upon sensible (and later imaginary) objects. This characteristic, intimated in the *Enquiry into Mental Illnesses* in the transformation of the slogans of a corrupt civil society into the "motivating forces of the will," entails that passions or "corrupt maxims" become the "drives of human nature." It also implies that the passions remain at a remove from both sensible perception and the sensible affects of pleasure and pain, an indispensable precondition for Kant's later argument concerning the imaginary character of the objects of the passions.

Before proceeding with the question of Kant's resumption of an explicit and consistent discussion of passions in the 1790s, it is necessary first to reflect on their near absence in the critical philosophy. Why is the discussion of passion largely absent from the analysis of physical nature in *The Critique of Pure Reason* (1781/1787) and *Metaphysical Principles of Natural Science* (1786) and the analysis of morality in *Grounding of a Metaphysics of Morals* (1775) and *Critique of Practical Reason* (1778)? The absence from the first critique is consistent with Kant's Newtonian conception of physical action. In his understanding physical action, Kant, as we saw, no longer subscribed to the traditional contrast of action and passion still defended metaphysically by Leibniz and physically by Wolff. Instead throughout the first critique he uses almost exclusively the Newtonian distinction between active and reactive force (*Wirkung und Gegenwirkung*).

In the critical philosophy the complement of action is no longer passion—there is no longer a subject that acts and one that suffers action—but an opposed force: action and passion are replaced by active and reactive forces. Even though Kant still very rarely uses the language of action and passion, it is no longer consistent with the overall direction of his analysis. Thus, while in the table of the categories of *Critique of Pure Reason*, community, or the third category of relation, is described in traditional terms of the interaction between action and passion ("Wechselwirkung zwischen dem Handelnden und Leidenden"), this reference to the tradition is extensively belied by Kant's use of the Newtonian discourse of force in order to describe physical action in the critical philosophy.[14] In the discussion of the second analogy, the contrast of action and passion is succeeded by one of action and substance—"Wherever there is action—and therefore activity and force—there is also substance."[15] Kant takes this step in order to argue for the infinite differences between force as substance, thus avoiding distinction between an active and a passive subject of force. Similarly, Proposition 4 of the chapter on mechanics in the *Metaphysical Foundations of Natural Science*, commenting on Newton's third law, argues that the reciprocal of action is not passion, but reaction: "every impact can communicate the motion of one body to another only by means of an equal counterimpact, every pressure by means of an equal counterpressure, and, similarly, every traction only by an equal countertraction."[16] In his philosophy of physical nature Kant has replaced the active and passive subject with active and reactive force.

The implications for the understanding of ethical action and passion are evident in the critical contributions to moral philosophy where passion hardly features. In both the *Grounding for a Metaphysics of Morals* and the *Critique of Practical Reason* the main concern is to distinguish the intelligibility of the moral law from sensible inclination. Kant separates the world of freedom and the moral law from the physical world governed by the laws of motion and force. The discussions of the feelings of respect for the moral law and its attendant humiliation do not add up to a constructive theory of the passions, for these feelings are precisely directed against the claims of the sensible world in the realm of morality. Indeed, at the end of the *Critique of Practical Reason* after the famous apostrophe to the "starry heavens above and the moral law within," Kant appeals to the analogy between the scientific analysis that resolves the "fall of a stone and the motion of a sling" into "their elements and forces manifested in them" and the analysis of moral judgments that separates the "empirical from the rational."[17] The separation of freedom from nature leaves little room for the passions.

Given this scenario, the absence of a discourse of passion in the critical philosophy is perhaps less surprising than its return in the writings of the 1790s. This revival of the passions has two interesting aspects. In the first—evident in the published writings of the 1790s as well as the lectures on anthropology—the theory of the passions is called to help explain moral pathology, while in the second it returns as part of the fundamental rethinking of the philosophy of nature that occupied Kant in the "transition-problem" of the *Opus Postumum*. The latter completed the movement away from a strictly Newtonian concept of nature already evident in the second part of the third critique on teleological judgment, and its consequences for the passions were already intimated in the changed orientation of freedom and nature implied in the aesthetic judgment of taste.

The dominant line of discussion of the passions in *The Critique of Judgement*, *Religion Within the Limits of Reason Alone*, the *Metaphysics of Morals*, and the *Anthropology from a Pragmatic Point of View* pursues their role in moral pathology. In the "General Comment on the Exposition of Aesthetic Reflective Judgements" in the *Critique of Judgement*, Kant explicitly distinguishes between affects and passions. He distinguishes them according to species, with the affects "related to feeling" and thus "impetuous and irresponsible" and the passions attributed to the "faculty of desire." As part of the latter, passions are described as "inclinations" (*Neigungen*) that "complicate or even prevent" the determination of the will by principles.[18] Kant notes further that the passions are "abiding and deliberate," adding that while affects may impede the freedom of the *Gemuet* (as in the case of stupidity discussed above), passions can completely "overcome" it.[19] Here the passions are accorded an entirely pathological role, but one that is complicated throughout the text by the emergence of a new relationship between freedom and nature exemplified by the aesthetic judgment. The rigorous distinction between affect and passion—based on the transcendental distinction between the lower faculty of sensibility and the higher faculty of understanding and reason—is also undermined in the course of the argument by the emergence of a concept of pleasure situated between the two faculties.

Of the three main texts published during the 1790s—*Religion Within the Limits of Reason Alone* (1793), *The Metaphysics of Morals* (1797), and the *Anthropology from a Pragmatic Point of View* (1798)—it is the last that contains the most extensive discussion of the pathology of the passions. Based on Kant's lectures on empirical psychology/anthropology, it contains material accumulated over decades of lecturing, and while it cannot be considered the last word on the subject of the passions, it does offer one of the most detailed reports on the development of his thinking on the topic. Much of the account of the passions in the *Anthropology from a Pragmatic Point of View* is consistent with that of the *Critique of Judgement* and those of the 1793 and 1797 texts, although much more detailed and comprehensive. The conceptual distinction between affect and passion remains central to all four texts, although the grounds given for the distinction are much richer in the latter three than in the *Critique of Judgement*. During the discussion of the "feeling of pleasure and displeasure" in the *Anthropology* Kant carefully distinguishes the affects of pleasure and displeasure from the passions, noting that while they have often been confused with each other, the passions properly belong to the faculty of desire and not that of sensibility.[20] This precise location of the passions within the philosophical architectonic is closely respected in the accounts of 1793 and 1797.

The discussion of the passions in the *Metaphysics of Morals* departs from the distinction between affect and passion, echoing the third *Critique* with the claim that "Affects and passions are essentially different."[21] The essential difference between them is manifest in a number of different ways. The affects belong to feeling—and are fleeting distractions—and succumbing to affects is "something childish and weak, which can indeed co-exist with the best will."[22] Affects can distract the moral work of the will, but do not necessarily damage it; they are more innocent than vicious. A passion, by contrast, is not fleeting but persists. It is understood genealogically as a *complication* of desire, a temporal extension of an inclination: it is a "sensible *desire* that has become a lasting inclination (e.g., *hatred* as opposed to anger)."[23] While the affect agitates and distracts, a passion emerges from a "calm" that "permits reflection" and allows the *Gemuet* to "form principles upon it," allowing it to become "deeply rooted" and, in the case of passions contrary to the law, to transport "evil" into the maxims of the will. While the pathology of the affect consists in momentarily distracting the will from doing good, the passion is potentially an enduring corruption of the will that inclines it to do evil.

The role of the passions in corrupting the maxims of the good will is also emphasized in *Religion Within the Limits of Reason Alone*, where passion is discussed in the context of "radical evil." In this version of his theory of the passions, Kant does not focus so much on the distinction

between affect and passion as upon the genesis of the passions. His genealogy assumes that passion forms part of the faculty of desire, and is characterized by the attempt to show how this faculty is vulnerable to corruption. He begins with a propensity (*Hang*) that is a predisposition to a
delight, which "once experienced, arouses in the subject an inclination to
it."[24] Here Kant is trying to explain how we can desire something of which
we have no experience—the "propensity" or "instinct" to enjoy something of which we have no concept becomes, when realized, the permanent "inclination" to enjoy the experience. The permanence of inclination, which may conflict with and be overcome by the maxims of the
moral law, is then contrasted with a further twist or "stage" in the faculty
of desire, namely "*passion* (not *emotion*, for this has to do with the feeling
of pleasure and pain) which is an inclination that excludes mastery over
oneself."[25] In this case, the fleeting desire made into a permanent inclination has succeeded in attaching itself to the determination of the will itself,
corrupting its maxims and convincing it to will evil. It is in this sense that
Kant in the *Anthropology* will compare the passions to "largely incurable
cancerous sores for pure practical reason,"[26] returning to the medical context of his precritical discussion of the passions and viewing the passions
within the submerged ethical healing mission of the *Anthropology*.

Predictably Kant's discussion in the *Anthropology* begins by distinguishing passion from affect, and in particular the affect of pleasure and
displeasure. Consistent with his other accounts, the passions are a state
of the soul—*Gemuetsstimmung*, literally a tuning of the soul—that form
part of the faculty of desire and are associated with reflection over extended periods of time. A new element in the version of the *Anthropology*
is the sustained medical metaphor—affects are momentary disorders,
while passions are powerful illnesses, with effects analogous to those occasioned by poison or severe injury. Such illness, Kant continues, requires
a "inner or outer soul-doctor" who, however, "knows only how to pre-
scribe palliative rather than *radical* medicine."[27] Later, in the chapter on
the passions, Kant returns to the question of medicine, describing affect
as a "rush" (*Rausch*) and passion as an illness (*Krankheit*) that shies from
any cure. The illness of the passions is now explicitly likened to "cancerous sores" (*Krebsschaeden*) of the will (pure practical reason), largely
incurable not just because only palliative medicines are available, but also
because the will is so disabled that the patient does not want to be cured
("der kranke nicht will geheilt sein").[28]

The chapter on the passions begins with a rehearsal of the distinctions
within the faculty of desire between propensity (*Hang*), instinct, and inclination (*Neigung*). In the context of these distinctions passion appears as
the inclination "that hinders the working of reason."[29] The pathological
relationship with reason makes passion in Kant's eyes a specifically

human pathology. Passion, he explains, "always presupposes a maxim of the subject to act according to ends prescribed by the inclination. It is thus always bound up with reason itself; mere animals cannot be attributed passions, as little as a pure rational being."[30] Kant then proceeds to outline the ways in which the passions are implicated with human reason and in particular with the human exercise of sensible imagination.

In the opening discussion of paragraph 77, Kant points to two pathological links between the passions and reason. The first is that the passions generate maxims in a way analogous to pure practical reason, mimicking pure practical reason and thus earning the epithet "cancerous." The second is the observation that (in German) the names for many of the passions are associated with the verb *Suchen* (to seek)—*Ehrsucht, Rachsucht, Habsucht* or the passions of pursuit of honor, revenge, and riches. Kant notes that by definition these passions can never be "completely satisfied"[31]—like simulacra of the ideas of reason, they can never be made fully present. They are, thus, like parodies of the moral law, the subject of an "endless task." Kant then moves to show that the mimicry of reason leads the passions to a fatal inconsistency, since while they are in fact partial—based on a particular inclination—they pretend to universality, a pretension that leads to a contradiction that Kant defines in terms of "stupidity" (*Torheit*)—meaning by this term something quite distinct from the earlier definition in the *Enquiry into Mental Illnesses*. The claim to universality on the basis of a particular inclination offers another distinction between the affects and the passions: the former do not pretend to universality, and while occasionally morally reprehensible, they are not essentially so. Passions, however, are not just pragmatically, but also morally, reprehensible; they do not represent a temporary loss of freedom and self-control, but rather extend the enjoyment of the feeling of slavery.[32] Passions, in short, are implicated in the masochistic pathology of freely electing to be a slave.

After these analyses of the relationship between reason and the passions, Kant proceeds to offer a classification of the particular passions. It is by no means complete, and is intended to make an important point concerning the distinction between natural and artificial passions. Abandoning the Rousseauian premises of the *Enquiry into Mental Illness*, Kant distinguishes between passions that arise from "natural (inborn)" and those that arise from "human culture (acquired)" inclinations.[33] The inclinations, it should be remembered, are not identical with passions; to become so they must in some sense become maxims guiding the operations of the will. Consequently, the natural inclinations of freedom and sexual attraction "bound with affect" may become passions, but not for intrinsic reasons. Kant's discussion of the natural passions focuses on freedom, distinguishing the affect of "freedom under moral laws" or "enthusiasm" from the inclination to remain in or extend external freedom that can become a passion. To be consistent with his definition—repeated during the discussion of the passion for freedom—that "Passions are actually only to do with humans and can only be satisfied through them,"[34] the passion for freedom will be fixed on the inclination to extend freedom at the expense of that of others, rather than in the name of the moral law.

The second class of acquired inclinations are intrinsically prone to become passions, since they are directed less by a desire for the enjoyment of objects than for the social reflection of the pursuit of such enjoyment— these passions are always, in Kant's words, directed by a desire issuing "from humans for humans."[35] Passions such as pursuit of honor, pursuit of power, and pursuit of possessions are largely independent of the affect provoked by the enjoyment of their objects, but "bound with the permanence of maxims tied to certain ends."[36] The maxim to act in order to achieve the end of possessing honor, or power, or wealth, is not in itself a passion. It becomes a passion when its realization is extended into infinity and the maxim of the passion universalized. In this case it is phrased thus: always act in order to achieve the end of possessing honor, power, wealth. In this formulation of the maxim it is implicitly acknowledged that for this kind of desire, the objects of honor, power, and wealth can never be attained, or rather their attainment is not the end desired. The passion consists more in the endless pursuit of a chimerical object than in its enjoyment.

Kant then classifies these passions according to whether they are ardent or cold, an example of the latter being avarice. However, most of his interest falls on the ardent and acquired cultural passions of the pursuit of the objects of honor, power, and money—thus encompassing the passions that characterize both feudal and commercial societies. The passionate pursuit of these inclinations is characterized by a number of contradictions—being social, the passions make their subjects dependent on others. They arise out of and provoke further "weakness"—the pursuit of honor depends upon the opinion others, that of power on fear of being dominated by others,[37] and the pursuit of wealth on self-interest in the expectation that others will do the same.[38] In the more extended discussion of the latter, Kant links possession of money with the desire for the possession of a universal means, by those whose passion is driven by the lack or fear of lacking means to achieve their ends.[39]

Kant ends his discussion of the passions in the *Anthropology* with a reflection on *Wahn* as the motive force of desire. His comments on the human craze for games and gambling nevertheless have some deeper implications for his understanding of the passions. He notes that "From time to time, nature desires to provoke strong stimulations of the feeling for life, in order to renew human activity so that they do not lapse into the mere enjoyment of the feeling of life."[40] Nature does so by making imaginary objects seem real and a source for passionate pursuits, namely honor, power, and gold. Kant thus links the passions with the development of culture (a development he sees as a natural one); mere affect or enjoyment of nature's objects will not promote the development of culture. For this end passion and its pathology are necessary. Thus in the end Kant insinuates that the pathological growths of the passions will indeed contribute to a constructive historical outcome of human history.

The indirectly constructive outcome of the passions that is hinted at in the *Anthropology* nevertheless assumes that the proper way to understand the passions is as a pathology of reason. With this Kant remains consistent with his separation of the causalities of freedom and nature—with action/passion banished from nature and replaced with action/reaction, passion found itself relegated to a pathology of the free will. However, the possibility of a constructive outcome points to an equivocation in Kant's accounts of the passions that may already be discerned in the third *Critique*. The vicious characteristics of the passions according to the *Metaphysics of Morals*—their universalizing a partial inclination (for Kant the fallacy of subreption) and the enjoyment of subjection—are given a different emphasis in the third *Critique*. The aesthetic judgment of taste is characterized by what might be described as a "virtuous" subreption—a partial experience rooted in the senses being experienced as if it partook of the universality of the concept.[41] The combination of the qualities of sensibility and the understanding is not considered to be pathological, but indeed opens the possibility of an experience that defies many of the laws of the critical philosophy—aesthetic pleasure. Similarly, the delight in subjection that the passions provoke is given a nonpathological significance in the discussion of the experience of the sublime, where the moment of subjection is part of a wider movement towards the enhancement of the feeling of freedom.[42] Thus the discussion of the aesthetic judgment in the first part of the third *Critique* opens up possibilities for a rethinking of the passions within and beyond the critical philosophy.

The tentative beginnings of an extension of the space opened by aesthetic judgment to the passions are evident in the third *Critique*, although their implications would not be fully realized until the *Opus Postumum*. Thus, the picture of the passions overcoming free will and judgment is cautiously modified in the *Critique* when Kant admits that the interest in the object of taste can "fuse also with all the inclinations and passions (*Neigungen und Leidenschaften*), which in society attain to their greatest variety and highest degree."[43] Initially consistent with his earlier commitment to Rousseau, Kant regards this fusion—a passion for the arts—as affording "a very ambiguous transition from the agreeable to the good" while conceding that this transition might "be furthered by means of taste

when taken in its purity."[44] This anticipates the possible constructive role
accorded the passions in the *Metaphysics of Morals*, although the discussion remains undeveloped. For this positive insight into the role of the
passions in promoting the good remains isolated in the writings of the
early to middle 1790s, with Kant inclining to an increasingly sophisticated
version of the first, pathological view of the effect of the passions on the
free will.

However, in Kant's late, indeed final, reflections on the theme in the
Opus Postumum it is possible to see the emergence of a new approach
to the passions, one surprisingly close to that of Spinoza (who is often
mentioned by name in these notes). In a note on the "Highest Standpoint
of Transcendental Philosophy" Kant observes that "Newtonian attraction through empty space and the freedom of man are analogous concepts to each other. They are categorical imperatives—*ideas.*"[45] He continues by describing them in terms that bring them close to Spinoza's
attributes of a unitary substance, with God almost being identified with
the universe: "There is one God and one universe. The totality."[46] In this
totality, humans are the subjects of the divine laws of nature and freedom—there is no longer a distinction between them: "A being who is
originally universally law-giving for nature and freedom is God."[47] At this
point, at the end of his life, Kant puts fundamentally into question the
premises of his life's thought, including the relegation of the passions that
these premises entailed.

Kant did not complete the adventure of thought upon which he em-
barked in the last years of his life, but its implications for his philosophy
were considerable. The relaxation of the rigorous distinction between nature and freedom and their unification in a divine/natural totality would
have many implications for his thought, not least concerning the passions.
Having long relegated them to the status of pathological, even if historically useful, perversions of the reason, the late Kant began a fundamental
rethinking of their role. His nascent doctrines of "self-positing" and
"auto-affection," in which we make ourselves the objects of our own
representations, promised to restore the concept of passion to the center
of the postcritical philosophy. Kant did not live to see this development
through to a conclusion, although it did, under other auspices, become
significant in the romantic, post-Kantian rethinking of the passions.

Beliefs and Emotions (from Stanley Fish to Jeremy Bentham and John Stuart Mill)

Frances Ferguson

From the time that eighteenth-century thinkers like Cesare Beccaria took up the project of demanding that laws answer to reason, government and governmentality have frequently been depicted as being at odds with emotion.[1] And it is true that, insofar as projects like Beccaria's and Jeremy Bentham's aimed to restrain the judgments of local justices, outlaws, or outraged private citizens, personal attachments were a target of the reformers' schemes. Rationalizing the law meant insisting that judgments look plausible to those who were not themselves parties in a dispute—or property-holders with enough land to feel that they were always parties to a dispute on or around their property. No longer, the legal rationalists argued, should it be possible for a property-holder who was justice of peace to decide that stealing from him ought to be punished more harshly than stealing from someone else. No longer should it be possible for the law to express the anger of the quickest-triggered, most easily offended, and most powerful. Legal rationalism depicted the law as important not so much because it exacted revenge after the commission of a crime as because it offered the law as a guide to action, to action that would be performed in the future. (Indeed, this commitment was so thoroughgoing as to have shifted discussions of punishment toward the question of deterrence.) The rationalized law would offer encouragement and discouragement, what Bentham called positive and negative incentives. Law, in Bentham's view, provided advice, made it easier for individuals to achieve happy outcomes from their actions, because it explicitly spoke on behalf of society at large. Statutory law—as opposed to the customary law of Blackstone that had always justified its decisions after the fact—would speak in advance of people's actions. Rationalized law would, in its own voice rather than the voice of friendly conversation or psychological observation, register the suggestion that an individual's parking her car in the middle of an intersection would be likely to make other drivers unhappy.

Now, although I think I have just given what I take to be a faithful translation of the project of rational law as Bentham presents it, I should immediately acknowledge that Bentham and political liberalism have for some time drawn criticism for ignoring individual beliefs and emotions. And it is certainly true that the rational law does not have emotional intonations. Its directives—"Don't leave your car in the middle of an intersection," for example—can appear irritatingly superfluous, like something that most people recognize as a good idea without feeling the need for any direction. For it aims to speak even to the insensitive, the obdurate, and the autistic. It aims to make it possible for even those with dull capacity for sympathy to develop the means for avoiding the wrath of others. Unlike libertarianism, which insists simply upon individual choice, liberalism tries to coordinate individual choice with government. That insistence on government has seemed to some commentators to exact a price from individuals. It has come to be a standard criticism of liberalism that, in abstracting from the beliefs and interests of actual persons, it insists upon a completely impersonal view, that it ignores the things that people care about and the strength with which their emotional attachments speak to them. In the following discussion, I will be contesting that view, and arguing instead that Jeremy Bentham's vision of government provides a capacious view of the complex of emotion and belief that goes under the notion of motivation. Bentham, who continually uses pleasure (and a comparison between pleasures) to gauge the appeal of differing choices, admits an extraordinarily wide range of emotions into his catalogue of motives, and insists that even frequently castigated motives are good if their consequences produce pleasure and avoid pain.[2] Indeed, in arguing that it is nonsensical to imagine that there is a bad pleasure or a good pain, Bentham aims to exempt motivating emotions from being stigmatized by dogmatic predictions about their consequences. Just as Foucault would later criticize the use of sexual typology as a predictor of behavior, so Bentham objects to trying to constrain behavior by evaluating motivating emotions rather than consequential actions (16–17). To do so, he argues, is to censor motivating emotions in advance of their having either positive or negative effects.

To many, it will be surprising to hear Bentham described in the ways in which I will be describing him. Yet my aim is less to present a startling counter to much of the received wisdom about Bentham than to point out the disadvantages under which that received wisdom has operated. Partially because Bentham wrote prolifically but saw comparatively little of his work through to publication, a substantial amount of his writing has only gradually emerged. Moreover, much of what was earlier published was significantly bowdlerized by his early editor, John Bowring, who sought to protect both Christianity and Bentham's reputation by deleting material critical of Christianity (xxxii). I hope to demonstrate in this essay that Bentham's emphasis on facts in no way excludes respect for beliefs and emotions and their interconnection. Yet I also mean to provide an exposition of his argument against granting religious belief an active role in government, and to explain why religious belief is not analogous to other sorts of beliefs. On Bentham's view, the argument against taking religious testimony about human affairs most importantly revolves around the question of power—specifically, whether a belief in an omniscient and omnipotent deity does not militate against all efforts to test and distribute human power. Although Bentham seconds Hume's skepticism about religious belief, he brackets the question of whether religious belief might be true and centers his argument on a different aspect of Hume's argument on miracles—its insistence that believing that miracles were once performed exacts a price from our own experience, and continually reinaugurates a world in which human experience is rendered nugatory.

The account of Bentham I am offering suggests how, in considering the influence of emotion and various types of beliefs on individuals and on government, he was attempting to respond to questions that both Hume and Rousseau had earlier broached. If Bentham regularly acknowledged Hume as having opened his eyes to the importance of pleasing and useful consequences that result from our actions, he was, like Hume, interested in identifying what kind of reason is at work in our subjective judgments. Like Hume, he saw emotions as a way of registering evaluations in a nonpropositional and nondoctrinal form. Moreover, this attentiveness to human experience as something that could never be named in advance was part and parcel of both Hume's and Bentham's arguments against the idea that individuals had unitary and stable identities. If both men see the evidence for motivations in the fact that people act (and must have moved themselves to act), neither of them imagines this as a matter of their having clear-sighted understanding of their own motivations and intentions. For the problem with the requirement that one know what one wants, as H.L.A. Hart once observed of John Stuart Mill, is that one perforce "endows [the normal human being] with too much of the psychology of a middle-aged man whose desires are relatively fixed, not liable to be artificially stimulated by external influences; who knows what gives him satisfaction or happiness; and who pursues these things when he can."[3] Because both Hume and Bentham reject such a constant model of the self who believes and desires, they obligate themselves to provide accounts of emotions through means other than those of direct testimony from the desiring agent.

Hume has been particularly important for various scholars tracing what Ronald de Sousa calls "the rationality of emotion" and explaining the defensible judgments implicit in emotions like jealousy or envy, and he has been embraced for the shrewd positivism with which he identifies and paraphrases actual and observable emotions.[4] Yet it has frequently seemed that Hume, for all his reflection on the history of government, did not fully coordinate individual beliefs and emotions with his account of government. Hume's account of beliefs and emotions highlighted the primacy of experience itself, but the force of Hume's observations seemed to suggest that human psychology would forever impede political efforts toward democracy. Although Hume is perhaps less insistent on the obdurately unregenerate character of the emotions than Slavoj Žižek, his picture of the emotions suggests the difficulties they present for political progress rather than the likelihood of their being harnessed for it.

Indeed, even a figure like Rousseau, at once intensely engaged with developing a notion of the general will and with attending scrupulously to the emotions, never fully articulated how the politics of the general will might have any positive connection to individual emotions, and continually noted the ways in which it was problematic for government that emotions became so pleasurable that people sought them at any price.[5] It was the French revolutionaries who tried to forge the strongest possible claim for a connection, as Robespierre demonstrated for years by carrying a copy of Rousseau's *Confessions* at his breast[6] and by enunciating Rousseau's message as a claim about the accuracy and transparency of the emotions.[7] In Robespierre's hands, Rousseau's recognition that the emotions are their own justification meant that the emotions offered the strongest possible mandate.

Bentham's understanding of the law as a positive system (rather than a set of inferences about customary practice) is, I shall argue, at base a claim that it is possible to identify not merely a general will but also collective emotion. If the operation of the law seems then to rest on the notion that law must be publicly stated, Bentham's account does not merely speak in the words of doctrine. Nor does it require public festivals of the sort that Rousseau proposed to advance a sense of participation in civil society. Rather, Bentham's view of law enables him to treat all actions as part of a system of mutual evaluation, in which the law and the behavior of individuals continually influence one another. Bentham's promulgation of the greatest happiness for the greatest number ought to be seen as a way of trying to depict collective emotion and to suggest how it might operate on individual emotions and opinions, how it might alter them so that the choices of individuals did not always look as though they could only be represented by individual position papers and statements of belief.

The argument I shall be making is a historical one, in that it seeks to describe a position that Bentham developed nearly two centuries ago. Yet the position that I shall be trying to capture is far from irrelevant to contemporary debates. Recently Stanley Fish has revived a version of the Robespierrean argument to claim that, since all beliefs and emotions are unjustifiable, all beliefs and emotions ought to have equal standing in political debates. He has specifically objected to what he sees as an inconsistency in liberalism. Although liberals claim to argue for the free expression of ideas, Fish says, they irrationally draw the line at admitting religious beliefs into political discussion. Thus, he argues (in "Mission Impossible: Settling the Just Bounds between Church and State") that the liberal project of establishing boundaries between church and state is a doomed enterprise, because all beliefs and emotions must be said to be self-justifying because they can have no other justification.[8] In that essay Fish rehearses an argument that can best be paraphrased as the assertion that notions like truth, justice, and fairness are simply empty abstractions and that they cannot provide any meaningful framework for deciding how to adjudicate between competing claims. Organizing his essay around the question of the tension between the claims of the state and the claims of religion, he portrays liberalism as essentially hypocritical: it professes disinterestedness and toleration while conspicuously failing to tolerate positions that are at odds with its own doctrines. What liberalism loses track of, in Fish's view, is that there is no such thing as disinterestedness. It thus attempts to substitute what he calls a theoretical framework (and what a constitutional or Rawlsian commentator would call a practical framework) for the actual beliefs that people hold.[9] Moreover, Fish thinks that liberalism (in the person of Thomas Nagel, for instance) can only pretend not to be committed to truth claims, for Fish takes the preference for one thing over another as an assertion of the truth of the preferred statement.[10] If liberals were honest with themselves and their readers, Fish thinks, they would recognize that they were claiming that their insights were true. But this assertiveness would, he also thinks, contradict a central self-perception of liberalism—that it can accept lots of views and not merely exclude them because they run afoul of liberal doctrine. What liberalism cannot acknowledge, Fish thinks, is that exclusion is constitutive of any governmental regime—or, for that matter, any perception. And liberalism is able to avoid achieving the clear-sightedness that Fish claims for himself because it fails to recognize that "beliefs are not what you think *about* but what you think *with*" and that "beliefs have *you*, in the sense that there can be no distance between them and the acts they enable."[11]

Beliefs, to rehearse Fish's view, are groundless because they cannot be justified, yet they are also the indispensable substrate of individual perception. For on Fish's account beliefs are essentially identical to emotions. They are the value-awarding elements in perception that we cannot alter through analysis. Beliefs—however groundless, and Fish insists that they are groundless or only accidentally justified—seem true to us because beliefs are essentially a version of emotions. They have perceptible force for us, and that perceptibility trumps analysis. There is nothing more to be said and nothing more that needs to be said. Yet having once made beliefs the equivalent of emotions that might as well be part of our DNA because they seem hard-wired, Fish proceeds to make an extraordinary claim—that true morality involves "playing to win" by pursuing your beliefs. In other words, we cannot choose or analyze our beliefs, but we can treat ourselves as moral agents if we define morality—which is usually conceived to be morality insofar as it revolves around making choices—as the single-minded pursuit of the things that seem true to us precisely because we were incapable of choosing them.[12]

It is at this point that we can see why Fish begins his essay by quoting from Locke's *A Letter Concerning Toleration*, in which Locke identifies the problem that liberalism has to confront in considering the question of the relationship between church and state: "For every church is orthodox to itself; to others, erroneous or heretical. Whatsoever any church believes, it believes to be true; and the contrary thereupon it pronounces to be error."[13] By the time that Fish has concluded his argument, it becomes clear that every individual is orthodox to herself. We are, on Fish's account, all churches of one. Fish recommends as a moral project that each of us engage in single-minded pursuit of ourselves—the beliefs and emotions (or belief-emotions) that make one's perceptions endlessly self-reinforcing—because one is honestly avoiding claiming any higher motives than self-affirmation. Yet even though he repeatedly announces in the essay that he is making the same point repeatedly, saying "You will have sensed before I say it that my argument has long since become repetitive" (2293), there are at least three points at which he makes affirmations that are hard to square with his announced position. His accounts of historical contingency, his understanding of change, and his representation of winning are all, to put it bluntly, highly abstract (2258).

First, there is the matter of sociological or historical contingency to which Fish refers. He observes, and correctly, that "if you believe something you believe it to be true, and perforce, you regard those who believe contrary things to be in error." Yet the very historical contingency in belief —aptly captured by a Marxist account like Raymond Williams's or John Barrell's—is its mutability over time.[14] Fish, however, continually speaks of one's beliefs as already fully identifiable and thus available to be acted on in the way that a game plan or a blueprint might be realized in action. Thus, he can take it as axiomatic that people can—and should—"testify" to "the truth as [they] see it" (2276). By converting the discussion into an ahistorical problem of individual standpoints and what they can and cannot acknowledge, Fish makes his argument on grounds that are at least as abstract as those of the writers whom he is criticizing.

Indeed, Fish's way of treating his central example—devout and indeed fundamentalist religious belief—may serve to illustrate my point. For it becomes apparent on a moment's reflection that the same liberal theorists whom Fish sees as having invented an insoluble problem out of merely theoretical commitments (or what he dismissively calls the give-and-take of a philosophy seminar) could not, if we were to take his account seriously, have invented the problem of toleration. Arguments about toleration may have had their particularly urgent origin in political struggles in which the state was constantly subject to turmoil as each new ruler tried to impose his or her own religion, but that version of the problem has long since ceased to have particular force for the western European countries that earlier faced it. Rather, the central issue has come to be that an increasingly small number of persons derive their sense of truth from religion. As John Stuart Mill eloquently observed in his essay "Utility of Religion" (published in 1874), "it has sometimes been remarked how much has been written, both by friends and enemies, concerning the truth of religion, and how little, at least, in the way of discussion or controversy, concerning its usefulness," and he went on to recognize the increase in accounts of the usefulness of religion as itself a symptom of its decline as a source of truth in everyday life.[15] Mill understood that "so long . . . as men accepted the teaching of their religion as positive facts, no more a matter of doubt than their own existence or the existence of the objects around them, to ask the use of believing it could not possibly occur to them" (403). The defense of religion itself does not so much defend religion, in other words, as reveal that religion stands in need of defense; and the multiplication of arguments for defending religion does not so much defend religion anew as show the insufficiency of previous defenses.

> The utility of religion did not need to be asserted until the arguments for its truth had in a great measure ceased to convince. People must either have ceased to believe, or ceased to rely on the belief of others, before they could take that inferior ground of defence without a consciousness of lowering what they were endeavouring to raise. An argument for the utility of religion is an appeal to unbelievers, to induce them to practise a well meant hypocrisy, or to semi-believers to make them avert their eyes from what might possibly shake their unstable belief, or finally to persons in general to abstain from expressing any doubts they may feel, since a fabric of immense importance to mankind is so insecure at its foundations, that men must hold their breath in its neighbourhood for fear of blowing it down. (403)

Yet where Mill makes a point that anticipates deconstruction's sense of the problematics of opposition and defense, Fish frames the matter abstractly: differences between liberalism and the devout are a direct standoff between two simply opposed viewpoints. What he does not acknowledge is that religious claims have retreated farther and farther from claims to truths that rest on religion—that, in other words, the assimilation that Mill is identifying under another name is not an assimilation required by a hegemonic liberalism but rather an assimilation performed from within by various religious sects. From the moment that prosecutions for witchcraft ceased (to use an example that Jeremy Bentham provided and Mill took up approvingly), one had evidence in behavior that religion had lost ground to science and law.[16] Moreover, the process was not a consecutive one in which beliefs were formulated and then implemented. Law and science increased their sway at the expense of religion not so much under the pressure of pleading or injunction as under the impulse of changes in belief that people did not quite register having had until the change was virtually universal. As long as people continued to believe in supernatural agency, prosecutions for witchcraft were always— and could only be—successful. No evidentiary grounds for overturning convictions could ever interfere. It still made sense to bring prosecutions for witchcraft while persons continued to believe that it was possible for a person to be a witch, consort with supernatural agents, and suspend the laws of nature.

The end to prosecutions for witchcraft may have reflected power struggles between religious and secular law and may thus have had political elements. But the struggles for jurisdiction and authority did not simply result from people's rallying about the views of a strong leader. Instead, charges for witchcraft ceased to be brought because prosecutors found themselves believing more strongly in the natural restrictions that underwrote law and the premium it placed on evidence that could be presented to the senses. Prosecutions for witchcraft, as Bentham observed, waned only when the law began to take seriously the notion of an alibi, with its implicit assertion that no individual could be in two different places simultaneously.

What I mean to insist upon here is that it is a very abstract way of proceeding to observe that actions such as filing suit in court to have one's child exempted from a school's training in critical thinking (which is what Vicki Frost did in the case of *Mozert v. Hawkins County Board of Education* that Fish features)[17] are evidence of beliefs and not to notice any kind of change over historical time in the cases that people bring in the name of their religious beliefs. The dilemma that confronted Edmund Gosse's father Philip, a distinguished Victorian scientist and devout member of the strict Calvinist sect the Plymouth Brethren, has ceased to be a dilemma for most of the devout. Indeed, even though Vicki Frost may be a member of the Christian Right, the observation that Mill made holds even for her. She is, thus, likelier to bring suit to protect her child against hearing that scripture seems questionable rather than sacred to some—and thus to stage a debate about how much belief should have to justify itself to or defend itself against the views of other people—than she is to urge a witch-craft trial or to plan on crossing the Red Sea by benefit of intense faith and her own two feet. As Bentham (and Mill) observed, religionists can-not restrict themselves to a defense of creationism or the argument that Christ walked on water; they must discard as well a great deal of the physical world and scientific accounts with some claim to regularity.

Fish, however, so accustomed to taking actual experience for granted that he can no longer see its claims, imagines that politics involves beliefs meeting beliefs in a contest between personal wills. Thus, he talks about how things might change and the devout "might bide their time and work to build up the political capital that would make success possible, just as the Christian Right is doing today when it elects members to school boards" (2305). In his view, their advantage is what liberals take to be a disadvantage: "they really *believe* something" (2292). But he is able to be so impressed by the intensity of the beliefs of the Christian Right only because he does not indicate exactly how limited their petitions are. Vicki Frost, like members of the Christian Right who get elected to school boards, ask that their beliefs be given a free ride, that people accord them a courtesy and treat their beliefs as if they were to be taken seriously. The content of this claim on behalf of one's belief is minimal—particularly since it applies to a belief that is very remote from the practices of every-day life. Whether you believe that god created the world in six days and rested, or whether you believe that the world gradually evolved without benefit of such divine purposive activity, you are talking about beliefs that are remote from thoughts about how you're going to spend your day.

Two points are worth underscoring here, and they are in fact related to one another. The first is that Fish imagines that the problem that people have with belief is merely with other people's belief, when it is often hard to identify the teams with the clarity that Fish would like. The second is that the very evangelism that Fish imagines that people ought always to engage under the banner of their beliefs—"biding their time," "building up political capital," working and waiting for their eventual success—seems most often to work in a different direction: the beliefs, on being distributed to ever greater numbers of persons over time, tend to lose their hard edge, the sharpness of definition that Fish admires in the beliefs of the Christian Right. While Fish suggests that liberals dismissively identify virtually everyone who falls outside their circle of agreement as crazy, the courtroom arguments over Mormon fundamentalist Ron Lafferty's sanity in his murder trial were arguments made in a Mormon state before what must have been a predominantly Mormon jury. It was they, rather than some collection of liberals, who were asked to accept the idea that funda-mentalist Mormonism really justified an individual in thinking that he had spoken with God and that he had been instructed to kill his sister-in-law under the doctrine of blood atonement. The real historical contingency at work in a situation like his is that his beliefs—however firmly and feelingly he holds them—look archaic to a jury of his peers. And no amount of working and waiting is going to help here because no view can "build up political capital" if it is essentially a monologue, with a believer speaking only to himself and a god whom no one else can hear.

The essential point is that Fish should take seriously his own opening remark: "If you believe something you believe it to be true, and perforce, you regard those who believe contrary things to be in error" (2258). That statement ought, I think, to cover not just what one might call active beliefs—the ones that you might list as ones that you espouse and act on—but also negative beliefs—the difficulty of being convinced that God is talking to Ron and Dan Lafferty or that a dog spoke to David Berkowitz. Liberalism has neither the commitment nor the ability to treat conflicting views as if they were equally valid and valuable, nor should there be any requirement for it to deliver on such an impossibility. To make this observation is to see that liberals like Amy Gutmann and Dennis Thompson (whom Fish criticizes for what he sees as their baseless exclusions) are not, as Fish charges, trying to decide on sets of true and untrue beliefs, are not expressing complacency about the correctness of their liberal views and smugly dismissing the mistakenness of slaveholding or religiously authorized violence as insane and therefore outside the realm of rational discussion.[18] They are instead being responsive to historical change and its impact on the availability of certain beliefs. If Bentham saw historical process at work when he observed that a human law that deals in alibis and evidence that was based on the proposition that an individual could only be in one place at one time had won out over a religious belief that does not recognize such claims, Gutmann and Thompson similarly make a practical historical observation. What they properly acknowledge is that defending slavery in the United States at the beginning of the twenty-first century has no real chance of counting as a creditable belief, that you can admit the plausibility of someone's being a Republican and holding various views associated with that position even if you are a Democrat but that you can only treat certain views as imaginable if you discount any account of historical shifts and believe that donkeys might fly.[19]

Indeed, although Fish is in the paradoxical position of talking about the possibility that archaic religious views—people who sound like seventeenth-century Calvinists who happen to be living in the twentieth and twenty-first centuries—might "win," liberalism has more plausible resources for addressing what Fish calls historical contingency. For perhaps the strangest aspect of Fish's position is that he imagines that "winning" has metaphysical existence that can be invoked in political conflict. As he talks about how "things might change" and the Christian Right might gain more political influence, it becomes difficult to suppress a question about exactly what he thinks winning involves. He says that "Winning is a dirty word in liberal theory; it is what is supposed never to happen, unless it is imagined as the impersonal outcome of some agentless mechanism like the marketplace of ideas of universal reason" (2330) and calls for a politics that would no longer subordinate "the truth to the process of debating it" (2331):

> Politics, interest, partisan conviction, and belief are the locations of morality. It is in and through them that one's sense of justice and the good lives and is put into action. Immorality resides in the mantras of liberal theory—fairness, impartiality, and mutual respect—all devices for painting the world various shades of gray. (2333)

If those remarks sound like the language of cheerleading, the reason may be that Fish is implicitly applying a very artificial notion of contests and victory to beliefs and is thinking less about how beliefs and arguments win out and more about the time clock of a football or basketball game and its standard mechanisms for displaying the actions of teams in competition with one another, evaluating them in a score, and demonstrating public opinion in an extraordinarily limited time frame. For while Fish thinks that winning is a dirty word in liberal theory, it's hard to know what it involves for him aside from an occasion for unbridled enthusiasm.

At the same time, however, Fish's announced commitment to the moral act of pursuing the views one actively and avowedly has comes to look like a complete self-contradiction when it starts seeming as if winning weren't simply the only thing but the inevitable thing. Thus, he describes Richard Rorty's replying to a question put to him after "a characteristically strong and polemical talk" by saying that he had heard that Donald Davidson had been working on "an argument that would go in a different direction from" his and that he would have to take seriously anything that Davidson had to say.[20] In Fish's presentation, the central element of this statement that emerges is not that Rorty and Davidson might have incompatible views but rather "that internal to the web of Rorty's beliefs is a belief in the importance of anything Donald Davidson says" (283). The construction that Fish produces is one in which you already have, as part of your internal network of beliefs, both those beliefs and their opposites. It thus becomes very hard to feel that the beliefs are the point, when even the possibility of feeling that you have been bested in an argument looks like a belief for which you should be given the credit of a victory. Fish seems to think that you could plausibly avoid noticing that the belief you had earlier been championing looked less tenable than an opposing view and could instead insist that you had somehow believed the opposite of your belief all along.

Indeed, trying to identify Fish's commitment to particular beliefs—or, perhaps more accurately, to see the relationship between one's particular beliefs and winning—is a project that is vexed at many points. In the "Mission Impossible" essay Fish uses exactly the opposite approach from the one he deployed in his commentary on Rorty's beliefs in "Beliefs about Belief": that is, he disagrees even with those with whom he would appear to agree.[21] Thus, he quotes a passage from Chantal Mouffe's *The Return of the Political* in which she rejects "the reliance of [liberal] theorists like Rawls on supposed 'self-evident' norms of neutrality and fairness" and goes on to say that "the easy invocation of these values, '[f]ar from being a benign statement of fact .. is the result of a *decision* which already excludes from dialogue those who believe that different values should be the organizing ones of the political order'" (2326). Fish quite rightly recognizes these views as familiar to the readers of his essay when he addresses them in a stage whisper: "(You will recognize this as the argument of the present Article.)" (2326). Yet the essay takes the peculiar turn of identifying people—Bonnie Honig, Steven Smith, and Chantal Mouffe—who share the views he has announced and proceeding to attack them as closet liberals because he thinks that they think that naming the inevitability of politics might "ameliorate it or make it easier to negotiate" (2332).

If you can agree with people whose positions are opposed to yours and disagree with people whose positions are extraordinarily close to yours, a significant problem arises for the notion of belief but, more importantly, for the notion of politics. For it becomes clear that politics cannot involve biding your time and building up political capital—if political capital involves any kind of common ground with other people. Indeed, this pattern of agreeing with those who contradict you and contradicting those who agree with you sounds like a version of liberalism simultaneously demotic and demonic. The injunction to "figure out what you think is right and then look around for ways to be true to it" turns out to be as useful as most general maxims of conduct. In this case, however, the passionate truth to beliefs turns out primarily to involve contradicting them oneself. Rawls could scarcely have asked for so strong an example of the "inevitability of dissensus."

My real aim here is not to disclose some "true" identity for Stanley Fish but to make an observation about belief and its connection to emotion— and to notice that while emotion begins in the role of an attachment to one's beliefs, it quickly comes to abandon the beliefs that it had earlier championed out of a sense of the greater appeal of the pleasures of feeling that one has won or is winning. The personalizing of the political that Fish means to promote by stressing passionate attachment to one's beliefs may secure groundlessness for belief. But it also gives those beliefs an increasingly indeterminate aspect and a decreasingly political impact, if politics involves any notion of action that extends past the person. To be absolutely explicit about the matter, I am not criticizing Fish's account of belief out of a sense that it is "unfair" to someone with unfashionable beliefs but because I think that Fish produces a remarkably abstract account of belief—one in which someone and his beliefs could win without developing any kind of consensus around them, and, most particularly, one in which beliefs always precede actions and are at some distance from them (as Fish suggests when he writes that "if it is within belief that deliberation occurs and evidence becomes perspicuous and reasons persuasive, then what you believe will, as James suggests, be determinative of what you see, of what you notice, and, down the road, of what you do," 2284).

My most strenuous objection to Fish's position revolves around that phrase "down the road," which makes it sound as though one gathered one's beliefs as if accumulating capital and then invested them "down the road" in actions. That formulation disguises the way in which Fish has emptied positions of their content, endorsed agreement with opposing views, and disparaged agreement with his announced views. By contrast with such a view, Jeremy Bentham's attack on theism, *The Influence of Natural Religion on the Temporal Happiness of Mankind*, presents an account of the competition between religion and secular law for morality that analyzes how we might understand what it means to be given reasons by our experience of the world and why law might plausibly find itself bracketing religious belief. The most important feature of Bentham's account is its attention to behavior, the actions that people take that can be observed by other people, externally and without direct testimony. Bentham, I shall argue, understands action to be especially important for offering a real but necessary simplification of belief, and his arguments are essentially directed at identifying the best choices with the greatest clarity. Bentham, imagining that religion can—and should—be argued against, imagines that religious belief is inimical to what people really want and really ought to want. Insofar as people act well, they do so, he thinks, not out of religious belief but out of a more immediately available social motive—that the desire for the regard of other humans operates as a positive sanction for our beneficial actions and a negative sanction for our injurious ones.

As is apparent from the analysis I have given of Fish's position, he essentially treats emotion and the person it resides in as the sole source of value. Agreeing with persons whose views differ from yours (as in the Rorty-Davidson example) and disagreeing with persons whose views correspond to yours (as in the example of Fish and Honig, Smith, and Mouffe) makes it seem that he is willing to collapse beliefs so thoroughly into emotions that he takes it to be disabling for agreements and disagreements to rest on externalizable reasons and actions that carry merely implicit reasons within them. Individual emotions and the beliefs they generate look mysterious or capricious, and since actions that might clarify them may still be idling and hoping to pick up steam, those emotions look as unpredictable as the deity that Bentham was deducing from the behavior of the devout in his *Influence of Natural Religion.*

Bentham, however, thinks that religion suffers from a real disability in not being able to rely on sensory evidence. The argument that he makes is, in the first instance, a familiar one—that religious belief, however sincere it may be emotionally, can only draw its evidence from what he calls the "extra-experimental," because it is not apprehensible by our senses. Yet if Bentham's basic position might seem to make religious belief look merely unverifiable in the way that many subjective judgments may be, he elaborates his view well past the basic agnosticism that one can see in Rousseau's or Kant's positions on the existence of a deity. He first notices the extraexperimental character of evidence in favor of religion, conceived as "the belief in the existence of an almighty Being, by whom pains and pleasures will be dispensed to mankind, during an infinite and future state of existence" (30) and then addresses himself to the question of the effect of religious belief on society in general *"in the present life"* (italics his, 31). He notices that people have often suggested that the belief in such a deity and such posthumous rewards and punishments stimulates virtuous behavior, but he argues most strenuously against that claim. For he insists that divine law and human law must inevitably serve distinct and opposed interests.

As Bentham lays out his argument, he anticipates a version of Luhmann's notion of the autopoesis of social systems, in which the ability to depict a field of social practice under the aspect of a system also involves recognizing the boundaries of the system—elements whose inclusion would undermine the internal operation of the system. Insofar as human law is a device for encouraging people to achieve happiness or recognition by having a better understanding of where their actions are likeliest to yield happiness and recognition, its very ability to serve as any kind of guide would be compromised and rendered completely incoherent were it to admit religious law. For religious law introduces the constant hypothesis of a suspension of our confidence in any experience. It suggests that, while the sea does not usually part, it might part now; that, while dead men do not usually rise and walk, they might rise and walk now; and that once should, in the words of the bumper sticker, "expect a miracle" as one goes through the world.

Insofar as secular law and public opinion constitute nothing other than a mechanism for distributing the praise and blame of society to particular individuals for their actions, secular law must necessarily rather than incidentally be intolerant of religion. For even if religious belief might well be true if unjustified belief, it profoundly skews the economy of praise and blame. The problem that Bentham sees between religion and the "virtuous pagan," then, is not one about how to imagine the posthumous fate of good people who had no access to religion. Rather, the existence of virtuous persons all over the world and in every era suggests that religious belief is inessential for virtue. "A Christian who visits a country where his religion has never been heard of, will doubtless expect to meet with just or vicious men, varying in frequence according to circumstances: but he will never once dream of discovering any Christians there" (64). Thus, Bentham argues, "if the injunctions of piety inculcated performance or abstinence merely according as the action specified was beneficial or injurious in the present life, religion would be precisely coincident with human laws" and "religion would command and forbid the very same actions as the legislator" (65)

Bentham sees religion, however, as positively harmful to society because it exceeds its authority and originates "peculiar duties [and] crimes" (65). Far from merely falling into line with the commands and interdictions of the legislator, the devout produce a plethora of additional duties and crimes. If they begin by endorsing a god whom their descriptions unintentionally depict as capricious and tyrannical in his infinite might and inscrutability, that impulse towards self-abasement contaminates their relations with others. Although it is impossible to see earthly evidence of divine favor, it is also impossible to disprove it, which makes it possible for some people to set themselves up as if they had a "general power of attorney from the Almighty to interpret his feelings" (147). And it is this tendency—the personalization of religion—that is pernicious. The devout, Bentham observes, particularly hate the atheist, not merely because the atheist does not believe in god but also because the atheist does not value their belief as they do. For the sake of exacting obedience to a god whose existence they cannot prove or even confirm for themselves (and obedience to those who claim to be most loyal to him), they place "each man . . . under the surveillance of the rest," creating public antipathy for impious conduct (83). Insofar as the devout conception of an infinitely powerful and unknowable deity commits them to thinking of him as a being "pleased with human obedience" and therefore "pleased with those faithful allies who aid him in obtaining it" (83), they allow power to override the praise and blame of popular opinion.

In articulating the reasons why democratic political government ultimately finds itself at odds with religion, Bentham finds the most important one to be that religion regularly involves the naked assertion of power. He argues that democratic government, as opposed to autocracies, can work effectively only when it consolidates the representation of popular opinion and its praise and blame so as to eliminate the muzzling effect that power introduces into the system. Even before one takes religion into account, Bentham thinks, there will always be a struggle between power that attempts to extend itself and popular judgments. Compulsory power of any kind distorts any useful relationship between actions and their evaluation. If praise and blame are sanctions, "vested in the hands of every individual, and employed by him for his own benefit; the former *remuneratory*, and destined to encourage the manifestation of kindness towards him; the latter *punitory*, and intended to prevent injurious treatment," our ability to employ these two kinds of sanction is "proportional to our strength or weakness" (48). Thus, for example, the planter need not "bestow any eulogy upon his slave, in return for the complete monopoly of his whole life and services" but considers himself "as entitled to *demand* all this, since he possesses the means of *extorting* its fulfilment" (49). In this view, power that can command unwarranted praise and avoid warranted blame does not merely perpetuate inequality, it also prevents the judgments that individuals pass on the value of actions from contributing to the public good in constituting an implicit recommendation for future actions.

Religion, however, exacerbates the unjust secular workings of power by claiming that there is a being who really can establish—and has established—"so complete a system of espionage, as to be informed of every word which any of his subjects might utter," that "the unlimited agency of the Deity is equivalent to this universal espionage" (53). While earthly tyrants have difficulty in effecting such a system of complete "espionage" and "supervision" (53), religion by its definition of the deity and his powers accords such power to him, in turn creating a society of lackeys and a standing army of enforcers in the priesthood.

Notice exactly how far Bentham's account runs counter to the views that Fish has advocated. First, he imagines that power of the kind that Fish describes is not political power in any meaningful sense but merely a means of borrowing "compulsory force" "from the society," a kind of embezzlement from the general fund of social authority that is rightly granted to judges on the condition that it can be revoked (60). Indeed, he thinks that power as Fish conceives it—as "winning" greater influence for your beliefs than for others, constitutes an active suppression of free speech, which he portrays not simply as the ability to express your opinions but the right of any member of a society continually to pass judgment on various aspects of her world. Since Bentham thinks that persons can be supposed to know what benefits and what injures them, any power that interferes with their registering their judgments "distort[s] or disarm[s] public opinion (112–13). Religion, as the supreme example of power that never has to answer to persons, "cheats the public into the offer of a reward for conduct always useless, sometimes injurious—and embezzles part of the fund consecrated to the national service" (114). Moreover, it particularly encourages the misapplication of the popular sanction by criminating and interdicting "any number of innocent enjoyments, like the eating of pork—or any acts however extensively useful, like loans of money upon interest" (114), because it establishes doctrines unrelated to the predictability of actual experience that make it seem right to praise "monastic stripes and self-denial, or ratify the cruelty which persecution inflicts upon the unhappy dissenter" (114).

Bentham here diverges from Fish's account—and must diverge from Fish's account—because he is not merely concerned with power as the relative power that different individuals hold, express, and exercise in promoting their ideas. He can be stunningly articulate about "the intense and universal thirst for power," describing "human beings" as "the most powerful instruments of production" and noting that "every one becomes anxious to employ the services of his fellows in multiplying his own comforts" (104). Yet he appreciates an "equally prevalent hatred of subjection" (104). The distinguishing difference between humans and machines as instruments of production revolves around the necessity that persons recognize that they must—ultimately—solicit the wills of other people. While—and because—each person seeks an endorsement of his or her will from others, every one "therefore meets with an obstinate resistance to his own will, and is obliged to make an equally constant opposition to that of others" (104).

Bentham thus basically endorses the importance of the Rousseauian conception of the "general will" as the only genuinely political authority. For if he had ridiculed Blackstone for deriving the authority of the law from "an original contract" that was a historicized and literalized version of the Rousseauian social contract, he continually describes popular opinion as the expression of a general will. The general will is an outgrowth of the fact that individuals, while not necessarily having a stake in their own virtue, wish virtue on others: "it is each man's interest that his neighbour should be virtuous" (85). Society for him thus exists as a political entity in the moment in which its members recognize what Halévy highlighted in the notion of "an artificial identity of interests," which is nothing other than the recognition that everyone has a stake in keeping one's fellows virtuous, preventing the operation of power from allowing one person to appropriate another person's power as her own.

In Bentham's *Influence of Natural Religion*, the particular purchase of this notion is to de-emphasize the significance of doctrines and beliefs. Thus, while Fish identifies the emotions that people have in the exercise of their belief-laden wills and takes it as a natural fact that people will act on their beliefs, Bentham suggests exactly how the notion of a general will or social whole ought to act as a constraint on the kinds of beliefs and wills people ought to be allowed to try to force on one another. While Fish constructs a world in which our emotional attachments to our beliefs makes us feel empowered to ask that other people live by them, Bentham questions the inevitability of our martyrdom for other people's beliefs.

If Fish were to describe Bentham's argument as I have been sketching it, he might well say that it is suspiciously abstract. Yet, far from being abstract, Bentham's position is both concrete and consequential. He articulates reasons why we should refuse to accept the idea that disputes over the relative weight of religious and secular authority amount to a mere jurisdictional quibble in which some people give priority to religious law and others to secular law because their preexisting beliefs and dispositions lead them to do so. Instead, he first demonstrates that there must be a choice between religion and law: one cannot act in accordance with both secular law and religious injunctions simultaneously, because conduct requires acting in terms of one and only one of two contradictory directives. (In this regard, action simplifies our beliefs. While we may be able to walk and chew gum at the same time, we cannot play two different games at the same time.) Second, he thinks that understanding the difference between secular law and religious law enables us to hold the law to certain standards. Bentham argues, as Sade did in *Philosophy in the Bedroom*, that there should be few laws and that they should be good ones. This view sweeps away dietary laws based on religion rather than nutrition, and it obviously denies the standing of religious injunctions for self-punishment and self-abasement (which come to look like irrelevant offerings to an unseen deity who, being omnipotent, could not possibly be influenced by human gestures of praise).

At the same time, moreover, Bentham's position militates against exactly the sort of doctrine that results in the hate crimes that have become so much a feature of modern law. This much is clear not just from his *Influence of Natural Religion* but also from the essay "Paederasty," which he wrote about 1785.[22] Undertaking an analysis of the historical evidence to test the belief that homosexuality weakens men, Bentham finds that the heroism of Themistocles, Aristides, Epaminondus, Alcibiades, and Alexander appeared completely uncompromised by their sexual preferences and that the "austere philosopher" Cicero "play[ed] at blind man's buff with his secretary for pipes and [made] verses upon this notable exploit of gallantry" (7). Weighing a variety of different charges, he concludes that homosexuality costs society nothing and proposes that sodomy be decriminalized and no longer treated as a capital offense.

Now such an argument may sound a bit remote from the subject of emotion, particularly because Bentham does not press his case in terms of individual or popular sentiment. Yet from the time of his *Fragment on Government* (1776), in which he attacked Blackstone's account of English law, Bentham described "involuntary errors of the *understanding*" as regrettable but forgivable. "The sinister bias of the *affections*," by contrast, he saw as justification for "rigid censure."[23] What he criticized in Blackstone was that he was so eager to be the chief expositor and proponent of the law that he lost track of the aims of law and thus stood "forth the professed champion of religious intolerance" (16). Blackstone thought that it was important to read out the scores that had been registered in the past and to act as though the scores were identical to the rules. It was this feature of Bentham's thought that H.L.A. Hart understood and continued in his *Law, Liberty, and Morality*[24] when he attacked James Fitzjames Stephen's view that the law was designed to congeal and codify emotions. Stephen had written in his *History of the Criminal Law*,

> The sentence of the law is to the moral sentiment of the public in relation to any offence what a seal is to hot wax. It converts into a permanent final judgment what might otherwise be a transient sentiment. . . . In short the infliction of punishment by law gives definite expression and solemn ratification and justification to the hatred which is excited by the commission of the offence and which constitutes the moral or popular, as distinct from the conscientious, sanction of that part of morality which is also sanctioned by the criminal law. . . . The forms in which deliberate anger and righteous disapprobation are expressed, and the execution of criminal justice is the most emphatic of such forms, stand to the one set of passions in the same relation which marriage stands to the other [sexual passions]. (Quoted in Hart, 64)

As Hart put it, "this justification of punishment, especially when applied to conduct not harmful to others, seems to rest on a strange amalgam of ideas" (65). It combines the notion that moral condemnation is a thing of value in itself with the sense that "venting or emphatically expressing moral condemnation" is so important as to push society "uncomfortably close to human sacrifice as an expression of religious worship" (66).

Bentham's and Hart's positions enable us to discern why some notion of disinterest is and ought to be part of our conception of law. For if, as Fish suggests, the beliefs that our emotions continually fund are the only resource we as individuals have, any society worthy of continuation has an obligation to keep us from requiring human sacrifice to congeal the hot wax of our emotions from "transient sentiment" "into a permanent final judgment" (64). Bentham differs very significantly from Stephen, moreover, precisely because he does not think that law should be in the business of giving permanence to our emotions. Rather, he imagines that law ought to create a framework in which one no longer conceives of society as an inflated individual who needs to state his emotional opinions with greater and greater volume. Law ought, he thinks, to concern itself less with "justifying" our emotions through punishment than with recognizing a societal continuity that allows us to acknowledge that our emotions are changeable things. Societies in his view need to assume that, just as people have developed greater knowledge than their forebears, so will their descendants have greater knowledge than they. Indeed, in the *Influence of Natural Religion*, Bentham takes particular aim at the retrograde influence of priests. He objects to a standing army of priests because of the advantages they directly derive from "depraving" "the human intellect" (148) when they ask people to discard experimental evidence in favor of a belief in the special powers of the priestcraft and when they perpetuate schemes in which men feel obliged to apply for divine assistance because they are too ignorant or incapacitated to accomplish their purposes on their own.

In the moment in which a certain set of persons seem the authorized spokesmen for either a deity or society as a whole, the force of Bentham's systematic approach is lost. Indeed, his notion of there being something like a general depository of social regard comes to naught as soon as one introduces an economy of indemonstrable credit that seems merely to supplement the economy of demonstrable regard. And even as Mill writes his essay "Utility of Religion" principally as an enthusiastic endorsement of Bentham's argument, he erodes the power of Bentham's emphasis on a positive system in extending public opinion to include not just "the love of glory; the love of praise; the love of admiration; the love of respect and deference; even the love of sympathy" (410) but also a religion of humanity in which we make conjectures about opinions that will never be available to us in the present: "the thought that our dead parents or friends would have approved our conduct is a scarcely less powerful motive than the knowledge that our living ones do approve it: and the idea that Socrates, or Howard or Washington, or Antoninus, or Christ, would have sympathized with us . . . has operated on the very best minds, as a strong incentive to act up to their highest feelings and convictions" (421). Even though Mill's "Religion of Humanity" takes humanity rather than divinity as godhead, it suffers from the same problem that a god-based religion does: it introduces the possibility of our awarding ourselves the favor of persons who, being dead, will never be able to demonstrate it to us.

Contributors

Nancy Armstrong is Nancy Duke Lewis Professor of Comparative Literature, English, Modern Culture and Media, and Gender Studies at Brown University. She is the author of *Desire and Domestic Fiction: A Political History of the Novel* (1987), *Fiction in the Age of Photography: The Legacy of British Realism* (2000), and *How Novels Think: The Limits of Individualism from 1719 to 1900* (2005). With Leonard Tennenhouse, she coauthored *The Imaginary Puritan: Literature, Intellectual Labor, and the Origins of Private Life* (1992).

Judith Butler is Maxine Elliot Professor of Rhetoric and Comparative Literature at the University of California at Berkeley. She is the author of *Giving an Account of Oneself* (Fordham University Press, 2005).

Riccardo Caporali teaches Moral Philosophy at the University of Bologna. He is the author of *Heroes gentium. Sapienza e politica in Vico* (Bologna: Il Mulino, 1992) and *La fabbrica dell'imperium. Saggio su Spinoza* (Naples: Liguori, 2000).

Howard Caygill is Professor of Cultural History at Goldsmiths College, University of London and the author of *Art of Judgement, A Kant Dictionary, Walter Benjamin: The Colour of Experience*, and most recently, *Levinas and the Political*.

Patrick Coleman is Professor of French and Francophone Studies at the University of California, Los Angeles. He is the author of *Rousseau's Political Imagination: Rule and Representation in the "Lettre à d'Alembert"* (1984), *The Limits of Sympathy: Gabrielle Roy's "The Tin Flute"* (1993), and *Mourning and Modernity in the French Novel, 1730–1830* (1998). He has edited texts by Rousseau and Constant for Oxford World's Classics, and is the coeditor of several critical volumes, including *Culture and Authority in the Baroque* (2005). His current project is a book on anger and gratitude in the French Enlightenment.

Daniela Coli teaches History of Philosophy at the University of Florence. She is the author of *Croce, Laterza e la cultura europea* (Bologna: Il Mulino, 2nd ed. 2002), *La modernità di Thomas Hobbes* and *Giovanni Gentile*, published by Il Mulino in 1995 and 2004, respectively. She is the editor of the journal *Palomar*.

Frances Ferguson is the author of *Wordsworth: Language as Counter-spirit, Solitude and the Sublime: Romanticism and the Aesthetics of Individuation, Pornography, The Theory: What Utilitarianism Did To Action*, and articles on eighteenth- and nineteenth-century topics and literary theory. She teaches at Johns Hopkins University, where she is a Professor of English and Mary Elizabeth Garrett Professor in Arts and Sciences.

John Guillory is the Julius Silver Professor of English and Chair of the Department of English at New York University. He is the author of *Poetic Authority: Spenser, Milton, and Literary History* and *Cultural Capital: The Problem of Literary Canon Formation*. He is currently working on two books, *Literary Study in the Age of Professionalism* and *Things of Heaven and Earth: The Figure of Philosophy in English Renaissance Writing*.

Timothy Hampton is Professor of Comparative Literature and French at the University of California at Berkeley. He is currently writing a book on literary representations of diplomacy in Europe in the fifteenth, sixteenth, and seventeenth centuries.

Victoria Kahn teaches English and Comparative Literature at the University of California, Berkeley. She is the author, most recently, of *Wayward Contracts: The Crisis of Political Obligation in England, 1640–1674* (Princeton, 2004).

John P. McCormick is Professor of Political Science at the University of Chicago. He is the author of *Carl Schmitt's Critique of Liberalism: Against Politics as Technology* (Cambridge, 1997), and the editor of *Confronting Mass Democracy and Industrial Technology: German Political and Social Thought from Nietzsche to Habermas* (Duke, 2002). He is presently working on two book projects: *Weber, Habermas, and Transformations of the European State: Constitutional, Social, and Supranational Democracy*, and *Machiavellian Democracy*, both forthcoming from Cambridge University Press.

Neil Saccamano is Associate Professor of English and Comparative Literature at Cornell University. He has published on eighteenth-century literature and philosophy, and his current research centers on the aesthetics and politics of force from Hobbes to Rousseau.

Leonard Tennenhouse, Professor in the departments of Comparative Literature, English, and Modern Culture and Media at Brown University, is the author of *Power on Display: The Politics of Shakespeare's Genres* (1986) and with Nancy Armstrong, *The Imaginary Puritan* (1992). He is now completing a book on transatlantic literary relations in the eighteenth century (Princeton University Press, 2006). He has edited four collections and published a number of articles on seventeenth- and eighteenth-century British and American literature and cultural history.

Notes

Introduction

1. Norbert Elias, *Power and Civility*, trans. Edmund Jephcott (1939; New York, 1982), 8, 238–47.

2. Max Horkheimer, "Materialism and Morality," *Telos* 69 (1986): 117. This essay was originally published in 1933.

3. Max Horkheimer, "Egoism and the Freedom Movement: On the Anthropology of the Bourgeois Era," *Telos* 54 (1982): 10–11. This essay was originally published in 1936.

4. Albert Hirschman, *The Passions and the Interests* (Princeton, 1977), 12.

5. Hannah Arendt, *The Human Condition* (Chicago, 1958), 43.

6. Michel Foucault, *The History of Sexuality*, trans. Robert Hurley (New York, 1978), 138.

Tempering the *Grandi*'s Appetite to Oppress

Originally presented at the New England and American Political Science Association meetings (Providence, May 2003, and Philadelphia, August 2003, respectively). For comments on, criticisms of, and assistance with earlier drafts, I thank Corey Brettschneider, Patrick Coby, Markus Fischer, Ellen Nerenberg, Anne Norton, Gia Pascarelli, Melvin Rogers, Rogers Smith, Lucas Swaine, and Justin Zaremby.

1. Niccolò Machiavelli, *The Prince*, trans. Harvey C. Mansfield, Jr. (Chicago, 1998), composed ca. 1513 and published in 1532, cited within the text as *P*, with chapter number, in parentheses. The question of its intent was raised almost immediately after it appeared: see Peter S. Donaldson, *Machiavelli and the Mystery of State* (Cambridge, 1988), 1–29, 87–110. But the issue was framed for contemporary scholarship by Hans Baron, "Machiavelli the Republican Citizen and Author of *The Prince*" (1961), in Baron, *In Search of Florentine Civic Humanism*, vol. 2 (Princeton, 1988), 101–54.

2. See, respectively, Mary G. Dietz, "Trapping the Prince: Machiavelli and the Politics of Deception," *American Political Science Review* 80 (1986): 777–99; and John Langton, "Machiavelli's Paradox: Trapping or Teaching the Prince?" *American Political Science Review* 81 (1987): 1277–88.

3. Translated and retitled as *Discourses on Livy* by Harvey C. Mansfield and Nathan Tarcov (Chicago, 1997); originally composed by Machiavelli 1513–ca. 1519 and published in 1531; cited as *D* within the text with book and chapter numbers in parentheses. Italian references correspond with Machiavelli, *Discorsi sopra la prima deca di Tito Livio*, ed. Corrado Vivanti (Turin, 2000).

4. For example, see Quentin Skinner, *Past Masters: Machiavelli* (New York, 1981), 49–50.

5. Indeed, I take very seriously Patrick Coby's caveats regarding the search for subsurface enjoinders to action or attempts at motivation in Machiavelli's writ-

ings, specifically, "the practical problem of how hidden instructions can have an effect": see J. Patrick Coby, *Machiavelli's Romans: Liberty and Greatness in the Discourses on Livy* (Lanham, Md., 1999), 5–6, 288 n. 33. Nevertheless, in this spirit, and in the effort to open space for my tentative reasonings on *The Discourses*, I engage specific aspects of the so-called Straussian school's interpretation of the book over the course of the essay, particularly in the notes. Leo Strauss and his students have paid the most careful attention to the "rhetorical situation" of the work, and have prioritized the centrality of "appetite" to it. While my reading shares affinities with theirs in these respects, it conflicts sharply with their understanding of Machiavelli's political intentions.

6. What do we make of the fact that the specific "potential prince," Hiero of Syracuse, whom Machiavelli names as the model for his dedicatees, became a tyrant after establishing a principality? It could be an indication of the harshness, the severity, the tyrannical quality of Machiavelli's republicanism—its modes and orders, or laws and institutions, as well as the disposition of its citizens and magistrates. See Mansfield and Tarcov, "Introduction," in *Discourses on Livy*, xxv–xxvi. But the fact remains that Hiero is a singular prince, an individual tyrant, and is *not* an example of "princes plural," a fact that perhaps foreshadows Machiavelli's argument for the necessity of individual authority in the establishment or reformation of a republic (e.g., I.9, III.30). A republic is governed normally by princes plural but founded and reformed by a princely individual. Nevertheless, the tyrannical or potentially antirepublican quality of the Hiero example is perhaps moderated by the amalgam of Machiavelli's references to the Syracusan in *The Prince* and *The Discourses*: Hiero rises from private citizen to captain to prince, and frees his city from dependence on unreliable mercenary forces (P 6, 13); and the institutions that he establishes in Syracuse lay the groundwork for a more popular (I.58) or free (II.2) appropriation of them in time. Ultimately, any suggested subordination of republicanism to individual tyranny in *The Discourses'* dedication may be overturned by Machiavelli's eventual revelation that, for all his "virtuous" efforts, Hiero's principality depended on the friendship of the Roman republic for protection (II.30).

7. Indeed, one of the dedicatees, Rucellai, may have died (in 1519) before Machiavelli finalized the work, in which case Machiavelli decided not to change the dedication. See Harvey C. Mansfield, Jr., *Machiavelli's New Modes and Orders: A Study of the Discourses on Livy* (Ithaca, 1979), 22 and 22 n. 5. It will become clear that my interpretation depends less on the specific identity of the dedicatees than the fact that they are plural, young, wealthy and are members of families with distinct oligarchic prejudices.

8. This is not to say that *The Discourses* would be of no interest or use to princes proper and peoples generally (nor that *The Prince* would be of no use for princes plural or peoples). Strauss alludes to the multiple perspectives that pervade each book; how some predominate, and some are subordinate or intermittent: see Strauss, *Thoughts on Machiavelli* (Glencoe, Ill., 1958), 49; cf., Mansfield and Tarcov, "Introduction," xlii.

9. Consult Felix Gilbert's research on the pro-oligarchic/antipopulist preconceptions of the Florentine ottimati in this era, including members of the Rucellai and Buondelmonti families: Gilbert, "Florentine Political Assumptions in the Pe-

riod of Savonarola and Soderini," *Journal of the Warburg and Courtauld Institutes* 20 (1957): 187–214; Gilbert, "The Venetian Constitution in Florentine Political Thought," in *Florentine Studies: Politics and Society in Renaissance Florence*, ed. Nicolai Rubinstein (Evanston, Ill., 1968), 442–62; and Gilbert, "Bernardo Rucellai and the Orti Oricellari: A Study on the Origin of Modern Political Thought," in Gilbert, *History: Choice and Commitment* (Cambridge, Mass., 1977), 215–46. For a roughly contemporary confirmation of these dispositions in Cosimo's and Zanobi's forebears, see Francesco Guicciardini, *The History of Florence*, trans. Mario Domandi (New York, 1970), 144–45 and 299, respectively.

10. See Skinner, *Past Masters*, 49, 50; Maurizio Viroli, *Founders: Machiavelli* (Oxford, 1998), 14, 159, and e.g., Mansfield, *Machiavelli's New Modes*, 21. The ottimati background of the dedicatees is more clearly presented in the historical and biographical literature: see *The Discourses of Niccolò Machiavelli*, ed. and trans. Leslie J. Walker, vol. 2 (London, 1950), 3; Roberto Ridolfi, *The Life of Niccolò Machiavelli*, trans. Cecil Grayson (Chicago, 1963), 168, 170, 174; and Viroli, *Niccolò's Smile: A Biography of Machiavelli* (New York, 2000), 185.

11. Ridolfi, *Life of Niccolò Machiavelli*, 22–130, 133–54.

12. On the ottimati's contempt for Machiavelli, see Robert Black, "Machiavelli, Servant of the Florentine Republic," in *Machiavelli and Republicanism*, ed. Gisela Bock, Quentin Skinner, and Maurizio Viroli (Cambridge, 1990), 71–99, here 97; John M. Najemy, "The Controversy Surrounding Machiavelli's Service to the Republic," in *Machiavelli and Republicanism*, 102–17, here 117; Felix Gilbert, *Machiavelli and Guicciardini: Politics and History in Sixteenth Century Florence* (Princeton, 1965), 172–74; and Ridolfi, *Life of Niccolò Machiavelli*, 130–32.

13. See Elena Fasano Guarini, "Machiavelli and the Crisis of the Italian Republics," in Bock, Skinner, and Viroli, *Machiavelli and Republicanism*, 17–40, here 20–21.

14. Najemy, "Controversy Surrounding Machiavelli's Service," 103, 113, 117.

15. See John M. Najemy, ed., *Between Friends: Discourses of Power and Desire in the Machiavelli—Vettori Letters of 1513–1515* (Princeton, 1993); and Gilbert, *Machiavelli and Guicciardini*.

16. See Ridolfi, *Life of Niccolò Machiavelli*, 174; and J. R. Hale, *Machiavelli and Renaissance Italy* (New York, 1963), 150.

17. Strauss emphasizes the fact that the dedicatee of *The Prince*, Lorenzo, was Machiavelli's "master." See Leo Strauss, "Niccolo Machiavelli, 1469–1527," in *History of Political Philosophy*, ed. Strauss and Joseph Cropsey (Chicago, 1972), 271–92, here 278 (twice). While Strauss acknowledges that the dedicatees of *The Discourses*, Machiavelli's "two young friends" (whom, if I'm not mistaken, Strauss names nowhere in any of his works), "compelled" Machiavelli to write the book, Strauss does not seem to consider the extent to which they too might be Machiavelli's "masters." There are indications that he rethought this when considering the young dedicatee discussed in his "How to Begin to Study [Maimonides'] *Guide of the Perplexed*" (1963), in Strauss, *Liberalism Ancient and Modern* (Chicago, 1995), 140–84, at 145–49.

18. It is obviously no accident that Machiavelli did *not* title the book dedicated to a prince proper *A Commentary on the Strategies and Actions of Successful and Almost-Successful Princes from Moses to Cesare Borgia*. Therefore, there must

be some significant differences among different kinds of princes for Machiavelli, even beyond those that the titles suggest obtain between princes proper and princes plural. In *The Discourses*, there seem to exist princes senatorial, tyrannical, military, plebeian, tribunate, philosophic, and even "the people" as prince. Are they all the same? Mansfield is fond of suggesting that, for Machiavelli, indeed they are: see, e.g., *Machiavelli's New Modes*, 139; and Mansfield, *Machiavelli's Virtue* (Chicago, 1996), 246.

19. On the issue of just how cultivated a grandi audience might be: I assume that Machiavelli's dedicatees or readers like them will have a general familiarity with Roman constitutional arrangements and Livy's history of Rome, Machiavelli's ostensible source, but *not* that they will be reading Livy along with *The Discourses*, carefully cross-comparing and contrasting the texts and the events described within each of them. On the contrary, Mansfield assumes that a "present-day" noble audience *will* conduct such comparisons while a more popular audience will not. See Mansfield, *Machiavelli's New Modes*, 49, 44, respectively. I assume that neither will, but do not rule out the likelihood that Machiavelli intends for some of his readers to do so.

20. Mansfield and Tarcov render "ottimati" as "aristocrats" (e.g., I.2), which, in English, is potentially too laudatory. "Optimates" is more literal, and, while still implying some connection to excellence, inclines less toward praise or respect in the English context than "aristocrats." If Machiavelli had wanted to use that word, there were Italian equivalents available to him, even if they were infrequently used.

21. Mansfield, *Machiavelli's New Modes*, 37.

22. Machiavelli states that the tribunes were "ordered" with "much eminence and reputation" (I.3). It is not too far-fetched to assume that Machiavelli's dedicatees would be familiar with the functions that the tribunes were famously empowered to perform, and from which such eminence and reputation would derive: the tribunes could veto consular, senatorial, and legislative measures; they could free plebs who were seized and confined by patricians for whatever reason; and their persons were sacrosanct, that is, they could not be touched physically by a noble. See Andrew Lintott, *The Constitution of the Roman Republic* (Oxford, 1999), 121–28. Machiavelli will emphasize their wielding of public accusations against magistrates and notable citizens (I.7).

23. In theory and in practice, see, respectively, Cynthia Farrar, "Ancient Greek Political Theory as a Response to Democracy," in *Democracy: The Unfinished Journey, 508 BC to AD 1993*, ed. John Dunn (Oxford, 1993), 17–40; and Danielle Allen, *The World of Prometheus: The Politics of Punishing in Democratic Athens* (Princeton, 2000). For significant qualification of the grounds for such anxieties, see Arlene W. Saxonhouse, *Athenian Democracy: Modern Mythmakers and Ancient Theorists* (South Bend, Ind., 1997), and Susan Sara Monoson, *Plato's Democratic Entanglements: Athenian Politics and the Practice of Philosophy* (Princeton, 2000).

24. Mansfield, *Machiavelli's New Modes*, 43.

25. Therefore, I disagree with Coby's assertion that Machiavelli distinguishes between the patricians of Rome, on the one hand, and the nobility of medieval and Renaissance Europe, including the Florentine ottimati, on the other. See Coby,

Machiavelli's Romans, 65, 304 n. 62. I do agree with Coby against Alfredo Bona-deo, however, that Machiavelli does not desire the elimination or demise of the grandi—except, I would aver, under very specific circumstances (see notes 30 and 49 below). Nevertheless, consult Bonadeo's provocative essays, "The Role of the People in the Works and Times of Machiavelli," *Bibliotheque d'Humanisme et Renaissance* 32 (1970): 351–78; and "The Role of the 'Grandi' in the Political World of Machiavelli," *Studies in the Renaissance* 16 (1969): 9–30.

26. Although Machiavelli concedes in *P* 9 that "libertà," seemingly a euphemism for a republic, is one of the possible outcomes of grandi-popular interaction.

27. Sullivan deems the characteristic pleb reaction "defection"; an apt indication of what Coby identifies as their basic "at-restness." See Vickie B. Sullivan, *Machiavelli's Three Romes: Religion, Human Liberty, and Politics Transformed* (Dekalb, Ill., 1996), 114; and Coby, *Machiavelli's Romans*, 97. However, Vatter may go a bit too far in characterizing the pleb demeanor as the appetite for "no-rule," as this seems to collapse the distinction between oppression, which Machiavelli states that the people seek to avoid, and government, which Machiavelli seems to suggest, when conducted through law, or, for instance, experienced in military service, the people will tolerate and perhaps even welcome (especially as they become aware of the necessity of ordered and legal government for the realization of their desire not to be oppressed). See Miguel E. Vatter, *Between Form and Event: Machiavelli's Theory of Political Freedom* (Amsterdam, 2000), 91–95.

28. Machiavelli's terms, "uomo da bene" and "uomo degno di fede," correspond closely with the self-attributions of Roman patricians.

29. Contiones were called and presided over by a magistrate, but its unclear whether only magistrates or nobles could actually speak in them. See Lintott, *Constitution of the Roman Republic*, 44–45, and Henrik Mouritsen, *Plebs and Politics in the Late Roman Republic* (Cambridge, 2001), 46–47. The first specific example of a concione invoked by Machiavelli is called and conducted by a plebeian dictator and a plebeian master of horse (I.5). Coby points out Machiavelli's failure to discuss the formal assemblies, or *comitia* (the *centuriata*, *curiata*, and *tributa*). See Coby, *Machiavelli's Romans*, 56. Yet Machiavelli does describe if not name the *concilium plebis* (I.18), and explicitly mentions the contiones quite often (e.g., I.4, I.5, III.34, and III.46). Machiavelli's suggestion that "any citizen at all" could speak out on laws, public policy, as well political and military appointments in these legislative (the concilium) and deliberative (the concioni) assemblies is a radical departure from Roman practice, which kept deliberation, especially popular deliberation, away from actual voting; and from Florentine aristocratic preference, which sought to forbid any deliberation in the popular assembly—if the ottimati couldn't disband the latter completely. On Rome, see Lily Ross Taylor, *Roman Voting Assemblies: From the Hannibalic Wars to the Dictatorship of Caesar* (Ann Arbor, 1990); on Florence, see J.G.A. Pocock, *The Machiavellian Moment: Florentine Political Thought and the Atlantic Political Tradition* (Princeton, 1975), 129, 253, 255.

30. But do all grandi have a desire to dominate, and hence do they all owe their wealth and status to this humor alone? No. Surely some gain the latter by inheritance or chance and try to maintain them slothfully, rather than through

continued domination. Machiavelli has a word for this subset of grandi, *gentilu-omi*, or gentlemen; and he explains what tends to happen to them among virtuous people (I.55). The implication is that such grandi do not remain great for very long. For the most thorough discussion of the grandi-popolo distinction in *The Discourses*, especially, the place of nature and circumstance within it, see Coby, *Machiavelli's Romans*, 13, 93, 96.

31. The prince should ponder why men (e.g., *P* 17) seem to have a different nature than the "people," according to the book (e.g., *P* 9), but we might assume that he does not. Machiavelli uses "men" to stand for the people or the plebs in I.47.

32. Consult the imagined conversations between the young ottimati and the low-born but highly accomplished Medici henchman, Bernardo del Nero, in Guicciardini's *Dialogue on the Government of Florence*, trans. Alison Brown (Cambridge, 1994).

33. See Bernard Manin, *The Principles of Representative Government* (Cambridge, 1997), 42–93, 132–60.

34. For representative views of Venice in the Florentine political imagination, see Gilbert, "The Venetian Constitution in Florentine Political Thought," and Guicciardini, *Dialogue on the Government of Florence*. On views of Venice more widely, see William J. Bouwsma, *Venice and the Defense of Republican Liberty* (Berkeley, 1968) and E.O.G. Haitsma Mulier, *The Myth of Venice*, trans. G. T. Moran (Assen, 1980).

35. Here I rely on arguments already elaborated in my "Machiavellian Democracy: Controlling Elites With Ferocious Populism," *American Political Science Review* 95, no. 2 (2001): 297–314; and "Machiavelli Against Republicanism: On the Cambridge School's 'Guicciardinian Moments,'" *Political Theory* 31, no. 5 (2003): 615–43 ; to be further developed in *Machiavellian Democracy* (Cambridge, forthcoming).

36. Mansfield, *Machiavelli's New Modes*, 46.

37. For instance, Livy, *The Rise of Rome: Books 1–5*, trans. T. J. Luce (Oxford, 1998), 226–28; and, in general, Charles-Louis, baron de Montesquieu, *Considerations on the Causes of the Greatness of the Romans and Their Decline*, trans. David Lowenthal (Indianapolis, 1999).

38. Coby points out that I.37 contradicts noble charges entertained by Machiavelli regarding the supposed limitlessness of the people's ambition. See Coby, *Machiavelli's Romans*, 97.

39. Perhaps unwittingly reading Aristotle in a Machiavellian fashion, Bernie Yack defines the "political" as the competition between differing perspectives on justice, domination, and class: see Bernard Yack, *Problems of a Political Animal: Community, Justice and Conflict in Aristotelian Political Thought* (Berkeley, 1993). This analysis shares much with Vatter's exciting examination of political conflict and libertà in Machiavelli: see Vatter, *Between Form and Event*, especially 108–9.

40. Interestingly, the grandi spokesman invokes the unsuccessful populist insurgent, Marius, rather than Caesar himself, who actually usurped the liberty of the republic. Perhaps Marius is the more hated by the nobles because, unlike Caesar, who is more to be feared, Marius was of notoriously low birth. Mansfield has

a different interpretation of Machiavelli's invocation of Marius here: see Mansfield, *Machiavelli's New Modes*, 47 n. 39.

41. One is tempted to explore the many discrepancies between Machiavelli's account of the episode and Livy's, but, for reasons mentioned above (note 19), I will resist this impulse here.

42. Mansfield accepts the nobles' response that the people and the dictator were acting "extraordinarily," but it is not clear on what grounds. See Mansfield, *Machiavelli's New Modes*, 48. If he means the use of the dictatorship itself, Machiavelli later identifies the office as an *ordinary* institution that addresses *extraordinary* circumstances (I.34). Moreover, Mansfield speculates that the plebeian dictator is seeking the consulship for himself, but Machiavelli's readers would likely know that dictators almost always previously served as consuls. See Arthur Kaplan, *Dictatorships and "Ultimate" Decrees in the Early Roman Republic, 501–202 BC* (New York, 1977), 2; and Richard E. Mitchell, *Patricians and Plebeians: The Origin of the Roman State* (Ithaca, N.Y., 1990), 137.

43. An added reason to suspect that Machiavelli assumes that a grandi audience might skip over this last section of I.5 is the very presence of a pleb dictator within it. At this point in *The Discourses*, Machiavelli has yet to persuade the grandi to allow the people their own magistrates, the tribunes. Moreover, his case that the plebs should be permitted to stand for noble-dominated offices like the consulate is made very gingerly and gradually over the course of Book I, culminating in I.60. Thus, if the grandi were to observe here that Machiavelli permits or advocates that the plebs assume the dictatorship—traditionally, the magistracy of last resort for grandi suppression of the plebs—they might not bother to read any further. Machiavelli assumes that the resolution of the debate over populist versus oligarchic republics and the elaboration of the imperialism issue in the next chapter are so compelling for the grandi, that he may be willing to risk losing their attention altogether with the contents of I.5's conclusion should they remain to read it.

44. See Strauss, *Thoughts on Machiavelli*, 110–14; Mansfield, *Machiavelli's New Modes*, 45–53; Mansfield, *Machiavelli's Virtue*, 85–92; Victoria Kahn, *Machiavellian Rhetoric: From the Counter-Reformation to Milton* (Princeton, 1994), 50–51, 261 n. 13; Sullivan, *Machiavelli's Three Romes*, 63–66; and Coby, *Machiavelli's Romans*, 39–41.

45. Paul Rahe emphasizes appetite in Machiavelli's ostensible endorsement of empire, Markus Fischer prioritizes glory, and Coby emphasizes greatness: see Paul A. Rahe, "Situating Machiavelli," in *Renaissance Civic Humanism: Reappraisals and Reflections*, ed. James Hankins (Cambridge, 2000), 270–308; Fischer, *Well-Ordered License: On the Unity of Machiavelli's Thought* (Lexington, 2000); and Coby, *Machiavelli's Romans*, 261–68.

46. Strauss notes that Machiavelli's Roman nobles are consumed by "the insatiable desire of each for eternal glory in this world." Strauss, *Thoughts on Machiavelli*, 134; cf., 250. But this is not an assumption that Machiavelli would make necessarily about either grandi in general, or his noble dedicatees a priori. Machiavelli's characterization of the Roman nobility in *The Discourses* is, in this respect, prescriptive not descriptive. The grandi appetite to oppress is *not* in and of itself the same as the desire for worldly glory, in particular, through imperial conquest.

Machiavelli labors to move them from the one to the other, the former to the latter, and in this essay I try to show that much of the argument and action of the early discourses strategically serves that attempted manipulation. And, again, as the history of ancient and early-modern city-states generally shows, most grandi prefer a predominance of men of virtue (read: wealth and title) in the magistracies, defensive security over empire, and domestic stability over class conflict. See Daniel Waley, *The Italian City-Republics* (London, 1969), 88–157; Raphael Sealey, *A History of the Greek City States, 700–338 BC* (Berkeley, 1976), 66–133, 238–68; and Anthony Molho, Kurt Raaflaub, and Julia Emlen, eds., *City States in Classical Antiquity and Medieval Italy* (Ann Arbor, 1991), 33–52, 93–169, 289–354, 565–640. In other words, the grandi of most oligarchies (which the overwhelming number of republics were and still are) were content with dominating their own, and acquiring modest renown within their own regime. The assumption that Machiavelli is encouraging his elite to follow their most basic nature, understood as a desire for glory, is then one step removed from what is actually their more fundamental inclinations. They have a humor to dominate, according to Machiavelli, *not* to be famous. The desire to oppress or command has no inherent link with the desire for glory; it pertains to the pure pleasure of making someone do something they might not have done otherwise, or of lording over them a privilege or status that they themselves do not possess. It does not mean having one's name revered eternally. Bullies do not ordinarily think about eternity. Machiavelli's gambit is to offer such bullies domination over *mortality and time* in exchange for some relinquishing of their domination over their own poorer citizens: include the latter in politics so you can conscript them into the army, expand your regime, and possibly achieve eternal fame for yourselves. Machiavelli's founders or would-be founders could be said to be driven naturally by a desire for eternal glory—for them the appetite to oppress and for glory are entwined—but it's less than clear whether history demonstrates, or Machiavelli assumed, that this also applies to the grandi as a class. Therefore, like Strauss, Mansfield and Tarcov may too easily collapse the grandi appetite to dominate with the appetite for glory: without qualification they equate "those whose natures insist on [ruling]" with "those who want glory." See "Introduction," xxviii; cf., Mansfield, *Machiavelli's Virtue*, 238.

47. In addition, the exclusion of the Swiss and the Athenians from the context of the debate over liberty, power, and greatness in I.6 is quite curious. Machiavelli's neglect of Athens cannot be attributed simply to the fact that, as he states in I.2, it is a "simple" popular regime or democracy as opposed to a "mixed" republic: after all, Machiavelli refers to Athens as a republic subsequently (e.g., I.28). And yet the Athenians are an example of a regime that entrusted the people with the guard of liberty, achieved greatness and fame commensurate with Rome's, and yet whose expansionary policies led to the enslavement of much of Hellas and a devastating collapse of the regime domestically. Athens is a populist republic that rivals Rome in greatness but highlights the drawbacks of expansion. The Swiss are an even more interesting case because Machiavelli sometimes intimates that he admires them as much as the Romans, and, given their historical and geographic proximity, fears them more. Read I.12, II.4, II.12, II.16 in light of Machiavelli's exchange with Vettori in Najemy, *Between Friends*, 156–75. The

Swiss are as powerful militarily as were the Romans, but do not expand, or at least do not expand imperially: they contract their troops to regimes who do not arm their people like France, and augment themselves through enlargement of their confederation—i.e., in a way that preserves or enhances the liberty of new territories, rather than extinguishing it. The Swiss are populist republics that rival Rome in power but highlight the nonnecessity of imperial expansion (but amplify the necessity of military might). Therefore, Strauss and his students may accept too readily Machiavelli's association in II.4 of the Swiss republican confederation with the ancient Etruscan ("Tuscan") one that Rome defeated. See Strauss, *Thoughts on Machiavelli*, 182; cf., Sullivan, *Machiavelli's Three Romes*, 173–74. Machiavelli's examples of how the ancient French seized Lombardy from the Tuscans and how the Romans overwhelmed the latter (II.4) may be, respectively, an ironic commentary on contemporary French-Swiss relations, and an angry underscoring of the present plight of republicanism in North Central Italy. Machiavelli often remarks how the French monarchy is now the virtual puppet of the Swiss republics; and Tuscan republicanism (under a league or a hegemonic city) is made impossible by the church's alternating collusions with France, Spain, and the German emperor to maintain and/or expand the papal states. On Florentine debates over expansion and imperial options, and Machiavelli's place within them, see Alissa Ardito, "Machiavelli's Madisonian Moment: The Tuscan Territorial State as Extended Republic," Ph.D. diss., Department of Political Science, Yale University, 2004. So why might not Machiavelli more openly support the Swiss model in *The Discourses*? Because there is no inducement for his grandi addressees to adopt it: it promises advantages for the people and none for them. Machiavelli must, on the contrary, entice them with a republican model that entails empire so as to encourage them to accept more egalitarian and participatory politics at home. With carrot (glory) and stick (necessity) Machiavelli compels his dedicatees to pursue empire, and so leverages a more populist domestic politics out of them in the process. But to what extent will the people abide by grandi direction of imperial expansion once they've been included in domestic politics in the long run? The grandi might be heartened by the elite manipulation of the plebs as citizens and troops that Machiavelli describes throughout *The Discourses*, but the people might learn how to resist it precisely on the basis of those descriptions. For a fine-grained examination of Machiavelli's estimation of the pros and cons of Swiss military policy, see Coby, *Machiavelli's Romans*, 119–20, 138–39. Ultimately, whatever the idiosyncratic advantages or inherent deficiencies of the Swiss confederate-republican model invoked by Machiavelli, they are no more peculiar or deleterious than those that he ascribes to the Roman imperial-republican model. Thus, if it remains an open question whether or not liberty trumps empire in *The Discourses*, then the former model would seem to remain a viable option.

48. In particular, Cosimo's family, the Rucellai, had close ties to the Medici: see the chapter "The Patriciate" in Gene A. Brucker's *Renaissance Florence* (Berkeley, 1969), especially 125–27. This relationship continued during the era of the Orti: see Gilbert, "Bernardo Rucellai and the Orti Oricellari," 218–22. Zanobi Buondelmonti, on the other hand, conspired in the unsuccessful plot to overthrow the Medici in 1524, but managed to flee to safety. See Ridolfi, *Life of Niccolò Machiavelli*, 203.

49. Mansfield suggests that Machiavelli's true teaching is that the tribunes were created and the accusations ordered by the Roman grandi for their own purposes—i.e., to "manage" the plebs—rather than negotiated by the people and instituted for their benefit. See, e.g., *Machiavelli's Virtue*, 242–43. This is a very intriguing reading, one that I cannot engage fully here. I would only point out some factors that might militate against such a conclusion. In the case of the tribunes: in the passages describing their establishment in I.2 and 3, the arrangement of the indefinite pronouns, the passive verb constructions, and certainly the suggestive context would all indicate that the tribunes were jointly created by the plebs and the senate. Moreover, Machiavelli declares that the nobles reluctantly agreed to the establishment of the tribunes; that they were "constrained to yield" to their creation (I.2). In addition, Machiavelli often describes the senate's desire to be rid of the tribunes altogether (I.40). This is hardly the disposition or behavior of those who are using the tribunes to their own ends on a consistent basis. In any case, nowhere does Machiavelli suggest that the senate would have created the tribunes without the people instigating their establishment in the first place. Also, Machiavelli gives clear examples where the tribunes act against the senate (e.g., I.7, I.51). So are they really the stooges of the latter in all cases? The accusations are a more complicated issue. Mansfield insists that Machiavelli presents them as a device whereby the nobility can deflect popular enmity from themselves as a class to a troublesome individual member of their group—a win-win situation in which the people as a whole are satisfied (*they* decide to absolve or convict) and the grandi as a class are preserved no matter what the outcome. Mansfield doesn't consider the extent to which a refined focus on and recourse against fewer prominent citizens or even one of them rather than large numbers of them is good for the people as well. What kind of "animus" would frequent trials and convictions of many grandi arouse in the latter against the plebs, and what would be the result? The cycles of vengeance described in I.7–8, which ensue absent formal accusation procedures, can hurt large numbers of the people, as well as the great. Ultimately, Machiavelli "pitches" the argument for accusations in terms of the grandi's interest because they are his declared audience, after all. However, on the other hand, Mansfield may exaggerate the extent to which Machiavelli himself would only like to see individual members of the grandi sacrificed, so that their class may endure. Sometimes a whole set of grandi seem to outlive their usefulness. Throughout both *The Prince* and *The Discourses* there are instances where the grandi as a class are wiped out, usually cut to pieces, and Machiavelli sheds no tears for them; in fact, there is an inferred justice to the event. For example, Clearchus, Hiero, and Baglioni cut to pieces or clearly should have, respectively, a city's nobility, a group of *condottieri*, and the prelates of the church (I.16, *P* 13, and I.27). These are, incidentally, the three kinds of grandi who, when corrupt (that is, when beyond ordinary account), most viciously oppress the people: oligarchs, officers, and priests. Machiavelli states that the "people" and "everyone" are satisfied, or would have been, by the actions of the individual tyrants in at least two of these three episodes. On the metaphoric import of these "cuttings to pieces," see McCormick, "Machiavellian Democracy," 298. I would be remiss if I didn't point out where Machiavelli shows that the people are capable of taking such matters into their own hands against the grandi, as in Corcyra, to the same

"satisfying" effect (II.2). It seems that Machiavelli wants his grandi audience to be aware of, if not dwell too long on, such episodes, and accept accusations as a much less inconvenient alternative, but one that might be equally beneficial to the people. Except when compelled to do so by the form of a commentary (as in *Machiavelli's New Modes*), Mansfield does not focus on these episodes in *Machia-velli's Virtue*, as if he wanted to protect the grandi from the possibilities of such outcomes. His motivation to do so may be significantly greater than was that of his principal object of investigation.

Difficult Engagements
Private Passion and Public Service in Montaigne's *Essais*

1. All citations will be from Montaigne's *Oeuvres complètes*, edited by Thi-baudet and Rat (Paris, 1962). Page numbers will be included in the text, along with the conventional letters (a), (b), and (c) to indicate the different "levels" of Montaigne's frequently revised text. The English passages, unless otherwise indicated, will be taken from the version by Donald Frame in *The Complete Es-says of Montaigne* (Stanford, 1967). I have here been quoting the king's letter, which may be found on page 1657 of the Thibaudet and Rat edition. The transla-tion of the letter is mine.

2. See, for example, the excellent accounts in Madeleine Lazard's *Montaigne* (Paris, 1992), 281–310, and Geralde Nakam's *Montaigne et son temps* (Paris, 1993), 302–24. Both scholars note that Montaigne's reelection was difficult, and that a number of ultra-Catholics, including several of Montaigne's own relatives, opposed him. On Montaigne's role as a political mediator during his term as mayor see Zachary Sayre Schiffman, "An Intellectual in Politics; Montaigne as Mayor of Bordeaux," in *Changing Identities in Early Modern France*, ed. Michael Wolfe (Durham, N.C., 1997), 307–24.

3. I have slightly modified Frame's translation here to make it conform more closely to the original.

4. Albert O. Hirschman, *The Passions and the Interests: Political Arguments for Capitalism before Its Triumph* (Princeton, 1977), 14–20.

5. The phrase "crisis of the aristocracy" comes, of course, from Lawrence Stone's well-known book of that name. On the vicissitudes of aristocratic identity in late-Renaissance France see Jonathan Dewald, *Aristocratic Experience and the Origins of Modern Culture: France, 1570–1715* (Berkeley, 1993). Themes of aris-tocratic identity and ethical choice in Montaigne's work have been explored with insight by a number of recent critics. See, in particular, David Quint, *Montaigne and the Quality of Mercy: Political and Moral Themes in the Essays* (Princeton, 1998), and Ullrich Langer, *Vertu du discours, discours de la vertu* (Geneva, 1999).

6. On the crisis of public life generally in late-sixteenth-century France see J.H.M. Salmon, *Society in Crisis: France in the Sixteenth Century* (London, 1974), chaps. 7–9.

7. On Montaigne's "Politique" moderation see Quint, *Montaigne and the Quality of Mercy*, chaps. 2 and 4, as well as Geralde Nakam, *Montaigne et son temps*, chap. 4.

8. In my use of the phrase "technologies of selfhood," I have in mind the late work of Michel Foucault on the construction of subjectivity through various historically contingent techniques of self-definition and strategies of self-transformation. See Foucault's essays "Technologies of the Self" and "The Hermeneutic of the Subject," in *Michel Foucault: Ethics Subjectivity and Truth*, ed. Paul Rabinow, trans. Robert Hurley and others (New York, 1997).

9. Cicero, *On Duties*, ed. and trans. M. T. Griffin and E. M. Atkins (Cambridge, 1991), 29. Panurge's comments to Pantagruel are in the eighteenth chapter of Rabelais's *Tiers Livre*.

10. On the importance of Ciceronian notions of public service for Renaissance moral philosophy see Peter N. Miller, *Defining the Common Good* (Cambridge, 1994), chap. 1.

11. Cicero, *On Duties*, 29.

12. *De Constantia* was first published in 1584, in Latin. I have consulted *De la Constance*, the French translation that appeared anonymously in the year of Montaigne's death, 1592. See the reprint of this version published by Noxia (Paris, 2000).

13. On the figure of the home in Montaigne, see Georges van den Abbeele, *Travel as Metaphor: From Montaigne to Rousseau* (Minneapolis, 1991), as well as George Hoffman, *Montaigne's Career* (Oxford, 1998), chap. 1.

14. I have altered Frame's translation. He lends the term "place" a mercantile coloration that it doesn't necessarily have in French by rendering it as "market place."

15. Quoted in Miller, *Defining the Common Good*, 23.

16. See Miller, *Defining the Common Good*, 27, as well as Maurizio Viroli, *From Politics to Reason of State* (Cambridge, 1992), chaps. 2 and 3.

17. There is some disagreement as to whether Montaigne advocates a notion of reason of state or not. See, in this context, Robert J. Collins, "Montaigne's Rejection of Reason of State in 'De l'Utile et de l'honneste,'" in *Montaigne's Message and Method*, ed. Dikka Berven (New York, 1995), 377–400. Collins is taking issue with earlier work by Quentin Skinner and Nannerl Keohane. David Louis Schaeffer engages similar topics in *The Political Philosophy of Montaigne* (Ithaca, N.Y., 1990), chap. 7.

18. I note in passing the fact that "De l'utile et de l'honneste" and "De l'inconstance de nos actions" are the opening essays in the second and third books, respectively. Both essays concern themselves with the problem of moral action in the public sphere—a theme introduced in the famous opening essay of Book I, "Par divers moyens on arrive à pareille fin."

19. Here again I have slightly altered Frame's version.

20. Rabelais's reflections on reading charitably, "in the best sense," may be found in the prologue to *Gargantua*. Augustine's discussion of charity and interpretation is in *On Christian Doctrine*, book 3, chap. 3. We might note as well that the plea to read "in the best sense" is frequently used as a rhetorical device. Thus in Montaigne's longest piece of official writing from his mayorship, a remonstrance to the king, he twice urges the king to "prendre en bonne part" his entreaties for help with various problems. See Thibaudet and Rat's edition, 1373 and 1377.

21. On Montaigne's juxtaposition of military and literary ideals see James Supple, *Arms versus Letters: The Military and Literary Ideals in the "Essais" of Montaigne* (Oxford, 1984), and David Posner, "Stoic Posturing and Noble Theatricality in the Essais," *Montaigne Studies* 4 (1992): 127–55. On the complex relationship between anger and virtue in the period see Gordon Braden's *Renaissance Tragedy and the Senecan Tradition: Anger's Privilege* (New Haven, 1985).

22. One of the few readings that links "De l'utile et de l'honneste" to "De mesnager sa volonté" is Schaeffer's, in *The Political Philosophy of Montaigne*, 364ff., who claims, however, that the two essays taken together constitute a moral argument for a very modern-sounding kind of "limited government."

23. The literature on the emergence of the modern "private" subject is, of course, immense. For a variety of perspectives one might consult the collection entitled *La problématique du sujet chez Montaigne*, ed. Eva Kushner (Paris, 1995). My own thinking has benefited from conversations with Timothy J. Reiss, and from his suggestive discussion in *Mirages of the Selfe: Patterns of Personhood in Ancient and Early Modern Europe* (Stanford, 2003), chap. 16.

24. For the changing history of oaths of fealty in the Renaissance see J. Russell Major, *From Renaissance Monarchy to Absolute Monarchy* (Baltimore, 1994), chap. 3.

25. On the traditional link between passion and rhetoric, see Gisèle Mathieu-Castellani, *La Rhétorique des passions* (Paris, 2000).

26. Reiss (*Mirages of the Selfe*, 444) argues that Montaigne's self-presentation in this passage constitutes an act of stripping himself of all private singularity, of presenting himself "qua magistrate" as "a man without qualities." This seems right to me. However, I would also want to take into account the rhetorical dimension of Montaigne's statements, the sense that this is *both* a performance that seals a compact *and* a moment of self-representation in the larger economy of the *Essais*. The whole point of Montaigne's discussions of public and private is that public actions have private consequences and vice versa. So while one may seek to divest oneself of one's particularity through a kind of speech act, that very act of negative self-description also constructs a moral portrait of the subject that connects up to Montaigne's many other descriptions of himself in negative terms (as a man without memory enough to lie in "Des Menteurs," as a man without the energy to sin in "De l'institution des enfans," and so on). The listing of what one doesn't have may empty the private self of content as it enters the public sphere, but it also constructs a literary self-portrait that Montaigne exploits elsewhere in the *Essais* in contexts that are often political.

27. For example, in the "Apologie de Raimond Sebond" (II.12, p. 498), Montaigne mentions Plato's "deciphering" of the allegory of Pluto's garden (a gesture of interpretation). And in "Observations sur les moyens de faire la guerre de Julius Caesar" (II.34, p. 715) he alludes to Caesar's description of his construction of the Pont du Gard ("de quoy il dechifre particulierement la fabrique").

28. I am indebted to Maurizio Vito for calling my attention to the importance of Palinurus in Renaissance depictions of political leadership.

29. The reference is to *Aeneid* 5.849–51.

THE BACHELOR STATE

1. Brian Vickers, ed., *Francis Bacon* (Oxford, 1996), 174; henceforth cited as Vickers. Where possible, I have used recent scholarly editions or translations of Bacon's writings. Otherwise I have quoted from the standard edition of James Spedding, Robert Leslie Ellis, and Douglas Heath, 11 vols. (London: Longman, 1857–59); henceforth cited as SEH.

2. In a letter to Lancelot Andrewes after his fall (Vickers, 328–31), Bacon takes counsel from the examples of Demosthenes, Cicero, and Seneca, remembered for their writing and not for the occasions of their expulsions from power. *New Atlantis* might also be said to belong to the genre of the "consolation of philosophy," for which Boethius would provide a pretext, but perhaps more powerfully Cicero's *Tusculan Disputations*. See also in this context Lisa Jardine and Alan Stewart, *Hostage to Fortune: The Troubled Life of Francis Bacon* (New York, 1998), 475. "As he manufactured an impressive body of scientific and philosophical writings . . . Bacon tacitly erased all signs that his 'thought' and his 'life' (in the political arena) had been intimately linked. Instead he constructed a 'before' and an 'after': before Francis Bacon was an active politician, caught up in the hurly-burly of court and parliamentary affairs . . . after, he was a patrician thinker, selflessly pursuing his scientific endeavours for posterity." I am indebted throughout this essay to Jardine and Stewart's definitive account of Bacon's life.

3. Bacon names two kings in the history of Bensalem, Solamona, who established Salomon's House nineteen hundred years before the present time of the narrative, and an earlier king, Altabin, who defended the island against an invasion by inhabitants of what is now Mexico. The lesser importance of the king after the reign of Solamona is suggested by the fact that the revelation of Christian doctrine, which the Bensalemites receive "twenty years after the ascension of our Saviour," is given first to a Fellow of Salomon's House. Bacon's point here is that the Fellows are entrusted by virtue of their knowledge of natural philosophy to distinguish between the natural and the supernatural, and so they are entrusted to certify the miraculous origins of the Bible contained in the mysterious ark on the waters; so the Fellow's reception of the sacred scripture would seem to indicate a priestly function as well as kingly. At various points in the narrative the Fellows seem to take on both roles. Other aspects of these systematic appropriations will be discussed below.

4. "Poesy Parabolical" in the same passage is said to involve "the secrets and mysteries of religion, policy, or philosophy." I do not intend to read *New Atlantis* with quite the hermeneutic freedom Bacon brings to his interpretation of ancient myths in *De Sapientia Veterum*, his chief occasion for explicating Poesy Parabolical. Bacon tends to associate secrecy with government in accord with the tradition of the *arcana imperii*. For an interesting study of this tradition, which does not concern Bacon, see Peter S. Donaldson, *Machiavelli and the Mystery of State* (Cambridge, 1988). Rawley calls *New Atlantis* a "fable" in his introductory note to the posthumous edition, which brings it into relation to the *De Sapientia Veterum*. Secrecy is a leitmotiv of *New Atlantis*, and often draws the attention of commentators. I locate secrecy in my own reading as one of the hinges between natural philosophy, which Bacon describes as "knowledge of Causes, and secret

motions of things" (Vickers, 480), and the claim to sovereignty implicit in the Father's control over the secrets of nature.

5. "The Fellows and Brethren of Salomon's House," Vickers, 471, and passim.

6. The honorific use of *Father* is familiar enough as the form of address for Catholic priests, or in the "Fathers" of the Church. Closer to Bacon's Fellow is the use of *Father* as the name for the sponsors of student candidates (that is, the bachelors) in the practice of formal disputations at Cambridge. See William J. Costello, S.J., *The Scholastic Curriculum at Early Seventeenth-Century Cambridge* (Cambridge, 1958), 17.

7. Jacques Le Goff, *Intellectuals in the Middle Ages*, trans. Teresa Lavender Fagan (Cambridge, Mass., 1993), notes a distinction current in the later Middle Ages between a *clericus* and a *philosophus*, but he also argues that the *philosophus* does not correspond to the later sense of the philosopher. Le Goff is interested in describing the emergence of university-trained "intellectuals" who are not exclusively clerics, but rather strongly involved in a variety of nontheological traditions and studies.

8. For an interesting study of friendship in the early modern period, see Alan Bray, *The Friend* (Chicago, 2003). Though I have learned much from Bray, I have some caution about his programmatic desexualization of friendship in early modernity. As will be apparent later in this essay, the sexualized friendship is a possibility Bacon had no choice but to acknowledge. Bray's work is indisputably valuable, however, as a countervailing argument to the tendency in some scholarship to regard all friendship as inescapably sexual, which also loses the tension between what is possible and what is actual in any given social relation.

9. The resolution of sectarian conflict is a corollary effect of separating natural philosophy from theology. On this point see the argument of Stephen Gaukroger, *Francis Bacon and the Transformation of Early-Modern Philosophy* (Cambridge, 2001), 74–83. This point has given rise to controversy because Bacon's separation of natural philosophy from theology has been confused with hostility toward religion. For a brief statement on this question see Perez Zagorin, *Francis Bacon* (Princeton, 1998), 49.

10. Still a very useful account of the character of the natural philosopher is Moody Prior, "Bacon's Man of Science," in *Essential Articles for the Study of Francis Bacon*, ed. Brian Vickers (Hamden, Conn., 1968), 140–63. Prior writes, 153, that in Bacon's "conception of the scientist there is a pronounced ethical element." The question of the character of the natural philosopher has more recently become the impetus for a productive area of scholarly research. In this context character or ethos bears its full classical signification as the self-presentation of a person in the rhetorical situation, that is, the situation requiring persuasion. The natural philosopher saw himself always in a rhetorical situation, in which he would necessarily have to appeal to his own public and private character as evidence for the credibility of his arguments. Recent scholarship has concentrated on two aspects of ethos cultivated by the early modern natural philosophers: (1) *civility* or politeness, usually associated with aristocratic cultural modes of verbal exchange, which tended to confirm on social grounds the credibility of the natural philosopher; and (2) *asceticism* or control over the passions, which confirmed the moral probity of the natural philosopher, and thus preempted invid-

ious comparison with the religious vocation, or moderated tensions between natural philosophy and theology. On the former theme see Steven Shapin, *A Social History of Truth: Civility and Science in Seventeenth-Century England* (Chicago, 1994); Christopher Lawrence and Steven Shapin, eds., *Science Incarnate: Historical Embodiments of Natural Knowledge* (Chicago, 1998); Mario Biagioli, *Galileo, Courtier: The Practice of Science in a Culture of Absolutism* (Chicago, 1993), and Mario Biagioli, "Etiquette, Interdependence, and Sociability in Seventeenth-Century Science," *Critical Inquiry* 22 (Winter 1996): 193–238. Biagioli's thesis in the latter essay, 205, is representative of this line of argument: "While in the long run the sociabilities of the republic of letters and court society diverged, I believe that the conditions of possibility of scientific etiquette remained framed by the processes through which authority and subjectivity were constructed within court society." On the latter theme of control over the passions, see in *Science Incarnate*, Steven Shapin, "The Philosopher and the Chicken: On the Dietetics of Disembodied Knowledge," 21–50; and Peter Dear, "A Mechanical Microcosm: Bodily Passions, Good Manners, and Cartesian Mechanism," 51–82. See also Gaukroger, *Bacon and Transformation of Philosophy*, 52: "Mastery of the passions was, in one form or another, not only a theme in philosophy but a distinctive feature of the philosophical persona from Socrates onwards, and Renaissance and early-modern philosophers pursue the theme of self-control with no less vigour than had the philosophers of antiquity. This, as we shall see, is the model, prominent in writers like Montaigne, around which Bacon wishes to shape his new practitioner of natural philosophy." Gaukroger adds in a footnote: "This is particularly evident in Bacon's posthumously published account of his scientific utopia, *New Atlantis* (1627), where self-respect, self-control, and internalized moral authority are central." Gaukroger rightly emphasizes the origin of these behavioral models in humanist thought, particularly in its complex reconsideration of ancient ethical systems such as Stoicism, inflected always, of course by Christian theology. Gaukroger is not concerned specifically with the question of bachelorhood, which I will argue below is not connected as directly as it may seem with the motive of asceticism. Shapin has a brief comment in *A Social History of Truth*, 165, on Robert Boyle's disinclination to marry. A more extended consideration of the bachelor scientist figure can be found in Robert Iliffe's contribution to *Science Incarnate*, "Isaac Newton: Lucatello Professor of Mathematics," 121–55, which examines Newton's abiding if tortured commitment to a life of chastity or sexual abstinence. The only book-length work on the connection between bachelorhood and the early modern philosopher, however, is Naomi Zack, *Bachelors of Science: Seventeenth Century Identity, Then and Now* (Philadelphia, 1996), though Zack is not concerned with Bacon in particular. Her argument will be discussed below, in the context of the distinction I propose between bachelorhood and ascetic motivations.

11. Friedrich Nietzsche, *On the Genealogy of Morals*, ed. Keith Ansell-Pearson, trans. Carol Diethe (Cambridge, 1994), 81. Just before the passage quoted, Nietzsche writes: "Thus the philosopher abhors *marriage*, together with all that might persuade him to it,—marriage as hindrance and catastrophe on his path to the optimum." And just after: "Every philosopher would say what Buddha

said when he was told of the birth of a son: Rahula is born to me, a fetter is forged for me."

12. Philosophy, of course, has produced its own critique of metaphysics along these lines, beginning with Nietzsche (or Schopenhauer? or Spinoza?). For a recent example, drawing upon the results of cognitive science, see George Lakoff and Mark Johnson, *Philosophy in the Flesh: The Embodied Mind and its Challenge to Western Thought* (New York, 1999).

13. See Diogenes Laertius, *Lives of the Eminent Philosophers*, 2 vols., trans. R. D. Hicks (Cambridge, 1972). Interest in the "lives and opinions" model of the history of philosophy persisted through the seventeenth century, exemplified best in England by Thomas Stanley's *History of Philosophy* (1655). Stanley continues to insist upon the importance of the philosopher's life. For a discussion of Stanley, see Giovanni Santinello et al., *Models of the History of Philosophy*, vol. 1, *From its Origins in the Renaissance to the "Historia Philosophica* (Dordrect, 1993), 163–203.

14. Pierre Hadot, *Philosophy as a Way of Life*, trans. Michael Chase (Oxford, 1995), 83. See also Pierre Hadot, *What is Ancient Philosophy?* trans. Michael Chase (Cambridge, 2002).

15. See Alexander Nehamas, *Nietzsche: Life as Literature* (Cambridge, 1985), and for a more general extrapolation of this conception of philosophy, Alexander Nehamas, *The Art of Living: Socratic Reflections from Plato to Foucault* (Berkeley, 1998).

16. Hadot, *What is Ancient Philosophy?*, 30: "He [Socrates] is *atopos*, meaning strange, extravagant, absurd, unclassifiable, disturbing. In the *Theaetetus*, Socrates says of himself: 'I am utterly disturbing [*atopos*], and I create only perplexity [*aporia*].'" The quotation is from *Theaetetus* 149a.

17. Today, of course, the philosopher is usually an academic, and though philosophers may have "disciples" of a sort, they need not lead a socially eccentric life, in Nietzsche's sense or Hadot's. The lives of academic philosophers signify largely in the context of a professional ethics, and the philosophy professor has much the same relation to this ethics as any other professor. Perhaps one ought as a rule to be wary of philosophers, however brilliant, who achieve a cultic status. But we should also not deceive ourselves about what has been given up with the modern construction of the philosopher. The recent return in philosophy to questions of ethics, or to "moral philosophy," suggests that philosophers themselves have become increasingly aware of what has been lost in the evolution of the philosopher's social identity. Hadot's forceful argument for understanding philosophy as a "way of life" is provocative, though it leaves unresolved the question of whether philosophers can or should move from this new reading of philosophy's history to a new practice of an implicitly cultic nature.

18. Willard Van Orman Quine, *From a Logical Point of View* (Cambridge: Harvard University Press, 1953; rpt. 1999), 20–46; J. L. Austin, *How To Do Things With Words* (Oxford, 1962).

19. Wittgenstein is perhaps the last philosopher for whom the unmarried state was integrally significant to his formation as a philosopher, as Ray Monk argues in his biography, *Wittgenstein: The Duty of Genius* (New York, 1991).

20. Instrumental arguments for celibacy have always had to contend with the fact that the clergy of the primitive church was generally married. Clerical celibacy has a long and complicated history. The church did not succeed in establishing it as the universal norm for the clergy until well into the third century; and even then, the practices of secret marriage and concubinage were not uncommon all the way down into the early modern period (and beyond). I am speaking here specifically of celibacy as a doctrinal concept, and not of other more opportunistic motives for its imposition, such as control over the inheritance of church property.

21. For princes and peers, such a choice was especially problematic. The case of Elizabeth is exemplary of the risks for monarchs, and it was perhaps only her sex that permitted her to remain unmarried and a monarch. More anomalous, because the subject is male, is the case of the earl of Southampton, whose mysterious refusal to marry was the occasion of much comment and perhaps also of Shakespeare's sonnets.

22. This kind of question belongs to a field that scarcely exists as yet, and which we might call the "social history of philosophy." Where something like this project does exist, it tends to be located either in individual biographies of philosophers, or in the history or sociology of science, though in my view it doesn't simply coincide with either project. What I would like to do in this argument is something rather different, since my concern is not exclusively with the individual lives of philosophers or with the history of science, but with the figure of the philosopher as such, as a social type. In addition to works cited below, I would invoke as precedent Michele Le Doeuff's concept of the "philosophical imaginary," in *The Philosophical Imaginary*, trans. Colin Gordon (Stanford, 1989).

23. Lawrence Stone, *The Family, Sex, and Marriage in England, 1500–1800* (New York, 1977), 377–80. See also Antoinette Fauve-Chamoux, "Marriage, Widowhood, and Divorce," in *Family Life in Early Modern Times, 1500–1789*, ed. David I. Kertzer and Marzio Barbagli (New Haven, 2001), 225–27; and Alan Macfarlane, *Marriage and Love in England, 1300–1840* (Oxford, 1986), 149–51.

24. See Stone, *Family, Sex, and Marriage*, 491, and Elizabeth Abbot, *A History of Celibacy* (New York, 1999), 304.

25. For a comment on the living arrangements in the ancient universities, see Stone, *Family, Sex, and Marriage*, 517. See also Alan Bray, *Homosexuality in Renaissance England* (Boston, 1982), 51–52.

26. For Gresham's will, see John Ward, *The Lives of the Professors of Gresham College* (London, 1740).

27. Shapin, "The Philosopher and the Chicken"; also Iliffe, "Isaac Newton: Lucatello Professor of Mathematics." And Susan James, *Passion and Action: The Emotions in Seventeenth-Century Philosophy* (Oxford, 1997), 183–207, on "dispassionate scientia."

28. Shapin, *Social History of Truth*, 165. Shapin discusses Boyle as the perfect type of the ascetic philosopher, who probably died a virgin. By contrast Robert Hooke was "notably unchaste."

29. I take up here lines of argument already well advanced by Shapin and Iliffe. Both Boyle (probably) and Newton (certainly) entertained philosophical and theological heterodoxies that, had they been public knowledge, would have invited closer scrutiny of their private lives. The prevalence of heterodoxy among philoso-

phers, including Descartes, Hobbes, Spinoza, Locke, and others hardly needs demonstration. What needs further inquiry is the social condition that enabled such "freedom of thought" while severely constraining its expression.

30. Bacon's consistent interest in this subject is confirmed also by a poem translating and expanding an epigram, possibly by Poseidippos, from the *Greek Anthology*: "Domestic cares afflict the husband's bed, / or pains his head. / Those that live single take it for a curse, / or do things worse. / These would have children; those that have them moan, / or wish them gone. / What is it then to have or have no wife, / But single thraldom, or a double strife?" (Vickers, 332). Vickers believes the poem was written in 1597–98.

31. Thomas Wilson, *The Rule of Reason* (London, 1551).

32. *Collected Works of Erasmus*, vol. 25, *Literary and Educational Writings*, ed. J. K. Sowards (Toronto, 1985), 129–48. See also his *Defense of His Declamation in Praise of Marriage* (1519), in *Daughters, Wives, and Widows: Writings by Men about Women and Marriage in England, 1500–1640*, ed. Joan Larsen Klein (Urbana, Ill., 1992), 65–138. For an important discussion of some of the issues surrounding the relation between celibacy and dangerous modes of sexuality— particularly in connection with Erasmus—see Alan Stewart, *Close Readers: Humanism and Sodomy in Early Modern England* (Princeton, 1997).

33. For accounts of the crisis, see J. S. Spink, *French Free-Thought from Gassendi to Voltaire* (London, 1960); René Pintard, *Le Libertinage erudit dans la première moitié du XVIIe siècle* (Geneva, 1983); Antoine Adam, *Théophile de Viau et la libre pensée française en 1620* (Geneva, 1965); and Richard H. Popkin, *The History of Skepticism from Erasmus to Spinoza* (Berkeley, 1979), chap. 5, 87–109.

34. This compound meaning is already registered in Randle Cotgrave's *Dictionary of the French and English Tongues* (London, 1611): "*libertinage*: m. libertinage, Epicurism, sensualitie, licentiousnesse, dissolutenesse." The two senses were later to diverge again, though never completely separate. The opening and closing over the next century of the distance between "free-thinking" and libertinism in the sexual sense is a subject of great interest, though beyond the scope of this chapter.

35. The trials and executions of Vanini and Bruno evidently prepared the ground for the panic. See François Garasse, *La Doctrine curieuse des beaux esprits de ce temps* . . . (Paris, 1623); Marin Mersenne, *L'Impiété des déistes, athées et libertins de ce temps* (Paris, 1624). For an exhaustive account of the libertine crisis, with particular reference to Théophile de Viau, see Frederic Lachèvre, *Le Libertinage au XVIIe Siécle*, vol. 1, *Le Procès du poète Théophile de Viau* (Geneva, 1968). For a general account of the types and sequence of libertine modes, see Claude Reichler, *L'Age Libertin* (Paris, 1987).

36. For Garasse's accusation of sodomitical sympathies against Théophile, see *La Doctrine*, 782. Joan DeJean, *The Reinvention of Obscenity: Sex, Lies, and Tabloids in Early Modern France* (Chicago, 2002), argues that the 1623 trial of Théophile was driven more by the issue of obscenity (specifically the famously misread "sodomitical sonnet" published in 1623 without Théophile's permission in a volume called *La Parnasse des Poetes Satyriques*) than by the issue of religious heterodoxy (Théophile was also a Protestant convert). The continuity of the panic

about the libertine freethinkers thus concealed a discontinuity for DeJean, a shift in concern from religious issues to a civil or "civilizing" obsession with the policing of printed speech. I thank Juliette Cherbuliez of the University of Minnesota for pointing out DeJean's work on Théophile to me.

37. Lachèvre remarks, *Le Libertinage*, xxiii, that the libertines were denounced for "raillant la religion, n'ayant autre Dieu que la Nature." Perhaps there is an argument to be made for the generalization that all early modern philosophy is natural philosophy. It is only the retroactive distinction granted to the experimenters that prevents us from seeing that figures such as Hobbes and Spinoza are just as much natural philosophers as Boyle or Newton. For an interesting discussion of the tactic of "dissimulation" as a response to the panic, see Perez Zagorin, *Ways of Lying: Dissimulation, Persecution, and Conformity in Early Modern Europe* (Cambridge, 1990), chap. 12, "Libertinism, Unbelief, and the Dissimulation of Philosophers."

38. But we might ask whether the type of the philosopher can already be seen in Erasmus, if we recall his "philosophy of Christ." In any case, the larger point to be grasped is that the recovery of the classical lifestyle philosophies is a condition for the appearance of the early modern philosopher as a distinct social type.

39. DeJean, *The Reinvention of Obscenity*, 22, points out that "beginning with Théophile de Viau, all writers' trials received immediate press coverage." Bacon would, however, have had many oral sources of information about continental scandals.

40. There was certainly much anxiety about sexual behavior in James's court, but the English seem not to have drawn the tight connection between sexual and intellectual libertinism common in France. When anxiety about sexual libertinism erupted in England, it came in with Charles II and a Francophile court. See David Foxon, *Libertine Literature in England, 1660–1745* ((New York, 1965); and James Grantham Turner, *Libertines and Radicals in Early Modern London: Sexuality, Politics and Literary Culture, 1630–1685* (Cambridge, 2002).

41. It was Descartes's opinion that the greatest contribution of philosophy is not speculative but practical. See his *Discourse on Method*, chap. 6, in *The Philosophical Writings of Descartes*, 3 vols., trans. John Cottingham et al. (Cambridge, 1985), 1:142–43. For a comparison of Bacon and Descartes on this issue, see Robert B. Pippin, *Idealism as Modernism: Hegelian Variations* (Cambridge, 1997), 196–97.

42. The ubiquity of the theme of charity in Bacon's work has often been noted, and its instances are too numerous to list. But see his essays "Of Goodness" and "Of Love." Bacon's use of the term tends to fuse the Christian virtue with the Greek concept of *philanthropia*, which he invoked in his famous "Letter to Lord Burghley" outlining his ambitions. For a discussion, see Ian Box, "Bacon's Moral Philosophy," in *The Cambridge Companion to Bacon*, ed. Markku Peltonen (Cambridge, 1996), 260–82.

43. For Bacon, to philosophize is not so much to learn to die as it is to learn how to prolong life. Jardine and Stewart remind us in *Hostage to Fortune*, 502–10, of Bacon's constant medical experiments upon himself, one of which very likely killed him. *Sylva Sylvarum*, to which *New Atlantis* was appended in publication, is concerned in part with such medical remedies for prolonging life, as well

as his *Historia Vitae et Mortis.* The Fathers of Salomon's House are described as conducting experiments on prolonging life.

44. *Novum Organum,* trans. Peter Urbach and John Gibson (Chicago, 1994), 14.

45. The emphasis on pity would seem to contradict Gaukroger's argument for the pervasive Stoic influence on the *New Atlantis,* as the Stoics were opposed to rulers who made decisions on the basis of pity rather than reason. See David Konstan, *Pity Transformed* (London, 2001), 114. Perhaps the point here, as always with Bacon, is that his dependence on the ancients was systematically unsystematic, never an identification with one figure or philosophy.

46. Benjamin Farrington in *The Philosophy of Francis Bacon* (Chicago, 1964), 104.

47. See René Descartes, *The Passions of the Soul,* trans. Stephen H. Voss (Indianapolis, 1989), 119–21, for a discussion of pity. This translation is illustrated by drawings of facial expressions from Charles Le Brun, *Conférence sur l'expression des passions* (1696). No drawing for the passion of pity is given.

48. Although Cassell's Latin Dictionary gives "calm, settled" as one definition of *compositus.* This meaning (which carries over into the English sense of "composed") may overlay the ordinary sense of *componere,* to put or place together. The Latin text hints at the indefinite duration of the expression of pity by associating it with the "settled" quality we might expect to accompany the demeanor of placidness or serenity.

49. For the relation between disposition or habit (*hexis*), virtue, and the passions, see Aristotle, *Nicomachean Ethics,* 1105b26. For Aristotle on pity, see *Rhetoric,* book 2, chap. 8; and *Poetics,* book 1, chaps. 6, and 12–14. For recent discussions of pity in Aristotle, see Amélie Oksenber Rorty, ed., *Essays on Aristotle's Poetics* (Princeton, 1992); and Stephen Halliwell, *The Aesthetics of Mimesis: Ancient Texts and Modern Problems* (Princeton, 2002).

50. Philip Fisher, in *The Vehement Passions* (Princeton, 2002), acknowledges pity among the passions, but excludes it from the vehement passions.

51. From *The Anti-Christ,* section 7: "Christianity is called the religion of *pity,*" in *Twilight of the Idols and the Anti-Christ,* trans. R. J. Hollingdale (London, 1968), 130. Konstan, *Pity Transformed,* 106, discusses the merging of *compassio* and *sumpatheia* with the concept of pity in the Hellenistic era. He also points out that a new word *eleomosunē,* "meaning both pity and an act of charity," appears during this period. Finally, one might observe that pity can be distinguished from the involuntary pain of sympathetic identification, such as that expressed by Miranda as she views the shipwreck in *The Tempest,* I, ii, 5: "O, I have suffered / With those that I saw suffer!"

52. In "Temporis Partus Masculus" (1603). The work is translated as "The Masculine Birth of Time" by Farrington, *Philosophy of Francis Bacon,* 61–72. The sentence quoted is from page 72. For a similar statement, see *The Advancement of Learning* (Vickers, 148). The trope of generation is so ubiquitous in Bacon that it is difficult to read more than a few pages of his work without coming across an example of it.

53. Michèle Le Doeuff, "Man and Nature in the Gardens of Science," in *Francis Bacon's Legacy of Texts,* ed. W. A. Sessions (New York, 1990), 119–38, argues, rightly in my view, that Baconian science is not modeled on industrial activity or machine technology, as is science in our modern cultural imaginary, but rather on

gardening. Bacon is not a "mechanical philosopher" in the Galilean sense. He is still oriented toward the vegetable and animal world for his conceptions of scientific effectivity. It should also be noted that while Bacon's ubiquitous recourse to metaphors of generation has often been taken as confirming a masculinist, or heterosexist ideology, at the basis of modern science, this notion is complicated by any reading of Bacon that takes the measure of his figures as figures. For a vigorous, if inconclusive attempt to come to terms with Bacon's metaphoric heterosexualism, see Evelyn Fox Keller, *Reflections on Gender and Science* (New Haven, 1985), 33–42.

54. Hyperbole carries the burden in *New Atlantis* of expressing such anxiety. By contrast the comparative degree, which is pervasive in the text, conveys a more assured sense of Bensalem's superiority. With remarkable consistency, Bensalem is described in the comparative degree, beginning with the parchment carried by the officials who approach the stricken sailors ("somewhat yellower than our parchment"). Here as elsewhere there is no obvious reason why the yellower parchment is the better parchment, and yet the ground for such invidious judgment is established by the grammatical choice. Elsewhere the comparative degree can explicitly signify superiority, as in the passage quoted above about making plants "more fruitful and bearing." Bensalem is like Europe in most respects, only better. Most of all, perhaps, in that its people live *longer*: "we have a water which we call Water of paradise, being, by what we do to it, made very sovereign for health, and prolongation of life" (Vickers, 481).

55. Simonds D'Ewes, *Extracts from the MS Journal of Sir Simonds D'Ewes, with Several Letters to and from Sir Simonds and his Friends* (London, 1783), 25–26. For the definitive account of this episode, with other citations, see Jardine and Stewart, *Hostage to Fortune*, 444–69. They consider not only D'Ewes but a number of ballads and pamphlets that were circulated after Bacon's fall, usually intimating sexual relations between Bacon and his many secretaries, ushers, and younger friends. John Chamberlain in his letters reports more discreetly on this gossip, *The Letters of John Chamberlain*, ed. Norman Egbert McClure, 2 vols. (Philadelphia, 1939), 2:356: "Many indignities are said against him, and divers libells cast abroad to his disgrace not worth the repeating as savoring too much of malice and scurrilitie."

56. *Aubrey's Brief Lives*, ed. Oliver Lawson Dick (London, 1950), 11.

57. The enigmatic hauteur of this political fable is confirmed by the obvious allusion in the figure of Joabin to the biblical Joab, King David's faithful but ruthless lieutenant and friend (recounted in 1 and 2 Samuel and 1 Kings). Joabin is a placeholder, a lieutenant, for Bacon himself, at once inside and outside Bensalem's protected enclosure (the symbolic burden of his Jewishness). Bacon too was a faithful and ruthless lieutenant. He helped James advance his favorites, destroy his ex-favorites, and he was thrown over by James in the end, just as Joab was repudiated by David.

58. Vickers cites a precedent in Plato, *Laws*, 12.948A–B, but it is difficult not to read this passage as extenuating Bacon's indulgence in the vice of his time. Few state officials were expected to live off their salaries, and the system of "tipping" was more or less institutionalized.

59. Bacon evidently maintained just such a show even after his disgrace, a "fabulous show" as Jardine and Stewart put it, *Hostage to Fortune*, 469. In these circum-

stances, disavowal and defiance collude. So Prince Charles implied upon one occasion of seeing Bacon's elaborate carriage and retinue pass by after his fall: "This man scorns to go out like a snuff." Charles captures the note of defiance that I understand as Bacon's assertion, despite all, of his right to lead a "libertine" life.

60. In this context, I follow Alan Stewart's argument in *Close Readers* that some of the suspicion expressed toward humanist scholars in the sixteenth century was incited by the way in which the humanist international—as a vast network of friends—bypassed the systems of kinship and dynasty. The humanist foundation of Bacon's Salomon's House is evident in its reliance on such nonfamilial bonds, but its bureaucratic organization is probably also descended from humanist models. For a study of one possible precedent for Salomon's House, Matthias Facius Illyricus's scheme for producing a definitive ecclesiastical history, see Anthony Grafton, "Where Was Salomon's House," in *Die Europäische Gelehrtenrepublik im Zeitalter des Konfessionalismus / The European Republic of Letters in the Age of Confessionalism* (Wiesbaden, 2001), 21–38. Bacon realizes a certain *plus ultra* for the humanist friendship network in his Salomon's House—not for the sake of humanism as such but for natural philosophy, at once a continuation of, and a break from, sixteenth-century humanist concerns. Joan DeJean, *Libertine Strategies: Freedom and the Novel in Seventeenth-Century France* (Columbus, 1981), notes the importance of friendship networks for the propagation of libertine thought in France. This point can be generalized in the context of a sociology of modern knowledge, with appropriate historical adjustments. Friendship networks sometimes function adversarially, but can also serve as the basis for institutionalization, as with the Royal Society.

61. Here at my own *plus ultra*, as opposed to Bacon's, I must acknowledge that the story I have told about Bacon is probably too circumscribed to sustain the larger historical narrative looming beyond it, and to which accordingly I only gesture. For an interesting if tendential version of an argument about the alienation of intellectuals from power in the post-Renaissance, see Reinhart Kosellek, *Critique and Crisis: Enlightenment and the Pathogenesis of Modern Society* (Cambridge, 1988). Kosellek's argument is similar to Joseph Shumpeter's account of the alienated modern intellectual in *Capitalism, Socialism, and Democracy*, trans. Tom Bottomore (New York, 1942). This theme circulates as either a sociology of intellectuals or a denunciation of them, depending usually upon one's politics. I accept the utility of the theme without endorsing Shumpeter's rather dark view of modern critical intellectuals. In any case, I hope to have limned a credible figure of the early modern (seventeenth-century) natural philosopher as in certain respects a successor to the humanist intellectual, mediating the transition to another kind of philosopher from whom the scientist will be split off. This narrative is indeed much farther than this essay can go.

HOBBES'S REVOLUTION

1. There is a vast and growing literature on the uses of *phantasia* in antiquity and late antiquity, and on its specific uses by each of the great ancient thinkers. From the last two decades, see M. C. Nussbaum, *Interpretative Essays to Aristotle's De Motu Animalium* (Princeton, 1978), 258–61; G. Rispoli, *L'artista sa-*

piente. Per una storia della fantasia (Naples, 1984); G. Watson, *Phantasia in Classical Thought* (Galway, 1988); M. Fattori and M. L. Bianchi, *Phantasia-Imaginatio, V. Colloquium Internazionale* (Rome, 1988); L. Formigari, ed., *Imago in phantasia depicta* (Rome, 1999). On the disputes between *ratio* and *imaginatio* in Western thought, cf. R. Bodei, *Geometria delle passioni. Paura, speranza, felicità: Filosofia ed uso politico* (Milan, 1991); and F. Piro, *Il retore interno. Immaginazione e passione all'alba dell'età moderna* (Naples, 1999).

2. On relations between Hobbes and the Royal Society, cf. Q. Skinner, "Thomas Hobbes and the Nature of the Early Royal Society," *Historical Journal* 12 (1969): 217–39. Cf. also S. Shapin and S. Shaffer, *Leviathan and the Air-pump: Hobbes, Boyle, and the Experimental Life* (Princeton, 1985).

3. Cf. B. Barry, *Democracy, Power and Justice* (Oxford, 1989), 424.

4. N. Bobbio, "Hobbes e il giusnaturalismo," in *Da Hobbes a Marx* (Naples, 1965), 57.

5. J. Tully, ed., *Meaning and Context: Quentin Skinner and His Critics* (Cambridge, 1988), 13.

6. See *The English Works of Thomas Hobbes of Malmesbury*, ed. Sir William Molesworth (London: John Bohn, 1837–45; reprint Scientia Verlag Aalen, 1966), 2:iv–v. Hereafter abbreviated *EW*.

7. Ibid., 3:91.

8. Cf. Q. Skinner, *Reason and Rhetoric in the Philosophy of Hobbes* (Cambridge, 1996), 426.

9. Cf. L. Strauss, *The Political Philosophy of Hobbes: Its Basis and Its Genesis* (Chicago, 1952).

10. "Itaque ob hanc rem, quod figuras nos ipsi creamus, contigit geometriam haberi et esse demonstrabilem." *Thomae Hobbes Malmesburiensis Opera Philosophica quae Latine scripsit Omnia in unum corpus nunc primum Collecta studio et labore Gulielmi Molesworth* (London: Joannem Bohn, 1839–45; reprint Scientia Verlag Aalen, 1966), 2:93. Hereafter cited as *Opera Latina*.

11. Ibid., 94: "Praeterea politica et ethica, id est scientia *justi* et *injusti, aequi* et *iniqui*, demonstrari a priore potest; propterea quod principia, quibus *justum* et *aequum* et contra, *injustum* et *iniquum*, quid sint, cognoscitur, id est, justitiae causas, nimirum leges et pacta, ipsi fecimus. Nam ante pacta et leges conditas, nulla neque justitia neque injustitia, neque boni neque mali publici natura erat inter homines, magis quam inter bestias."

12. "Per intuitum," writes Descartes in *Regulae Ad Directionem Ingenii*, in *Oeuvres de Descartes*, ed. Charles Adam and Paul Tannery, vol. 10 (reprint, Paris, 1974), 368, "intelligo, non fluctuantem sensuum fidem, vel male componentis imaginationis judicium fallax; sed mentis purae et attentae tam facilem distinctumque conceptum, ut de eo, quod intelligimus, nulla prorsus dubitatio relinquantur; seu, quod idem est, mentis purae et attentae non dubium conceptum, qui à sola rationis luce nascitur, et ipsamet deductione certior est, quia simplicior, quam tamen etiam ab homine malé fieri non posse supra notavimus. Ita unusquisque animo potest intueri, se existere, se cogitare, triangulum terminari tribus lineis tantum, globum unicâ superificie, et similia, quae longe plura sunt quàm plerique animadvertunt, quoniam ad tam facilia mentem convertere dedignantur."

On this point, cf. also G. Israel, "Dalle Regulae alla Géometrie," in *Descartes: Il Metodo e i Saggi*, ed. G. Belgioso, G. Cimino, P. Costabel, and G. Papuli (Rome, 1990), 441–47; and G. Rodis-Lewis, *Descartes et le rationalisme* (Paris, 1985), 11.

13. *EW* 1:viii.

14. Cf. K. Popper and J. Eccles, *The Self and the Brain* (Berlin, 1977).

15. T. Hobbes, *Troisièmes Objections*, in *Méditations*, in *Oeuvres de Descartes*, ed. Charles Adam and Paul Tannery, vol. 9 (reprint, Paris, 1973), 134.

16. Cf. *EW* 4:28.

17. Ibid.

18. Ibid.

19. "[S]ense," writes Hobbes in *Leviathan*, "is nothing else but original fancy caused . . . by the pressure that is, by the motion of external things upon our eyes, ears and other organs." *EW* 3:3.

20. *EW* 3:35.

21. Ibid., 1:7.

22. Ibid., 16. Cf. also *Opera Latina*, 1:14, where names are defined as "vox humana arbitratu hominis adhibita."

23. *EW* 1:20.

24. Ibid., 38.

25. See ibid., 3:85. Cf. also *Opera Latina*, 2:103.

26. Cf. J. Hampton, *Hobbes and the Social Contract Tradition* (Cambridge, 1986), 18.

27. *EW* 3:38.

28. Ibid., 39.

29. Ibid., 4:2–3.

30. Ibid., 3:4–5.

31. Cf. ibid., 4:9.

32. Ibid., 3:5–6.

33. Cf. ibid., 4:12–13.

34. Ibid., 3:19.

35. Ibid., 13.

36. Ibid.

37. Cf. also J. Plamenatz, *Man and Society* (London, 1963), 121.

38. Cf. *EW* 3:57.

39. Cf. Albert O. Hirschman, *The Passions and the Interests: Political Arguments for Capitalism before its Triumph* (Princeton, 1977).

40. See *EW* 4:50–51.

41. Ibid., 24.

42. Ibid., 50–51.

43. Ibid., 51.

44. Cf. ibid., 56.

45. Ibid., 3:45.

46. Ibid., 3:45.

47. Cf. ibid., 4:51.

48. Ibid., 85.

49. Ibid., 85–86.

50. Cf. E. Canetti, *Die Provinz des Menschen—Aufzeichnungen 1942–1972* (Munich, 1969).

51. Cf. *EW* 3:48.

52. Ibid., 48–49.

53. Cf. ibid., 5:78–81.

54. Ibid., 4:32.

55. Ibid., 3:61.

56. Ibid., 4:25.

57. Ibid., 3:146.

58. Ibid.

59. Ibid., 251.

60. Ibid., 335.

61. Ibid.

62. Cf. ibid., 3:xi–xii.

63. Cf. Bobbio, *Da Hobbes a Marx*, 60.

64. On the originality of Hobbes's model, cf. C. Galli, "Guerra e Politica: Modelli di interpretazione," *Ragione Pratica* 8, no. 14 (2000): 163–95.

65. Ibid., 175.

66. *EW* 3:85.

67. Ibid., 85–86.

68. Ibid., 208.

69. Ibid., 321.

70. Ibid., 321–22.

71. Ibid., 209.

72. Cf. C. Galli, "Guerra e Politica," 175.

73. Cf. Strauss, *Political Philosophy of Hobbes*, 22–23.

74. *EW* 3:62.

75. Ibid., 4:40.

76. Ibid., 41–42.

77. Ibid., 3:45–46.

78. Cf. ibid., 112.

79. Cf. M. Bertmann, "God and Man: Action and Reference in Hobbes," *Hobbes Studies* 3 (1990): 18–34, 19.

80. J.-J. Rousseau, *Émile*, in *Oeuvres complètes*, vol. 4 (Paris, 1969), 249 ("A citizen of Rome was neither Caius nor Lucius, he was a Roman; he loved his country better than his life. . . . A Spartan mother had five sons with the army. A Helot arrived; trembling she asked his news. 'Your five sons are slain.' 'Vile slave, was that what I asked thee?' 'We have won the victory.' She hastened to the temple to render thanks to the gods. *That* was a citizen.")

81. N. Machiavelli, *Discorsi sopra la Prima Deca di Tito Livio* (Milan, 1984), i, vi, 77–78. ("If anyone therefore should want to establish a new republic, he should have to consider if he should want it to expand in dominion and power as did Rome, or whether it should remain within narrow limits. In the first case, it is necessary to establish it as Rome, and to give place to tumults and general dissensions as best he can; for without a great number of men, and [those] well armed, no republic can ever increase, or if it did increase, maintain itself." If on the other hand he wants a state incapable of expansion he should follow the exam-

ple of Venice, which "having occupied a great part of Italy, and the greater part [obtained] not by war but by money and astuteness, when it came to make a test of her strength, everything was lost in one engagement").

Happy Tears
Baroque Politics in Descartes's *Passions de l'âme*

1. The epigraph is taken from a text of Descartes called the *Praeambula*, which appears in *Oeuvres de Descartes*, ed. Charles Adam and Paul Tannery, 12 vols. (Paris, 1996), 10:213.

On this understanding of philosophy, including its studied indifference to politics, see Raymond Polin, "Descartes et la philosophie politique," in *L'Adventure de l'esprit: Mélanges Alexandre Koyré*, 2 vols. (Paris, 1964), 2:381–99, esp. 397.

2. Just in the last few years, however, there has been a revival of interest in Descartes's *Passions*. The best recent book-length treatment is that of Carole Talon-Hugon, *Les passions rêvées par la raison: Essai sur la théorie des passions de Descartes et de quelques-uns de ses contemporains* (Paris, 2002). For briefer discussions, see Charles Taylor, *Sources of the Self* (Cambridge, Mass., 1989), 143–58; Amélie Oksenberg Rorty, "Descartes on Thinking with the Body," in *The Cambridge Companion to Descartes*, ed. John Cottingham (Cambridge, 1992), 371–92; Stephen Gaukroger, *Descartes: An Intellectual Biography* (Oxford, 1995), 384–417; Susan James, *Passion and Action: The Emotions in Seventeenth-Century Philosophy* (Oxford, 1997); Peter Dear, "A Mechanical Microcosm: Bodily Passions, Good Manners, and Cartesian Mechanism," in *Science Incarnate*, ed. Christopher Lawrence and Steven Shapin (Chicago, 1998), 51–82; Jerome Schneewind, *The Invention of Autonomy* (Cambridge, 1998), 184–93; John Marshall, *Descartes's Moral Theory* (Ithaca, 1998); Timothy J. Reiss, *Mirages of the Selfe* (Stanford, 2003), 469–518 ; and the essays in *Passion and Virtue in Descartes*, ed. Byron Williston and André Gombay (New York, 2003). Older, still useful works include Pierre Mesnard, *Essai sur la morale de Descartes* (Paris, 1936); Martial Gueroult, *Descartes' Philosophy Interpreted According to the Order of Reasons*, 2 vols., trans. Roger Ariew, with the assistance of Robert Ariew and Alan Donagan (Minneapolis, 1952; rpt. 1985); Roger Lefèvre, *L'Humanisme de Descartes* (Paris, 1957); Alexandre Matheron, "Psychologie et politique: Descartes," in *Dialectique* 6 (1974): 79–98; Hugh M. Davidson, "Descartes and the Utility of the Passions," *Romanic Review* 51 (1960): 15–26; Anthony Levi, S.J., *French Moralists: The Theory of the Passions, 1585–1649* (Oxford, 1964); Nannerl O. Keohane, *Philosophy and the State in France* (Princeton, 1980); and Richard Kennington, "Descartes," in *History of Political Philosophy*, ed. Leo Strauss and Joseph Cropsey, 3rd ed. (Chicago, 1987), 421–39.

3. Theodor W. Adorno and Max Horkheimer, *Dialectic of Enlightenment*, trans. John Cumming (1944; New York, 1969), 30.

4. Hugo Grotius, *De jure belli ac pacis*, 2 vols., ed. James Brown Scott, trans. Francis W. Kelsey et al., Classics of International Law (Oxford, 1925), prolegomena. The literature on seventeenth-century materialism is enormous and cannot be canvassed here. On the challenge to Aristotle, see James, *Passion and Action*.

5. Thomas Hobbes, *Elements of Law*, in *Human Nature and De Corpore Politico*, ed. J.C.A. Gaskin (Oxford, 1994), Epistle Dedicatory to William, Earl of Newcastle, 19.

6. See chapter 16 of Hobbes's *Leviathan*; and my discussion of this chapter in *Rhetoric, Prudence, and Skepticism in the Renaissance* (Ithaca, 1985), chap. 6.

7. I discuss this nonmimetic relation in *Rhetoric, Prudence, and Skepticism*, as well as in "Hamlet or Hecuba: Carl Schmitt's Decision," *Representations* 83 (Summer 2003): 67–96.

8. In his travels in Europe in his twenties, Descartes was also briefly a member of the duke of Bavaria's staff. See Adrien Baillet, *Vie de Monsieur Descartes* (1691; Paris, 1946), 23–74. See also Descartes's letters of June and July 1648 on the troubles of La Fronde.

9. I quote the Lettre-Préface to the French edition of Descartes's *Principes* (1647) from René Descartes, *Oeuvres philosophiques*, ed. Fernand Alquié, 3 vols. (Paris, 1973), 3:780. Despite his emphasis on epistemology, Descartes was not immune to the practical import of his philosophy, but he tended to locate that import in his method. In part VI of the *Discours sur la méthode*, Descartes claimed that philosophy will make us "the lords and masters of nature." In the Lettre-Préface to the French edition of his *Principes* he asserted that "this study is more necessary for ordering our morals and guiding us in this life than the use of our eyes is for guiding our steps" (771). He also claimed that the principles of metaphysics themselves would have beneficial political consequences (783). Scientific principles and scientific method would themselves provide a new objective language—one that would preclude ideological dispute and thus provide the basis of international concord. But because Descartes was eager—even zealous—to "render service to the public," he had published his preliminary results—"the principal rules of logic and of an imperfect morality" in his *Discours de la méthode* (780).

10. Of course, in one way, the contractual account of society is not incompatible with obeying the laws and customs of one's country. As Hobbes remarked in *Philosophical Rudiments Concerning Government and Society*, "no civil law whatsoever, which tends not to a reproach of the Deity . . ., can possibly be against the law of nature" (Hobbes, *Man and Citizen*, Bernard Gert, ed. [n.p., 1972], 278).

11. Descartes's relation to Stoicism is complicated. He is not a Stoic if we equate Stoicism with a suppression of the passions. On the other hand, his ideal of self-government has much in common with the Stoic philosopher Epictetus, whom Descartes admired. See A. A. Long, *Epictetus: A Stoic and Socratic Guide to Life* (Oxford, 2002), 264–66. It may also be that Descartes's various Stoic-sounding pronouncements in his correspondence are part of a provisional morality. On this point, see Richard Kennington, "Descartes and Mastery of Nature," in *Organism, Medicine, and Metaphysics*, ed. Stuart F. Spicker (Dordrecht, Holland, 1978), esp. 214–15.

12. I quote the letters from René Descartes, *Lettres sur la morale*, ed. Jacques Chevalier (Paris, 1935), here the letter of October 10, 1646, p. 155. All page references are to the Chevalier edition. The letters also appear in volume 4 of the Adam-Tannery edition of Descartes's works. Unless otherwise indicated, translations of Descartes's letters are from *The Philosophical Writings of Descartes*, 3 vols. (Cambridge, 1991), vol. 3, *The Correspondence*, trans. John Cottingham,

Robet Stoothoff, Dugald Murdoch, and Anthony Kenny. Translations of Elisabeth's letters are my own.

13. Elisabeth was the daughter of Elizabeth of Bohemia, sister of Charles I of England. I take the phrase "deposed 'Winter King'" from Dear, "A Mechanical Microcosm," 57. Descartes offers advice about Elisabeth's depression in his letters of July 8, 1644, and May, June, and July 1645. See also the letter of January 1646, in response to Elisabeth's anger over her brother's conversion; and the letter of February 22, 1649, on the execution of Elisabeth's uncle, Charles I, in England.

14. Descartes, letter to Elisabeth, May 19, 1645; and Seneca, *De vita beata* in *Moral Essays*, 3 vols., trans. John W. Basore (Cambridge, 1965), 2:149, 179. Descartes discusses Seneca's essay in his letters to Elisabeth of August 4 and 18, as well as those of September 1 and 15, 1645. His chief objection seems to be that Seneca's philosophical vocabulary is insufficiently precise. For Seneca's pejorative use of the theatrical metaphor to convey the flux and inconstancy of human experience, see e.g. Seneca, *Epistulae morales*, trans. Richard Grummere, 3 vols. (Cambridge, Mass., 1967), 1:31, 87, 105, 189, 211. On Seneca's use of theater or "spectaculum" as a metaphor for self-reflection, see *Epistulae morales*, 1:185, 3:395 and Gordon Braden, *Renaissance Tragedy and the Senecan Tradition* (New Haven, 1985), 25–26 and passim. See also Descartes's letter to Elisabeth of May 1646, whose concluding paragraph declares his incapacity as a philosopher to pronounce on political matters: "I lead such a retired life, and have always been so far from the conduct of affairs, that I would be no less impudent than the philosopher who wished to lecture on the duties of a general in the presence of Hannibal if I took it on me to enumerate here the maxims one should observe in a life of public service." However, the disavowal is more complicated than it looks at first glance, since it can be found as well in the preface to Gentillet's *Contre Machiavel*, in which Gentillet compares Machiavelli the armchair political theorist to the philosopher advising Hannibal.

15. Descartes to Elisabeth, October 6, 1645, Chevalier ed., 101.

16. See Descartes's letter to Elisabeth of September 1646. In his letter of October or November 1646, Descartes writes, "I have recently read his discourse on Livy, and found nothing bad in it."

17. In conclusion, however, Descartes politicly rejected Machiavelli's argument in the preface to *Il Principe*, that to know a prince well, one must be of the people. Instead, he withdrew again behind the mask of the philosopher, demurring that only princes can know what it is like to be a prince, so the advice he offers should be taken as mere "divertissement."

18. Pierre Mesnard makes this point in his *Essai sur la morale de Descartes*, Excursus: "La morale et la politique," 190–212, esp. 209–10.

19. Quoted by Keohane, *Philosophy and the State in France*, 133.

20. In Corneille's plays, generosity ideally involves the sublimation of the passions in the service of personal and political glory. In practice, however, as Corneille shows, generosity is itself a passion or ambition that needs to be channeled if it is not to have catastrophic political consequences.

21. Guillaume Du Vair, *La Philosophie morale des stoïques*, quoted in Descartes, *Les Passions de l'âme*, ed. Geneviève Rodis-Lewis (Paris, 1994), 219.

22. Charron, *De la Sagesse*, 1. book 3, chap. 2; cited in Mesnard, *Essai sur la morale*, 194.

23. Descartes links force and artifice in his letter on Machiavelli of September 1646, in *Lettres sur la morale*, 146. See also See Charron, *De la sagesse*, book 2, chap. 2 on the prince's performing his role, and book 2, chap. 8 on the spectacle of majesty.

24. Descartes, *Traité de l'Homme*, in *Oeuvres de Descartes*, ed. Adam and Tannery, 11:130–31; quoted in Alain Vizier, "Descartes et les automates," *MLN* 111 (1996), 695. I quote from the translation in *The Philosophical Writings of Descartes*, trans. John Cottingham, Robert Stoothoff, and Dugald Murdoch, 3 vols. (Cambridge, 1985), 1:100–101. In this somewhat murky comparison, it would make sense to think that God or nature is the engineer of the body while the soul is its sovereign. In fact, Descartes collapses the engineer with the sovereign-soul, both of which are located in the royal seat of the pineal gland.

25. Descartes, *Traité de l'homme*: "And finally, when a *rational soul* is present in this machine it will have its principal seat in the brain, and reside there like the fountain-keeper who must be stationed at the tanks to which the fountain's pipes return if he wants to produce, or prevent, or change their movements in some way" (11:131–32, quoted by Vizier, "Descartes et les automates," 705).

26. See Stephen M. Fallon, *Milton Among the Philosophers* (Ithaca, 1991), 48: "Descartes's admission of corporeal, mechanical causation into the domain of what we call psychology highlights the vulnerability of soul within a mechanical theory of nature."

27. Vizier, "Descartes et les automates," 702. See also *Passions*, art. 21 and Descartes's letter to Newcastle, November 23, 1646: "As for the movements of our passions, even though in us they are accompanied by thought because we have the faculty of thinking, it is nevertheless very clear that they do not depend on thought, because they often occur in spite of us. Consequently they can also occur in animals, even more violently than they do in human beings, without our being able to conclude from that that animals have thoughts" (cited in *Les passions de l'âme*, 17).

28. See Elisabeth's letter of September 13, 1645, and Descartes's letter of September 15, 1645, both in *Lettres sur la morale*, 85–86, 92. In the following pages, I quote from the English edition of *The Passions of the Soul*, ed. Stephen H. Voss (Indianapolis, 1989). I have omitted Voss's capitalization of "passion" and of individual passions, which does not appear in the French text. I have consulted the French text of *Passions de l'âme* in René Descartes, *Oeuvres philosophiques*, ed. Fernand Alquié, 3 vols. (Paris, 1973), vol. 3.

29. Keohane, *Philosophy and the State in France*, 191.

30. See J.-F. Senault, *De l'usage des passions* (1641; Paris, 1987), dedicatory epistle to Richelieu, 9–10; preface to the reader, 27, 32. In addition to these traditional analogies, there are also elements of Senault's analysis that anticipate the mechanistic politics of the Cartesian body, such as the suggestion that the prince appeal to the people's passions to manipulate them without their knowledge: "approaching men by their passions, you will make them serve your designs, without their knowledge: They act by your movements, and are unaware of your inten-

tions" (8). On Senault, see also Keohane, *Philosophy and the State in France*, 196–97.

31. In *Essai sur la morale de Descartes*, Pierre Mesnard called attention to Descartes's preoccupation with method as the link between his letter on Machiavelli and the treatise on the passions. Mesnard argued that Descartes's interest in reason of state is analogous to his interest in providing a mechanical explanation of the passions. In both cases, Descartes wanted to do away with the Aristotelian or scholastic emphasis on final causes. His goal, instead, was to dissect the mechanisms of politics just as it was to describe the mechanisms of the body. Only after such mechanisms had been analyzed could other moral or spiritual considerations—such as the agent's intention or the sanction of divine right—be reintroduced (211–12). For a critique of the view that Descartes was sympathetic to Machiavelli, see Polin, "Descartes et la philosophie politique." For a different view of the incompatibility of reason of state and Cartesian philosophy, see Henri Gouhier, "Le nouvel humanisme selon Descartes et la politique," in *Cristianesimo e ragion di stato* (Rome, 1952), 77–86, esp. 83–85.

32. In discussing these classes of perception, Descartes uses the verb *rapporter*, usually translated as "refer." Thus a more precise formulation would be that some perceptions are referred (*rapporté*) or attributed to external objects; some are referred to the body, and some are referred to the soul itself. As Descartes writes in article 25 of *Passions*, "The perceptions that are referred to the soul alone are those whose effects are felt as in the soul itself, and of which no proximate cause to which they may be referred is commonly known. Such are the sensations of joy, anger, and others like" (32). It is hard to know what it means for passions to be felt "in" the soul, since the soul has no extension in space. Talon-Hugon, *Passions rêvées*, calls attention to this phenomenological definition: we experience the passions *as though* located in or caused by the soul, but really they are caused by the body (126).

33. See James, *Passion and Action*, 92–93, for a lucid discussion.

34. The relationship between the force of the passions and their representation in the soul is the subject of article 94, which explains the pleasure we receive from all sorts of sensations, even painful ones, in terms of the strength of the body to withstand these same powerful sensations: "What we call a titillation or delightful sensation always consists in the fact that objects of the senses are exciting some movement in the nerves which would be capable of harming them, if they did not have enough strength to withstand it or the body were not well disposed. This produces an impression in the brain which, being instituted by Nature to testify to this sound disposition and this strength, represents it to the soul as a good which belongs to it, insofar as it is united with the body, and so excites joy within it." And he goes on to compare this delightful experience to watching a play, where the representation of adventures is pleasing both because it excites the passions and—as Elisabeth had insisted—because it cannot harm the spectator in any way: "For nearly the same reason one naturally takes pleasure in feeling moved to all sorts of passions, even sadness and hatred, when these passions are caused only by the unusual adventures one sees represented on a stage or by other similar matters, which, not being able to harm us in any way, seem to titillate our soul in affecting it."

35. As this definition makes clear, generosity is the place where the morally indifferent passion of wonder or admiration is moralized. Generosity involves wonder (a morally neutral passion) at one's moral capacity to use one's free will.

36. In this passage, Descartes enters the early modern debate on the nature of catharsis, specifically on whether pity is purged or merely moderated in the experience of tragedy. One of the best short treatments of this debate, with particular reference to Descartes, is Earl Wasserman's "The Pleasures of Tragedy," *ELH* 14 (1947): 283–307. See the note on this passage in Descartes's *Oeuvres philosophiques* on how, as a Christian, Descartes can't give up pity, so he distinguishes between sad pity and happy pity. Another source for this distinction between good and bad kinds of pity is Seneca's *De clementia*, 2.5.1, which opposes effeminizing pity and Stoic mercy, misericordia, and clementia. In *De constantia* (1584), Lipsius's Stoic "Langius" distinguishes between pity, which is a positive good, and compassion, which is a form of weakness.

37. On *émotions intérieures*, see the helpful comments in Levi, *French Moralists*, 276–81, 284–86; and James, *Passion and Action*, 197.

38. For the moralizing reading, see James, *Passion and Action*, who renders the distinction between passion and reflective intellectual joy this way: if the widower's joy were prompted by "an involuntary memory of his wife's complaining, together with his realization that he will never have to humour her again," his joy would be a passion caused by the movement of the pineal gland. "But if it accompanies a judgement based on a reflective assessment of his marriage, it may stand at one remove from these bodily events and be said to lie in the soul alone. The widower's joy is then an intellectual joy" (198). For a different sort of moralizing interpretation, which is compatible with the interpretation of the mourning husband as a hypocrite, see Seneca, *Epistulae morales*, 63: "Do you wish to know the reason for lamentations and excessive weeping? It is because we seek the proofs of our bereavements in our tears, and do not give way to sorrow, but merely parade it. No man goes into mourning for his own sake. Shame on our ill-timed folly! There is an element of self-seeking even in our sorrow."

39. See Wasserman, "The Pleasures of Tragedy."

40. See John Cottingham, "Cartesian Ethics: Reason and the Passions," *Revue internationale de philosophie* 195 (1996): 193–216. Cottingham argues that "Examining the passions *en physicien*, from the point of view of a natural scientist, reveals the full extent to which their influence depends on factors below the threshold of consciousness. . . . Coming to terms with the essential opacity to the conscious mind of the operation of the passions now becomes the chief task of what might be called Descartes' 'anthropologically informed' ethics" (210–11).

41. In this account, *émotions intérieures* have the same relation to the passions as the primary passion of *admiration* has towards its objects. Both involve a theatrical or aesthetic distance, and in both cases, theatrical distance involves a fundamental indifference to the object or primary passion.

42. Wasserman, "The Pleasures of Tragedy," 288. Hobbes adopted a similar materialist perspective when he explained aesthetic pleasure in terms of the physical distance that ensures the spectator's personal safety. (This materialist argument about the link between self-preservation and aesthetic pleasure was regularly associated with Lucretius in the early modern period.) See Baxter Hathaway, "The

Lucretian 'Return upon Ourselves,' " *PMLA* 62 (1947): 672–80; and Eric Rothstein, "English Tragic Theory in the Late Seventeenth Century," *ELH* 29 (1962): 306–23.

43. See *Passions of the Soul*, art. 152: "I observe but a single thing in us which could give us just cause to esteem ourselves, namely the use of our free will and the dominion we have over our volitions. For it is only the actions that depend on that free will for which we could rightly be praised or blamed; and in making us masters of ourselves, it renders us like God in a way."

44. As though to illustrate this point, Descartes returns to the example of fear in the conclusion to the treatise, and shows how one can also argue that "it is better to make an honorable retreat or beg for mercy than expose oneself sense-lessly to certain death."

45. Dear, "A Mechanical Microcosm," 75, addresses a similar tension in Descartes's defense of free will in *Principes*. See also Rorty, "Thinking with the Body," 384: "While admitting that 'it is to the body alone that we should attribute every-thing that can be observed in us to oppose our reason' (*Passions*, art. 47), Descartes nevertheless also shows how will depends on the cooperation of the body to correct or check its deviations."

46. In internalizing baroque politics, Descartes also differed from some of his followers, who attempted to apply his insights about the passions to the realm of politics. In his contribution to *The Cambridge History of Political Thought, 1450–1700* (Cambridge, 1991), ed. J. H. Burns with Mark Goldie, Noel Malcolm gives the example of the brothers Johan and Pieter de la Court, who combined "Tacitus and Machiavelli with a Cartesian theory of the passions, so that the task of political philosophy was seen as that of constructing the state as a mechanism to regulate the passions of individuals and force both rulers and ruled to identify their individual interests with the common good" (547). This is a far more conven-tional understanding of the body politic than Descartes's internalization of poli-tics in the body.

The Desire to Live
Spinoza's *Ethics* under Pressure

1. Benedict de Spinoza, *A Spinoza Reader: The "Ethics" and Other Works*, ed. and trans. Edwin Curley (Princeton: Princeton University Press, 1994), IIIP6, 159. Note: All further citations to this text will occur within parentheses, including reference to Spinoza's text, as it is usually cited, followed by the page number of the Curley translation.

2. Gilles Deleuze, *Expressionism in Philosophy: Spinoza*, trans. Martin Joughin (New York: Zone Books, 1990).

3. Sigmund Freud, *Civilization and Its Discontents*, ed. and trans. James Stra-chey (New York: W. W. Norton, 1961), 78–79.

4. See Freud, "Triebe und Triebschicksale" (1915), in English as "Instincts and Their Vicissitudes," *The Standard Edition of the Complete Psychological Works of Sigmund Freud*, vol. 14, ed. and trans. James Strachey (London: Hogarth Press, 1957), 109–40.

5. Jean Laplanche, *Life and Death in Psychoanalysis*, trans. Jeffrey Mehlman (Baltimore: Johns Hopkins University Press, 1976; reprinted 1985).

6. "... eine psychologische höchst merkwürdige Überwindung des Triebes, der alles Lebende am Leben festzuhalten zwingt." See "Mourning and Melancholia," *Standard Edition*, 14:246; translation mine.

7. "The Economic Problem of Masochism," *The Standard Edition of the Complete Psychological Works of Sigmund Freud*, vol. 19, ed. and trans. James Strachey (London: Hogarth Press, 1961), 163.

8. Richard Kearney, "Ethics of the Infinite," an interview with Emmanuel Levinas (1982) in *Face to Face with Levinas*, ed. Richard Cohen (Albany: SUNY Press, 1986), 21.

9. Emmanuel Levinas, *Alterity and Transcendence*, trans. Michael B. Smith (New York: Columbia University Press, 1999), xxx.

10. See *The New Spinoza*, ed. Warren Montag and Ted Stolze (Minneapolis: University of Minnesota Press, 1997).

11. "The mind can neither imagine anything nor recollect past things, except while the body endures. . . . it conceives no body as actually existing except while its body endures" (VP21 and P21D, 255).

12. Emmanuel Levinas, *Ethics and Infinity: Conversations With Philippe Nemo*, trans. Richard A. Cohen (Pittsburgh: Duquesne University Press, 1985), 87.

13. Primo Levi, *The Drowned and the Saved*, trans. Raymond Rosenthal (New York: Vintage, 1989), 76.

A MIND FOR PASSION

1. Gary Wills, *Inventing America: Jefferson's Declaration of Independence* (New York, 1978), summarizes the popular view when he writes, "Locke's *Essay Concerning the True Original, Extent, and End of Civil Government*, known as the *Second Treatise* . . . was one of the canonical books of nineteenth-century liberalism. This has led us, looking back through the period of John Mill and Ricardo, to forget how equivocal was the work's status in the eighteenth century" (169). Wills and others point out, however, that during the eighteenth century, Locke was best known for his *Essay Concerning Human Understanding*. As the *Second Treatise* grew in importance during the nineteenth century, the *Essay* suffered intellectual disrespect as it came to be understood as hopelessly mired in the rationalist model of eighteenth-century philosophy. On this point see Hans Aarslef, "Locke's Reputation in Nineteenth-Century England," in *From Locke to Saussure: Essays on the Study of Language and Intellectual History* (Minneapolis, 1982), 120–45. For the reception of Locke's *Second Treatise* in the eighteenth century, see John Dunn, "The Politics of Locke in England and America in the Eighteenth Century," in *John Locke: Problems and Perspectives*, ed. John W. Yolton (Cambridge, 1969), 45–80.

2. John Rawls, *Lectures on the History of Moral Philosophy*, ed. Barbara Herman (Cambridge, Mass., 2000), 8–11. This opposition is particularly clear in Rawls's discussion of Hume's argument with Samuel Clarke, 69–83.

3. Étienne Balibar in "Subjection and Subjectivation," *Supposing the Subject,* ed. Joan Copjec (London, 1994), 1–15, argues that the current tendency to find the modern subject before Locke "is a mere retrospective illusion, which was forged by the systems, the philosophies of history and the teaching of philosophy in the nineteenth century. Neither in Descartes nor in Leibniz will you find the category 'subject' as an equivalent for autonomous self-consciousness (a category which itself was invented by John Locke) a reflexive center of the world and therefore a concentrate of the essence of man" (6).

4. In *Bodies, Masses, Power: Spinoza and His Contemporaries* (London, 1999), Warren Montag points out that Locke was haunted by the figure of "the multitude," as "the destructive or destroyed double" of "the people." According to Montag, the multitude "is that force partly inside and partly outside the political nation [of property owners] that either, as in Locke's early writings, causes the destruction of government or, as in the *Second Treatise*, is the result of a dissolution of society, the sum of dissociated individuals 'without order or connection,' deprived of any juridical status except a purely negative one" (113). This figure, we would argue, is closely linked to the notion of "factionalism" that Jean-Jacques Rousseau puts forth in "The Discourse on the Origin and Foundation of Inequality among Men," in *The Discourses and Other Early Political Writings*, trans. and ed. Victor Gourevitch (Cambridge, 1997). In *The Theory of Moral Sentiments* (Amherst, 2000), 219, Adam Smith, like Rousseau, associated factionalism with the spontaneous and collective emotional responses for which the Hobbesian body politic was known. The self-enclosed individual offered a conceptual resolution to this problem. In large part for this reason, Smith was as insistent as Locke on maintaining such an individual as the foundational unit of the modern state.

5. John Locke, *An Essay Concerning Human Understanding*, ed. Peter H. Nidditch (Oxford, 1975), II.i.2. Citations of the text are to this edition.

6. Since the Middle Ages, international law—following Roman law—could recognize a nation's legal occupation of a foreign territory by declaring it *res nullius* or *terra nullius*, a blank land over which no one yet had dominion. Andrew F. Burghardt, "The Bases of Territorial Claims," *Geographical Review* 63 (1973): 225–45; and Merete Borch, "Rethinking the Origins of Terra Nullius," *Australian Historical Studies* 32 (2001): 222–39. In *Lords of All the World: Ideologies of Empire in Spain, Britain and France c. 1500–c. 1800* (New Haven, 1995), Anthony Pagden explains the use of the related term, *res nullius*: "In the absence of a sustained argument to the right of occupation grounded on the supposed nature of the indigenous inhabitants, the British . . . were driven to legitimize their settlements in terms of one or another variant on the Roman Law argument known as *res nullius*. This maintained that all 'empty things,' which included unoccupied lands, remained the common property of all mankind until they were put to some, generally agricultural use. The first person to use the land in this way became its owner" (76).

7. We discuss this point in *The Imaginary Puritan: Literature, Intellectual Labor, and the Origins of Personal Life* (Berkeley, 1992), 169–74.

8. In "Rousseau: the Social Contract," Louis Althusser explains how this modern version of the contract refutes Grotius's notion of collective alienation, i.e., that just as an individual can sell himself into slavery, so a whole nation can submit

to a monarch. According to Rousseau's argument, the slave's choice is more reasonable than that of the subjects of monarchy: where the slave gets sustenance in exchange for servitude, subjects are guaranteed nothing. Rousseau's contractual model renders submission to a monarch null and void: "To renounce liberty is to renounce being a man." As Althusser points out in commenting on this line from Rousseau, however, "total alienation is the solution to the state of total alienation," or the state of the people under monarchy (*Montesquieu, Rousseau, Marx*, trans. Ben Brewster [London, 1982], 127). The figure of the contract—as opposed to the logic of the contract—turns "a forced total alienation" into "a free total alienation," whereby each individual consciously and voluntarily submits to the general will in exchange for negative rights, or the protection of his person and property (128).

9. Peter Harrison, "Reading the Passions: The Fall, the Passions, and Dominion over Nature," in *The Soft Underbelly of Reason: The Passions in the Seventeenth Century*, ed. Stephen Gaukroger (London, 1998), 49–78.

10. In "Governing Conduct," in *Conscience and Casuistry in Early Modern Europe*, ed. Edmund Leites (Cambridge, 1988), 12–71, James Tully offers an especially clear historical explanation of the logic linking the modern state and the formation of the individual subject to it. Arguing against Nietzsche's notion of "conscience" as the product of the administrative practices of the early modern period, Tully contends that "[t]he new practice of governing was [in fact] an attack on the conscience as both too radical and too submissive, and an effort to create habits that would replace the conscience and guide conduct" (13). From Lipsius to Locke, Tully continues, the objective of the new model of government was not to propagate the true faith but to ensure the good life; carried over from early modern culture were chiefly "those rights and duties of subjects compatible with or derivable from the objective of preservation of life" (15). Such a government rejects "any theory that assent or belief is governed by a natural disposition or telic faculty to the true and the good." As a faculty of a mind that has been swept clean of innate ideas, thus indifferent to truth or falsehood, good and evil, conscience has to be a "non-dispositional power of judgment," and belief must be the product of "acquired dispositions" (16).

11. David Hume, *An Enquiry Concerning Human Understanding* (Oxford, 1975), 17–22.

12. In "What is an Author?" in *The Foucault Reader*, ed. Paul Rabinow (New York, 1984), 101–20, Foucault explains, "when I speak of Marx or Freud as founders of discursivity, I mean that they made possible not only a certain number of analogies, but also (and equally important) a certain number of differences. They have created the possibility for something other than their discourse, yet something belonging to what they founded." Freud, he explains, "made possible a certain number of divergences—with respect to his own texts, concepts, and hypotheses—that all arise from the psychoanalytic discourse itself" (114–15).

13. Robert Burton, *The Anatomy of Melancholy*, ed. Thomas C. Faulkner, Nicolas K. Kiessling, and Rhonda L. Blair (Oxford, 1989), 1:249.

14. Important, too, for this model of the early modern mind is the fact that the body and its humors were affected by climate, diet, and other conditions of the environment. See Nancy Siresi, *Medieval and Renaissance Medicine* (Chicago,

1990); Gail Kern Paster, *The Body Embarrassed: Drama and the Disciplines of Shame in Early Modern England* (Ithaca, 1993), 1–15; Lester S. King, "The Transformation of Galenism," in *Medicine in Seventeenth-Century England*, ed. Allen G. Debus (Berkeley, 1974), 7–31.

15. Locke's proposal stands in stark contrast to the popular notions of memory assumed by his contemporaries. Late-seventeenth-century English writers, contrary to Descartes, thought that memories and ideas were physically present to the individual experiencing them. According to Kenelm Digby, for example, ideas were like little bodies cast off by objects that hit the brain, while Robert Hook described them as "material and bulky." See, John Sutton, "Controlling the Passions: Passion, Memory, and the Moral Physiology of Self in Seventeenth-Century Neurophilosophy," in Gaukroger, *Soft Underbelly of Reason*, 115–46.

16. To account for the fact that we receive information about an object from the various senses and from that information still formulate a single idea, or holistic image, of the object, Locke gives the neurological components of the early modern body only a minor role to play: "If . . . external objects be not united to our Minds, when they produce *Ideas* in it; and yet we perceive *these original qualities* in such of them as singly fall under our Senses, 'tis evident, that some motion must be thence continued by our Nerves, or animal Spirits, by some parts of our Bodies, to the Brains or the seat of Sensation, there to produce in our *Minds the particular* Ideas *we have of them*" (II.viii.12).

17. Beginning with such early readers as Edward Stillingfleet, bishop of Worcester, in 1697–98, there has been an ongoing debate about what Locke means by the term *idea*, given the very different uses to which he puts it in *An Essay*. For summary accounts of this debate, see R. S. Woodhouse, *Locke's Philosophy of Science and Knowledge, a Consideration of An Essay Concerning Human Understanding* (Oxford, 1971), 33–45, and Michael Losonsky, "Locke on Meaning and Signification," in *Locke's Philosophy, Content and Context*, ed. G.A.J. Rogers (Oxford, 1994), 123–41. Paul Schuurman, *Ideas, Mental Faculties and Method: The Logic of Ideas of Descartes and Locke and Its Reception in the Dutch Republic, 1630–1750* (Leiden, 2004), 4–33, offers an overview of Locke's debt to Descartes on the logic of ideas. Locke does indeed try to have it both ways, when he defines "ideas" as both the ideational response to pleasure and pain and as the internal stimulus (comparable in this respect to "sensation") to such complex ideas as "love" and "envy." We see this slippage as one among many rhetorical consequences of his effort to dislodge the mind—including its irrational faculties—from the early modern body.

18. See Tully, "Governing Conduct," for an explanation of Locke's use of the concept of "uneasiness" to deal with the question of how an absent good could influence human volition, a concept that transforms his notion of desire in the first edition of *An Essay* (48).

19. In "Locke on the Freedom of the Will," in Rogers, *Locke's Philosophy*, 101–21, Vere Chappell reminds us that having revised chapter xxi of Book II, "Of Power," substantially for the second edition (1694) "Locke made significant further additions to it both for the fourth edition, published in 1700, and for the fifth, which came out after his death in 1706" (101–2). In "Locke's Desire," *Yale Journal of Criticism* 12 (1999): 189–208, Jonathan Kramnick discusses the diffi-

culty Locke had in writing about desire in "Of Power," its length almost doubling from the first to the fifth editions. Hans Aarsleff summarizes many of Locke's revisions in "Of Power" in his "The State of Nature and the Nature of Man," in Yolton, *John Locke*, 99–136.

20. In a statement that suggestively echoes Tully's description of Locke's transformation of the early modern notion of "conscience," Richard Tuck points out what modern discipline obviously drew from Stoic tradition: the interests in Seneca and the study of Stoicism in the Renaissance for Montaigne and Lipsius was based on a concern for "the fundamental character of self-preservation, the preservation of the self not only from external attack" but also "from the passions that might leave it open to attack." *Philosophy and Government, 1572–1651* (Cambridge, 1993), 51.

21. Katherine Bradfield, "How Can Knowledge Derive Itself? Locke on the Passions, Will, and Understanding," *Locke Studies* 2 (2002): 81–102. See also Peter A. Schouls, *Reasoned Freedom: John Locke and the Enlightenment* (Ithaca, 1992), 92–114.

22. Francis Hutcheson, *An Inquiry into the Original of Our Ideas of Beauty and Virtue; in Two Treatises. I. Concerning Beauty, Order, Harmony, Design II. Concerning Moral Good and Evil* (London, 1734; rpt. Charlottesville, 1986), xvi. Citations of these essays are to this edition.

23. Francis Hutcheson, *On the Nature and Conduct of the Passions with Illustrations on the Moral Sense*, ed. Andrew Ward (Manchester, 1999), 24. Citations of these essays are to this edition.

24. In arguing that desire for the general good is the first and formative human desire, Hutcheson is not really contesting Locke so much as trying to define the general will as something already embedded in each individual. This effort did not succeed. When, for example, Rousseau claims "'the law of majority voting is itself something established by convention, and presupposes unanimity,'" as Althusser points out, "Rousseau is rejecting the Lockean theory of the 'natural' character . . . of the law of the majority. The majority does not belong to the social body as weight does to the physical body." *Montesquieu, Rousseau, Marx*, 117.

25. Hutcheson writes, for example, "Let physicians or anatomists explain the several motions in the fluids or solids of the body, which accompany any passion," "On the Nature and Conduct of the Passions and Affections" (*Nature and Conduct of the Passions*, 36). This is one of several passages where he allows that conditions of the body sometimes influence how we feel. At no point, however, does he indicate that the body is in charge. Nor does understanding its physiology help us to understand the interaction of reason and what he calls "the selfish appetites." For such understanding, he looks strictly to the internal senses.

26. On the principle of countervailing passions, see Albert O. Hirschman, *The Passions and the Interests: Political Arguments for Capitalism before Its Triumph* (Princeton, 1997), 20–31.

27. Hirschman observes that "in his most important and influential work [Adam] Smith sees men actuated entirely by the 'desire of bettering [their] condition,' and he further specifies that 'an augmentation of fortune is the means by which the greater part of men propose and wish to better their condition.' There seems to be no place here," he observes, "for the richer concept of human nature

in which men are driven by, and often torn between, diverse passions of which 'avarice' was only one" (ibid., 107–8). In setting the idle man of inherited wealth against the man who must "think of increasing [his] wealth," Hutcheson begins the task that his student Smith will finish, namely, that of revising the passions to animate and authorize the man of commerce.

28. On this point, it is important to recall that Hume argued against Locke's notion that ideas are the springboard of emotion. Hume claimed that both emotions and ideas derive from one's ability to transport him- or herself imaginatively back to sensations and, by means of association and custom (rather than logic), come up with the idea, for example, that fire is hot (*Enquiry*, 43–46). When Smith develops the idea of sympathy, he indeed draws on Hume's notion of imaginative association to argue that we are naturally disposed, upon witnessing the spectacle of another's pain, to imagine how we would feel in that individual's position. As we witness repeated scenes of the joy and suffering of others, however, we not only gain a progressively clearer sense of how our own emotions look to other people. We also double our inner spectator, so that the spectator who responds with inappropriate feeling and would impetuously spring to action is tempered by an "impartial spectator" who looks upon the scene with indifference and responds sympathetically to the cause of joy or pain (*Theory of Moral Sentiments*, 164–92). With the figure of the impartial spectator, Smith pulls the feelings that arise from sympathetic identification back in line with the Lockean faculty of reason.

29. Thomas Malthus, *An Essay on the Principle of Population*, ed. Antony Flew (London, 1985), 70. All citations of the text are to this edition.

30. Étienne Balibar locates a significant modification of the modern subject during the period when Malthus was writing. Where Locke had posited a state of free subjectivity prior to one's entry into the civic arena, authors writing a century later subtly reversed those priorities. Balibar describes the difference as the end of the belief that the subject is naturally endowed with free subjectivity, "an originary source of spontaneity and autonomy, something irreducible to objective constraints and determinations." Instead, "'freedom' can only be the result and counterpart of liberation, emancipation, becoming free." In this case, then, we understand subjection "as the condition, or even the guarantee of future salvation" ("Subjection and Subjectivation," 9). Under these circumstances, "citizenship is not one among other attributes of subjectivity, on the contrary: it is subjectivity, that form of subjectivity that would no longer be identical with subjection for anyone." This, as Balibar observes, poses the problem with which citizens would be grappling for the next two centuries, "since few of them, in fact, will achieve [subjectivity] completely" (12).

31. This act of imagination, as we have elsewhere explained at some length, performs exactly the reversal of the dynamic of power shaping and reproduced by the early modern stage, whereby the monarch, thus those in proximity to his or her body, embodied the gaze for the nameless, faceless spectators who were dependent on aristocratic body. Foucault's chapter details how "the spectacle on the scaffold" endangered the exclusive power of aristocratic performance over invisible spectators by putting the criminal in a spectacular position center stage in a grisly performance that inspired popular riots. Equally telling is how the stage itself, during this same period, sought to reverse its cultural gears and empower

292 • Notes to Pages 149–153

the spectator; see Tennenhouse, *Power on Display: The Politics of Shakespeare's Genres* (Methuen, 1986), 13–15; and Armstrong, *Fiction in the Age of Photography: The Legacy of British Realism* (Cambridge, Mass., 2000), 75–123.

32. Joanna Baillie, *The Dramatic and Poetical Works of Joanna Baillie* (London, 1853), 3. Citations of the text are to this edition.

ROUSSEAU'S QUARREL WITH GRATITUDE

1. Jean-Jacques Rousseau, *The Reveries of the Solitary Walker*, trans. Charles E. Butterworth, in *The Collected Writings of Rousseau*, ed. Roger D. Masters and Christopher Kelly (Hanover, N.H., 1990–2003), 8:49 (Sixth Walk). References to volumes of the *Collected Writings* will henceforth be abbreviated as *CW*. For the French text, see *Les Rêveries du promeneur solitaire*, in Rousseau, *Oeuvres complètes*, ed. Bernard Gagnebin and Marcel Raymond (Paris, 1959–95), 1:1050. All references to Rousseau's French texts are to this edition, henceforth abbreviated *OC*.

2. *Reveries*, 78 (*OC* 1:1054).

3. The distinction between gift and contractual exchange is a difficult one and the subject of an important contemporary debate that cannot be summarized here. Today, we do not think of gratitude as a "passion," but Descartes does list it as such in his *Les Passions de l'âme* (art. 193). As Carole Talon-Hugon has reminded us in *Les Passions rêvées par la raison: Essai sur la théorie des passions de Descartes et de quelques-uns de ses contemporains* (Paris, 2002), Descartes's work stands at the intersection of different languages about the emotions—medical, Thomist, Stoic, and Augustinian—and this discursive complexity continues into the eighteenth century, when the scope of the terms *passion*, *affection*, and *sentiment* often overlaps or is hard to distinguish. I will use the word *emotion* in this essay because I wish to focus on the relational aspect of feeling and because in today's speech it allows for a range of meanings from the physiological to the cognitive.

4. Daniel Gordon, *Citizens without Sovereignty: Equality and Sociability in French Thought, 1670–1789* (Cambridge, Mass., 1994).

5. François de Sales, *Introduction à la vie dévote*, in *Oeuvres*, ed. André Ravier (Paris, 1969), 141. The book was first published in 1609, with a final revised edition in 1619,

6. Descartes, *Meditationes de prima philosophia/Meditations on First Philosophy*, trans. and ed. George Heffernan (Notre Dame, 1990), 149. The work was first published in 1641.

7. Philip Fisher, *The Vehement Emotions* (Princeton, 2002).

8. I use *men* rather than *human beings* because Rousseau's focus is on males. He speaks very little of women in the state of nature, and minimizes mothers' attachment to their children, a bond that according to his logic lasts only a short time.

9. Rousseau, *Discourse on Inequality*, in Rousseau, *The "Discourses" and Other Early Political Writings*, ed. and trans. Victor Gourevitch (Cambridge, 1997), 155 (*OC* 3:157). All translations from the *Discourse* are from this edition.

10. "As justice dependeth on antecedent covenant; so does gratitude depend on antecedent grace; that is to say, antecedent free gift; and is the fourth law of

nature, which may be conceived in this form: that a man which receiveth benefit from another of mere grace endeavour that he which giveth it have no reasonable cause to repent him of his good will. For no man giveth but with intention of good to himself . . . of which if men see they shall be frustrated, there will be no beginning of benevolence or trust, nor consequently of mutual help, nor of reconciliation of one man to another; and therefore they are to remain still in the condition of war, which is contrary to the first and fundamental law of nature which commandeth men to seek peace." Hobbes, *Leviathan*, chap. 15, par. 16. I have used the edition of Edwin Curley (Indianapolis, 1994), 95. See also *De Cive* iii.8. In this text, gratitude is the third "law of nature." Note that in Samuel Sorbière's French translation of 1649, Hobbes's Latin "fiducia," translated by Michael Silverthorne as "good faith" (Hobbes, *On the Citizen*, ed. and trans. Richard Tuck and Michael Silverthorne [Cambridge, 1998], 47) is rendered as *reconnaissance*. Since it is likely that if Rousseau read Hobbes directly, it would have been Sorbière's version of this text, the passage is worth quoting in the French text: "La troisième loi de nature est qu'on ne permette point que celui qui, s'assurant de notre reconnaissance, a commencé le premier à nous bien faire, reçoive de l'incommodité de sa franchise, et qu'on n'accepte un bienfait qu'avec une disposition intérieure de faire en sorte que le bienfaiteur n'ait jamais un juste sujet de se repentir de sa bénéficence. Car sans cela, celui qui se mettrait le premier à bien faire aurait peu de raison de prodiguer et de voir périr la plus belle chose du monde, qui est sans doute un bienfait. D'où il s'ensuivrait qu'il ne se trouverait plus de courtoisie parmi les hommes, et que toute l'amitié et la fidélité qui les lient seraient ôtées." See Thomas Hobbes, *Le Citoyen, ou les fondements de la politique,* ed. Simone Goyard-Fabre (Paris, 1982), 117.

11. Catherine Larrère, "Rousseau," in *Dictionnaire de philosophie politique,* ed. Philippe Raynaud and Stéphane Rials (Paris, 1996), 590.

12. Samuel Pufendorf, *On the Duties of Man and Citizen,* trans. Michael Silverthorne, ed. James Tully (Cambridge, 1991), 35.

13. Ibid., 64.

14. Ibid., xxi.

15. Ibid., 3.

16. *Discourse,* 114 (*OC* 3:111). Rousseau had in fact lost his Genevan citizenship because he had converted to Catholicism as a young man. At the time of writing, however, he was preparing to recover his status and adopt the stance of a loyal Genevan.

17. *Discourse,* 120 (*OC* 3:118).

18. Cf. the preface to the *Letter to d'Alembert,* trans. Allan Bloom, in *CW* 10:255 (*OC* 5:6).

19. *Discourse,* 120 (*OC* 3:118). When his son was ten years old, Rousseau's father exiled himself from Geneva rather than submit to censure for an armed quarrel with an army captain.

20. *Discourse,* 177 (*OC* 3:182). Rousseau cites Locke and Sidney for support on this point.

21. *Discourse,* 152–54 (*OC* 3:154–56). The literature on Rousseau's notion of pity is extensive. See notably Jacques Derrida, *De la grammatologie* (Paris, 1967).

22. Pierre Force, *Self-Interest Before Adam Smith* (Cambridge, 2003), 24–25.

23. It has been claimed that the omission only shows how Rousseau always focuses on the self at the expense of any real acknowledgment of the other's reality. See John Charvet, *The Social Problem in the Philosophy of Rousseau* (Cambridge, 1974). Given Rousseau's anxious awareness of the other's gaze, this otherwise shrewd explanation falls short of the mark.

24. *Letter to d'Alembert*, CW 10:269 (OC 5:24).

25. The sarcastic remark in the *Discourse* about the "philosopher" who "only has to put his hands over his ears and to argue with himself a little in order to prevent nature ... from letting him identify with [a] man being assassinated" (*Discourse*, 153; OC 3:156) may have been inspired by Diderot, but it expresses Rousseau's resentment at what he thought was the complacency of the freethinking intellectuals of his day.

26. Paul Henri Thiry, baron d'Holbach, *Système Social* (1773) (Paris, 1994), 130.

27. Ibid., 221.

28. Ibid., 100.

29. Niccolò Machiavelli, *Discourses on Livy*, trans. Harvey J. Mansfield and Nathan Tarcov (Chicago, 1996), 64 (book 1, chap. 29).

30. Gabriel Bonnot de Mably, *Entretiens de Phocion, sur la rapport de la morale avec la politique, traduits du grec de Nicoclès, avec des remarques* (1764). The book was published anonymously.

31. See B.A. Gerrish, *Grace and Gratitude: The Eucharistic Theology of John Calvin* (Minneapolis, 1993).

32. See Helena Rosenblatt, *Rousseau and Geneva: From the First "Discourse" to the "Social Contract"* (Cambridge, 1997). For contemporary reflections on the evolution of Reformed theology on this issue, see Nicholas Wolterstorff, *Educating for Life: Reflections on Christian Teaching and Learning* (Grand Rapids, Mich., 2002). On the Catholic side, it is interesting to note that Pascal's *Pensées*, which deploy a rich variety of emotional strategies in their effort to convert secular libertines, do not mention gratitude among the "reasons of the heart" to which they appeal.

33. *Social Contract* IV.8, 142 (OC 3:468).

34. *Social Contract* IV.8, 142 (OC 3:468).

35. "Obedience to the commandments of love *is* thanksgiving, which for Calvin is not only a liturgical but an ethical concept" (Gerrish, *Grace and Gratitude*, 126).

36. Consideration of Hobbes's treatment of religion in the last part of *Leviathan* lies beyond the scope of this essay.

37. In this respect Rousseau is closer to Spinoza, who declared that "Scripture demands nothing from men but obedience." See Baruch Spinoza, *Theological-Political Treatise*, trans. Samuel Shirley, 2nd ed. (Indianapolis, 2001), 154. This was a radically revisionist reading of the Bible, but one that is consistent with Spinoza's view of God as the impersonal necessity of nature. In the absence of a reciprocal personal relationship, gratitude is meaningless. Cf. Hobbes: "The right of nature whereby God reigneth over men, and punisheth those that break his laws, is to be derived, not from His creating them, as if He required obedience as

of gratitude for His benefits, but from His irresistible power." *Leviathan*, 235 (chap. 31).

38. In the *Letter to d'Alembert*, Rousseau does offer a vision of moral intimacy in his depiction of the Genevan festivals, but even there it must be tempered by the vigilance of the authorities—authorities (religious and secular) whose rule is not to be made the object of scrutiny. One can have social intimacy and clarity about its political foundations, but not both.

39. *Social Contract* IV.8, 43 (*OC* 3:460–61).

40. For an interpretation of the curious frequency of references to Caligula in the *Social Contract*, see Felicity Baker, "La peine de mort dans le *Contrat Social*," in *Rousseau and the Eighteenth Century: Essays in Memory of R.A. Leigh*, ed. Marian Hobson, J.T.A. Leigh, and Robert Wokler (Oxford, 1992), 163–88.

41. *Social Contract* IV.8, 142 (*OC* 3:460).

42. *Social Contract* II.6, 68 (*OC* 3:380).

43. *Social Contract* II.7, 69 (*OC* 3:381).

44. Rousseau does not mention Jesus as one of these "impostors," but not, I believe, only for reasons of prudence. Unlike Moses or Mohammed, Jesus did not found a people in the political sense.

45. *Social Contract* II.7, 71 (*OC* 3:383).

46. *Social Contract* II.7, 69 (*OC* 3:381). One wonders to what extent this duality reflects the ghostly influence of the long debate about the two natures of Christ.

47. *Social Contract* II.7, 72 (*OC* 3:384).

48. In the *Letter to d'Alembert*, Rousseau warns that a play in Geneva commemorating the Escalade—the day in 1602 when Savoyard invaders were successfully repelled—would stir up too much warlike spirit amongst the people. See *CW* 10:340n. (*OC* 5:110n).

49. Rousseau, "Preface of the New Heloise or Conversation about Novels between the Editor and a Man of Letters," in Jean-Jacques Rousseau, *Julie, or the New Heloise. Letters of two lovers who live in a small town at the foot of the Alps*, trans. Philip Stewart and Jean Vaché, *CW* 6:16. All references to Julie give first the book and letter number, then citation from this edition, followed by a reference to the French text (here *OC* 2:23).

50. *Julie* I.24, *CW* 6:70n; *OC* 2:85n.

51. *Julie* II.18, *CW* 6:211; *OC* 2:258.

52. *Julie* VI.6, *CW* 6:549; *OC* 2:668.

53. "The Loves of Milord Edward Bomston," *CW* 6:614; *OC* 2:751. In contrast with the translators, I will refer to the character as Edouard, the name he bears in the novel.

54. *Julie* III.18, *CW* 6:288; *OC* 2:349.

55. *Julie* II.6, *CW* 6:170; *OC* 2:208.

56. *Julie* IV.12, *CW* 6:403; *OC* 2:491.

57. *Julie* IV.12, *CW* 6:403; *OC* 2:492.

58. *Julie* IV.10, *CW* 6:367; *OC* 2:446.

59. *Julie* V.8, *CW* 6:500; *OC* 2:611. Cf. 1 Chron. 29:34.

60. *Julie* V.1, *CW* 6:431; *OC* 2:525–26.

61. *Julie* VI.3, *CW* 6:534; *OC* 2:649.

62. *Julie* II.19, *CW* 6: 215; *OC* 2:262.

63. We find the same kind of empowering gratitude in Rousseau's relationship with Madame de Warens—an elective relationship, determined neither by blood nor by legal ties. See Felicity Baker, "The Object of Love in Rousseau's *Confessions*," in *Representations of the Self from the Renaissance to Romanticism*, ed. Patrick Coleman, Jayne Lewis, and Jill Kowalik (Cambridge, 2000), 171–99.

64. *Julie* V.5, CW 6:484; OC 2:591.

65. La Rochefoucauld, *maxime* 223, in *Moralistes du XVIIe siècle*, ed. Jean Lafond (Paris, 1992), 154 (my translation).

66. *Julie* V.5, CW 6: 483; OC 2:590.The lovers of *Julie*, like their creator, are also admirers of Archbishop Fénelon, whose doctrine of "pur amour" radicalized the basic Christian idea that God should be loved for himself by claiming that any self-interest (ultimately, even interest in one's own salvation) tainted that love. In doing so, Fénelon transformed an idea that had long been invoked by Christian mystics as a kind of theological paradox into a principle of general application. The notion of *pur amour*, and the "quietist," almost impersonal attitude toward salvation associated with it, left little room for gratitude at all.

67. For details of Rousseau's views of gender differences in this regard, see his discussion of Sophie's education in *Emile*, Book 5.

68. For a discussion of the social accommodation of emotion in the period, see William M. Reddy, *The Navigation of Feeling: A Framework for the History of Emotions* (Cambridge, 2001).

69. See Robert Darnton, "Readers Respond to Rousseau: The Fabrication of Romantic Sensitivity," in *The Great Cat Massacre and Other Episodes in French Cultural History* (New York, 1984), chap. 6; Claude Labrosse, *Lire au XVIIIe siècle: La Nouvelle Héloïse et ses lecteurs* (Lyon, 1985).

70. The best recent interpretation of the work is Laurence Mall, *Emile ou les figures de la fiction*, SVEC 2002:04.

71. For a provocative treatment of this issue, see Susan Meld Shell, "Émile: Nature and the Education of Sophie," in *The Cambridge Companion to Rousseau*, ed. Patrick Riley (Cambridge, 2001), 272–301.

72. *Emile*, trans. Allan Bloom (New York, 1979), 221 (OC 4:503). Unless otherwise indicated, all references are to book 4 of *Emile*.

73. Recall that for Rousseau what distinguishes God (or the legislator) is that he loves without need.

74. For Rousseau's wariness about the identification with the national community, see Patrick Coleman, "'Aimer les lois': L'objet de l'éducation républicaine chez Rousseau," in *Republikanische Tugend: Ausbildung eines Schweizer Nationalbewusstseins und Erziehung eines neuen Bürgers. Contribution à une nouvelle approche des Lumières helvétiques*, ed. Michael Böhler, Etienne Hofmann, Peter H. Reill, and Simone Zurbuchen (Geneva, 2000), 459–70.

75. *Emile*, 233–34 (OC 4:520–21).

76. *Emile*, 235 (OC 4:523).

77. If the tutor is not likely to abuse his power, it is because he is an exceptional individual, of course, but also because he is not Emile's father. His position is socially marginal and also limited in time.

78. *Emile*, 260 (OC 4:558).

79. *Emile*, 264 (OC 4:562).

80. *Emile*, 278 (OC 4:583).

81. For Rousseau, it is lack of power that generates ill will.

82. There has been much discussion about where conscience as a normative voice fits within Rousseau's conception of human nature, but the issue cannot be addressed here. See Henri Gouhier, *Les Méditations métaphysiques de Jean-Jacques Rousseau*, 2nd ed. (Paris, 1984). For a different interpretation of Rousseau religious views, see Victor Gourevitch's challenging essay "The Religious Thought," in Riley, *Cambridge Companion to Rousseau*, 193–246.

83. *Emile*, 293 (OC 4:604–5).

PARTING WITH PREJUDICE

1. David Hume, *A Treatise of Human Nature*, ed. L.A. Selby-Bigge, revised by P. H. Nidditch (Oxford, 1978), 415. Hereafter abbreviated as *T* and cited in the body of my text.

2. Norman Kemp Smith, *The Philosophy of David Hume* (London, 1941), 147–55, 193–202.

3. See the opening line of Hume's *Enquiry Concerning Human Understanding*: "Moral philosophy, or the science of human nature," in the edition of L.A. Selby-Bigge, revised by P. H. Nidditch (Oxford, 1975), 5. This volume also contains the *Enquiry Concerning the Principles of Morals*, hereafter abbreviated as *EM* and cited in the body of my text. Hume's enumeration of the sciences of human nature is taken from his "Abstract" of the *Treatise*, included in the Oxford University Press edition (*T*, 646).

4. Letter of March or April 1734, conjectured to be addressed to Dr. George Cheyne, in *The Letters of David Hume*, 2 vols., ed. J.Y.T. Greig (Oxford, 1932), 1:16.

5. In *Religion and Faction in Hume's Moral Philosophy* (Cambridge, 1997), Jennifer Herdt addresses this same issue through an analysis of Hume's changing understanding of the nature and function of sentiment. Her chapters "'Poetical Systems' and the Pleasures of Tragedy" and "Sympathetic Understanding and the Threat of Difference" (82–167) are closest to my own essay and the best treatment of the interconnections of aesthetics, ethics, and politics in Hume's writings.

6. In the *Enquiry Concerning Morals*, Hume cites the social and universal character of sentiments "dependent on humanity" as frequently capable of controlling and limiting the disorderly passion of self-love responsible for "popular tumults, seditions, factions" and civil wars in which, on the example of Solon "who punished neuters," there are only friends and enemies (*EM*, 274–75). See Jean-François Lyotard, "Anamnesis of the Visible, or Candour," in *The Lyotard Reader*, ed. Andrew Benjamin (London, 1989), 237.

7. Carl Schmitt, *The Concept of the Political*, trans. George Schwab, with comments by Leo Strauss (New Brunswick, N.J., 1976), 54–55; first published in 1932.

8. Ibid., 26–27. For Schmitt, "The political enemy need not be morally evil or aesthetically ugly," but "he is, nevertheless, the other, the stranger, . . . and in the extreme case conflicts with him are possible" (27), conflicts, singularly, involving

life and death, war and sacrifice. In his comments on this book, Leo Strauss remarks that Schmitt insists the political is both autonomous and "authoritative": "In this sense, it is to be understood that the political is 'not equivalent and analogous' to the moral, the aesthetic, the economic, and so on" (86).

9. See, for example, Étienne Balibar's "Subjection and Subjectivation," in *Supposing the Subject*, ed. Joan Copjec (London, 1994), 1–15; Chantal Mouffe, *The Democratic Paradox* (London, 2000); Pheng Cheah and Bruce Robbins, eds., *Cosmopolitics: Thinking and Feeling Beyond the Nation* (Minneapolis, 1998); Steven Vertovec and Robin Cohen, eds., *Conceiving Cosmopolitanism* (Oxford, 2002).

10. Timothy Brennan, *At Home in the World: Cosmopolitanism Now* (Cambridge, Mass., 1997), 25. Brennan considers recent progressive claims for cosmopolitanism as failing to acknowledge its use in the ideology of imperialism and globalization and the resistance to imperialism that nationalist movements still provide.

11. "[D]ie Skeptiker, eine Art Nomaden, die allen beständigen Anbau des Bodens verabscheuen, zertrenneten von Zeit zu Zeit die bürgerliche Vereinigung": Immanuel Kant, *Critique of Pure Reason*, trans. Norman Kemp Smith (New York, 1965), 8; *Kritik der reinen Vernunft* (Wiesbaden, 1956), 12.

12. James Noxon, "Hume's Opinion of Critics," *Journal of Aesthetics and Art Criticism* 20 (1961–62): 157–62.

13. For an account that tends to stress the "law of the heart," see Terry Eagleton, *The Ideology of the Aesthetic* (London, 1990), 31–69.

14. On the tension between self-correcting passions and the mediating effects of reason in Hume, especially with regard to justice as civic virtue, I have benefited from the following works: Smith, *Philosophy of David Hume*; Éléonore Le Jallé, *Hume et la régulation morale* (Paris, 1999); Barry Stroud, *Hume* (London, 1977).

15. Kant, *Critique of Pure Reason*, 44.

16. David Hume, *Essays Moral, Political, and Literary*, ed. Eugene F. Miller (Indianapolis, 1987), 259 n. 8. Hereafter abbreviated by *E* and cited in the body of my text.

17. As has often been noted, Hume's stress on sympathy as the medium productive of humanity and especially benevolence in the *Treatise* tends to disappear in the second *Enquiry*. "It is sufficient," Hume remarks there, that "we have humanity or a fellow-feeling with others" for it "to be a principle in human nature," and he advocates a "party of humankind" on the basis of such an original and universal benevolence (*EM*, 219 n. 1, 272–76). In the introduction to his edition of the second *Enquiry*, for example, Selby-Bigge notes: "In the *Enquiry*, sympathy is another name for social feeling, humanity, benevolence, natural philanthropy, rather than [as in the *Treatise*] the name of the process by which the social feeling has been constructed out of non-social or individual feeling"; in eliminating the psychological "machinery" of sympathy in the later work, Hume "abandoned perhaps the most distinctive feature of his moral system" (xxvi).

18. Philip Mercer, *Sympathy and Ethics* (Oxford, 1972), 12–16, 35–36.

19. Hobbes and Locke had preceded Hume in this inquiry into the problematical referentiality of moral language derived from affective subjectivity. In *Leviathan*, Hobbes argues that the terms good and evil do not refer to constant qualities of objects but only to the variable sensations of the "person[s] that useth them,"

who by these terms name "such things as affect us, that is, which please or displease"; hence, to speak of good or evil as if they were "in the nature of the objects themselves" is either to employ a metaphorical discourse or, more abusively, to ignorantly mistake or deceptively substitute figural for literal language. The inconstancy of reference in moral language that results from its affective condition necessarily precipitates for Hobbes the instituting of a sovereign as absolute arbiter to prevent contradiction and conflict as well as error. See *Leviathan* (Harmondsworth, 1968), 109, 120, 122. Similarly, in detailing the imperfection of words in the *Essay Concerning Human Understanding*, Locke ascribes to the terms of morality—or what he calls the names of mixed modes—"various and doubtful" signification because "they want *Standards* in Nature," being but "assemblages of *Ideas* put together at the pleasure of the Mind, pursuing its own ends of Discourse, and suited to its own Notions." To counter the instability of reference in moral language for individuals, "who have scarce any standing Rule to regulate themselves" but their own pleasure and displeasure, Locke, of course, does not introduce an absolute sovereign but gestures (rather weakly) toward common use to regulate meaning. See *An Essay Concerning Human Understanding* (Oxford, 1975), 478, 479. 514.

20. Étienne Balibar, "Ambiguous Universality," chap. 8 in his *Politics and the Other Scene*, trans. C. Jones, J. Swenson, and C. Turner (London, 2002), 160.

21. Theodor Adorno, "Refuge for the Homeless," in *Minima Moralia: Reflections from Damaged Life*, trans. E.F.N. Jephcott (London, 1974), 39; "[E]s gehört zur Moral, nich bei sich selber zu Haus zu sein" (*Minima Moralia* [Frankfurt am Main, 1951], 45). Perhaps we could translate this to mean that the feeling of not belonging is what belongs to morality.

22. Hume's "general point of view" has received considerable attention in recent scholarship that argues it does not constitute an abstract, ideal position that can be occupied and resolve contradiction and conflict. See, for example, Annette C. Baier, *A Progress of Sentiments: Reflections on Hume's "Treatise"* [Cambridge, Mass., 1991], 181–83); Herdt, *Religion and Faction*, 70–81; and Geoffrey Sayre-McCord, "On Why Hume's 'General Point of View' Isn't Ideal—and Shouldn't Be," in *Social Philosophy and Policy Foundation* 11.1 (1994): 202–28.

23. To acknowledge that self-parting is felt as violence is perhaps to complicate the arguments of those who, like Seyla Benhabib, proceed as if the recognition alone of the historical truth of "hybridity" at the origin of cultural identity would apparently render misguided any discussions of incommensurability (of peculiar cultures) and practices of cultural translation. See "'Nous' et les 'Autres' (We and the Others): Is Universalism Ethnocentric?" in her *The Claims of Culture: Equality and Diversity in the Global Era* (Princeton, 2002), 24–48. On the other side, see Hent de Vries' and Samuel Weber's stress on a violence that occurs in the very constitution of apparently autonomous individual and collective subjects in their introduction to *Violence, Identity, and Self-Determination* (Stanford, 1997).

24. Compare Schmitt: "The concept of humanity is an especially useful ideological instrument of imperialist expansion, and in its ethical-humanitarian form it is a specific vehicle of economic imperialism" (*Concept of the Political*, 54).

25. Mouffe, *The Democratic Paradox*, 123. Mouffe's analysis of the salutary effect of the tension in liberal democracy is worth recalling in this context: "The

democratic logic of constituting the people, and inscribing rights and equality into practices, is necessary to subvert the tendency towards abstract universalism inherent in liberal discourse. But the articulation with the liberal logic allows us constantly to challenge—through reference to 'humanity' and the polemical use of 'human rights'—the forms of exclusion that are necessarily inscribed in the political practice of installing those rights and defining the 'people' which is going to rule" (44–45).

26. Judith Butler, Ernesto Laclau, and Slavoj Žižek, *Contingency, Hegemony, Universality: Contemporary Dialogues on the Left* (London, 2000), 207. Hereafter abbreviated by *CHU* and cited in my text. In the following brief references to this work, I do not mark the shifting fault-lines of agreement and disagreement to be found across the intricate and engaged essays contributed by these writers.

27. Derrida, *Specters of Marx*, trans. Peggy Kamuf (New York, 1994), 65. See also Werner Hamacher's incisive analysis of the aporetic structure of this promise of democracy in "Lingua Amissa: The Messianism of Commodity-Language and Derrida's *Specters of Marx*," in *Ghostly Demarcations*, ed. M. Sprinker (New York, 1999), 168–212.

28. Donald W. Livingston has strenuously argued for a conservative Hume whose commitment to "established authority" based on "tradition, custom, and prejudice" places Hume "outside the liberal democratic tradition of Locke, Rousseau, Kant, and Mill" (*Hume's Philosophy of Common Life* [Chicago, 1984], 337). I tend to agree, however, with John B. Stewart's assessment that "the priority Hume gives to the individual, the preeminence and consequent independence he gives to the economy, [and] his faith in the natural harmony of society," among other characteristics, "are all notable marks of liberalism" (*The Moral and Political Philosophy of David Hume* [Westport, Conn., 1977], 323–24), and with Duncan Forbes's emphasis on intertwined political strains in Hume's thought: "there are strikingly 'liberal' features in what is usually regarded as Hume's final 'conservative' or even 'reactionary' phase, and 'conservative' features in the early Hume"—a tension between what Forbes settles on calling "vulgar" and "scientific" or "skeptical" Whiggism (*Hume's Philosophical Politics* [Cambridge, 1975], 139–40).

29. Howard Caygill, *Art of Judgement* (Oxford, 1989), 100–101.

30. Balibar, *Politics and the Other Scene*, 165.

31. Jean-Jacques Rousseau, *Letter to M. d'Alembert*, in *Politics and the Arts*, trans. Allen Bloom (Ithaca, 1960), 17; *Lettre à M. d'Alembert sur son article Genève* (Paris, 1967), 67.

32. Rousseau, *Letter*, 119; *Lettre*, 124.

33. David Hume, *The Natural History of Religion* (New York, 1993), 176.

34. Jean Racine, *Théâtre complet* (Paris, 1960).

35. Pierre Corneille, *Oeuvres complètes* (Paris, 1963), 3.3.950–51.

VICO, "TENDERNESS," AND "BARBARISM"

1. F. M. Pagano, *Saggi politici* (Naples, 1784–85).

2. B. Croce, *Intorno alla vita e al carattere di G.B. Vico* (1909), subsequently in Croce, *La filosofia di G.B. Vico* (1911) (Bari, 1973), 256.

3. G. Ferrari, *Corso sugli scrittori politici italiani* (Milan, 1862), 710. On Vico's "standing" in Italy and the rest of Europe between the end of the eighteenth century and the first half of the twentieth, cf. F. Nicolini and B. Croce, *Bibliografia vichiana* (Naples, 1947–48); P. Rossi, "Giambattista Vico," in *I classici italiani nella storia della critica*, ed. W. Binni, vol. 2 (Florence, 1970), 1–41.

4. I am thinking in particular of the important works by N. Badaloni, G. Giarrizzo, and B. De Giovanni, for which I refer the reader to my own review "La politica in Vico. Note sugli attuali orientamenti storiografici," *Il Pensiero Politico* (1983): 3–18.

5. Cf. as an example of the former view, F. Vaughan, *The Political Philosophy of Giambattista Vico: An Introduction to "La Scienza Nuova"* (The Hague, 1972); and, representing the second, M. Lilla, *G.B. Vico: The Making of an Anti-Modern* (London, 1993), and U. Galeazzi, *Ermeneutica e storia in Vico. Morale, diritto e società della "Scienza Nuova"* (L'Aquila, 1993). On the complexity of the relations between Vico and modern political philosophy, it is worth mentioning at least B. Haddock, *Vico's Political Thought* (Swansea, 1986); M. Montanari, *Vico e la politica dei moderni* (Bari, 1995); and G. Carillo's recent *Vico. Origine e genealogia dell'ordine* (Naples, 2000).

6. Among the few exceptions, cf. G. Cantelli, *Mente Corpo Linguaggio. Saggio sull'interpretazione vichiana del mito* (Florence, 1986); A. O. Hirschman, *The Passions and the Interests* (Princeton, 1977); G. Cacciatore, "Passione e ragione nella filosofia civile di Vico," in *Bollettino del Centro di Studi Vichiani* 31–32 (2001–2002): 97–114; and—although they do not directly address the political dimension—also see A. Battistini, "Vico and the Passions," in *Teorie delle passioni*, ed. E. Pulcini (Bologna, 1989), 113–28, and S. Contarini, "La tela di ragno e la farfalla: Vico e le passioni dell'anima," in *Momenti vichiani del primo Settecento*, ed. G. Pizzamiglio and Manuela Sanna (Naples, 2001), 37–74.

7. I have modified the English version, which translates the Italian word *tenerezza* as "affection," a term that I do not find very appropriate in this case.

8. In the 1730 edition *tenerezza* (tenderness) occurs only once (cf. infra, first paragraph), and in the 1725 edition not at all, while *barbarie* appears eleven times and *barbaro* sixty-two. Quite legitimately P. Girard includes the second term in his *La vocabulaire de Vico* (Paris, 2001) and leaves out the first. *Tenerezza*, moreover, is given no space even in the meatiest commentaries on the *Scienza Nuova*: cf. F. Nicolini, *Commento storico alla seconda Scienza Nuova*, 2nd ed., 2 vols. (Rome, 1978), and A. Battistini, "Introduzione" and "Note" to G. B. Vico, *Opere*, ed. A. Battistini (Milan, 1990).

9. "Ma essendo passato l'Impero de' nobili al popolo, perché la plebe pone tutte le sue forze, ricchezza, e potenza nella moltitudine de' figliuoli, i quali, finché si maritano, sono di frutto e giovamento a' loro padri, s'incominciò a sentire dalle leggi la tenerezza del sangue e i pretori incominciaron a riguardarlo con le *bonorum* possessioni, cominciaron a sanare co' loro rimedi a vizi, o difetti de' testamenti, perché si divolgassero le ricchezze, le quali sole ammira il volgo." G. B. Vico, *Principj d'una Scienza nuova d'intorno alla comune natura delle nazioni* (1730), ed. P. Cristofolini and M. Sanna (Naples, 2004), 340.

10. G. B. Vico, *Principj d'una Scienza nuova d'intorno alla comune natura delle nazioni* (1744), trans. D. Marsh as *Principles of the New Science concerning the Common Nature of Nations*, 2nd ed. (London, 2001). All the citations in the

text, with the number of the paragraph given in parentheses, refer to this edition. In a few cases I have made slight alterations to the translation.

11. Cf. also pars. 592, 985, and 1021.

12. The addition continues as follows: "In this early age, the large number of plebeians posed a threat to the aristocracies, which are based on and named after the minority. But later they contributed much to the greatness of democracies and even more of monarchies, which is why imperial laws compensate women so generously for the dangers and pains of childbirth. In the age of popular liberty, praetors began to recognize the rights of blood relations."

13. Here too the reference is to the successions, to the "heroic Roman successions," which for Vico excluded women, including daughters.

14. Croce, *La filosofia di G.B. Vico*, 169.

15. "But Vico is not only a moral philosopher or a metaphysician; he is also and (at least for us moderns) above all an anthropologist" (Battistini, "Vico and the Passions," 121). A picture of Vico as forerunner, if not the actual founder, of modern "cultural anthropology" is presented by M. Vanzulli in "Caso e necessità nella nuova scienza vichiana," *Quaderni Materialisti* 1, no. 1 (2002): 7–39.

16. A. C. 't Hart, "La metodologia giuridica vichiana," *Bollettino del Centro di Studi Vichiani* 12–13 (1982–83): 20.

17. The only positive aspect, in a manner of speaking, that Vico sees in the "brutish wandering" is its role as an early factor in the distribution of humanity over the earth: "first, during their brutish wanderings through the earth's inland regions; then under heroic law on both land and sea, and finally through the Phoenicians' maritime trading" (736).

18. On the figures and structures of Vico's "brutish wandering," cf. F. Nicolini, "L'erramento ferino e le origini della civiltà," in *La religiosità di Giambattista Vico* (Bari, 1949), 67–99; and L. Bulferetti, "L'ipotesi vichiana dell''erramento ferino,'" in *Annali della Facoltà di Lettere-Filosofia e Magistero dell'Università di Cagliari* 12 (1952).

19. Cf. also pars. 248ff., 284, 521–22. Among the fuller and more profound investigations of Vico's "poetic wisdom," it is worth mentioning at least J. Trabant, *Neue Wissenschaft von alten Zeichen: Vicos Sematologie* (Frankfurt am Main, 1994). But see too J. Mali, *The Rehabilitation of Myth* (Cambridge, 1992).

20. Useful considerations on the subject can be found in B. Pinchard, "Diis manibus ou Vico chez les morts," *Archives de Philosophie* 56 (1993): 549–60, who defines the new science in general as "science des morts," contrasting it with "panthéisme fusionnel."

21. "Finally, to appreciate the importance of my third principle, that of burial rites, let us imagine a brutish state in which human corpses are left unburied as carrion for crows and dogs. Such bestial behavior clearly belongs to the world of uncultivated fields and uninhabited cities, in which people wandered like swine, eating acorns gathered amid the rotting corpses of their dead kin" (337).

22. These aspects have been emphasized in various ways by E. Garin, *La filosofia* (Milan, 1947), 950; F. Vaughan, *The Political Philosophy of Giambattista Vico*, 34ff.; J. Morrison, "Vico's Doctrine of the Natural Law of the Gentes," *Journal of the History of Philosophy* 16, no. 1 (1978): 47–60, and Morrison,

"Vico and Machiavelli," in *Vico: Past and Present*, ed. G. Tagliacozzo (New York, 1981), 2:1–14; B. A. Haddock, *Vico's Political Thought*, 174ff.

23. P. Cristofolini, *Scienza Nuova. Introduzione alla lettura* (Rome, 1995), esp. 35–57, is of particular interest on these themes, pointing out the (theoretical and *philological*) complexity of the problem and avoiding simplistic secularist short-cuts, but also showing the basic impracticability of any dominance of sacred over profane history.

24. "If, then, the fundamental principle of Providence, which is 'architect of this world of nations,' remains unchallenged, it should also be remembered that, according to Vico, this same Providence gives rise, not only to the world of nations, but also its rule, which is that of 'vernacular wisdom'": G. Cacciatore, "Giambattista Vico: L'ordine della 'comunità' e il senso comune della 'differenza,'" in *All'ombra di Vico: testimonianze e saggi vichiani in ricordo di Giorgio Tagliacozzo*, ed. F. Ratto (Ripatransone, 1999), 194.

25. According to K. Löwith, Vico's theory is "rather classic than Christian": "The cyclic recurrence provides for education and even 'salvation' of mankind by the rebirth of its social nature. It saves man by preserving him. This alone, but not redemption, is the 'primary end' and providential meaning of history": *Meaning in History: The Theological Implications of the Philosophy of History* (Chicago, 1949), 158. Likewise D. Faucci declares that Vico "emerges from the confines of the religious problem of divine help, which is a problem of salvation: grace saves the soul. By contrast, Vico's providential aid intervenes to preserve 'the human race,' human society": "Vico e Grozio 'Giureconsulti del genere umano,'" in *Vico e l'instaurazione delle scienze*, ed. G. Tagliacozzo (Lecce, 1968), 109. Similar considerations are found in A. Momigliano, "La nuova storia romana di G.B. Vico," *Rivista Storia Italiana* 77 (1965): 788: "the Incarnation plays no guiding part in the New Science"; in Vaughan, *Political Philosophy of Vico*, 43; and in G. Bedani, *Vico Revisited: Orthodoxy, Naturalism and Science in the "Scienza Nuova"* (Oxford, 1989).

26. On these aspects I will take the liberty of referring the reader to R. Caporali, *Heroes gentium. Sapienza e politica in Vico* (Bologna, 1992), 109ff.

27. The key moments in this process in Rome appear to have been the Publilian Law (by which plebiscites acquired legal value for all Roman citizens, and which "marked a turning-point in Roman history, for it proclaimed the shift of the Roman constitution from aristocracy to democracy"), and the Poetelian Law, which "released the plebeians from feudal liability for debt, which previously had made them liege vassals of the patricians and compelled them to labor in their private prisons, often for life" (104 and 115).

28. "Vico takes the idea of the three ages from the ancient Mediterranean tradition (an Egyptian cosmogonic division into periods reconciled with Platonic psychology and Augustinian theology), but reverses their original axiological order: in the age of the gods he sees primitive creatures at the mercy of unbridled passions or imaginary terrors, in the heroic one bellicose ambitions . . . and in a manifestly reappraised 'age of men' the time when 'fully developed human reason' gained the upper hand": G. Prestipino, "Sulle fonti e sulla fortuna di Vico pensatore mediterraneo," *Critica Marxista*, n.s., 12, nos. 5–6 (2002): 81.

29. It is partly for this reason that I continue to find reductive all those interpretations of Vico's philosophy as a yearning for a restoration of religion: cf., among the more recent and stimulating studies, Lilla, *G.B. Vico*, and U. Galeazzi, *Ermeneutica e storia in Vico*. R. A. Miner sees Vico instead as engaged in the construction of an unprecedented reconciliation of Catholic tradition and modernity, in the name of a supremacy of morality that emerges "genealogically" over the course of historical development: *Vico: Genealogist of Modernity* (Notre Dame, Ind., 2002).

30. Rather than the "primitivist" interpretations that locate the zenith of Vico's nation at its beginning (after which any change would necessarily take the form of a retardation, an enfeeblement), I feel that those authors who see the crisis as an "awareness of the dangers inherent in the very civilization whose development was theorized by Vico" have come closer to the mark: N. Badaloni, introduction to G. B. Vico, *Opere Filosofiche*, ed. P. Cristofolini (Florence, 1971), xiii; similar views can also be found in N. Abbagnano, "Il concetto della storia dell'illuminismo italiano," *Rivista di Filosofia* 56 (1965): 283–96. Among the interpreters who insist instead on the primacy of the imagination and see the age of men as decadence (each from his own perspective of course), cf. I. Berlin, *Vico and Herder: Two Studies in the History of Ideas* (London, 1976); D. P. Verene, *Vico's Science of the Imagination* (Ithaca, 1981); M. J. Mooney, *Vico in the Tradition of Rhetoric* (Princeton, 1985); E. Grassi, "The Priority of Common Sense and Imagination: Vico's Philosophical Relevance Today," *Social Research* 43 (1976): 612–24.

31. Clear echoes of Plato, *Republic*, VIII.

32. Too well known for it to make sense to examine in detail here, the dispute with Descartes runs all the way through Vico's theoretical research, at least from the time of the *De ratione* (the last and most important of the inaugural lectures). To summarize it very briefly, Vico accuses the "tyrant Renée Descartes" of having raised the cogito from the status of a particular and subjective certainty on the part of the refined and civilized man to that of a universal and absolute "method," the sole and indisputable criterion of truth in every sphere of knowledge. In this way Descartes ignored the empirical dimension of sensibility and sentiment, of imagination and fantasy, which, decisive and predominant in the first two ages of the course of nations, not only did not disappear in the phase of "developed humanity" but remained the crucial litmus test for the possibility of *ratio* getting a grip on the ethical, political, and social dynamics of the "age of men." By eliminating the sensible from the realm of science, the Cartesian cogito loses sight of the inalienable emotional connections, the inescapable passionate relations that fortify the "individual," the modern "subject." Vico holds that a similar limitation applies to contract theory, which he sees as represented not so much by Hobbes (with whose work he had only a sketchy and indirect acquaintance) as by the Tribonian tradition of the *lex regia*, a presumed but in reality imaginary act of formal handing over of the *imperium* to Augustus on the part of the senate and on behalf of the Roman people. The hypothesis of the "pact" is misleading and simplistic, because it aims to explain the origin of power by a transparent act of that reason which is instead a mature and climactic historical product of the tensions and contradictions of power. On Vico's anti-Cartesian polemic cf. in particu-

lar G. B. Vico, *De nostri temporis studiorum ratione* (1708), trans. E. Gianturco as *On the Study Methods of Our Time*, 2nd ed. (London, 1990), and *Vita di Giambattista Vico scritta da sé medesimo* (1723–28 and 1731), trans. M. H. Fisch and T. G. Bergin as *The Autobiography of Giambattista Vico*, 3rd ed. (Ithaca, 1975). On the *lex regia* cf. G. B. Vico, "Ragionamento secondo d'intorno alla legge regia di Triboniano," in *Opere*, ed. F. Nicolini, vol. 2 (Bari, 1928), 299–306. From the historiographical perspective, the critical literature on Vico's polemic against Descartes is endless; so I will limit myself to mentioning an essay by B. De Giovanni, who does not lose sight of its political implications: "Corpo e ragione in Spinoza e Vico," in B. De Giovanni, R. Esposito, and A. Zarone, *Divenire della ragione moderna. Cartesio, Spinoza, Vico* (Naples, 1981), 93–165. On his rejection of contractual theory cf. N. Bobbio, "Il modello giusnaturalistico," in N. Bobbio and M. Bovero, *Società e Stato nella filosofia politica moderna* (Milan, 1979), 29ff.; A. C. 't Hart, *Recht en Staat in het denken van Giambattista Vico* (Alphen aan den Rijn, 1979), 211–13.

33. Naturally the comparison of recurrence to the postmodern is valid only in a suggestive and approximate sense, without any pretense to real historical and philological credibility, as an indication of the disintegration of the functional order of modernity under the centrifugal impulses of its own constituent categories: the subject and the state, freedom and authority, order and conflict. In any case, I do not find very convincing the considerations of D. P. Verene, in *Vico nel mondo anglosassone*, ed. by M. Simonetta (Naples, 1995), 37–43, who identifies the "barbarism of reflection" with "criticism of the modern era." Nor, more in general, the interpretation of E. Voegelin, *History of Political Ideas: Religion and the Rise of Modernity*, ed. J. L. Wiser (Columbia, 1998), chap. 3, who claims that Vico is opposed *tout court* to modernity, as the first of the great diagnosticians of the crisis of the West. Formulations that do not explain how the denunciation in the *Scienza Nuova* of the dangers faced by humanity "in the present civilized age" (29) is able to coexist with its evident, explicit celebration: useful indications on the twofold character of Vico's position can be found in A. Pons, "Vico et la 'barbarie de la reflexion,'" in *La pensée politique* 2 (1994): 178–97. But see too T. S. Holmes, "The Barbarism of Reflection," in Tagliacozzo, *Vico: Past and Present*, 2:213–22.

34. This is a variant that does not appear in the final version: cf. Vico, *Opere*, ed. Nicolini, 2:258.

35. Cf. also pars. 737 and 1025.

36. Cf. also par. 1087. Carillo comes up with a different interpretation, in which Vico's democracy appears "destined *ab initio* to be superseded," a mere parenthesis "between the government by the few (the degeneration of aristocracy into oligarchy) and the perfect government, by one" (*Vico. Origine e genealogia dell'ordine*, 214).

37. P. Cristofolini, on the other hand, holds that Vico became the champion of "an ideal eternal republic" founded on "feudal relations that were perpetuated and recurrent through the historical vicissitudes of the nations": *Vico pagano and barbaro* (Pisa, 2001), 62–63.

38. And it is, incidentally, also the essence of the other "solution" to the crisis, the submission to another nation, which preserves the conquered one by turning it into a "province" (1105).

39. "Monarchs represent their entire subject nations" (998).

40. Cf. also the "Ragionamento secondo d'intorno alla legge regia di Triboniano," in Vico, *Opere*, ed. Nicolini, 2:304. It is the procedural and spontaneous character of this convergence between *rex* and *multitudo* that lies at the root of Vico's aversion to Tribonian's tradition of the existence of an act of explicit delivery of power into the hands of Augustus by the senate on behalf of the people: cf. P. De Francisci, "L'antitribonianismo di G.B. Vico," *Rivista Internazionale di Filosofia del Diritto*, 2nd ed. (1931–32), 128–36.

41. I have modified the translation here, which originally said simply: "affection for one's wife and children."

KANT AND THE RELEGATION OF THE PASSIONS

1. *Plato's Cosmology: The Timaeus of Plato*, ed. & trans. Francis M. Cornford (Indianapolis, 1997), 143.

2. Aristotle, *On the Soul*, 403b.

3. Harry Austryn Wolfson offers a helpful characterization of three senses of passion in Aristotle that he links with Descartes's and to a lesser extent Spinoza's accounts: "(1) in the general sense of accident (*sumbebekos*), (2) in the sense of the emotions (*kineseis*) of the soul which are also called by him the qualities (*poiotetes*) of the soul, and (3) in the general sense of suffering as the opposite of *ergon*." *The Philosophy of Spinoza* (Cambridge, 1962), 2:193–94.

4. René Descartes, *The Passions of the Soul*, trans. Stephen H. Voss (Indianapolis, 1989), 34.

5. *Ethics*, Book III, def. 2, in *The Collected Works of Spinoza*, ed. and trans. Edwin Curley, vol. 1 (Princeton, 1985), 493.

6. Ibid., def. 3.

7. Ibid., 531.

8. Kant, *Versuch über die Krankheiten des Kopfes*, in *Immanuel Kant Werkausgabe*, ed. Wilhelm Weischedel (Frankfurt am Main, 1982), 2:889.

9. Ibid., 890.

10. Ibid., 898.

11. Ibid., 889.

12. In the seminal text of eighteenth-century German metaphysics, Christian Wolff's *Vernunftige Gedancken von Gott, der Welt und der Seele des Menschen Auch Alle Dinge Ueberhaupt* (1719) (Halle, 1751), passion is defined in the section on ontology as "a change, whose ground lies in another object from the one so affected" no. 104).

13. Immanuel Kant, *Lectures on Metaphysics*, trans. and ed. Karl Ameriks and Stephen Naragon (Cambridge, 1997), 48 (*Metaphysik L*, mid-1770s).

14. *Immanuel Kant's Critique of Pure Reason*, trans. Norman Kemp Smith (London, 1986), A81/B107. Kant even refers casually to the "derivative concepts (*actio, passio*)" as featuring in Aristotle's original list of the categories.

15. Ibid., A204/B250.

16. *Metaphysical Foundations of Physical Science*, trans. James W. Ellington (Indianapolis, 1985), 109.

17. Kant, *Critique of Practical Reason*, trans. Lewis White Beck (New York, 1989), 168.

18. Kant, *The Critique of Judgement*, trans. James Creed Meredith (Oxford, 1973), 124.

19. Ibid.; this marks one of Kant's rare uses of the term *Aufgehoben*.

20. *Anthropologie in pragmatischer Hinsicht*, in *Immanuel Kant Werkausgabe*, 12:557.

21. *Metaphysics of Morals*, trans. Mary Gregor Cambridge, 1991), 208.

22. Ibid.

23. Ibid.

24. *Religion Within the Limits of Reason Alone*, trans. Theodore M. Greene and Hoyt H. Hudson (New York, 1960), 24.

25. Ibid.

26. *Anthropologie in pragmatischer Hinsicht*, 12:600.

27. Ibid., 581.

28. Ibid., 600.

29. Ibid., 599.

30. Ibid., 600.

31. Ibid.

32. Ibid., 601.

33. Ibid., 602.

34. Ibid., 605.

35. Ibid., 602.

36. Ibid.

37. Ibid., 610. Kant follows this point with a discussion of the struggle for domination between the sexes.

38. Ibid., 608.

39. Ibid., 611.

40. Ibid., 612.

41. The entire discussion of the quantity, quality, relation, and modality of aesthetic judgments of taste depends on sensuous experiences somehow possessing conceptual qualities without being subsumed by the understanding.

42. This sublime movement also informs the famous encounter of the starry heavens and the moral law at the end of the second critique. The abasement experience in contemplating the immensity of the heavens is there converted into an even stronger experience of the majesty of the moral law.

43. *The Critique of Judgement*, 156.

44. Ibid.

45. *Opus Postumum*, trans. Eckart Foerster and Michael Rosen (Cambridge, 1993), 237.

46. Ibid., 239.
47. Ibid., 221.

BELIEFS AND EMOTIONS

1. Cesare Beccaria, *On Crimes and Punishments*, ed. David Young (Indianapolis, 1986). See Michel Foucault's discussion of Beccaria in *Discipline and Punish: The Birth of the Prison*, trans. Alan Sheridan (New York, 1977), 90–91.

2. Jeremy Bentham, *Deontology together with A Table of the Springs of Action and The Article on Utilitarianism*, ed. Amnon Goldworth (Oxford, 1992).

3. See H.L.A. Hart, *Law, Liberty, and Morality* (Stanford, 1963), 33. There Hart makes a serious argument in favor of restricting government so that the law is not merely a positive expression and intensification of social morality. He thus joins Bentham in imagining that law should not be merely customary but should exercise a critical function.

4. Ronald de Sousa, *The Rationality of Emotion* (Cambridge, Mass., 1987).

5. Rousseau, "Lettre a M. Philopolis," in *Du contrat social; Ecrits politiques*, ed. Bernard Gagnebin and Marcel Raymond (Paris, 1964), 230–36.

6. See Gregory Dart for the information that it was the *Confessions* rather than the overtly political writings that Robespierre kept with him as his constant companion. *Rousseau, Robespierre and English Romanticism* (Cambridge, 1999), 43–75.

7. For a discussion of the political resonances of emotional terms like *terror*, see George Armstrong Kelly, *Moral Politics in Eighteenth-Century France* (Waterloo, Ont., 1986), 51, 292–311.

8. Stanley Fish, "Mission Impossible: Settling the Just Bounds between Church and State," *Columbia Law Review* 97, no. 8 (1997): 2255–2333.

9. John Rawls's *Political Liberalism* was perhaps his most concerted effort to explain why his views were not simply abstract universal accounts (New York, 1993).

10. Fish cites Thomas Nagel's "Moral Conflict and Political Legitimacy," *Philosophy and Public Affairs* 16 (1987): 215–40.

11. Fish, "Mission Impossible," 2257. Fish is here quoting his earlier *Doing What Comes Naturally: Change, Rhetoric and the Practice of Theory in Literary and Legal Studies* (1989), 326.

12. Sade takes a similar view in his *Justine* to make a very different point—namely that character, being built into persons, is unalterable (and therefore should not be punishable); he basically argues that morality is irrelevant for humans because they, in having the individual characters they have, have no freedom of choice.

13. Quoted in Fish, "Mission Impossible," 2258.

14. See John Barrell, *The Idea of Landscape and the Sense of Place: 1730–1840: An Approach to the Poetry of John Clare* (Cambridge, 1972); and Raymond Williams, *Culture and Society, 1780–1950* (New York, 1983).

15. John Stuart Mill, "Utility of Religion," in *Collected Works of John Stuart Mill*, vol. 10 (Toronto, 1963), 403.

16. Jeremy Bentham, *Analysis of the Influence of Natural Religion on the Temporal Happiness of Mankind*, ed. Delos McKown (Amherst, N.Y., 2003), 42, 129–30.

17. Fish discusses the case in "Mission Impossible," 2288–89. The case is 827 F.2d (6th Cir. 1987).

18. Fish focuses his attack on Amy Gutmann and Dennis Thompson, *Democracy and Disagreement* (Princeton, 1996), 63–69, cited in "Mission Impossible," 2289–98.

19. This is not to say that there is no such thing as slavery in the contemporary world, but merely to register that identifying a particular situation as slavery would be tantamount to beginning the process of its demolition.

20. Stanley Fish, *The Trouble with Principle* (Cambridge, Mass., 1999), 282–83.

21. "Beliefs about Belief," in ibid.

22. "Paederasty," though written about 1785, was not published until almost two centuries later. It first appeared in the *Journal of Homosexuality* 3, no. 4 and 4, no. 1 (1978).

23. Jeremy Bentham, *A Fragment on Government*, ed. J. H. Burns and H.L.A. Hart (Cambridge, 1977), 15.

24. Hart, *Law, Liberty, and Morality*, 64–66.

Index

Adorno, Theodor W., 93, 185–186
aesthetics, 4–5, 175–195
affect, 218, 224–226
Althusser, Louis, 132, 287–288n8
appetite, 84
Arendt, Hannah, 3, 92
Aristotle, 34, 66, 75, 81, 84, 86, 94, 218, 219; *Ethics*, 84; Poetics, 66, 94; *Rhetoric*, 75, 94
asceticism, 267n10
Aubrey, John, 70
Augustine, Saint, 39, 156, 167; *De Doctrina Christiana*, 39
Austin, J. L., 54
avarice, 24
aversion, 84

Bacon, Francis, 49–74; *The Advancement of Learning*, 50; *New Atlantis*, 49–74; *Valerius Terminus*, 64
Baillie, Joanna, 148–150
Balibar, Etienne, 184, 188, 287n3, 291n30
Balzac, Guezde, 98
barbarism, 196–216
Barrell, John, 236
Barry, Brian, 76
Bayle, Pierre, 166
beauty, 142, 179–180
Beccaria, Cesare, 231
belief, 231–250
Benhabib, Seyla, 299n23
Bentham, Jeremy, 133, 231–234, 238, 239, 240, 243
Berkowitz, David, 240
bio-power, 5
Blackstone, Justice, 231, 247, 249
Bobbio, Norberto, 76
body, 125–127, 137, 140, 148, 149, 219, 290n25
body politic, 101–102
Borwing, John, 232
Boyle, Robert, 58
bribery, 70, 72
Brutus, Junius, 28

Burton, Richard, 134–135, 139
Butler, Judith, 187, 188

Calvin, John, 158, 159; *Institutes of the Christian Religion*, 158
Canetti, Elias, 84–85
Caygill, Howard, 188
celibacy, 56–59, 63–64, 72
charity, 65–67, 73, 272n42
Charron, Pierre, 97–98, 109
Cicero, 13, 33, 34, 35, 37, 40, 42, 45, 94, 151, 178, 248; *De Officiis (On Duties)*, 35, 45, 94, 151
civility, 267n10
Coby, Patrick, 253–254n5
compassion, 156
conscience, 117
constancy, 38, 39, 42, 45
contract, 45, 94, 95
Corneille, Pierre, 98, 192, 195
cosmopolitanism, 179, 186
Croce, Benedetto 196
curiosity, 83

Davidson, Donald, 241, 243
death, 203, 205
death drive, 111, 116, 118, 126–127
decadence, 212–213
Delbo, Charlotte, 128
Derrida, Jacques, 188
Descartes, René, 62, 76, 78–80, 93–110, 152, 217, 218–219, 304n32; *Dioptrique*, 78–79; *Méditations*, 79,152; *Passions de l'âme*, 93–110, 218; *Traité de l'homme*, 99–100, 101
desire, 82, 87, 88, 90, 131–150, 164
D'Ewes, Simonds, 70
Diderot, Denis, 157
Du Vair, Guillaume, 97–98

Elias, Norbert, 2
emotions, 32, 231–250
empire, 19, 22–24, 26–27
envy, 137, 170
Epicurus, 63